ACTION RESEARCH
for Teachers

Traveling the Yellow Brick Road

in alphabetic order

Joanne M. Arhar
Kent State University

Mary Louise Holly
Kent State University

Wendy C. Kasten
Kent State University

Merrill
Prentice Hall

Upper Saddle River, New Jersey
Columbus, Ohio

Library of Congress Cataloging-in-Publication Data

Arhar, Joanne M.

 Action research for teachers: traveling the yellow brick road/Joanne M. Arhar, Mary
Louise Holly, Wendy C. Kasten.—1st ed.

  p. cm.

 Includes bibliographical references (p.) and index.

 ISBN 0-13-769225-0

 1. Action research in education. I. Holly, Mary Louise. II. Kasten, Wendy C.
III. Title.

LB1028.24 .A75 2001
370'.7'2—dc21
 00-041129

Vice President and Publisher: Jeffery W. Johnston
Editor: Linda Ashe Montgomery
Editorial Assistant: Jennifer Day
Production Editor: Mary M. Irvin
Design Coordinator: Diane C. Lorenzo
Text Design: Rose Mary Votta
Production Coordination: Carlisle Communications, Ltd.
Cover Design: Rod Harris
Cover Art: Artville
Production Manager: Pamela D. Bennett
Director of Marketing: Kevin Flanagan
Marketing Manager: Amy June
Marketing Services Manager: Krista Groshong

This book was set in Palatino by Carlisle Communications, Ltd., and was printed and bound by R. R. Donnelley
& Sons Company. The cover was printed by The Lehigh Press, Inc.

10 9 8 7 6 5
ISBN 0-13-769225-0

To all of our teachers, past and present, who have accompanied us on this journey to Oz.

Acknowledgments

We would like to acknowledge the many students, teachers, and other colleagues who have contributed to our growing understanding of teaching and learning and action research. Through them we are made aware of the challenges and triumphs possible for those who persist in pursuing questions and matters of consequence. We include examples from their studies in this text. Beyond their immediate work, however, is the power of their message: that through heart, mind, courage, and action, teaching and learning can be transformed. Not, however, without the company of our friends, those critical colleagues who, in the spirit of collegiality on this journey we call teaching and learning, have challenged our thinking. They are the wizards we celebrate throughout this book.

Our four case studies are drawn from the work of Jill Zuckerman Braun, Janice Schelat, Teresa Sopko, Rosemary Rudesal, and Angela Langstaff. We thank them in particular, for their willingness and courage to share some of their personal insights AND frustrations.

From Joanne Arhar's action research classes over the years, she would like to thank the Master's in Arts of Teaching (MAT) students and classroom teachers whose work she has included in this book: Angela Langstaff, Pam Donaldson, Rosemary Rudesal, Deb Friesen, Antoinette Hampton-Wheeler, Tracy Kilfoil, Erika Weliczko, Gayle Buck, Darlene Mitroff, Andrea Nixon, Meridith Niecamp, Andrew Glasier, Trish Yakovich, Lorinda Koss, Matt Naska, Mary Schwartz, and many others who are not mentioned here.

From Wendy Kasten's action research classes over the years, she would like to thank the following graduate students whose work she has included in this book: Kathleen Ruttan, Bonnie Hood, Kelly McDougal, Kelly Chaboudy, Kim Gerdes, Patricia Whittaker, Cheryl Goldstein, Lisa Wood, Leann Laure, Lore Hawkins, Misse Farinacci, Brenda Greene, Perrine Robinson Geller, Jodi Dodds Kinner, Lynda Cornett, Nancy Dunker, Maureen Coe, Victoria Tapp, Vickie Greguric, Meredith Maurer, Tina Seese, Christine Crosslands, Mary Kirt, JoAnn Carter, Marjorie Braddix, Mark Tanski, Allyson Meyer, Vicki Kendra, Lisa Leone, Pam Russomanno, Pam Vanaags, Maren Koepf, Sandra Gardner, Karen Taylor, Suzanne Burkhardt, Georgia Darrah, Melisa Carlson, Joan Diamond, Jennifer Kadilak, Carol McIntosh, Diane Ingersoll, Barbara Martanovic, Debora Austin, Beth Souers, Carol Young, Kathleen Miller, Ann Ritchie, Sandra Hartman, Kelly DiThomas, Debra Lipnos, Christine Barkhurst . . . and all of the others whose work contributed in many ways to the writing of this book.

Mary Lou Holly would like to thank students and teachers over the years who have taught her about action research. Chuck Coleman, in 1969, at age 6, in a rural Michigan primary school classroom, taught a young teacher the need for humility, empirical evidence, and collaboration. Martha MacLure, a six-year-old twenty-odd years later in Norwich England, taught lessons of imagination and the will to create, and their power in any learning experience. Maggie MacLure brought substantive critique of action research. John Elliott's passion, commitment, and action on behalf of students and teachers to furthering the profession through Action Research have long been contagious. The Collaborative Action Research Network (CARN) which he founded, and people associated with it, Marion Dadds, Christine O'Hanlon, Bridget Somekh, Chris Day, Jack Whitehead, Richard Winter, Stephen Rolland, Pam Lomax, Kathe Greene, and colleagues Rob Walker and Michael Schratz and their work on qualitative methodology for social change as well as colleagues from Deakin University including Collin Henry, Helen Henry, Richard Davis, and Helen Modra who have each contributed in their own way to this work—though they surely wouldn't know it! Bev Bruneau, Rich Ambrose, Beth Swadener, and the Master's Cohort teachers in Early Childhood Education at Kent State University, especially Cathy Reiner, Gwendolyn Bryant, Carol Law, and Becky Miller, who contributed to the manuscript, Thank you. Helen Hulbert, thank you.

We would also like to acknowledge the reviewers of our manuscript: Carla Eide, College of Notre Dame at California; Robert J. Fallows, Northern Arizona University; Ochieng' K'Olewe, Western Maryland College; Pricilla M. Leggett, Fayetteville State University; Leanna Manna, Villa Maria College; Karen E. Mayo, Stephen I. Austin State University; and Tonja L. Root, Valdosta State University. We would also like to acknowledge two contributors whose insights and suggestions have enriched our thinking and made this a better book. Charles Avery Blackman, emeritus professor from Michigan State University, made sage suggestions and gave perceptive comments at just the right moments. Michael Lee provided critique, suggestions, and support throughout the journey. Students at Kent State University in selected *Introduction to Research in Education* classes over the last few years provided useful suggestions and critique. Chrys Bouffler, from Queensland, Australia, suggested we journey to Oz in this book. Thank you all.

Although there are many contributors to our thinking, what we have made of their contributions remains solely our responsibility.

Contents

Invitation and Road Map for Conducting Action Research: A Journey to Oz

66 *The road to the City of Emeralds is paved with yellow brick,"*
said the Witch; "so you cannot miss it. 99

The Wonderful Wizard of Oz
L. Frank Baum (1900)

Ah, but it's easy to miss! Especially if you are looking for a superhighway rather than a road paved with yellow brick. The Yellow Brick Road, circuitous and enchanted, may not be the most direct route to the rainbow, but it may be the *best* route to finding out what works or does not work in your classroom teaching.

Over one hundred years ago, Dorothy found herself in a strange land and started an adventure that would change her life and enable her to see her everyday surroundings with new eyes. The challenges of the 20th century were no less daunting to Dorothy than challenges are to 21st-century teachers. We invite you as a 21st-century educator to join us as we journey on the Yellow Brick Road with all its surprises and intriguing adventures. Our journey will be the action research journey.

Why This Narrated Expedition?

As teacher-educators, we wanted to find a way to describe and facilitate action research as the journey that it is, not as a set of methods and techniques, a way to get from A to B by the shortest possible trip. Trips are fast and easily forgotten, but a *journey?* That's an entirely different way to move and be, filled with exploration, mystery, and challenge. Our pre-service and graduate students wanted a clearly narrated expedition that made practical sense, a grounded how-to guide with many examples. We wanted a book that would enable and support teachers to become experts in their own practice as well as articulate spokespersons, critics, and colleagues able to communicate to others their appreciations and understandings. We wanted a book that made use of *all* the colors of the rainbow. We wanted AR in technicolor and motion, where curiosity, play, imagination and creativity as well as informed and disciplined method were used in the service of social and educational aims.

We couldn't find just the right book, so we began writing. One of our aims, in addition to bringing more of the colors of the rainbow together, is to further develop our action research skills as we guide others in the process. This, we hope, will lead to more professional practice for all of us, practice which is defined by educators who recognize and more fully grapple with the complexities of teaching and learning and with the conditions under which these take place.

This book is intended for educators committed to improving life through education. While most examples in this book are drawn from classroom teachers, the process we are advocating is equally relevant to all who teach: parents, administrators, supervisors, community and agency people, those in the helping professions such as theologians and nurses, professional organizations, and business people.

This book is designed to make conducting action research a natural part of teaching, drawing on all the resources and talents we possess. It links together the practical aspects of how to conduct action research with the scholarly tools that support the cycle of reflective practice. You will find out how you come to different understandings, and how you and your colleagues can become more articulate spokespersons for educating young people and adults. You will find illustrations of how other teachers have become researchers, and how they have learned to focus selectively, take action, document, analyze, and come to better understand some of the day-to-day and recurrent challenges of teaching.

In an era in which we are becoming increasingly involved in partnerships and consortia with a myriad of people, including parents, students, community members, and youth-serving agencies, our journey through *Action Research for Teachers* provides us with a framework for problem solving in collaborative contexts. In collaborative problem posing and problem solving, we will find that action research is a powerful method for documenting, developing, and evaluating the curriculum. Simultaneously, AR is a formidable process for accountability and professional growth.

Acknowledging these same points, Tripp (1990) and his Australian colleagues describe AR as "a family of activities in curriculum development, professional development, school improvement programs, and systems planning and policy development. These activities have in common the identification of strategies and planned action which are implemented, and then systematically submitted to observation, reflection, and change" (p. 159). AR is a powerful process!

How often have we looked to wizards for answers we could have found within ourselves? And, much to the point of AR, answers we can find with the help of our colleagues. So, while we are off to see the Wizard on what might seem to be a perilous adventure, we are well suited to the challenges we will face.

We will soon find ourselves, along with Dorothy and her friends, traveling the Yellow Brick Road. We will follow our hunches and discover that by sticking together, putting our *minds* and *hearts* and *courage* to the task, not only will we feel success along the way, but we will become wizards in our own lands of Oz.

Road Map of the Journey

Now that we have discussed some of the reasons for the journey and who will come along, we'd like to offer a road map for both the process of AR and the organization of this book. The AR process is cyclical, and one part can lead either forward or backward. In fact, some parts are done simultaneously! For example, analysis occurs during data collection, leading to another part of the cycle—trying out other solutions. If this all sounds confusing, never mind. This fluid process will prove to be the very thing that enables us to creatively pursue our AR questions. This process will become clearer as we continue.

The title of this book, *Action Research for Teachers*, directly and simply captures the main thrust of the book. It also forms an acronym, *ART*, which aptly expresses our belief in the creative artistry of teaching. We think that good teaching, learning, and research, by their very natures, are forms of scholarship which are distinguished by what John Dewey termed an attitude of scientific inquiry. We also see it as an artful and creative process. As teacher-educators we concur with educational scholars John Elliott and Alan Tom who identify teaching as a *moral craft* that demands action on behalf of the students whose education we shape.

And why have you selected the theme of Oz?

In addition to the similarities we find between the journey implied by conducting action research and the journey to Oz taken by Dorothy and her friends, we feel that *journey* is a good metaphor for the processes involved in doing action research. If you recall, Dorothy and her friends use courage, mind, and heart to meet and overcome the many challenges and obstacles on the road to Oz. We think you will see the parallels in the journey we are about to undertake. As you travel through this text you will see that each section begins with a quotation from *The Wonderful Wizard of Oz* (Baum, 1900). In addition, explorations and exercises in each section are included for those of you who want to complete your own action research journey along with us.

We begin Section 1 with the larger context of the journey, the times in which we live, and why this—the scholar's journey—is necessary. In Chapter 2 we look into professional learning and action research in particular as a key method of learning from our teaching experience. At the conclusion of each section of the book, "Exploring the Forest" provides exercises, explorations and a few "data collection excursions" to develop our tools of inquiry.

Section 2 is designed to define and put action research into larger perspectives: paradigms and research, orientations to knowledge, and historical context. We think that this section is important because this is also what the action researcher does: puts research into specific contexts.

In Section 3 we explore a key element, one without which the journey cannot be made, the selves who make and narrate the journey. We will begin by taking ourselves into account, in a process called *autobiographical inquiry*. Although this process forms an important basis for all aspects of the journey, it is linked quite closely with the narrative process that is the focus of Section 7.

Section 4, "Developing an Inquiring Mind," addresses how to take a curiosity or problem and develop it into an action research study.

Sections 5 and 6 take us through three of the four phases of the action research process, including planning and designing action research projects, and making sense out of the data we collect by analyzing and interpreting it.

Section 7 focuses on portraying and sharing the story with a variety of other people and finding media and methods appropriate for different audiences. Although we portray this journey as a straightforward one for the sake of simplicity, we will show how each phase is part of all the other phases. We conclude our journey from a spot somewhere over the rainbow where we can begin to look back at our journey and put it all together. We will derive lessons from Oz—what we have learned from our journey and what it means for us as professionals. We include a Glossary of terms at the end of the text. That's it—our road map.

The Yellow Brick Road beckons. Let's begin!

SECTION 1

The Scholar's Journey

"... You must go to the City of Emeralds. Perhaps Oz will help you."

"Where is this City?" asked Dorothy.

"It is exactly in the center of the country, and is ruled by Oz, the Great Wizard I told you of."

"Is he a good man?" enquired the girl, anxiously.

"He is a good Wizard. Whether he is a man or not I cannot tell, for I have never seen him."

"How can I get there?" asked Dorothy.

"You must walk. It is a long journey, through a country that is sometimes pleasant and sometimes dark and terrible. However, I will use all the magic arts I know of to keep you from harm."

The Wonderful Wizard of Oz
L. Frank Baum (1900)

We begin the scholars's journey in Chapter 1 with reasons for the journey and a call to all wizards to meet the challenges we will face. In Chapter two we explore how educational wizards learn, and we learn about a few of their tools.

CHAPTER ONE

Why Journey to Somewhere over the Rainbow Now?

We begin our journey with jubilation and . . . perhaps skepticism.

Jubilation? Speak for yourselves, authors. What's this all about?

It's about a special kind of research—research that is like a journey—one that can help us grow personally and professionally.

Is this just one more effort to reform us? We have all been in schools a very long time. We know quite a bit of the territory. We've all been students, too. Pardon our skepticism, but . . .

Well, er, um, yes. This journey is an effort to reform us. *All* of us. And no, this isn't just "one more effort." This action research (AR) journey has more power than any of its predecessors. In fact, it draws strength and grows from those reform efforts. So this journey isn't exactly new. In fact, some of its elements are very old and have much wisdom to impart to us.

Come on, authors. How can something be both old and new? Your words are like a riddle!

It is new in the sense that it involves people who usually have not been involved in research. And it is old because its roots go back to the time of Aristotle. The journey is powerful because it is a process which, when used, can become a teaching way of life.

Relax. We're not about to inoculate or retrain. Rather, we are about to embark on a research journey together that will take us "over the rainbow"— and back home again. While each of us begins her or his journey wishing for a bit more courage, brain power, and heart, what we really need is a spirit of wonder and commitment to the students we teach (and will teach), to our own professional growth, and to cultural evolution. It is with this sense of wonder . . . apprehension . . . and adventure . . . that we anticipate our journey.

It's still not clear about why we need to take this journey. There are so many daily chores and demands to keep us frazzled right where we are!

True enough. And it is these daily chores and demands, as you call them, that this journey is all about. We will learn to see them in different ways. The action research journey offers many ways to make daily practice more professional:

1. It is a potent form of *professional development*—and lifelong learning.
2. It is a form of *reflective practice* that can become a natural part of teaching and learning.
3. It enables us to *learn consciously from experience*.
4. It is a potent force for continuing *staff development, cultural change,* and *educational improvement*.
5. It is a potent force for *research-enabled curriculum and program development*.

And, key to those chores and demands you mention,

6. The action research journey enables our work to be more efficient and targeted so that we actually *save time*.

Let's look for a few minutes at the larger context and some of the challenges that follow from them that make today's action research journey for educators so important.

Challenges A-plenty!

We are evolving—consciously and unconsciously. We can see and feel that we are in a time of significant change, that we are "in process," and that change is a normal part of life.

Yes. It's hard to accept that life isn't likely to "slow down" or "go back to 'normal'" anytime soon.

Old worlds are closing and new worlds are opening. With advances in human and environmental research, our knowledge is growing. Few people would argue that advances in technology enable change in how and what we know, and in the ways we live our lives. The availability of a vast and growing library over the Internet as well as shopping and communication with people next door and across the planet has implications almost beyond our imaginations. We want to hold on and to let go. We are skeptical, yet aware of enormous opportunity.

The long era of certainty is over. And that is disconcerting! The modern era, "based on the premise that the world is objectively knowable, and that knowledge so obtained can be absolutely generalized" (Havel, 1992), has overextended its shelf life! We now know that we don't know—nor will we ever know—*all*. Our perspectives are inevitably partial. We know that the earth and its resources are finite. We are coming to understand the truth of what many Native Americans and artists have long known: We must learn to love the journey more than the destination. Said another way, life is a process, it is *all* journey. Destinations are not separate from the journey, they are markings—small or large—within the journey.

The end of the modern era has enormous implications for education, not the least of which is the need for continuous scholarship and learning. The scholar's life is one of continual inquiry and growth, and that is what this book is about. A scholar is one who brings a questioning stance to life. A scholar is committed to making life better through education, bringing a little light to darkness, and learning from both darkness and light.

The challenges we face in the postmodern world are of many kinds. The light from our research enables us to see into the darkness created inadvertently by previous levels of awareness and development. Our home, the earth, for example, is threatened by the very "progress" of the modern era that brought us to "the world's first global, planetary, technical civilization" and to "a final crisis" for which we have reached the limits of modern thought to bring us back from the brink" (Havel, 1992). The conclusion of the 20th century and its environmental and social problems brought with it humility, and the awareness that we need more than knowledge to save our global community and planet.

Human Understanding and Community

We need different ways of thinking, different kinds of education and scholarship. We need, as Havel says, to *try harder to understand than to explain.*" While much more is known about the world and its peoples, their physical, social, and cultural functioning, than was known in the previous era, making sense of it is problematic. "There is too much to know . . . [Information and knowledge] can no longer be fully grasped and understood, let alone contained" (Havel, 1992). Mostly, we need *human understanding* and *connection.* We need to see and be in relationship—with the land, with ourselves, and with others. Although we may not be able to control the future in the ways we once thought we could, the good news is that with historical consciousness, sensitivity, and social purpose, together we *can* influence and help to shape it.

By the late 19th century, John Dewey had called for the creation of democratic communities where learning, individually and collectively, would be everyone's responsibility. For most of the 20th century we focused on the individual. The democratic societies we sought would be comprised of informed, caring, and thoughtful citizens. Although the individual was key to social development, we didn't fully understand the importance of Dewey's concept of community.

We human beings are inextricably related; we live and breathe shared social practices, beliefs, and values. Just as the earth provides a physical foundation for life in its many forms, culture provides the social and emotional medium through which we grow and evolve. Erik Erikson, a contemporary of John Dewey, took seriously the social context within which people lived. As a social scientist, he contributed to us the concept of identity and the theory of psychosocial development, central to which is the idea that social context shapes who we are—as individuals and as groups. We will address his ideas later.

The person, the group, their *contexts* and cultures are fundamental to social change in a democratic society. In the chapters which follow we will explore the contexts within which we find ourselves as action researchers, and as we do so, we develop the educational scholar's tools for social change. You may wish to consult a book entitled *Research as Social Change: New Opportunities for Qualitative Research*

(1995) by Michael Schratz and Rob Walker. These authors present many ways to think about and do educational research, including action research, for social change.

Challenges to Educators

Current social and environmental changes place high demands on educational systems. These demands call attention to what educators have long known, that the whole child, adolescent, or adult—and family—comes to school, and that school forms communities that reside within other communities. Some of our more enlightened legislators and members of the business community are working with schools to attack problems associated with poverty and the declining health and welfare of some of our most vulnerable students. Although these problems are not restricted to our urban areas, there is a significant trend toward community, toward partnerships and collaboration on behalf of students in our cities. No one group, including teachers, can bring about the kinds of change that are needed to enable our children and youth to march confidently into the decades ahead.

In conjunction with the many necessary changes in the environmental and social conditions within which our children and their families live, work, and learn, there is general agreement on the importance of knowledgeable, caring, and committed teachers in helping students learn. The emphasis has shifted from reforming schools to simultaneously reforming teacher education *and* schools, and thus attending to culture, the shared social practices and values which guide educational life inside and outside schools.

Reform and evolution take time, sometimes a l o n g time to act and for us to see the results of our actions. Often we haven't given enough time and attention to the cultures within which reform can take place and continue to develop; but now, increasing numbers of people are networking to make cultural change possible. There is good news: They are us! The challenge is to continue to develop professionally in the face of rapid and needed change. The National Commission on Teaching for America's Future, for example, calls for "reinventing teacher preparation and professional development, overhauling teacher recruitment, encouraging and rewarding teaching knowledge and skill, and creating schools that are organized for student and teacher success."

A pretty tall order, wouldn't you say? Even for a wizard! Is this possible?

Calling All Wizards!

We think so. An alternative to the image others might have of us—standing and rusting, or quietly and patiently awaiting the next wizard—is to work together to develop the tools of our trade. And in so doing, we further develop not only our schools and classrooms, but also our profession. As John Gardner (1962) so aptly asked, "How do we fashion a system which continuously renews itself?" In our own terms, how do we fashion a system in which, as a matter of course, people and groups of people, classrooms, schools, and other educational and social institutions function as innovative, self-renewing, learning communities?

Let's zoom to the end of our journey for a few minutes. Will we, like Dorothy, end our journey able to see with new eyes, consciously, the sights we missed or could not have imagined even a short while earlier? Let's imagine for a minute. What might a profession full of wizards be like? What attributes might characterize the profession, its people, its structure, and its functioning?

OK. So what will we, a profession of wizards, look like, know, and do?

Visions of a Profession of Wizards

We're glad you asked!

- Our moral commitments to justice and equity will drive our work, including its technical and practical aspects.
- We will be a community of learners, each teaching and learning.
- We will be scholars whose commitment to the profession and to students will be palpable; it will be seen, heard, and felt.
- We will work well in partnerships and consortia designed for specific purposes, some ad hoc, others continuing over years and even a career.
- We will have resources, know what to ask for, and know how to use them.
- We will learn from what we do—individually and collaboratively.
- We will know who we are and what we stand for as professionals and as a profession.
- We will look with a scientist's observing eyes and speak with an artist's sensitivity and expression.

And what will the profession be like?

- The conditions under which we practice will support our scholarship and our partnerships, and the most important beneficiaries will be our students and their families.
- Teaching will be generally acknowledged as a process of continuous professional inquiry; the scholarship of teaching, a normal part of work.
- Education will be everybody's business, and schools and educational institutions will exemplify the best of what we know about learning.
- The words of Martin Haberman will be common practice in our educational institutions:

> Learning is good—it feels good.
> It is right, it is natural,
> It can be enjoyable,
> And it is what we do here.
> It is a natural act—like eating, sleeping, or breathing.

CHAPTER SUMMARY

We began our journey with the admonition that we must walk to the City of Emeralds. "It is a long journey," good witch Glinda informed us, but one worth the effort. The journey contains "all the magic arts" Glinda knows. We talked about the challenges that confront us as we move from modern to postmodern societies, and of the challenges for those in education. The profession of wizards that we envisioned is reason enough for the journey.

To bring our images into being, we must journey, and somewhere over the rainbow we will look back, and as wizards, know what we have learned. And just how will we learn?

How Do Educational Wizards Learn? With Professional Tools.

Dorothy: Who are the wizards?

Authors: *We* are the wizards Dorothy. Although most of us in education were not *born* wizards (unlike Harry Potter), and that includes our august Wizard of Oz, we can become wizards through professional learning. Scholarship is the fuel that keeps us wizards, and action research is a form of scholarship for learning in a dynamic social system. In this chapter we address professional learning and action research, and we introduce a few tools of the educational scholar—the professional journal and portfolio—that we will use on our journey to Oz.

Professional Learning and the Development of Scholarship

Teachers engage in a special kind of learning—professional learning. Its focus is on the integration of three educational processes necessary to pedagogical success: human development, curriculum development, and teaching. How do people learn and grow? What do they need to learn and grow and to increase their capacity for further learning and social evolution? John Dewey makes important distinctions among three kinds of learning: educational, noneducational, and mis-educational. While learning is involved in each, the end results vary.

Noneducational learning denotes that the learning doesn't change anything; a few days after the test what was learned either is gathering dust in the mind's recesses or has departed. *Mis-educational* learning means that deeper learning on the topic is either sidetracked or subverted; picking apart poems for parts of speech can extinguish the desire to read poetry. *Educational* learning increases the capacity for further learning toward socially worthwhile goals; while bank robbing skills are surely learned, Dewey would not consider them educational.

Professional learning has been a goal for educators since the teaching profession first began. The basic goal has remained the same: to grow and develop professionally as a result of experience. From the early days of in-service training institutes, to more recent workshops and grant activities, the goal has been to improve what happens in classrooms and between educators and students. See, the world *is* changing! While professional learning has always been aimed toward the improvement of practice, it must now be directed toward a larger, more adequate, complex, and robust process: *scholarship*.

Over the years, educators have become a larger and more diversified group. Our roles and responsibilities have expanded. While we have talked and read about working with others in more collaborative and participatory ways, until recently there have been very few sustained collaborative efforts from which to learn, and more than a few organizational constraints to doing so. Narrow, rigid, and linear uses of space, time, and scheduling, for example, have mitigated against the very collaborative relationships which might help us meet the demands of social and environmental changes. Consequently, needed changes have been difficult to make.

Not long ago scholarship was considered to be the sole purview of specialists located at universities and research organizations. Classroom educators were not respected for scholarship and had few opportunities for recognized teacher research. Whether it was true or not, there was a general view that researchers should be removed from the "real world" of practice. Many researchers prided themselves on self-imposed isolation and the *objectivity* that could attend their removal from the daily world of practice and from the people and systems they studied. More recently, in the social sciences and education in particular, the number of researchers choosing to enter the real world of practice, where they embrace their own senses and *subjectivity,* has grown. Slowly, subjectivity has become, if not always desirable, at least not antithetical to the research process. There are several other changes taking place, including:

- A growing realization that objectivity is a myth, that we each see and interpret from a point of view
- A growing number and diversity of people conducting research
- Researchers straying into more complex and "messier" questions, topics, and terrains
- Research conducted closer to the subject of inquiry (such as in classrooms, in addition to laboratories)

Traditionally, scholars in education were people outside the schools. They conducted research in schools on teaching and learning, curriculum, administration, and organizational and professional development. But these scholars were not answering the pressing questions posed by teachers about everyday work. We teachers wanted these scholars to be like Sherlock Holmes, an investigator we could summon at will to solve thorny educational problems. But teachers cannot afford to wait for the results of expensive studies, often presented in a style and manner that makes translation into practice difficult at best.

In 1975 a British scholar named Lawrence Stenhouse published a book entitled *An Introduction to Curriculum Research and Development* in which a central chapter, and indeed the theme of the book, was the "teacher as researcher" and the genesis of a new professional. The same year, *School Teacher,* a sociological study by a U.S. sociologist, Dan C. Lortie (1975), brought another major contribution to the discussion. From his book we learned more about who we were as teachers, why we decided to become teachers, and how we developed as a profession. These two key works enable us to better understand the roots and profile of the profession. These works and others offer a foundation for charting the future of an evolving profession, one which is directed as much by its *internal* (professional teachers) as by its *external* influences and environments (business community, legislatures, and others). Since the time of those works and others, we have seen a flurry of activity related to teachers and to research:

- from research on *teachers→*
　　- to research in the company of *teachers→*
　　　　- to research with *teachers→*
　　　　　　- finally to research by *teachers,*
　　　　　　　　with teachers, students, and others.

It is this last and most recent shift in research that is the subject of this book. A relatively small but fast-growing group of practitioner researchers in this country and elsewhere practice a form of scholarship called *action research.*

Introducing Action Research

Action research implies an orientation to research, a form of professional practice, a research process, and, for teachers, a reflective way of teaching. Teachers who ask questions of their practice such as, How can I improve my practice? (Whitehead, 1996), who try out some of their ideas in response to that question, who systematically observe and collect evidence related to their actions, and who then analyze and talk with others about it—these teachers are engaging in reflective practice. They are following the same kind of cyclical process that characterizes action research. We might say that they are using professional (informed) eyes to observe their own practice; they are facing the challenges they meet with action and analysis; and they are sharing the results with others—perhaps their students, their colleagues, parents, the larger community of the school, and the discipline. What makes action research a form of scholarship is the tenaciously inquisitive, purposeful, systematic, critical, self-critical, and collaborative ways one explores and changes one's practice.

Not only can teaching and learning be characterized by an attitude of scientific inquiry, but they can be conceptualized as a moral craft that demands action on behalf of students whose education we shape. Alan Tom (1997), a noted U.S. educator, has long referred to teaching as a moral craft. A British colleague, John Elliott (1991), has long emphasized the foundation and purpose of our work—the moral nature of our professional commitment to teaching. They refer to the democratic ideals of a profession whose purpose is to educate for freedom and an informed citizenry. Teaching involves the intimate, helping, and democratic relationship of teachers and students; of caring, knowledgeable, and skilled teachers who use their gifts on behalf of each child, adolescent, or adult they teach. What could be more important (and intimate) to a democratic society than consciously shaping environments that influence the development of the hearts and minds of our students? The curriculum is the vehicle for opening, creating, building, and serving as a catalyst in educational space; learning is the process through which the curriculum is made manifest. Opportunities and tools to learn can shape their—and our—worlds ever after. This is reason enough for us to develop the tools of scholarship through action research.

We believe, along with the late Lawrence Stenhouse, that "It is teachers who, in the end, will change the world of the school by understanding it." We believe that this understanding will come about through reflective practice. In this reflective form of practice, or *praxis,* our way of thinking changes as a result of our experience. Praxis is a form of educational scholarship, a critically reflective dialogue that takes place continuously between the professional and her or his practice. It places practice into larger contexts including one's purposes as well as earlier and future experiences. As agents of change, professionals commit themselves to educational scholarship. This is the basis of professional teaching. Teaching well is inquiring well. Our commitment to students' learning *is* the purpose for our scholarship. Developing educational scholarship is the subject of this book. In the last section of this chapter two major tools for developing scholarship journals and portfolios are addressed. Such tools will be useful in documenting and learning from experience.

Exploring the Forest
Developing Tools for the Journey

To make this journey *ours*—not as spectators but as explorers—we can engage ourselves in it. This engagement can be facilitated by the journal, an important personal and professional tool for scholarship and research. A journal is a place in which to document and describe experience, to explore, to gather insights, and to give voice to our interpretations. Thus, each journal is unique.

Here, in the first "Exploring the Forest" section of the book, we present general information about *journals,* and *portfolios;* a way to conceptualize and relate these two tools; and ways to write about and make sense of our work through documentation and reflection on it. There are many excellent books and articles on these subjects, and different ways that journals and portfolios are defined and used. We present some definitions here and lay out the way we will use the journal and portfolio in this book. Later, in Section 5, we further develop the contents you may find useful to include in your journal and portfolio. In this chapter, and in each of the chapters that follow, we have designed and numbered explorations and exercises to help develop research tools over the length of our journey together. Try them out and watch (and feel) your capacity for scholarship expand! You will need the following:

- *An object such as a loose-leaf binder, bound journal, and/or computer to house your writing* (with a loose-leaf binder you can add, subtract, and move materials around) and a box or other case for objects that do not fit into the binder, journal, or computer. Many objects can be scanned into a computer.
- *Writing tools:* pens, markers, pencils, and/or technological or electronic devices such as tape recorders, notepads, electronic journals, computers.
- *A computer, scanner, and printer.* These are not essential but *highly* recommended. There are distinct advantages to having an electronic journal, not necessarily to replace a paper journal, but to work with it. You can transfer important notes on paper to your computer via typing or scanning—or even by talking into your computer, or uploading them from the notepad you write on. But a more important quality of an electronic journal is that you can add, copy, subtract, and move around parts of your journal whenever you want or need to. You can develop an idea over time and use online resources and quickly move these into your journal as well as move things out of your journal to other places (such as a report).

- *Scissors, glue, tape, paints,* and whatever you may wish to use in some of the nonword exercises. Disks, videos, and other supplies may be useful as your imagination lets loose along the way.
- *Creativity, energy and enthusiasm,* and whatever else you want to use.

There are many different ways that we can plan, document, and learn from our work. We will house and cultivate the fruits of our study in the professional journal. The scholar's tools for our journey are many (they include methods of data collection such as observing, interviewing, and artifact collection as well as methods for analysis and interpretation). We will explore these in subsequent chapters.

The *professional journal* is a rich, evolving database within which the scholar can converse with herself or himself. It is a private document "owned" by the scholar and used to inform practice. It is also a rich source to draw upon for constructing a purpose-specific *portfolio,* which is intended to be a public document used to communicate professional practice to others through narrated illustration.

The Professional Journal

The *professional journal* is a living document. We distinguish it from other kinds of journals (calendar and chronological elaboration, dialogue, reader response, buddy, and content journals used in science, mathematics, and other disciplines) as a working document that is intentionally reflective. As such, it is returned to. In a professional journal you can incorporate any of the kinds of writing contained in the other types of journals including diary and logs (which we will soon define). It is a potent tool for scholarly reflection and professional development; for collecting data, analyzing, synthesizing, interpreting, and extending it. Although most journals are written documents, they can also contain drawings and other forms of documentation and expression such as pictures, charts, diagrams, lists, and excerpts from other materials. The professional journal can include objects and artifacts that could not typically fit into some other kinds of journals such as reports, pamphlets, videos, compact disks (CDs), and audio tapes. As a personal document, the journal can be organized to suit the author's needs and purposes. When we refer to journals in this book, we are referring to professional journals as described here, unless otherwise indicated.

If you are going to use a journal on this journey, you may want to start it now. Let's start with some reflection (and gather baseline data).

1. Make two drawings, one of your thoughts and feelings about *research* before you picked up this book and one after you read the first two chapters. After each drawing, write freely to explain in words what the drawings might say if they could talk. Date these and place them in your journal.
2. Make two more drawings, this time one about your thoughts and feelings about *action research* before you picked up this book and one after you read this chapter. After each drawing, write freely to explain in words what the

drawings might say if they could talk. Date these and place them in your journal.

There are many different kinds of writing that we will find useful, among them, log and diary-type writing.

Log sheets are descriptive and "objective" types of writing in the sense that more than one person could record and understand what is entered (logged). For example, a log might be used to record the questions asked by students during a discussion. Who is speaking? What kinds of questions are they asking? Who is not speaking? You may find it useful to keep a researcher log to record events as they occur, to keep a running record that you can return to for analysis.

Diary-type entries are often written as stream of consciousness. The authors normally hold no illusions of objectivity. As many journal keepers find, diary writing is a good way to "let it all hang out." These entries can be filled with emotion as the author usually doesn't edit feelings and thoughts. As a result, diary writing can be quite therapeutic as well as a good source to return to and locate oneself (if rather vividly at times) in the circumstance.

Journals contain both kinds of entries and many others. They can be used to record observations, describe events and experiences, write creatively, and make sketches; to analyze and synthesize. Writing can be objective, subjective, creative, and expressive. All these kinds of information are important to the action researcher. As researchers, we can return to our entries often and think further about what they contain. For now, try these exercises and invitations to reflect.

3. Keep a *log* of something that would be interesting or useful for you to focus on over the next week (hour, day). It could be of every time you see a lightbulb go off in a student's mind (when, who, what are the circumstances?). It could be to record each time the telephone rings (when and who and why), or that your studies are interrupted (when and who and why). It might even be each time you find yourself automatically wending your way to the refrigerator (time and object sought?). When the designated time is over, sit down and read all that you have written. Think about what happened over that time period. What can you learn from it?

4. Write a *diary* entry about something recently that didn't seem fair to you and about which you could be justifiably critical. It could be a policy or piece of legislation, something that happened to you or to someone around you. Let all your thoughts and feelings out. You may find that after your emotions are addressed, your thoughts will become clearer.

5. Write freely and quickly about something meaningful that you recently learned on your own. Don't think too much or edit—even in your mind—as you write. Give it a title. Describe it. Now list all the benefits to you from that learning (now and potentially). Next, write about how you learned it. Why is it

important to you? Can you learn anything from it about how you learn? If so, write this down as a summary statement.

6. Do the same thing as in number 5 for something you learned with other people. What similarities and differences between learning on your own and learning with others do you find? As you process your writing, it becomes a *journal*.

In numbers 5 and 6 you were engaged in what is called *free-writing;* it simply means writing freely. Peter Elbow (1973), a scholar on writing, distinguishes two processes of writing: *growing* and *cooking*. Once you grow your writing, you shape it into something. This process is much like growing tomatoes and lettuce and making them into a salad. Much diary-type writing is of this growing sort. Don't mentally process it. Instead, let your fingers write or type as fast as they can, and don't hinder them by talking to them as they go. Let them talk to you. You have probably heard the statement "How do I know what I think until I see what I say?" Say it on paper, and then look to see what you said. Set a time limit and write until you reach it. You may want to start with 5 or 10 minutes and expand to 15 or 20, 30, or more. We will provide a few ideas to get started with free-writing.

As with quick sketches (with words), you will find some terrific writing and some that isn't so great; it does not matter. The important part is to get the creative juices flowing and ideas percolating. Most people we know who have tried this find the process to be enjoyable and productive. If you do, there are some good books to spark more ideas and deepen your writing and thinking. Natalie Goldberg, author of *Writing Down the Bones* (1986), and *Wild Mind: Living the Writer's Life* (1990), fear-busting, seed-planting, humorous books about writing with lots of ideas for free-writing, says that there are seven rules of writing practice. They happen to be useful for reflective writing (and getting ideas for proposal development):

- Keep your hand moving.

- Lose control (Say what you want to say. Don't worry if it's correct).

- Be specific. Not a car, but a Cadillac.

- Don't think.

- Don't worry about punctuation, spelling, grammar.

- You are free to write the worst junk in America.

- Go for the jugular. If something scary comes up, go for it. (That's where the energy is.) (1990, pp. 3–4)

Although it may seem strange, free-writing, with as little thinking as possible, is an excellent way to learn to think beyond the surface. We will be talking more in the next few chapters about a very important process that some people call "problematizing our practice." Free-writing is especially good for doing this. When we free-write, we pass right over the heads of our editors, the monitors that keep us on our path. The trouble with editors is they often keep us on a path that is too straight and narrow. While it is important to be heading in a direction, we need to have the freedom to let our thoughts and imaginations range more freely than the straight and narrow permits. Free-writing lets us do this. It gives us access to parts of ourselves that can usefully be employed and questioned, parts of ourselves that run for cover when the monitors peek in.

7. Do a 10-minute free-write on an idea triggered by something in this chapter.

Portfolio

In 18th-century Italy, the portfolio was described as a *porto folio* coming from "portare," meaning to carry, and "fogli," meaning leaves or sheets of paper. According to the *Oxford English Dictionary,* it has a long history and can be defined as:

> A receptacle or case for keeping loose sheets of paper, prints, drawings, maps, music, or the like; usually in the form of a large book-cover, and sometimes having sheets of paper fixed in it, between which specimens are placed.

The portfolio, as we now refer to it, has its roots in these early uses which included collections of drawings and art, legal and official documents of an agency or government, and financial holdings. Today, the portfolio is used in all these ways and takes on a professional orientation in educational settings. It is more (and less) than an archive or general collection of items. It is a composition: *a carefully selected, constructed, and narrated collection of work pertaining to a special topic.* At Deakin University in Australia, for example, this document, which they call a folio, is a carefully constructed and portable document that contains and illustrates the development of a thesis. In universities throughout the world, portfolios are used to put forward carefully crafted programs for review and certification by outside experts. In schools, the portfolio is increasingly being used to document the learning and development of pupils. Some schools use portfolios to present professional development for review by professional development councils. In an increasing number of school districts in Ohio, for example, local professional development committees (called LPDCs) are using portfolios in review for licensing. In all these cases, the portfolio is a tool for educational learning, development, and evaluation.

The kind of portfolios we create depends on our purposes. For example, we might want to create a portfolio to illustrate our work in a course we teach. This is called a *course portfolio,* and it is becoming an important way to study one's course and to share it with others. As the *scholarship of teaching* evolves over time, we will see more and more of this type of portfolio. We study a specific course or topic (What are the topic and area of study? My aims, goals, and/or objectives? What did I do and how did it work? What were student roles, responsibilities, actions, and reactions? What did I learn? So, what does this mean for the future of my teaching this course?), and we present the results of our study in an illustrated document for others. We might develop a portfolio to document and highlight important aspects of teaching over a term or a year or to document benchmarks in or to document benchmarks in a career. These are often referred to as *teaching portfolios*. We would include such things as our aims, documentation of our teaching in different areas over time, and commentary including our interpretations and future directions which follow from the work we illustrate. The portfolio can serve as an illustrated resume, an evaluation tool, a promotion document, or a story of progress and completion of an action research project.

You need not think too much about a portfolio yet; we will collect and construct materials for it in our journals over time. Then we will construct portfolios of the action research process as we near the end of our journey. For now, we explore how others define and use portfolios and we collect some data to put into it.

8. Ask four people for their thoughts on portfolios and how they use, or might use, them.
9. Free-write about possible purposes you might have for a portfolio. Think about potential benefits of developing a portfolio which tells a story and illustrates key points in your action research project.

CHAPTER SUMMARY

We started this chapter with the realization that in order to be educational wizards, we would need to engage in a special kind of learning—scholarship. We traced the development of research *on* teachers and teaching to research *by* teachers on teaching. Action research, we found, is both a process and an orientation to research; it is a moral craft. And, like any moral craft, it takes learning and using tools of the trade. In our case, we laid the foundation for our wizardry with tools for documentation and learning with the professional journal and portfolio. We will come back to these tools and further develop our scholarship at the conclusions to each section of the book.

SECTION SUMMARY

With challenges enough to fill the rainbow, and tools for the journey, let's find out more about action research, what it is, and how it came into being.

Defining and Putting Action Research in Context

"Ah. My party's just beginning!" said the Wicked Witch of the West.

The Wonderful Wizard of Oz
L. Frank Baum (1900)

Dorothy: Egads. I shudder at the word *research*, and here we are with a wicked witch, smirking about a party!

Authors: Would it help if we tried to demystify the word *research?* If we explored some of the wonderful consequences of doing research? And the fun we can have in so doing?

Dorothy: Wonderful consequences? Fun? Research?

Authors: Yes. And by learning about what the word really means, we will be preparing for our own party.

Dorothy: OK. I'll be open-minded if you go easy on the jargon.

Authors: You have a deal. Occasionally we may use terms unfamiliar to you. When we do, we'll define them. There is a Glossary at the end of the book if things still seem unclear.

In this section we will discuss some general terms, concepts, and kinds of study associated with knowledge and research, which will provide a larger context from which we may better understand AR. We will further define action research, its characteristics, and its history, and we will close with exploring the parts of the forest through which we have just traveled. We will begin to find our way within the forest . . . and to identify companions for the journey.

23

CHAPTER THREE

The Bigger Picture: Paradigms, Theories, and Research

In Chapters 1 and 2 we talked about current challenges facing educators and directions for the future of the profession. We talked about the modern and postmodern worlds, and about the end of the modern age as we knew it. Today we are caught between (and living in) modern and postmodern paradigms, or world views, each of which is vying for our attention. According to David Elkind (1997), these two paradigms characterize two distinct periods and can each be described by three different, general beliefs:

Modernity	Postmodernity
Progress	Difference
Universality	Particularity
Regularity	Irregularity

Although there are many different ways to characterize the two paradigms, Elkind provides a general and clear description of each. He notes that Dewey ushered in the modern era in education with his argument that educational progress was developmental. Dewey argued that a progressive educational pedagogy was called for in which students were viewed as active participants rather than the passive participation that characterized most school activity and curricula of the late 19th and early 20th centuries. The curriculum was organized so that simpler concepts *progressed* into more complex concepts. Dewey's suggestion that students of any age learned best by doing, was a *universal* belief—we learn better by doing than by being "done to." Finally, Dewey also believed that education was *regular* in that there was a "predictable sequence in the acquisition of skills, values, and knowledge" (1997, p. 29). While many of Dewey's early ideas lead also into the postmodern era (e.g., in addition to progress, he stressed *difference*), it may make the case more clearly to turn to the work of Jean Piaget, who worked in the modern era but while doing so, heralded in the postmodern era for education (Elkind, 1997, p. 34). Not all children, he showed, progress at the same time and in the same way. *Particularity* and *difference* were more the rule than the exception. Each individual has a unique biological endowment and circumstances which interact to make experiences unique—*not* "regular." In schools, postmodern beliefs have been translated to attention to individual differences, diversity, multiple intelligences, multiple ways of knowing, children's rights, fewer boundaries between public and private life, children and adults, and other forms that make schooling more complex than it was in modern times.

Dorothy: Hmm. In Chapter 1 you said, "We will look with a scientist's observing eyes and speak with an artist's elegance." Are these two paradigms?

Yes, they can be considered paradigms. They are world views that people develop when they learn within a discipline. People in a scientific discipline hold many things in common and can be said to come from a scientific paradigm. We will talk more about these and other world views later in this chapter. From the scientific paradigm we learn to observe very carefully and analytically. From the artistic paradigm we construct meaning, drawing intentionally from the interaction of inner as well as outer landscapes. Artists interpret and portray their work in creative ways which enable others to derive insights from their portrayals. We will be developing both of these abilities throughout this book.

In this chapter we started out with *paradigms*. Next, we will look at *theories* and *research*. A scholar generally functions from a frame of reference, or *paradigm*, within a larger group whose perspective the scholar shares. Within this larger group there may be several *theories*, each focusing on a specific phenomenon, be it broadly (i.e., psychosocial development) or narrowly (bee pollination in southwest Georgia) focused. The *research* that takes place within this frame of reference and in conjunction with a theory, whether implicit or explicit, in turn can inform both the theory and the paradigm.

> **Paradigm:** A world view or model ascribed to a group of people who hold certain beliefs, knowledge, and understandings in common
>
> **Theory:** A systematically organized explanation of a phenomenon.
>
> **Research:** Systematic self-critical inquiry made public (after Lawrence Stenhouse).

In general, *we are concerned with the utility of a paradigm and the quality of the explanation generated from a theory and the research that informs it.* Implicit in paradigms are values, whereas the theories that researchers construct may come from their value orientations and a particular paradigm (which may motivate them to raise issues and investigate them using specific methods), but the theories themselves are articulated as a carefully constructed set of principles which hold true no matter what the reader's values. As we defined *log* in Chapter 2, readers of a ship's log can understand the principles regardless of their points of view. So, too, with the theory. However, we interpret the *meaning* and possible *application* or *implications* of the theory according to our values. Theories can bring new meanings and coherence to our understanding of a phenomenon, and they help us to interpret what we see and wonder about.

Theories provide frames of reference. "Whatever problem we face, the most useful frame of reference will be the one that most adequately helps us to understand and use all of the facts before us" (Combs and Snygg, 1959, pp. 8–9). Scientists in the physical sciences and the human, or social, sciences use theories to explain phenomena as diverse as the origin of the universe, motivation, and school change. We will focus here on a few theories that help us to better understand the complexity of teaching and learning and how we can study it.

We will look at two theories that are particularly important to educators. According to Robert Kegan, these theories have shaped and "influenced nearly every aspect of intellectual life in the last hundred years" (Kegan, 1982, p. 8). One big idea—or theory—is *constructivism*. The other is *developmentalism*. Both have influenced our understanding of how people learn.

Constructivism.   The name most often associated with this theory of cognitive development is that of the Swiss genetic epistemologist (a person who studies the nature of knowledge), Jean Piaget. He developed a comprehensive theory of cognitive development based upon lifelong research in this area. There are other theories of cognitive development, and many (including Robert Kegan's theory) are built upon Piaget's constructivist theory. In essence, constructivism means that persons (and systems) constitute and construct their own reality. We are meaning-making beings. And what do we make meaning from? Our experiences. And how do we make sense of those experiences? By reflecting upon them. We do this all the time. People who develop public theories, some of which are referred to as *grand* theories because their scope is broad, do so by careful and systematic study which they make understandable to others. Piaget's theory of cognitive development is one such public, or grand, theory. We each have our own theories about life. Because we do not study and organize them into theories for public use and scrutiny, they are referred to as *personal* theories. Through the action research process we become aware of tacit elements of our personal theories.

According to Piaget, we function and make meaning using a fundamental process that is part of life from our earliest to our final days. Throughout a lifetime, we *assimilate* information that fits into already existing ideas, and we *accommodate* information for which we have to amend existing ideas or to develop new ones. Assimilation and accommodation are processes that involve multiple ways of knowing. For example, a baby might use a wall to pull herself up. One day she tries this and the wall moves! This seemingly familiar object becomes something it wasn't—a door. Now she can push it at will and learns that this door makes a certain sound when it swings open. It also looks different when it moves. Very quickly she has come to know this object in multiple ways: through sight, touch, and sound. Life itself is a continuous process of bringing assimilation and accommodation into equilibrium. Too much assimilation would be boring; too much accommodation, frustrating.

Dorothy: How did Piaget figure this out?

By very careful observations and analysis. For one thing, he watched babies discover new things. It took a very long time. Piaget started out studying insect and plant life in ponds, and he moved to using some of his skillful methods of observation and question-posing to study children—his own and other children. He developed a method of questioning children that went beyond prevalent methods used by researchers of his time. This process of gathering data is termed the *clinical method.* He took children very seriously and asked them open-ended questions. Instead of categorizing their responses as right or wrong, he paid attention to the reasoning behind their responses. The answer itself, he found, was only a small part of their reasoning.

Children's art provides a good example of this. Watch a 4-year-old child paint. If you are lucky, you will hear the child talk about what he is doing and you will discover a story. What may look like a muddy or scribbled mess to an unskilled eye may be a wonderful imaginary adventure to the child. Let's take a real example. Martha created this picture (Fig. 3.1) and talked about it as she drew. Here is how Martha's observant mother, Maggie, described the picture:

> This is Disneyland. If you look closely (or imaginatively), you will see
> Princess Jasmine in the castle, Aladdin, the monkey, and the magic carpet.
> Also a rainbow. And see your name on the back?

If we see only scribbles, we miss so much, and it was the "much" that interested Piaget. We do not want to go into depth regarding constructivism or Piaget's theory here—there are many books to do that. We want only to point out that through careful and systematic study, a new theory evolved that changed how we look at child development, schooling, teaching, learning, and curriculum development. Understanding constructivism can make a significant difference in our work. Whether we view Martha as a passive *tabula rasa* (blank slate) on which we

FIGURE 3.1

write what we want her to learn, or whether we view her as a dynamic sense-making being makes a considerable difference in our approach to her. Anyone who knows Martha even remotely would find the word *passive* 100 percent inappropriate. Piaget would say that we have a lot to learn from her, and as teachers we can always learn from our students. Yetta Goodman (1991) calls observing children "kidwatching." Martha is a dynamic child who constructs her own knowledge from the environment and her interactions in it.

How would you like your teachers to treat you? As a blank slate or as someone given credit for having an active and creative brain?

Dorothy: Tabula rasa? No thanks. I'm changing all the time.

Yes, we all are. That is what Piaget discovered. He discovered that we change considerably over time, and he called that change *development*, which brings us to the other *big* idea and related theory.

Developmentalism.   On the most fundamental level, life is comprised of entities in motion over time. *Development* is defined as change over time. As Kegan explains, "Organic systems evolve through qualitatively different eras according to regular principles of stability and change" (1982, pp. 13–14). Once we know a little about this theory, we can see examples of it all around us.

Authors: Can you think of any examples of development, Dorothy?

Dorothy: Sure. Before I learned to write, I scribbled. Like Martha, I drew and wrote more and got better at control and detail.

Authors: Good example. You probably learned to crawl before you learned to run, too? And as you start to think about research, you might think of yourself as a beginner. That might account for the feelings of trepidation?

There is another aspect of theories we can think about. If you place *ing* on the end of the word *theory*, the meaning is changed.

Dorothy: Theorying?

Authors: Sorry. No. Take off the *y* and add *izing*.

Dorothy: Theorizing. Hmmm.

Authors: Theorizing is the process of forming a *theory*. Today we use the word more generally to mean conjecturing, or speculating. It is what researchers do. In fact, action researchers spend a great deal of time speculating and trying things out. They make their best guesses (hypotheses), and then they test them to see what happens.

Action Research in the Context of Research

Since action research is a special kind of research, a look at research in general may provide a basis from which to understand its special qualities. The *action* part is central. We note three general types of research for the context they provide:

Basic research.   Basic research is usually conceived of in relation to the physical (sometimes referred to as the *hard*) sciences from which it draws its ideas about the nature of knowledge. Knowledge is conceived of as separate from practice; and knowledge can be discovered through the application of rigorous, experimental research methods that include sampling, controls, and manipulation of variables. The goal of this type of research is the development of theories through the discovery of broad generalizations or principles. Basic research advances the frontiers of knowledge; it is less concerned with the application of ideas to the concerns of people. A prime example of the fruits of basic research is Einstein's theory of relativity. While few teachers are unfamiliar with Einstein's equation $E = MC^2$, fewer still understand the implications of its meaning for everyday life. Nor was this potential "use value" likely on Einstein's mind as he unraveled the fundamental mysteries of physics.

Applied research.   In contrast, applied researchers can use principles and theories but supplement them with informal discovery methods for the purpose of generating practical results. Applied research is more concerned with a direct application of its findings to the concerns of real people and their planet. Leonardo da Vinci did applied research, although he would not have called it that. In fact, he was one of the most notable applied researchers of all time. His notebooks contain countless examples of diagrams and plans for things that can be constructed for real-world use. For example, he created the flintlock, a mechanism for generating the spark for gunpowder. His design was used until the mid-1800s!

Dorothy: I like his flying machine better.

Authors: Yes, that is a better example, especially as we are aiming at a special kind of applied research that has to do with improving the quality of life and circumstances—presumably to solve real-world problems. Perhaps a current and concrete example might help? Take food production and farming. The application of fertilizers and crop rotation can improve a farmer's yield and efficiency.

Dorothy: It can also put toxins in produce and ultimately in our stomachs!

Authors: True enough. That's thinking critically. Our point is that both basic research and applied research are valuable. Leonardo da Vinci and Albert Einstein were geniuses who did fundamentally different kinds of research.

Action research.   Action research is a type of applied research that contributes to the generation of principles and theories *and* is at the same time action-oriented. It is also a form of professional development. Thus, knowledge, practice, and development are not separated. It uses a problem-solving approach to improve social conditions and processes of living in the real world. Action research involves an ethical commitment to improving society (to make it more just), improving ourselves (that we may become more conscious of our responsibility as members of a democratic society), and ultimately improving our lives together (building community).

There is no attempt on the part of the action researcher to maintain an illusion of objectivity or to remain value-neutral. Rather, an action researcher's job is to bring to light assumptions, beliefs, and actions; to examine them; and to bring their actions into closer alignment with their values.

In collaboration with one another and their students, action researchers often develop and test theories about their work in a continuing cycle of action, observation, and reflection on the consequences of action. Theorizing includes self-critique: Action researchers constantly examine their actions in light of both their values and an ethical commitment to improving their lives with others.

We will meet many action researchers in the following chapters. They are trying to create classrooms that are responsive to students' needs for belonging, academic achievement, language acquisition, responsibility, and participation in democratic life, to name a few areas of inquiry. These action researchers also demonstrate their increasing awareness of the roles they play in the learning environment.

As you can see, AR is distinct from basic and other forms of applied research in several ways: (1) It is conducted mainly by insiders (practitioners) rather than outsiders. (2) It has an explicit value orientation and doesn't espouse "objectivity" in the traditional sense. (3) It is geared toward the improvement of the practitioner-researcher as well as practice. (4) It is self-critical inquiry, undertaken by the participants themselves.

There are many reasons for engaging in educational action research, not the least of which is to enable the profession, and the professionals who comprise it, to establish methods for continuous growth toward socially constructive ends. From their earliest participation as students in schools which are collaborative, inquisitive, and reflective communities, to likewise engaging in teacher preparation and continuing education institutions and schools, constructive change can be cultivated and supported. Action research can be a potent tool to do so.

CHAPTER SUMMARY

We began this chapter by discussing the bigger picture, the move from modern to postmodern times, and some of the paradigms, theories, and research that provide a context for action research. We looked in particular at constructivist and developmental theories which have been, for good and ill, highly influential to intellectual life during the past century. Action research necessitates theorizing, speculating, and acting. We placed AR in relationship to basic research and applied research, and we noted its distinction in four areas: It is conducted by insiders, it has an explicit value orientation, it is geared toward improvement of the researcher as well as the practice, and it is self-critical inquiry. In the next chapter, we will continue to develop the context of AR with three orientations to knowledge and the methods used by researchers within these orientations.

CHAPTER FOUR

Three Orientations to Knowledge and Methods of Research

Action research (AR) is a process of theorizing and testing our own, as well as other people's, ideas and theories in practice. It is grounded in ideas about how knowledge is generated (AR is a process of developing theories by practitioners who test those theories against their own values) and in the relationship between the knower and what is known (the researcher and what is being studied are connected in an interactive way—the values of the researcher influence what is learned).

Thomas Kuhn, a well respected scientist, wrote a fascinating (and now classic) book about paradigm shifts and changes entitled *The Structure of Scientific Revolutions* (1970). In this book he describes how we need to think "outside of the box" (theory and/or paradigm) when a system of thinking no longer works and there is an anomaly that cannot be explained by the current theory or paradigm. When this happens in our teaching, it can lead to AR. While the contemplation of competing paradigms and theories can absorb (and waste) a considerable amount of energy, it can also provide the impetus to further develop our perspectives. Open discussions and debate can enrich us as we develop multiple perspectives. However, as Dewey pointed out, arguing against another's perspective can also narrow our thinking; reacting against any *ism*, he taught, is a trap or game in which energy is usually wasted. The three orientations to knowledge that we will discuss here each have their paradigms, theories, and methods of scholarship.

The world view of the knower is rarely made explicit, even to the knower; but it is of no small consequence, for such paradigms determine how knowledge is approached and defined. It is a model of sorts, a description of how a system works. It is a way of organizing one's thinking and making sense of the world. A paradigm is broader than a theory; it is a birthplace for theories. In the sections which follow, we will discuss a few dominant paradigms and their ways of knowing. Like any way of categorizing experience and ways of understanding it, the paradigm is not a static way of looking at a phenomenon. The paradigm evolves and changes over time, as we can see with the modern and postmodern eras. Two other paradigms, probably familiar to you, that have evolved over the last century are the behavioristic and humanistic paradigms.

Now, let's go to another level of discussion and explore some ideas about how knowledge is constructed and acquired. We will find that different views of knowledge construction and discovery result in different purposes and methods for conducting action research.

Dorothy: This is sounding a great deal like philosophy—are you sure you want to take us down that path? You seem to keep forgetting that it is a solid Yellow Brick Road that we are traveling to Oz. How will philosophy get us there?

The study of knowledge is a philosophical quest. And, yes, as action researchers, we *do* want to go there. But *there* is not as amorphous as you might think. In fact, when we engage in professional work, we are *doing philosophy*. That's pretty concrete, wouldn't you agree?

According to Jurgen Habermas, a noted philosopher, knowledge is related to the way people orient themselves to the world (Habermas, 1972). He offered a succinct framework outlining three basic orientations to the world and to knowledge, each of which has a particular interest in mind.

Habermas's three basic orientations to knowledge

Orientation:	Material well being	Communication	Freedom
Governed by:	Technical interest	Practical interest in understanding	Emancipatory interest, liberation from oppression
Produces:	Empirical knowing	Situational knowing	Critical reflective knowing

The first orientation, toward material well-being, is "governed by a technical interest in acting on the world. This produces an empirical knowing in the form of facts and generalizations" (Carson, 1990, p. 168). The next orientation, toward communication, "is governed by a practical interest in understanding others . . . [It] is situational and interpretive, rather than generalizable and empirical" (Carlson, 1990, p. 168). The third of Habermas's orientations is toward freedom and the liberation of those who are oppressed. Paulo Freire (1970) is a good example of this, as he taught people in a small South American village to read with materials that enabled them to become conscious of the ways in which they were oppressed. This third orientation "produces a critically reflective knowledge" (Carlson, 1990, p. 168). In the United States, Miles Horton (1993) used a similar method of education in the civil rights and labor union movement to empower persons who would not otherwise have had access to educational opportunities. A fascinating account of education and social change from this critical perspective is found in a book of conversations between Miles Horton and Paulo Freire called, aptly, *We Make the Road by Walking* (Bell et al., 1990).

Each of these orientations to the world—technical, practical, and emancipatory—can be seen in the ways in which practitioners approach improving themselves, their work, and their work lives. Using the ubiquitous example of how we use time in classrooms, we can illustrate these three orientations.

- Those with a *technical orientation* toward time might ask, How can I use my time more efficiently so that my students will have maximum learning time, which may result in increased achievement on standardized tests?
- Those with a *practical orientation* toward time might ask, How do my students think about the time they spend on computers in the classroom?
- Those with an *empancipatory interest* might ask, How just is the expenditure of time used in preparation for tests that will disenfranchise some students (by not allowing them to graduate if they do not pass the test) and some teachers (by withholding monetary rewards when their students do not pass the test)?

Not only are these distinctions important in terms of understanding the orientations and questions asked by practitioners, but also these orientations and ways of knowing determine to a large extent the research methods that are used in conducting an inquiry. These methods have been termed *empirical analytic* (for those whose interests are technical), *naturalistic* (for those whose interests are interpretive and practical), and *critical* (for those whose interests are emancipatory). Let's look more closely at the methods associated with these orientations.

Experimental methods. Experimental methods are normally associated with technical and empirical orientation to research. Researchers from this orientation use various methods for experimentation and observation of the empirical world—the world that can be seen, heard, touched, tasted, and felt. Hypotheses are tested for verification (can they be verified?) and variables are manipulated (which of these competing explanations of the phenomena under study can be eliminated?). Experimental methods are used to understand a phenomenon that is relatively simple—an atom, for example—in which there are limited variables that must be taken into account as alternative explanations for a change in the atom.

The research setting, often a laboratory, is contrived, and the conditions can be controlled to the extent that it is possible to avoid the influence of variables that are not part of the study. The purpose of the research is to generalize, predict, form laws, and derive cause-and-effect explanations for how and why this thing happens the way it does. This is accomplished by taking things apart to see how the parts fit together, which explains why this method is also referred to as analytic.

Because the researcher manipulates variables to determine causal relationships, the outcomes have been manipulated as well. Reality exists in the behavior or appearance that can be experienced; a person using the experimental method seeks to study this reality. Experimental methods have often been used in classrooms to study the effects of different treatments (e.g., sometimes curriculum and teaching techniques). Pretesting and posttesting students who have been assigned to a treatment group (a new method of teaching mathematics), to a nontreatment group (continuing with the same mathematics program), or to various kinds of treatment groups (divided into groups, each using a different mathematics program) provides evidence (or doesn't!) of learning and/or change between or among treatment groups.

Experimental studies (or, as some would say, "quasi-experimental"—acknowledging that true experiments cannot be conducted with human beings) of teaching conducted in the 1960s, 1970s, and 1980s, called *process-product research*, have contributed to understanding specific ways in which basic skills can be taught (e.g., through the use of direct instruction), ways to develop orderly classrooms (e.g., through the use of rewards for positive academic and social behavior), and ways to encourage higher levels of thinking (e.g., through the use of open-ended questions).

Naturalistic methods.   Methods are considered naturalistic when they occur in natural settings (such as classrooms, as opposed to laboratories) where there is relatively little intervention to the normal flow of events. For the most part they are nonexperimental. That is, naturalistic researchers are not interested in manipulating or controlling the situation, and they are not interested in studying interventions in the traditional sense of experimental study. When the purpose of research is to understand *what is* rather than to study that which has been manipulated and controlled, naturalistic research methods are appropriate. In naturalistic research, questions are developed in a cyclical, repetitive process of interaction between the researcher and the researched. Results are compared and contrasted to arrive at understandings that are more sophisticated than those at the outset of the study and result in generating new questions or hypotheses. When the researcher wants to understand something that is complex, socially influenced, dynamic, and interactive with many variables, naturalistic approaches are more appropriate because they enable the researcher to look more contextually and comprehensively (some would call this holistically) at what is occurring.

Understanding how students learn, for example, is an entirely different matter from understanding how the atoms of which students are comprised operate. Given that classrooms are socially complex places, naturalistic approaches are often useful. Reality as we know it is not just what appears on the surface of behavior (or even in the movement of atoms!). Reality is seen in the complex dance of beings in relationship on multiple levels, and it is, in part, created by people. Naturalistic methods enable researchers to seek meaning to enhance human interactions in complex social settings.

For example, one might set out to study how teachers grow. That is a pretty broad question! One of us designed a study to explore that territory. She did not expect to find an answer to that question, but she did expect to gain insights into the nature of professional growth and the conditions that seem to support it. Her study was phenomenological. She wanted to find out about how people (seven teachers) perceived their own development and those aspects of their practice which constrained, supported, or had little effect on their development. She was particularly interested not in other people's views of the teachers, but in their own views—how teachers' worlds felt to them and how they interpreted their experiences (their phenomenal worlds).

The study began in 1980 and lasted well over a year. The researcher participated with and observed the teachers in their classrooms, analyzed their journals, collected and analyzed artifacts, and held weekly seminars during which the teachers talked about their teaching lives and experiences. As in many naturalistic studies, there were mountains of data. (This could happen to us! Don't be concerned; we will discuss ways to handle large amounts of data in Chapter 13.) An unexpected finding was that writing about practice was a powerful tool for professional development. The power of writing as a tool for professional development is now well known, but at the time it had been used by many qualitative researchers as a way to peer into another's world (Holly, 1989). While the study was designed from a naturalistic perspective with the intent to intervene as little as possible in the participants' lives, the unintended consequences of the data-gathering tools (journals and discussion groups in particular) were considerable and contributed valuable means for critique and for professional development. During this same period, researchers in the field of English were exploring the power of writing as a cognitive process (Perl, 1981; Flower, 1981; Flower and Hayes, 1980, 1981). We now have a rich base of studies which illustrate the many benefits of writing about practice.

Critical methods.   Although the word *critical* to many people means "finding fault" and thus has a negative connotation, we are using the word *critical* in the sense that Habermas and others (e.g., Carr and Kemmis) use it—as an emancipatory orientation to the world. Critical theorists claim that the quality of interaction that is sought by those whose orientation is practical cannot be reached without emancipating people who have been constrained from pursuing a better life by one or more of the following: race, class, gender, ability, and age.

The purpose of socially critical research is to improve the lives and environments of those who have been disenfranchised or marginalized, those whose voices are not heard. A teacher, for example, who wonders why the out-of-school suspension list is filled with students of color and why the gifted and talented program is filled with white students may be critiquing current practices which value and privilege contributions of a dominant culture over those of nondominant cultures.

Improvement, according to critical theorists, is accomplished by examining our own *false consciousness* (the inability to see the constraints that have shaped us and have been placed on us by dominant forces of oppression); by exposing inequalities in relationships, social structures, and practices such as female subordination, authoritarian power relations between teachers and students and between administrators and teachers, and ability grouping; and by seeking to change those conditions to improve the quality of life for those who have been oppressed. According to critical theorists, reality is created over time by social, historical, political, cultural, psychological, economic, ethnic, and gender factors. Giroux and McLaren (1986) and other critical researchers have documented that the dominant professional orientation in education has been and still is *technical*. This dominant view is challenged by the critical. Figure 4.1 outlines this discussion of the three orientations to research.

The purposes of action research emerge from the purposes of research in general. As action researchers, we come to our practice with *technical, practical,* and

FIGURE 4.1 *Three approaches to research: experimental, naturalistic, and critical*

	Experimental	Naturalistic	Critical
Philosophical foundations	*Logical positivism:* concerned with facts or causes of phenomenon rather than the perspective of those involved with the phenomenon.	*Phenomenology:* concerned with understanding human behavior from the perspective of the participants.	*Social critical theory:* concerned with emancipatory political interests, i.e., empowering human beings to transcend the constraints placed by race, class, gender, etc.
Interests served	Technical	Practical	Emancipatory
What is the nature of reality?	Reality exists and can be studied by trying to discover the laws that govern it.	Reality is what individual people or groups of people experience, think it is, and agree that it is.	Reality is created over time by social, political, cultural, economic, ethnic, and gender factors so that what is now considered real was not always so.
What is the relationship between the knower and what can be known?	The researcher and the object of the investigation are considered independent so that the researcher does not influence the object of study.	The researcher and the object of study are interactively linked so that the finding (reality) is created as the research process unfolds.	The researcher and the object of study are interactively linked. The values of the researcher influence what is learned.
What is the purpose of research?	Generalize, predict, form causal explanations.	Contextualize, interpret, and understand perspective of the participant.	Critique the social injustices in society to improve the lives of those who have been disenfranchised.
What are the methods used by the researcher to find out what she/he wants to know?	*Quantitative:* Questions and/or hypotheses are empirically tested to verify them, by manipulating the variables so that competing explanations can be eliminated.	*Qualitative:* Questions are answered in a cyclical, iterative process of interaction between the researcher and the researched. Constructions are compared and contrasted to arrive at understanding that is more sophisticated than at the outset of the study.	*Critical:* The researcher and the participants in the inquiry engage in dialogue in which the goal is transforming consciousness from one of ignorance of the impact of race, class, gender, etc. toward informed consciousness, with the understanding that oppressive structures can be changed.

Adapted from Curriculum: *Perspective, Paradigm and Possibility,* © 1986. Reprinted with permission of Prentice Hall, Inc., Upper Saddle River NJ.

emancipatory purposes. Many teachers and students begin with questions of a technical or practical nature: improving classroom discipline, student skills in cooperation, effective use of time, or trying to apply the theory of multiple intelligences. As we and our students reflect openly on our work, we can begin to ask ourselves questions of a more critical and social nature, especially if we are challenged to do so (by a reading or colleague who poses questions). The more we critique our work, the more we can come to see injustices done in the name of helping. We can begin to understand the ways in which we are implicated in perpetuating these injustices. And, as we grow in our abilities to entertain more complex perspectives on our own actions, there are reverberations in social and psychological domains also. We address these in Section 3.

As we examine underlying assumptions about learning and teaching (both our own assumptions and those of the institutions in which we work), we often find ourselves critiquing the beliefs, structures, and practices that get in the way of creating the quality of classroom life that we seek. If we keep in mind the ethical, moral, and democratic commitments we make when we decide to become educators, we will begin our action research from a more critical stance. With this critical stance and the questions that follow from it, we find ourselves continuing to ask technical and practical questions, but we put them in the service of new understandings. For example, we may still want to find ways to use time more efficiently, but *what we consider to be efficient* may have changed: Giving young children precut papers instead of providing them with the opportunity to cut their own papers may "get the project completed faster," but it also becomes more the teacher's projects than the children's, and it does nothing to help children develop skills that will help them to become independent. Additionally, it sends the child clear—if implicit—messages about power and what is valued.

Characteristics of Action Research

Four elements characterize action research: ethical commitment, cycle of reflective practice, public character, and collaboration.

Ethical commitment. The foundation for any action research project is commitment to professional practice and to the democratic principles that undergird it. How best can I serve the students I teach? How can I improve my practice? a teacher-researcher may ask. Or one might ask, Does this curriculum privilege a few at the expense of others? and Whose needs are *not* being met? Whatever the question, the researcher is motivated by a concern for examining the social consequences of teaching practice.

For John Dewey, this commitment meant building a democratic learning community, one which values both the general social welfare and the full development of human beings as individuals (Dewey, 1916). According to Dewey, democracy requires the participation of every mature human being in the formation of values that regulate the community. Communities are formed when they allow the development of common aims, beliefs, aspirations, and knowledge—a common understanding (Dewey, 1964). This common understanding implies oneness and respect for alternative perspectives, negotiation, deliberation, and discussion.

Embedded within Dewey's ideas of a democratic learning community is the *BIG* idea we addressed earlier—developmentalism. In a democratic community developmentalism is expressed as a belief that human beings, independent of the range of their personal endowment, have the right to develop their gifts (Dewey, 1938).

For the action researcher, improvement means moving toward a more democratic learning community. This entails creating conditions that ensure the participation and development of individuals within the community. Students and teachers develop toward common understandings of what it means to be a valued member of a community.

If these are the goals and values that action researchers hold as they work to improve their teaching, what are the working principles that guide their actions? Stringer (1996) provides some useful guidelines:

- Relationships are equal, not hierarchical. Leadership shifts and depends upon expertise and the challenge at hand, rather than by position.
- Communication is authentic, sincere, and open.
- Participation is focused, active, and supportive of group aims and direction.
- All participants are involved and function in cooperative and inclusionary ways. (p. 38)

The promise of power and control that undergirds hierarchical and bureaucratic ways of organizing schools makes the enactment of these principles difficult to achieve. Traditionally, schools have been organized in ways that allow those "on top" (superintendents, supervisors, and principals) to control those "on the bottom" (teachers and students) so that schools run "efficiently" and so that students and teachers are accountable to state and national standards. Anyone who is familiar with what actually happens in schools (or any social organization for that matter) knows that human beings are relatively unpredictable, and that attempts to control them meet with little success. The consequence of being controlled (for those on the bottom) is increased frustration and alienation as they try to produce outcomes within the restrictive environment of policy and procedures. The consequence for those on top is increased stress as they try to follow the mandates from "above" and deal with the resistance from "below," trying to solve complex problems associated with education (Stringer, 1996). Without the active support of school administrators, community members, and government officials, these democratic values will be difficult to achieve.

Dorothy: This reminds me of the Wicked Witch of the West. She tried to control everything!

Authors: Yes she did. And you know what happened to her! We have a better path to chart—one which is more dynamic and reflective than that poor, disgruntled witch could fathom.

Cycle of reflective practice. According to Stenhouse, the impulse behind research is *curiosity.* For those of us who teach, this means taking a look at something in our practice which intrigues us. We follow this curiosity, preferably with some ferocity, into its den in the forest and abide there until we can begin to formulate potentially useful ways of engaging with it and learning about it. We plan our path (which becomes our design and "proposal"), to find out more about this curiosity, and we consider how we can protect our inquiry from the myriad of distractions which invite themselves into our teaching days. So, we start out with curiosity, we stick with it until we can describe it as *inquiry,* and we plan how we can conduct our studies.

In many forms of research we follow the plan (design), collect information (which we sort out as our data), analyze it, and write up our findings. Generally, the project is complete after we have written and presented the report. In action research, the process proceeds somewhat differently. It includes trying out our ideas, observing, and documenting ourselves and the consequences of our actions. As the process continues, we try out other ideas and continue the cycle of *acting, observing,* and *reflecting,* which ultimately takes us to other questions and new cycles. In a sense, AR is less linear, less tidy, and messier than what we normally think of as research. It doesn't often have a neat beginning, middle, and end. Action researchers can begin anywhere in the cycle depicted in Figure 4.2, and they can proceed in a number of ways. They can revisit parts of the cycle as the study evolves.

The research cycle includes acting and finding the consequences intriguing, observing (looking at) something that begs attention, and reflecting (thinking) on teaching. One part of the cycle can lead into any other. The process itself is *educational.* To be a professional educator, Stenhouse said that *teachers must inevitably be intimately involved in the research process,* which when used, becomes educational.

As a basic principle, action research is designed to improve practice. It is conducted by a person or people, or a small group, who want to bring their actions more in line with their aims and intentions. They want their practice to be congruent with their values, and they build themselves into the research. As the philosopher Sartre put it, research is undertaken by intellectuals, persons whose

Figure 4.2 *Cycle of reflective practice.*

"minds watch themselves." Action researchers design their watching into their work, not only as an afterthought, such as an epilogue or "reflections on the process," but also as a documented reflective process throughout. This is the important *self-critical* part of Lawrence Stenhouse's definition.

Authors: Dorothy, is this making more sense?

Dorothy: I guess so. It still doesn't sound very inviting—all this self-critical stuff.

Authors: Although often it is not acknowledged, development into a professional realm has been this way for a very long time. Few, if any, great journeys have been accomplished without self-critique. Even Aristotle, the great 4th-century philosopher, was self-critical.

Dorothy: So, action research is the process of acting, observing, reflecting, and being self-critical.

Authors: Well (pause) . . . yes, but there are two more characteristics.

Public character.   For it to be research, Stenhouse says that it must be shared with others. In his words:

> Research . . . is systematic and sustained inquiry, planned and self-critical, which is subjected to public criticism and to empirical tests where they are appropriate.

His shortened version is *systematic self-critical inquiry made public.*

If this terminology sounds intimidating, remember that the action research journey includes colleagues, ruby slippers, and the good witches—all useful. The last key component of AR is collaboration.

Collaboration

Dorothy: I don't know about you, but I feel pretty alone on my journey.

Authors: You are not as alone as you think. Look around you. What about the Scarecrow? The Tin Man? The Lion? Toto? And what about those Munchkins? That's alone?

Dorothy: So how do they help? What does this have to do with anything?

Authors: The beginning of this journey has to do with listening to those around you (especially your students) in seeking out different kinds of information (data) and support (collaboration). Involving others can take many forms— from asking students for their perceptions and opinions about what we are doing in school, to full-blown community development projects in which all members participate in a research process that is mutually beneficial. To put this into action and to start down the Yellow Brick Road, you have to summon a little courage and take a few steps.

Dorothy: Let's stop here for a minute. We have covered a lot of ground, but I think that I am beginning to understand what action research is.

Scarecrow: Me, too. Let me see if I can summarize it. Action research is a process of democratizing research and educational practice. It is a democratic orientation to professional practice, a way of learning and improving oneself and one's practice. It is a process that employs systematic and sustained inquiry, and it is made public. It is a self-directed journey, guided by a commitment to building a democratic learning community; and it is leading us toward greater professionalism!

Authors: Yes! You have all your "its" in a row. We would add only one: It is work in collaboration with your students and/or colleagues. We couldn't have put it better.

CHAPTER SUMMARY

Now that we have a better understanding of the three orientations to knowledge; the technical, practical, and emancipatory interests served; and the experimental, naturalistic, and critical methods used; we can place AR in a broader context. People with an emancipatory or critical approach use a diversity of methods, as long as the methods are directed at emancipation. With a commitment to social change, action researchers engage in a cycle of reflective practice, public discussion, and collaboration. These are the elements of AR. The final contextual perspective we will address in a brief historical excursion in Chapter 5. In that chapter we will define several different kinds of teacher research and conclude with AR as critical reflection.

From a Meandering Path to the Yellow Brick Road: A Brief History of Action Research

Our road begins long before it was paved. In fact, you might as well call it a dirt path for most of its history. You are about to meet quite an interesting group of people, whose work as thinkers and researchers paved the way for early teacher research and eventually action research. You will notice how researchers often go against the grain of what is common knowledge. Through careful observation, data collection, analysis, and interpretations that they discuss publicly, they make possible new ways of seeing and understanding.

Being skeptical enables new ways of seeing and understanding, Dorothy. These are our new eyes! Remember Galileo? Just think how much courage Galileo needed. Galileo's careful research provided concrete (observable) evidence and provided the basis for laws which would change our understanding of the cosmos and earth's place in it. Unfortunately this ran against the beliefs of the time and ran contrary to the beliefs held in the Catholic Church, so he faced ridicule and was threatened with death for his "grounded theories." His published work *Dialogue on the Two Chief World Systems* was an attempt to deal with official resistance to his ideas and factual observations. He recognized that doing the research wasn't the hardest part—getting people to consider his ideas was.

For Galileo to do research that supported Copernicus's theory that the sun (not the earth) was the center of the universe was to take a radically different point of view from the prevailing views of his time. Never mind that it took 300 years for others to recognize his brilliant contributions! (Better late than never.) And besides, we can learn from his mistakes—the one most pertinent to us here is that the researcher (like Copernicus) cannot expect the research to speak for itself. Only on Star Trek do people consistently give a fair hearing to all points of view before coming to a conclusion. As researchers, we have to make the results and implications of our research understandable to others.

Dorothy: Hmm. I see. It took considerable courage for Galileo to do his research and look what odds he went up against to speak his truth. I can at least be a pioneer into my own practice.

Trailblazers of action research.   That you can be, Dorothy. Now let's look at how action research can be connected to a broader, more inclusive type of research—or: *teacher research.*

Dorothy: Teacher research? Now you have lost me. I thought that we were talking about teachers' research all along. Teachers' action research. Is teacher research different than teachers' action research?

Yes again. We have been talking about teachers' research, and AR is a type of teachers' research. Some people use the two terms interchangeably, but we think that it is worth making a distinction between them. *Teacher research* is a broader term and incorporates research that does not satisfy (nor would its researcher normally want to) the four criteria we set forth in Chapter 4. It need not be a cyclical kind of research; nor need it be conducted in collaboration with anyone, for example. It can be individual or group research, and it can include all kinds of systematic inquiries conducted by teachers. Many, though not all, people agree with Stenhouse that for it to be research, it must be made public.

Action research, on the other hand, is carried out by teachers who have an explicit agenda based on the four characteristics we outlined earlier. We don't want to muddy the already murky waters here, but perhaps a chart might help—even if it has new terms.

Dorothy: At the risk of being cheeky, may I offer an observation?

Authors: Certainly.

Dorothy: You said that action research is a subset of teacher research.

Authors: Yes, we did.

Dorothy: Isn't it also true that teacher research can be a subset of action research? Isn't it true that lots and lots of types of action research take place outside of classrooms and schools and that teacher research, and classroom research for that matter, is only a small part of the larger category of action research?

Authors: Yes. That is true. It all depends on your point of view. You *are* using an analytical and critical eye! For now, look at action research as a subset of teacher research. Now, before we lose the thread completely, let's get back to the trailblazers.

Galileo was just one of the trailblazers who prepared the way for teacher research and eventually action research. Thinkers such as Aristotle, Copernicus, Galileo, and Newton went against the grain of accepted beliefs of their time. Newton, for example, was so upset with the lack of acknowledgment of his book *Principia Mathematica* that he simply stopped publishing his work at all for a long time. He delayed publication of the law of gravity for 20 years!

Types of Research Teachers Do

Teacher Research

Any kind of research undertaken by a teacher or a group of teachers and others.

Classroom Research

Any kind of research undertaken by a teacher, or teachers, or others, in and about classrooms.

Action Research

Research undertaken by individuals or groups which is founded on an active ethical commitment to improve the quality of life of others, is critically reflective in nature and outcome, is collaborative with those to be affected by actions undertaken, and is made public.

Teacher Action Research

Action research conducted by a teacher or teachers.

Classroom Action Research

Action research that takes place within and is focused upon life and practices (teaching and learning) within classrooms and schools.

Collaborative Action Research

Action research undertaken by individuals or groups in concert with, or with a common focus with, other individuals or groups.

Other thinkers went against the grain of accepted research methods. Whereas naturalistic methods of research were used primarily in studying the natural world, Comenius, Rousseau, Pestalozzi, Montessori, and Ashton-Warner applied naturalistic methods to the study of children. And they used their observations to study the consequences of their actions on the children they taught. It is easy to see why it took such courage for these teachers to become researchers. By observing children and developing teaching strategies based on these observations, these thinkers and teacher-researchers were challenging the accepted tradition that research be conducted by trained outsiders and under controlled conditions.

John Dewey holds a special place in the development of teacher research and action research. A progressive educational philosopher, he was critical of the traditional separation of knowledge and action. Dewey applied the scientific method of problem solving to education. He believed that teachers needed to test their ideas in action—while they were teaching. He believed that by bringing a healthy skepticism to their teaching, rather than jumping uncritically from one technique to another, teachers were better able to reflect on their practice. He was critical of education that simply taught students to fit in and to follow the status quo. Rather, he believed that it was our duty to help students become increasingly more complex, socially aware and responsible citizens, and active participants in a democratic society. To Dewey, the classroom was a democratic community. His thinking was considered revolutionary because he integrated child development, the purposes of schooling (social and democratic ideals), and the curriculum. He exalted experience itself as a teacher and deepened the teachers' role to include study of the child as a foundational element for curriculum development, teaching, and evaluation. Figure 5.1 outlines the development of the teacher researcher.

Constructing the Yellow Brick Road.   Dewey offered us a way to think about teaching as reflective and scholarly practice. He offered a way to improve teaching through reflective practice. Kurt Lewin, a social psychologist and a contemporary of John Dewey, developed the methods and principles to enable any social organization, including schools, to act as an agent for democratic change. Constructing the Yellow Brick Road formally began with Kurt Lewin's work in the 1930s and 1940s.

Lewin was a consultant for various groups. He developed experiments that compared the products of groups working under different degrees of participation in decision making (Adelman, 1993). One of Lewin's greatest contributions to social change was his use of action research (a term coined by a man named Collier just a few years before Lewin started his experiments) to help participants "learn to become detached and objective in examining the foundations of their biases" (Ebbutt, 1985, p. 154). For example, Lewin helped a group of managers at a new factory to examine their belief that newly hired, unskilled female trainees would not be able to perform their tasks as efficiently as already skilled men. Lewin helped us to see the importance of recognizing the biases, opinions, prejudices that we all have, and that when they go unexamined, impede us from seeing ourselves and our situations in new ways.

At the same time as Lewin was conducting his research, other people in psychology and psychiatry were trying to find ways of communicating more adequately. Part of their efforts were aimed at helping people to "see gaps and discrepancies between their perceptions and actions in their relationships with others" (Holly, 1989, p. 152). They were trying to uncover problems in personal and interpersonal communication which prevented them from recognizing and challenging their own biases and distorted perceptions (Lippitt, 1949). So, instead of continuing the tradition of focusing on changing *others,* research was turned toward changing one's *own behavior* and understanding. The research itself was empowering to the person and group conducting it, and it contributed to knowledge about social relations and change.

Today's action research, sometimes referred to as *educational action research,* grew from these earlier forms of inquiry and AR in the social and psychological professions. It pertains to individuals trying to monitor and learn from reflection on action and trying to become aware of discrepancies among perceptions, values, and actions. It contains elements of individual and group self-study, and social action.

FIGURE 5.1 *Trailblazers on the path: The roots of teacher research and action research*

Scientist/Thinker	Contribution to Research	What We Derive for Teacher Research
Aristotle (384–322 B.C.)	Valued observer's role in constructing reality; morally informed action clarifies belief and deepens understanding.	Importance of observation for learning; importance of basing our action on a morally grounded belief system.
Copernicus (1473–1543)	Went against common thought and created a firestorm; replaced the earth with the sun as the center of the cosmos.	Simplicity, harmony, and order are aesthetic goals.
Galileo (1564–1642)	Investigated physical causes and established celestial physics on firmer ground; careful observation and documentation.	Follow your instincts, collect documentation, use diplomacy, and do question the powers that be!
Newton (1642–1727)	Developed the law of gravity.	We cannot be deterred from making public what we learn, even though others may be critical of our ideas.
Comenius (1592–1670)	Conducted empirical observations of how children learn.	Child-centered observation as a basis for teaching methods; one of the earliest teacher researchers.
Rousseau (1592–1670)	Applied naturalistic methods of inquiry (which had been used for centuries to observe nature) to the study of children.	Use of naturalistic methods of observation as a basis for forming educational principles.
Pestalozzi (1746–1827)	Tested and applied his ideas of child rearing in educational settings.	Use of inquiry method of observation to address needs of students.
Montessori (1870–1952)	Conducted naturalistic methods of observation with teachers and students. Trained teachers to be observers of the effects of their teaching on students.	Use of observation to help us understand the effect of our actions on students.
Ashton-Warner	Saw teaching as an art form. Role of the teacher as calling on children's resources and having the patience to listen, watch, and wait; harnessing of creative energies as the agent of change.	Use of diary to record observations of students as a way of understanding the resources they bring to their own learning.

Dorothy: Whoa. Can you put that a little more simply please?

Surely. AR is about making changes. If we weren't still developing as teachers and researchers in social and physical environments where all our students were enabled to do wonderful and amazing things, there would be no reason to improve ourselves, our teaching, or the lives of our students.

Today, there are networks and AR groups that provide forums for discussion, support, and collaboration all over the world. There are core groups in Bath, England, associated with Jack Whitehead, and at Deakin University in Australia, where Stephen Kemmis, Robin Mc Taggart, and Collin Henry have been instrumental in the growth of AR. The network that we are most familiar with is that which has been developed from the works of British action researchers Lawrence Stenhouse and his colleague John Elliott. John Elliott founded the Collaborative Action Research Network (CARN) which, since 1967, has been comprised of an international group of teachers, administrators, and teacher educators involved in AR.

In Lawrence Stenhouse's 1975 book, *An Introduction to Research and Curriculum Development*, he traced the development of research in classrooms and research on teaching, including interaction analysis and what has been called *social anthropology* among other areas of inquiry. While AR had its origins in the experimental, psychological studies of Kurt Lewin, most action research studies developed from a more qualitative orientation and employ both naturalistic and experimental methods. As we reflect on the purposes of action research and observe its evolution over time, this makes sense. Inquiry which focuses on self-study, social improvement, and collaborative action naturally lends itself to a mode of inquiry that values individual and social interpretation as a basis for developing knowledge. The most important factor to remember is that *the context, questions, purposes, and participants* drive the appropriateness of methods, not preconceived notions about whether a study should be more quantitative or qualitative.

Dorothy: Speaking of questions, I've got lots of them right now.

That's not surprising. Let's continue and see if we can enlarge the context, which might help with some of your questions. If this doesn't help, we will address your questions later. Although it would be tempting to go into greater detail about the history of AR and to look at the various ways it has developed throughout the world, it would delay us from getting on to more practical matters of how to conduct action research. Instead, in Figure 5.2 we provide a few brief portraits of a few notable contributors and groups which illustrate some of the breadth and depth of the AR process as it evolved.

Today: AR as Critical Reflection

We who claim education as our calling need to critically reflect upon what we do. We have come to a time in history where we can begin to see our professional roots and where we reside in history, and we can consciously, if humbly, influence, at least partially, where we are going. As professionals, we can choose to become connoisseurs

FIGURE 5.2 *Pavers of the action research road*

Thinker/Action Researcher	Noted Position	Contribution to Action Research
John Dewey American	Educational philosopher; progressivism	Connected theory and practice through critical reflection—teachers must study the consequences of their actions. Conceived of teaching as an ethical and moral enterprise in which teachers educate students for responsible citizenship.
Kurt Lewin American	Social psychologist	Coined term *action research* to mean research conducted by scholar-practitioners to improve their social situations; participants must become objective in examining their own biases; saw AR as a way of describing professional development in social situations.
Stephen Corey American	Curriculum theorist	Applied AR to education as a means of reconceptualizing curriculum from a top-down efficiency model (most efficient way to achieve outcomes) to a curriculum developed by teachers with the goal of promoting a critical social consciousness of the impact of power in society.
Joseph Schwab American	Curriculum theorist	Emphasized the importance of group practical deliberation in curriculum development by teachers; based on the idea that the process of education is more important than the outcomes and the possibilities that curriculum action can make things "right."
Lawrence Stenhouse British	Director of the Humanities Curriculum Project	Teaching should be based on research carried out by teachers rather than by specialists; teaching is improved by teachers studying the effects of their actions.
John Elliott British	Director of the Ford Teaching Project and founder of Classroom Action Research Network (CARN)	Educational research is a moral endeavor in its attempt to realize values in practice; teachers develop theories as they teach. Developed a model of the action research process that includes a sequential cycle of action and reflection.

FIGURE 5.2 *Continued*		
Thinker/Action Researcher	**Noted Position**	**Contribution to Action Research**
Wilf Carr and Stephen Kemmis Welsh; British-American	Professors of education at the University of North Wales and Deakin University, Australia, respectively	Carr and Kemmis developed the term *educational action research;* developed a model for critical-emancipatory AR which is based on the belief that research should focus on developing just and democratic forms of education.
Jean NcNiff British	AR consultant and writer in England	Believed that teaching *is* research and that AR is a professional development activity; developed a model of AR that includes continuing spirals of action and reflection.

and to look critically at our practice. Inherent in action research is a commitment to do just that—to look with new eyes at the everyday and special occasions of our educational practice. Action research offers a framework within which to explore that wonderful and terrifying world we inhabit inside as well as outside ourselves.

The brief history we recounted in this chapter brings us to modern and post-modern times in which change and complexity are recognized as inevitable and constant. We are moving away from the *modern* world where life was thought to be a bit more manageable than we now know it to be. We thought we could straightforwardly attack and solve many of our problems. Researchers from outside our schools could do research and curriculum development for us. The best disciplinary minds could together produce excellent curricula. Unfortunately these curricula didn't work in many classrooms. For example, "Man, a Course of Study" was one of the most professionally staffed and creative curriculum design projects in recent history. It was more consistent with constructivist and developmental theories than most other curricula. Historians, scientists, artists, and others were involved in designing this innovative and integrated social studies curriculum. The materials included excellent suggestions for highly active and creative student and teacher participation. Unfortunately, the materials were out of step with the people they were to benefit. Had teachers been involved in the design and development process, the story would likely have been entirely different. Collaborative action research can have a marked effect in part because it involves those who stand to benefit from change.

Ours is a time in which teachers and researchers expose multiple dimensions of a "problem," where one "solution" leads to other "problems." Not only do we *see* more complexity, but also there is more complexity to see! This makes teaching in a postmodern world challenging. The world that most of us grew up in is different from the world in which we are called to teach. If we don't try to understand the new one, our teaching won't fit! Simple reflection won't do.

Critical reflection means looking beneath surfaces, asking questions, raising issues, exercising and judging merit. It means questioning practice with respect to larger social issues, ones to which we contribute. A critical theorist would ask, Whose interests *are* being served by this approach to teaching science, art, or literature? How did this happen? Does this curriculum serve all the children in my classroom—or does it privilege a few at the expense of others? In other words, whose needs *are not* being met? This is what Wilf Carr and Steven Kemmis mean by *critical reflection* in their book *Becoming Critical* (1986). Critical reflection can be defined as "being able to understand, analyze, pose questions, and affect and effect the socio-political label and economic realities that shape our lives" (Leistyna et al., 1996, p. 334).

We can become critical as we are able to move beyond "surviving" as teachers. Francis Fuller (1969), through her research on teacher professional development, was able to document what happened to teachers' concerns over time. She developed a theory that described three phases of a teacher's growth over time. In the first phase the teacher was concerned with survival: What do I do on Monday? How can I plan enough to fill the day? In the second phase the teacher focused on curriculum development and learning to teach more knowledgeably, efficiently, and effectively. In the third and last phase, the teacher focus was So what? What are the social, political, economic, and educational consequences of what I do?

This last phase is more typical of the critical theorist orientation. The teacher at this point is concerned with larger social issues and long-term consequences. It is not automatic that teachers go through these phases throughout a career. Some teachers *begin* their teaching careers with a socially critical eye toward practice, especially if they have colleagues who support a questioning stance. Like you, Dorothy, these teachers may walk a very different path in their development.

CHAPTER SUMMARY

After discussing several types of research that teachers do in schools today, we made an excursion into the past. We saw the seeds of teacher research in the relentless quest for learning exhibited by scholars from Aristotle to Galileo to Newton. Empirical investigation was conducted at great cost to the researchers who went against common knowledge and blind adherence to professed certainty that ruled across the Dark Ages. From dirt path to John Dewey and Kurt Lewin and to the paving of the Yellow Brick Road, scholars have challenged current thinking. With Kurt Lewin's research, AR had a start with an overtly social purpose: The people affected by research were to have a say in the conduct of that research. Discrimination in the workplace was fought with empirical evidence. Stephen Corey worked to demonstrate to educators the power of AR to improve education. The movement in education gathered momentum when Lawrence Stenhouse, John El-liott, and others in the United Kingdom worked with teachers in growing numbers and built networks for AR. Today those networks continue to grow. Critical AR is no longer the purview of the few, but the calling of many! While new teachers were characterized, not so very long ago, by survival, critical reflection and inquiry take practice to a new level, one where social change is not only possible, but probable from entry into the profession.

SECTION SUMMARY

Action research is an orientation to and a form of professional practice. It is, in many respects, a logical outgrowth of humankind's inquisitive constitution. Over the ages, from long before Aristotle to postmodernity and beyond, humankind has asked fundamental questions and sought ways to make life better. Action research is one way we can collectively do so. As a systematic, sustained, and publicly shared way of learning and improving oneself and one's practice, it has the power to perpetuate continuous renewal and creative experience. As a self-directed *and* collaborative journey, AR leads inexorably toward greater professionalism within ourselves and for shaping the conditions of our profession. This development in our professional lives and work is guided by critical reflection as we examine ourselves and our practice with an eye toward improving the social consequences of what we do. Teachers are agents of change—movers and shakers, rather than re-actors.

As you can see, AR includes an inward process of examining our assumptions and beliefs more carefully and critically on the lifelong journey of professional teaching. That is why the next section is devoted to taking an in-depth look at ourselves in this profession.

Dorothy: This inward journey is not something I had bargained for. But you have piqued my interest. I understand now what you mean by a cyclical journey!

To complete this part of the journey and to explore our own contexts and invite companions to continue the journey with us, we step into the forest to gather a few tools.

Exploring the Forest
Finding Our Way

Contexts and Companions

We have covered considerable ground in this section. We have touched briefly on some of the people and contexts which surround and shape action research, because we think this knowledge gives us a clearer picture of AR, its roots, and its uses. Whole books have been written on this subject, and we urge you to peruse some of them. Robin McTaggert provides two sources: *Action Research: A Short Modern History* (Deakin University Press, 1991) and an edited volume, *Participatory Action Research: International Contexts and Consequences* (State University of New York Press, 1997). For now, let us reflect on some of the ideas presented in this chapter.

1. *Research experience.* What are your experiences with research? How could your experiences with research hinder and help you in pursuing your area of interest?

2. *Definitions of research terms.* Begin a section of your journal set aside for definitions related to research. Using the text, define the following, and include any other terms that occur to you:
   - Theory, theorize, theoretical
   - Paradigm
   - Naturalistic research
   - Experimental research
   - Basic research
   - Applied research
   - Action research
   - Research methods

3. *Theories.* There are many theories that will be useful to you as a professional educator during your career. These theories inform the development of the most important theory—your own. Three salient theories to us in this book are *constructivism, developmentalism,* and *critical theory.* As a supersleuth researcher, try to do the following two things. Do the first before you read the second.
   - Draw a symbol and do a free-write for each theory.
   - Now write a brief definition of each. Give an example of each. Use your free-write for ideas, and consult this text and any other sources you might find useful.

4. *Critical colleagues.* As we discussed, professionals engage in critical reflection. Collaboration is a defining aspect of our professional lives. With whom (and how) do we form working relationships? *Critical colleague* is the term we will use to describe a person or persons with whom to share, discuss, and give and receive critical feedback. By *critical* we mean feedback that is challenging, collegial, respectful, and useful.

   Talk with another person, preferably a critical colleague, about these three theories and your current understanding of them. What are her or his thoughts on them? What place do any of these theories have in your teaching? Do you find any relationships between and among these theories?

   These theories give us a language to talk about experience, and if we hold on too tightly—as we can to our own theories—they narrow rather than open our perspectives. If we only understand the mechanics, we won't grasp enough to enrich our perspective.

   These theories describe, in a systematic way, many things that we observe and relate to in everyday life. What do we do in schools that has a developmental basis? We don't expect a 6-year-old to have the same experiences in school as a 12-year-old. What do we do in school that is *constructivist* in orientation?

5. *Three purposes of AR.* Material well-being, communication, and freedom are the three ways of knowing described in this chapter. We have used these ways of knowing as a means to frame three purposes of action research. Each is necessary to our personal and collaborative well-being. Without each we cannot be professional. While research is certainly possible without the primary goal of creating more just, equitable, democratic classrooms, professional practice is not.

   Referring to the discussion of these three purposes in the text, use your journal to jot down a few ideas and an example of when each is important to you. Are there times when your primary concern is with acting in such a way as to maintain your (and your students') material well-being? Are there times when the efficiency and effectiveness of your practice are of utmost importance? Are there other times when your primary concern is with a practical interest in understanding? And are there times when your primary concern lies in understanding the relationship between your goals and values and what your students are learning, with educational goals, activities, and experiences that lead to a more just, equitable, democratic classroom? Are there times when your goal is to liberate your students (and perhaps yourself) from oppressive situations?

   Use these jottings to start a conversation with your critical colleague(s). When you have finished this conversation, spend 15 minutes recording key ideas from it in your journal. What ideas, questions, or thoughts do you have as a result of this conversation? Highlight one or two that you might want to revisit.

The final exercises for Section 2 are designed to explore the historical and current contexts of your professional work.

6. *Journals.* What are the key journals in your area? *Childhood education* (for teachers of young children), *Middle-school journal* (for middle-school teachers), and the *Language arts* and **The Reading Teacher** (for teachers of literacy) are a few examples to get you started. Search your library for a list of relevant journals. Select one that seems most relevant to your work, and starting with the earliest issue in your library, scan the tables of contents and articles to see how it has developed over time. What were the topics in the earliest journals? What research methods, if any, were referred to in early articles? What topics are addressed today? What research methods are used for what types of research? Do you find AR among them? Are the topics and issues different in the later journal issues? If so, in what ways? Why might this be so? Theorize a bit. Why has it not shifted in topics and issues?

7. *Influential or significant people.* What people have influenced you most in your education? In what ways have they been influential or significant? You may feel a kinship or connection to someone from your past or present. Write a portrait for your journal of that person, and use stories to illustrate the ways in which they have affected you. Write as many portraits as you wish. Write about one in depth or several in less depth. Might it be worthwhile to share this with the portrayed person or with another colleague?

SECTION 3

Exploring Researcher Selves and the Profession

"Won't you go with me?" pleaded the girl, who had begun to look upon the little old woman as her only friend.

"No, I cannot do that," she replied; "but I will give you my kiss, and no one will dare injure a person who has been kissed by the Witch of the North."

She came close to Dorothy and kissed her gently on the forehead. Where her lips touched the girl they left a round, shining mark, as Dorothy found out soon after.

"The road to the City of Emeralds is paved with yellow brick," said the Witch; "so you cannot miss it. When you get to Oz do not be afraid of him, but tell your story and ask him to help you. Goodbye, my dear."

Dorothy: Where am I? This doesn't look like Kansas!

The Wonderful Wizard of Oz
L. Frank Baum (1900)

That's a good question. And where did I come from? Who am I? Where am I going? And what do I want? What is *my story?* Who am I as a professional? In this section we address some of these questions and others related to professional development with the aid of autobiographical writing. In the first sections of this book we explored the contexts of action research. Now it is time to focus on the person who conducts action research (AR). We will see how the professional and political spheres interact with and shape the personal domain which in turn influences professional and political life.

How can I return home to Kansas? you ask. We each have a "round shiny mark" inside, and it will help us to navigate. Returning home is a powerful incentive, one that will lead us on a journey which is sometimes frightening, sometimes difficult. In this journey we meet new people; explore our roots, human nature, and life; and gain insights we never could have predicted at the start of the journey.

Steven Brookfield, a specialist in adult learning, says that asking challenging questions is important, *especially* when they take us into unknown territory.

> Taking the risk to think critically, and to realize in our actions the insights we gain through this, is one of the most powerful activities of adult life. The reason we persist in doing this, even when it seems to produce only frustration, perplexity, and anxiety, are the rewards it produces . . . we are engaged in a continual process of creating and re-creating our personal, work, and political lives. We do not take our identities as settled; rather, we are aware of the scope for development in all areas of life. We see the future as open to our influence [and] . . . the world as changeable through our own individual actions and through collective action . . . We do not accept the idea that because things are the way they are now, they must always be this way . . . [Nor] that we (or anyone else) have the ultimate answer to life's ambiguities and problems. But we do have confidence in knowing that . . . the actions we take arising out of beliefs, spring from a process of careful analysis and testing against reality—in other words, from critical thinking.
>
> *Stephen Brookfield (1984)*

Just as Dorothy finds, and as we, too, will discover, the ultimate answers to our questions do not come from external wizards. While help from external sources at the right time is useful, we need to rely on judgments we have developed based on our experiences and critical inquiry into them. This is the point that Brookfield is making.

Authors: It takes courage to ask questions like, Where am I? Or Where are we? Don't you agree, Lion?

Lion: Oh, yes. You betcha. That's why I am here. I want to develop courage— enough courage to ask, Who am I? and Why did I do that?

Authors: It takes courage to ask these questions *and* to stick around long enough to find out the answers. It also takes humility and caring to motivate the search for answers. But if we keep our students' and our own professional learning on their behalf foremost in our mind, we know that we must engage in the search. Eh, Tin Man?

Tin Man: Yes, we need a reason to change things because change is hard to do.

Authors: Scarecrow, we need you, too. Just *asking* critical questions, let along figuring out ways to respond to them, takes intelligence.

Scarecrow: Count on me!

Authors: The success of this journey depends on examining our beliefs, gaining confidence in our own knowing, and ultimately discovering that we know more and less, than we think we know.

Our journey begins at home, with who we are and how we have gotten to be who we are. As Socrates put it, "Know thyself." The success of the AR journey depends on our abilities to explore these and other critical questions.

CHAPTER SIX

Journey of the Self: There's No Place Like Home

There is no place like home, and we take home with us most places we go. Early in Dorothy's journey, she examines the importance of home, a place she has taken for granted. Our journey, too, entails an examination of our roots, of what we value, believe, and hope to accomplish. As we continue, we will explore forests, encounter witches, be seduced by poppy fields, visit castles, and discover nasty flying creatures. This is the yet undiscovered landscape into which action researchers embark. Our work in this chapter includes discussion of the multiple selves who inhabit us and find their way into our teaching, and ideas for autobiographical explorations.

Home is a place inside of us. It is our base; it is a security we feel and a nest from which to reflect, act, and observe. While we take home with us, and feel confident and secure with its familiar wisdom, we also challenge its certainty and introduce it to new ways of being. This stretches us in sometimes uncomfortable ways. We learn about ourselves when our assumptions and beliefs are challenged. So, as we speak about the roles and responsibilities of our professional selves (teacher, colleague, student, decision maker, etc.), we will keep in the back of our minds the compass that guides us.

Dorothy: This is all very nice, but will this self-knowledge help me find my way back to Kansas?

Authors: Yes, and you will see it with new eyes.

Ways to Explore Our Teaching Selves

Not only are our identities not settled, but our journey toward self-direction is complex. The formation of our identities is intertwined with many social, political, and cultural forces of which we are not conscious. That is, while we want to shape who we are and who we become, we realize that teachers, schools, parents, churches, the media, and many other social and political forces weave their influences into our identities and our teaching selves. Becoming conscious of those influences is an essential part of becoming self-critical.

As we explore our identities, we get a more complex picture of ourselves. Self-exploration is challenging because we rarely want to face the parts of ourselves that are in conflict or that do not satisfy us. But it is exactly these parts that can act as catalysts for meaningful change. Change is often possible *only* when we face those aspects of our teaching selves. To make a more orchestrated chorus out of the dissonance created by these different parts, or selves, we need to build ways to bring them into conversation.

There are many ways to gain self-knowledge. In the following pages we explore a few of these ways which can be useful for action researchers.

Doing Self-Talk.   Have you ever noticed any private conversations taking place inside your head? Although these inside characters rarely rest, we aren't usually conscious of their debates. When we listen carefully, however, particularly at times when we are making decisions, we can tune into revealing conversations. Let's listen in on one such conversation. We will give each of the *selves* a different number (Self 1, etc.). The problem under consideration is "I'm hungry!"

Self 1: Let's go and get a hot fudge sundae with lots of nuts and whipped cream!
   (A more health-conscious self counters with:)

Self 2: It would be better if I had a salad with tofu and bean sprouts.

Self 1: Oh, yuck!

(Another more mediating voice offers a compromise:)

Self 3 (eagerly): How about a lowfat, fruit-flavored frozen yogurt?

Self 1 and **Self 2**, while not exactly jubilant, react with relief and go along with the compromise.

We often have these kinds of inside self-talk sessions concerning our teaching lives. Joanne recently engaged in self-talk about a student who was upset that "rules were being changed" midstream on an assignment. During a class discussion of an assignment, several students brainstormed possible ways to do the assignment. When Joanne encouraged them to use these new insights in their work, one student objected, saying, "I have already done the assignment, and now you are asking me to change my writing! I am extremely busy and finished it early so I wouldn't have to deal with it again!"

One voice told Joanne: Being a teacher means being flexible and adapting to new ideas—a lesson the student could better learn now than later. Another voice said: This student needs to read her syllabus more carefully and stop whining! Another voice said: I want to be an understanding teacher. This student is under a great deal of stress. And yet another thought occurred to Joanne: As a teacher, have I provided adequate structure and still allowed for flexibility in my assignments?

All this internal talk can influence our behavior. If we become aware of the chorus within, and hear what they say, we have the possibility of taking a new and possibly more insightful perspective. In this case, Joanne chose to react to the student in a way that minimized the student's stress (later the student confided that she was experiencing some difficulties at home on top of a hectic school schedule) *and* to examine the manner in which she presented assignments.

Critical reflection on her identity as a constructivist teacher helped Joanne recall the frustration she (and her colleagues) often felt in similar situations. As a teacher, she wants to provide sufficient structure to help students grow, without stifling their creativity and sense of responsibility with too many required rules and procedures. Many students resist this approach, wanting more specific guidelines. Thus, committing herself to a constructivist approach to teaching—and *living it* —will continue to be a challenging journey.

Interviewing others.   In exploring our roots, we can interview mothers, fathers, older siblings, extended family, friends, and colleagues. Often the comments of these others will spur memories of particular events or patterns and add multiple perspectives to emerging self-understanding. For example, as one part of her educational autobiography, Wendy interviewed her mother. Her mother shared stories of how Wendy liked to "organize her work space" prior to beginning a project and recalled her excitement at learning to read. This information helped her make sense of her career choices and her ways of operating as a teacher.

Examining personal artifacts.   In sharing the development of herself as a teacher, Margo, a preservice teacher, created an album of photographs. She traced the multiple identities she explored during adolescence. From a shy, overweight kid, to a prom queen, to a mother, she demonstrated how her multiple selves and the pain of making transitions from one to another would ultimately lead her to become a more sensitive and empathic teacher of young adolescents. The seeds of our emerging selves can be found in report cards, letters, photographs, program notices, and dried flowers—musty reminders of our formative experiences and the persons we are becoming as teachers.

Recalling significant others.   Uri Bronfenbrenner, a noted child development specialist, once said that the one thing that every child needs for healthy development is at least one person who is crazy about her or him. That one crazy-about-you person becomes a significant other. Pam, a preservice teacher, wrote a poem (see next page) that illustrates the power of a significant other in shaping her life.

People teach by example, by the ideas they explore with us, by their insights, by their expectations, and by the questions they ask. Teachers influence our thinking not only directly through the courses they teach, but indirectly through sharing themselves and how they see the world. Friends, family, teachers, students, and strangers can fill this role.

Generating metaphors.   Metaphor is a form of symbolic language in which one thing is used to describe another. The AR journey, for example, is a metaphor for the developmental journey of improving ourselves as teachers. Using metaphors can help us gain self-knowledge because metaphors form "the basis of the conceptual systems by means of which we understand and act within our worlds" (Taylor, 1984, p. 5). Metaphors capture images that crystallize meaning. Metaphors

My Teaching Self

by Pamela Donaldson

The following poem gives accounts of my elementary school years. I did terrible things, starting in first grade, when I decided to hide between two closets for 4 hours. Not only did the fire department and police come, thinking I was kidnapped, but they called my mom from work. I did it for attention—the same reason I did every other terrorizing thing that I decided to do. Then, in first grade, after being kicked out of my assigned classroom by the teacher, I was sent to Mrs. Harvey's class. Her beautiful and nurturing personality changed my behavior, and I decided I wanted to be the same kind of influence on children that she was on me.

Soo Badd

I was soo badd
So bad, teachers feared me,
I was the one they sent to someone else's class,
The desk always next to the teacher's,
The one who placed tacks in your chair,
Who put paint in your hair,
I was soo badd.

Soo badd, they knew my mother by her first name,
"Mary, Mary, why is your daughter so scary!
Maybe she should go to a special school,
Go learn with the other fools,
She's just soo badd!"

One day, they sent me to Mrs. Harvey's class
Once again, there were tacks on someone else's
As (usual) I thought, boy am I in trouble again,
Instead she said, "Why don't you grin?"

She said, "You're smart, and beautiful, why don't you show it?"
She said, "You're not that bad and I do know it."

She made a difference in my life the first day I met her,
And I can promise you I won't forget her,
But instead remember her always! Thank you, Mrs. Harvey, for all my good days!!!!!!!

of teaching enable us to capture essences of our teaching identities and to observe changes in those identities.

For example, one middle school teacher described different phases of her teaching career by comparing them to other occupations. One year, for example, she termed her *butler* phase because she felt like a servant to institutionalized systems and to her students—"serving knowledge to them on a platter." She referred to another era as her *train conductor* phase, when she was passing out things and collecting them. After reviewing his own long-term journal entries, another teacher realized that his metaphor was that of a *policeman,* leading him to reexamine his commitments and attitudes toward teaching and the conditions in which he found himself functioning.

Evoking metaphors from the arts to describe teaching can bring about surprisingly fresh insights. Letishia, for example, selected jazz as a metaphor for her teaching style. She compared the improvisational nature of jazz to the spontaneity and creativity involved in her teaching. While she was always well prepared for her lessons, she learned to follow the lead of her students and let the lesson take its own natural course. Another teacher reported feeling like a theatrical *stage manager,* responsible for much of what happens in a play but always behind the scenes, supporting actors.

Metaphors that define the self (teacher) also define the *other* (student) in revealing ways. For example, the metaphor of a teacher as policeman could suggest that students are unmanageable. Defining ourselves as train conductors could suggest that students are passengers. Defining teaching as *improvisation* could imply that students are an *ensemble* of creative and not always predictable musicians.

Critical incidents.   A critical incident is typically considered an event or situation that marks a significant turning point in our lives. Small and seemingly insignificant events can be *made* critical by the way we look at them. By probing and challenging underlying assumptions behind our actions and statements, an incident can become critical.

A recent discussion in a student teaching seminar may help to illustrate this kind of thinking. Into his second week of student teaching, Tom was overwhelmed with discipline problems in his middle school science class. In the seminar he described the students as rude and uncooperative to the point where he felt he was unable to teach science. He described the classroom rules that he made up to ensure a manageable environment and his frustration that students seemed to mock his rules, and test him every step of the way. He told of his mentor teacher's reaction: "You waver between being too strict and too easy on the students. They are getting mixed messages and getting confused." Recalling this recurring situation, Tom confessed, "I don't know who I am anymore! I am a nice guy. I hate being mean to them—it does no good anyway!"

Students in the student teaching seminar asked Tom questions about how he started class, his tone of voice, how he gained his students' attention. Many ideas emerged, but none more powerful than the question, Do you feel that this is *your* class—or your *mentor's?* Tom smiled, almost sadly. "Perhaps I am trying to please my mentor more than I am trying to figure out a way to be with my students." This was a critical incident for Tom. It ushered in a new way of thinking about his dilemma. He began to wonder if he was being fair to his students and to himself. It also offered him the potential to "regroup" and to approach this problem from a more authentic self. As critical colleagues, or mentors, we hope that this reflective process leads him to consider **student** roles and responsibilities, in addition to his own. **Whose** class is this? What are each of our roles and responsibilities.

Time line of incidents and people.   By creating a time line of our lives, marking the influence of critical incidents and people, we can coax the emergence and profile of our teaching selves. While some people feel as if they were born to be teachers, for many of us, the journey to teaching has been a circuitous one. Thinking about our lives historically can yield patterns and insight. One teacher who did this exercise discovered how important and influential her family was to her. Another teacher found a pattern of struggle against injustices that he was sure became manifest in his decision to work with children with special needs.

Developing a philosophy of teaching.   Our philosophies evolve as we gain experience and understanding. According to the Merriam-Webster Dictionary (1974), philosophy is "a critical study of fundamental beliefs and the grounds for them" (p. 522). So, as we develop professionally as action researchers, we expand the grounds for our beliefs.

While most of us function quite well from our own set of beliefs and hypotheses about what teaching is without a formal philosophy, to be able to articulate our orientation and the assumptions which guide our work is both useful and necessary. When we make a claim, for example, what is our rationale for making it?

Few educators have developed a written philosophy of education the likes of John Dewey's philosophical treatise "My Pedagogic Creed," written around the turn of the century when he was a young scholar (Archambault, 1964). Yet it can be quite helpful to our research and development to record our beliefs about the purposes of schooling, how children learn, the roles and responsibilities of teachers and of students. We, too, can use this as a foundation for our thinking about testing, approaches to discipline, and other issues confronting teachers today. The more we read, study, discuss, and cogitate over educational issues, problems, and dilemmas, the more articulate we can become in putting forth our own evolving points of view. As professionals we can ask ourselves and our colleagues to articulate the grounds of our beliefs and to make tacit beliefs and assumptions visible.

In Chapter 4 we described Habermas's technical, practical, and critical orientations to the world. Age, motivation, experience and situations including school norms, and culture influence how one's orientation and beliefs develop over time. Many teachers, for example, began practice with a technical or practical orientation and did not consciously take on a social advocacy role associated with the critical orientation toward teaching until late in their careers. Because AR is overtly democratic and social change is foundational to it, action research has the potential to enhance social advocacy in our schools and to do so from the beginning of one's career. Along with John Dewey, many prominent scholars, notably Maxine Greene, suggest that philosophy is not an entity; it is not something you *have*—it is a process, something that you *do*. You *live* it.

CHAPTER SUMMARY

The journey of the self begins long before we can be conscious of it. To become aware of this journey, and of some of the forces that shape who we are, is to make it possible for us to influence both the present and the future. There are many ways we can do autobiographical exploration. Although each return to previous experience is a reconstruction of that experience (there is no finished or static experience to return to), each reflection can be informative and even emancipating. Perhaps Aunt Ethel didn't understand that there are many ways to plant a garden; we needn't keep planting in narrow rows! And Uncle Edgar didn't understand that there are many reasons why people may not keep their shoes polished; we needn't question the character of those who don't.

Each foray into the past that leads to understanding today promotes a new way of looking at not only the phenomenon, but the larger context of learning and value. Teachers we have been taught by, social customs over time, critical events that leave a lasting impression—there are many influences that shape how we observe others, the way we teach, why we teach, and what we decide is important to research. Developing a philosophy of teaching is a way to integrate past learning and values with today's consciousness and commitment and provides a foundation for making decisions. Most of us function with an implicit philosophy; making this explicit enables us to bring the past into congruence with our current understandings and commitments. In the next chapter we will take autobiographical explorations one step further with a continuum which will enable us to look over many years of experience in a short time.

The Developmental Journey: Self and Action Research

While we have often been reminded to take the "whole child" into consideration in our teaching and curriculum development, how many times have we heard of the need to take into account the "whole teacher"? The lifelong developmental nature of professional growth (this is why it takes a lifetime to live a philosophy) necessitates looking at the personal dimensions of teaching and not separating teaching from being. Teachers, like students, learn and grow differently, at their own pace, and in the context of what each is ready to learn. As students of teaching, we must construct and be in charge of our own learning.

We learn when people and situations challenge us and provoke us to think. For example, we may see clearly a behavior or practice that is problematic in someone else that we have yet to see in ourselves. Such situations can be gifts to our professional growth.

To take a real-life example, Mary Lou, as a classroom teacher, noticed that Barb, her teaching mate, had a terrible time wrapping up lessons so that the second-grade children in their classroom could be on time for the bus to take them home. Barb was absent one day. Much to her surprise and chagrin, Mary Lou found herself taking more than a few children home after they all missed the bus. Many winding, bumpy country miles later, the realization dawned on her that *she*, too, had "a terrible time wrapping up lessons." Numerous chances to confirm or disconfirm her hypothesis presented themselves: Getting the children ready for lunch and recess provided a wealth of confirmations which, although not comforting, did stimulate useful change!

There are other basic developmental principles which can be useful as we look at our professional lives. The most basic is that *development is movement toward more complex, differentiated, and inclusive perspectives.* As we learn, we become able to see new things in our physical and social worlds. Where we at first saw only green, now we see many shades of verdure: olive, kelly, lime, and some we have yet to name, soft, sharp, dull, and mottled. We discriminate between objects, and between ideas. The last part of the principle, *inclusive*, refers to the ability to see and be more comprehensive and expansive in our understandings. We learn to embrace all living things as part of the earth, for example.

Dorothy: Wait a minute. To *differentiate* means to be able to see differences, to discriminate between objects or ideas and thus to see greater complexity in what we are looking at. I understand that. *Inclusive* sounds as if it is the opposite, being able to lump everything together—to *not differentiate*. Are you saying that this principle means we grow in the abilities to do both of these?

Yes! We don't usually do both at once (sometimes we do), but we do grow in the ability (and the capacity) to do both. Let's look at embracing diversity, for example. We grow in the ability to understand other people's perspectives, to cherish cultural rituals which are different from our own, while at the same time we can gain appreciation of similarities and see that we are all children of the earth.

This principle applies to all domains of development:

Physical and motor. We start out tiny and by fits and starts and uneven spurts grow to be large; we learn to walk before skipping; to scribble before drawing.
Social and emotional. We arrive in the world with reflexes and relatively undifferentiated feelings. We become able to distinguish between tears of laughter and sorrow. From "Mommy and I are one" to "I am a separate person," to ever more sophisticated social relationships, we grow.
Cognitive. To use language as an example of this domain, we enter this world with a broad array of sounds. Within the first years of life we begin to differentiate sounds and to use some and let some go. We put the sounds we use into shapes called words, and before you know it, we move from sentences to elaborate discourse—all within the early years of childhood!

This basic principle has much to teach us about how we grow and learn. Development is not a smooth journey! It is predictable in some ways, yes. But an odd thing happens with this process called *growth:* There are complex and interconnected processes taking place, and they are not always easy to see or to understand. For example, when something is learned, much of that learning takes place where we can't see it. Yet, when learning comes to fruition, we know it! As teachers, we don't always see development occurring in others either—especially our students. Here's an anecdote to illustrate our point.

A delightful 6½-year-old chap named Chuck was paying attention to a squirrel and some birds outside the back window of his classroom, when his frustrated teacher (who felt like jumping out the same window) decided instead to make an example of Chuck for not paying attention to the math lesson she was so painstakingly (and unsuccessfully) trying to teach: "Chuck? (!) Perhaps you can come finish the numbers on the board for the boys and girls? (!)" Slowly, calmly (as was his modus operandi), Chuck sauntered to the board—a l l t h e w a y u p t o t h e f r o n t o f t h e c l a s s r o o m, without saying a word or having eye contact with another human being, but seeming to study with a 60-year-old scientist's eyes several things outside of normal vision along the way. Picking up the chalk with a purpose and no wasted effort, he completed the math problem, turned around to face the class, and with his eyes meeting theirs, explained in simple, clear, direct, and understandable terms what the teacher had failed to teach.

FIGURE 7.1 *Chuck and friends*

Chuck's learning of mathematics certainly wasn't visible to his teacher. In fact, the teacher may have assumed he wasn't learning anything at all. Perhaps the main learning here was the teacher's! Learning is more complex than meets the eye.

A Developmental Continuum: Do We Get to Oz All at Once?

No, as you know by now, Dorothy and friends, we certainly do not. If we did we would miss the fun. To map aspects of our growth visually, from the time we were young to recent years, we might draw a continuum with phases or categories like this:

Developmental Continuum by Age Ranges					
1	2	3	4	5	6
0–5	6–10	11–14	15–18	19–26	27–
Early childhood	Middle childhood	Early adolescence	Adolescence	Early adulthood	Adulthood

We created these categories because they parallel general periods in development. Depending on the theory studied, categories vary slightly by age. Later in this chapter we will describe a continuum and theory that spans the entire life cycle. For now, these general categories will serve our purposes. There are many ways to explore our earlier years by using a continuum such as this. What, for example, are your earliest memories?

Using the same basic continuum, we can chart our formal education:

Structured Learning Continuum					
1	2	3	4	5	6
Early education	Elementary	Middle	High school	College	Continuing education

Return to this continuum later and write about some of your school experiences. Which school experiences can you remember most easily? Which are most difficult to recall? Why? What didn't happen?

We can look at many kinds of growth chronologically. We can describe development by domain. For example, we might chart our development as social beings. Let's take a total life perspective, sometimes referred to as a life span approach, and borrow from Erik Erikson's theory of psychosocial development (Erikson, 1950, pp. 247–74), to build a continuum. By putting our lives into a broader context, we can take the edge off the stress we face today. What seemed to be the end of the world at age 18 gets a different interpretation at ages 23 and 34 and 56½. We can use this principle when we look at some of today's challenges. A broader perspective enables us to address a phenomenon from multiple perspectives. This is what we will do as action researchers—view phenomena from multiple perspectives. As you read through Erikson's eight stages which follow, keep in mind that the tensions for each stage are never "resolved" or completed. We come to terms with them during the time indicated, but we meet them in different circumstances throughout the life cycle. Whenever we find ourselves in a new situation, for example, most of us struggle a bit with trust.

Which of these tensions are most prominent in your life today?

For those of us who have been teaching a while, we can create our own teaching continuums to describe how we've grown and changed, starting with our own teacher preparation and student teaching experiences.

Since action research can be viewed as a developmental process, we can use the same kind of continuum to make sense of it. We can see where AR might start: with a curiosity. The question we form as a result can be developed into an action research project. Dorothy, for example, might start with the comment, "Toto doesn't listen to me very well!" But perhaps the problem lies within her as well: "I wonder how can I improve my communication skills with Toto?"

Dorothy: No! I have a more important curiosity than that. How can I improve my chances of getting home?

A life span continuum for psychosocial development							
1	2	3	4	5	6	7	8
Birth–1 year	2–3 years	4–5 years	6–11 years	12–18 years	Young adulthood	Middle adulthood	Old age

1. *Basic trust versus basic mistrust* is the dominant tension negotiated in the first year of life.

   Consistency, continuity, and sameness of experience provided by the caregiver lead to the infant's first social achievement: congruence of inner certainty and outer reality that needs will be met.

2. *Autonomy versus shame and doubt* are the alternative basic attitudes in tension during these 2 years.

   The opportunity to try out his or her skills in a secure and supportive environment enables the young child to gain a sense of autonomy, and the ability to hold on and to let go.

3. *Initiative versus guilt* becomes a tension as the young child enjoys new mental and locomotive powers.

   Pleasure and confidence in the launch and conquest of carrying out her or his activities are the achievements secured by the child whose questions are met with affirming responses.

4. *Industry versus inferiority* becomes the focus as the child moves into the world, production, and education.

   Being encouraged to make and do things and to be recognized for her or his efforts and accomplishments leads to a sense of industry as the child learns to handle the tools of the "big people."

5. *Identity versus role confusion* is a central tension as the body and mind change rapidly and basic competence with tools and production has been achieved.

   The adolescent's ability to integrate multiple identifications, aptitudes, and new social roles with confidence, inner stability, and strength leads to a successful transition to career and adulthood.

6. *Intimacy versus isolation* becomes the focus of social development as one attains a more stable sense of self and competence in the adult world.

   With commitment to others—to love—and to causes beyond one's self—to work—one develops the capacity for intimacy which results in a stronger and larger sense of self as well.

7. *Generativity versus stagnation* is present when one confronts the future.

   The achievement here lies in establishing, creating, and supporting others and the environment.

8. *Ego integrity versus despair* is the summing up of one's one and only life cycle.

   Acceptance of one's life, love, and work leads to authenticity, congruence, and completeness.

Adapted from: Erikson, E. H. (1950). *Childhood and Society* New York: W. W. Norton Co.

Yes, of course. Your insistence just shows how important it is for each person to address her or his own curiosities. Using the following action research continuum, think through your own interest.

Action Research Continuum					
1	2	3	4	5	6

We will start with the simplest process, developing one's curiosity, and progress to a more complex inquiry until we arrive at an AR project as described in number 6.

1. *Curiosity:* Posing questions and musing: "I wonder why I dread Mondays!"
2. *Problem solving:* "Next Monday I'm going to notice what is happening when I feel frustrations, and then maybe I can change it."
3. *An inquiry:* Deciding on a strategy to come to an answer: "I'm going to keep a running record each day for two weeks and see if I can find anything unusual that happens on Mondays."
4. *I-search:* Gathering information (data) and following through to some action are considered to be an I-search: "What do I know about Mondays? In what ways are they different than other days? I wonder if other teachers feel this way. I'll ask my colleagues. I will take each time I feel dread and am frustrated and write about it in two ways: (1) I will describe it carefully, what is happening; and (2) I will write about my thoughts and feelings and actions. Then I will put all this information together, analyze it, and see what I find."
5. *Research into practice:* "I will take what I have learned in my I-search and design and carry out a study to see if my earlier findings are supported."
6. *Action research:* "I will extend my study to include myself as well as my students. I will proceed systematically, using a variety of data collection methods and analyzing data in a way that will help me verify my findings. I will collaborate and share with others. For example, I am going to work with my students and two of my colleagues to study my teaching with a focus on Mondays. My colleagues will study their classes and involve their students. Then we will meet and compare data. When we find trouble spots, we will discuss them, pool our suggestions, and try doing things differently, documenting them and see what happens. We will get into a cycle of trying things out to see what works."

Dorothy: That last one sounds more like *collaborative action reseach.*

Authors: Right you are.

In the next chapters, you will follow along the action research journeys of teachers in a variety of subjects and settings. These teachers and student teachers have been our students, and we have shared parts of their journeys with them.

We want to offer a word of caution here about continuums. While the modernist notion of development as a general movement toward greater complexity and inclusivity (inclusivity means that we are more open to diversity *and* that each part of the continuum includes previous parts) can be useful, postmodernists caution that this is only a part of the picture, and that we rarely progress evenly or in only one direction. Growing is more complex and multiply faceted than that! That's why the term *recursive* is often used to describe AR—not only do we move back and forth along a continuum in our practice, but within action research itself, we move back and forth between and among collecting data, analyzing data, and drawing tentative conclusions.

Dorothy: Wait a minute! I think you lost me. This sounds like a difficult journey. You said that development is movement toward more *complex, differentiated, and inclusive perspectives.*

Authors: Yes.

Dorothy: And you gave us a road map so we can chart our development.

Authors: Yes.

Dorothy: And now you say we don't go in only one direction?

Authors: Hm. Yes. That does sound confusing doesn't it? How can we explain this?

Lion: With courage! Especially if you have headed off in the wrong direction!

Scarecrow: No! With intelligence! Intelligence helps you move in useful directions—even if it means cycling back.

Tin Man: But ya gotta have a heart. The heart helps you *feel* the right direction.

Authors: You each have a point. What do you think *courage* has to do with this?

Lion: Everything! I mean that growing takes *courage*! Every little step along the way takes GAuUTtSZz! Especially if you have to hold two seemingly conflicting ideas at the same time. You often have to let go and move away from what you know, and *that* is Skscarey. Sometimes you don't even know what direction you are moving in until you look back!

Authors: What do you have to say, Tin Man? What has *heart* got to do with this?

Tin Man: Lots! A continuum is linear and neat, but it leaves out the most important part—the heart. Feelings! And emotions! And they aren't neat and tidy! It also implies that one end of the continuum is better than the other, as if a baby is worth less than an adult; as if an adult should not cry as a baby does. Numbered categories go only so far. I know in my heart—if I had one—that stages are not fixed. And not only that, but your heart may lead you to answer your own questions.

Authors: What you say makes sense. What do you have to say, Scarecrow?

Scarecrow: I think Lion and Tin Man are both right. It takes courage to try new things and ask questions for which you don't have answers or direction. And you have to put your heart and soul into framing the questions and finding the answers. A commitment to teaching is both affective and cognitive. As Einstein would say, "Imagination is more important than knowledge." Both Einstein and Tin Man agree: We have to trust our instincts and our imaginations and the messier parts of our creative selves—that is intelligent.

Lion: Yeah. First you have to prove yourselves worthy of making a discovery. And sometimes that means standing tall and not running away when your stomach says EeeYuCK! It's called *body knowing.* Your stomach and heart and brain can really help if you pay attention to them. They can stop you before you do something you'll wish you hadn't.

Authors: Thanks. We will think about what you all just said as we move along. The main point is that as a developmental process, the AR examples we use along the road represent many different points along the journey. We do not claim that each is a full-blown or sophisticated AR project. We will claim that each is an honest and authentic attempt at change and understanding. Each incorporates characteristics and qualities of mature AR.

Three Domains of Development

When we conduct action research, we develop simultaneously in three domains. These three domains, adapted from the research on adult and professional development by Sharon Oja (1989), parallel the journey of the Scarecrow, the Tin Man, and the Lion.

Cognitive and conceptual complexity. As with you, friend Scarecrow, the developmental journey starts wherever a person is and moves toward greater complexity and simplicity, creates a larger repertoire from which to draw, and develops problem-solving, research abilities, and reflective processes.

Moral, ethical, and social responsibility. And as with you, dear Tin Man, in your quest for a heart, the action research journey deepens consciousness and awareness, respect for diversity, and understanding of others. It also promotes collaboration, community, and valuing others.

Psychological and emotional maturity. Like your courageous journey, brave Lion, the AR journey can move us from closed, protective, defensive, rigid positions to more open, creative, and inclusive perspectives toward others. The journey is toward higher self-acceptance and self-esteem, and toward increasing the capacity and ability to nurture these characteristics in others.

Dorothy: So now let's get on with the *doing* so that we can become kinder, smarter, and more open!

CHAPTER SUMMARY

Using a continuum to chart development enables us to see a phenomenon over time. We can begin to see patterns and how one event can influence and relate to others. We can zoom in on one period in our lives, when we were the age of the people we teach (if they are younger), for example, or chart certain aspects of our lives over the time we have lived so far, our educational experiences, for example. Our professional capabilities and dispositions can be explored; what were our main intellectual achievements of the last 5 years? What were our most important social experiences—those that have had the greatest impact upon us—over the years in which we were in preparation to teach? How might those experiences influence the research we develop and conduct today? What educational experiences have had the greatest impact on our assumptions and beliefs about teaching and learning? How might the action research journey influence the complexity we see in teaching and learning? How might it affect our social responsibility to students or colleagues, and our psychological maturity?

Dorothy: It sounds a bit optimistic in scope! If AR can do all this, why aren't all teachers doing it? I'll be happy if it gets me back to Kansas. It's time to think about and develop a plan.

SECTION SUMMARY

We hope that by the end of this section, you have had a chance to focus on yourself as a prospective or practicing teacher. When you began the study of research, you might not have imagined how personal and professional growth might be part of the journey. You might want to return to this section later as you construct your own lessons from Oz at the conclusion of this book.

In the next leg of our journey, we will be your travel guides along with many former student-researchers who have generously agreed to share their questions, experiences, anxieties, studies, triumphs, surprises, and reflections about their journeys.

It's time for those ruby slippers!

Exploring the Forest
Finding Our Roots

Personal and Professional Journeys of the Self

We have many possible explorations on this leg of our journey. There are suggestions throughout this section that you might find useful. We will highlight a few here and direct you back into the chapters for other ideas. This is an important part of the journey, as we are making conscious some of the experiences which have shaped and continue to shape us as persons who choose to be professionals. The writings and creations we do in our journals here are foundational to what follows in other chapters. Building on this foundation not only will enhance and make the rest of the journey easier, but also will make our progress visible.

David Tripp uses the word *autopilot* to refer to our often uncritical business-as-usual stance toward our interactions and decision making. This is fine for most of our functioning, but many professional decisions call for a more conscious process. By building a better understanding of who we are and how we got to be this way, we can shift from functioning on autopilot to a state of consciousness, and even to critical consciousness. As Maxine Greene might say, we move toward a state of being *awake* and our life becomes *doing philosophy*. You might even say we can *be our philosophy*. Being fully who we are can only happen when we are awake! Functioning on autopilot often has to do with responding to someone else's agenda. We might agree with what we have been taught to do; then again, we may not. The key is to make *conscious decisions* on matters of consequence. Only then are we free people. And that is what we mean when we talk about being professional: making critical decisions and using our educational imaginations to make learning more worthwhile.

1. *Doing self-talk.* Begin to pay more attention to some of the conversations taking place inside you. Think back to a recent time when you debated with yourself about an action you were contemplating. Record the options you considered. Give these different options tags, such as self 1, self 2, and self 3. Or create names such as Tim(id), Win(Win), Care(less), Ms. Prim, Master Controller, and Wise Guy. What would each of these characters (or personalities) say? What might each be lobbying for and why or toward what ends? What would be the main trait of each?

   Take these to the extreme. Which personality "won"? What were the consequences?

Now, see if you can pay closer attention to some of the conversations that take place inside you as they happen, and record a few in your journal. How many such discussions do you think take place in a day?

2. *Self-in-a-bag.* Take 10 or 15 minutes to think about who you are. What artifacts and symbols could you put together that would give people a sense of who you are? Now, find a bag that is appropriate to you—plastic, paper, cloth of any kind—and put into it five to seven artifacts, metaphors, or symbols that give a good sense of who you are. After you have done this, do the interviews suggested below. You may wish to add an item or two to the bag.

3. *Interviews.* Who are the people who knew you well when you were a child? List them. Who were the people who knew you best as an adolescent? As a young adult? List them. Select a few from each category (categories may overlap), and write a brief portrait of each person you select; include an example of something you did with this person.

   Which of these people are still in your life? Select one, two, or three who are, and have a conversation with them related to the years in which they knew you. What do they remember about you and about the times? What few words, symbols, or artifacts would they use to describe who you were then? Place them in your bag.

4. *Bag-write.* Now, with these artifacts and symbols all together in your bag, write a brief portrait of yourself using the artifacts. Look back at the personalities you wrote about in self-talk. Do you see any sign of them within the bag? If so, write about them.

5. *Time line of critical incidents and people.* Create a time line of critical incidents and significant people who have influenced your life and your teaching self. Write a paragraph or two about each incident and person and how they influenced you and your teaching. Include the consequences of their influence on you. Keep your writing brief. You can always go back later and elaborate.

6. *Teaching philosophy.* What is your philosophy of teaching? A teaching philosophy can be a set of beliefs about the purposes of schooling, how children learn, the roles and responsibilities of teachers and of students. Theoretically this philosophy guides the actions we take. It can provide a foundation to return to, to reflect upon, and to develop. Write a one-page statement of your teaching philosophy.

7. *Development and learning continuum.* Go back to the continuum presented in Chapter 7, and construct a continuum for your life by age and by level of schooling. For each, begin to do some free-writing about memories related to each marker. They need not be exhaustive, and you can return to explore different phases later on.

   Hopefully through these explorations, you have a slightly different perspective on your history and your present selves. To conclude this section and to make use of the professional contexts we began to build in Chapter 2 with disciplinary explorations, as well as to lead into the next leg of the journey, think about the last exploration in this section.

8. *Your own action research questions.* Revisit the last explorations in Chapter 2 about journals and significant people, and generate a few questions related to your own work. If, for example, you were going to publish a paper in the journal you reviewed, what might the title of your paper be? What questions and methods might you employ? At this point, do not be too specific or overly concerned with the *how* of it. Just think about what you are interested in and what you might be able to do in your own practice related to it. In fact, it might be a good idea if you limited this exploration to 15 or 20 minutes so that you get fairly spontaneous and creative ideas without getting bogged down. You will not have to *do* any of them if you choose not to.

Would any of the influential people you cited earlier have any ideas for you to consider related to the research topic(s)? It might be useful to generate a few topics—maybe more. Perhaps after you have played a bit with possible ways to improve your practice, one will become more feasible or more valuable for you to study at this time.

Developing an Inquiring Mind

. . . with Toto trotting along soberly behind her, she started on her journey.

There were several roads near by, but it did not take her long to find the one paved with yellow brick. Within a short time she was walking briskly toward the Emerald City, her [ruby slippers] tinkling merrily on the hard, yellow roadbed

* * *

"How far is it to the Emerald City?" asked the girl.

"I do not know," answered Boq gravely, " . . . it is a long way to the Emerald City, and it will take you many days. The country is rich and pleasant, but you must pass through rough and dangerous places before you reach the end of your journey."

The Wonderful Wizard of Oz
L. Frank Baum (1900)

Dorothy: I feel better now that I am on the Yellow Brick Road and at the same time apprehensive about these dangerous places!

Authors: These feelings are understandable. The Yellow Brick Road reminds us that we have questions and a topic to pursue. But there are inevitable obstacles we must face.

Dorothy: Like wicked witches?

Authors: Yes, and nasty flying creatures—we will have our wits about us.

Dorothy: Courage, heart, and intelligence?

Authors: Yes. As we focus our energies on specific questions, we will be surprised at how rejuvenating the journey will be! As the title of this section suggests, we are going to generate a topic and then explore questions to guide our studies. We will also look at our questions (and our practice) problematically, trying to explore the hidden assumptions and biases that color our thinking. You may want to skip to the "Exploring the Forest" section in the back of this section so that you can work through some of the exercises as we go along. Some of the exercises will help you to identify topics and questions. The questions that underlie our work in this chapter are:

What is my research interest?   To explore that research interest, we offer some additional questions that you may want to consider:

Why am I interested?   What values and beliefs do I want to live out in my teaching? (Think about the work you began in the last section.) A philosophy of education is a good starting point for examining our practice. Is our philosophy a living part of what we do? If we claim to be developmentalists or constructivists, are these beliefs enacted in our daily work? If we consider ourselves to be critically oriented, are we aware of the social, cultural, political, and economic contexts that shape our work and the lives of our students?

What is my question?   How can I bring my teaching more in line with my values and beliefs?

What do I already know?   What do my experiences tell me about this classroom, these students, this school, this curriculum, the politics surrounding decisions that are made?

What do others know?   What can I learn from scholars who have explored this topic and whose theories and research are made public? What can I learn from other colleagues—teachers, school support staff, youth-serving agencies? From families, community members, business people, legislators, lawyers, doctors?

What do I expect to find?   In combination with what I know and what I learn from others, what are my informed hunches (and biases) about my topic of interest?

By the end of this section, you will have the opportunity to explore these questions for yourself and to see how the teachers in our case studies have explored them. And, in the process, you may find out some important things about yourself as well as about your research interest. "Exploring the Forest" at the end of Section 4 will offer additional ways for you to develop your questions.

Scarecrow: I am glad we are going to explore this. For a head full of straw, mine sure feels overloaded!

Tin Man: I have an idea, but it certainly isn't a "research question"!

Authors: *Relax.* Most of us feel uneasy at the beginning. We will shape our question(s) into more succinct, doable, researchable questions. There is no end to what you might study—the trick is to focus on one idea and to develop it. We have our entire careers to ponder and research other questions and topics. Often, as we conduct research, new avenues of research open up—we can record these to do *later.*

Lion: I don't know . . . I am feeling a little cowardly.

Authors: That's okay. In fact, that's fine. You have the chance to take something that you are curious about—perhaps it is how to solve a problem you are facing—and allow us and your critical colleagues to help you to develop it. As you think about the topic, the values and beliefs that shape your interest in it, and what you and others know about it, the focus of your scholarship becomes clearer. Thinking about what we *expect* to find helps us to be realistic as we define our question(s). It is also important for us to be *aware* of our expectations. By stating what they are, we may bring to the surface hidden biases that we may want to examine and perhaps even challenge in our studies. These expectations are a basis for our personal hunches and hypotheses. When they are combined with what we learn about our topic from others (scholars and practitioner-scholars), we can reformulate these into more scholarly hunches and "test" them by looking for "evidence" that either confirms or disconfirms them.

As we challenge ourselves by talking and writing about our topics in new ways, we will come to a deeper appreciation of them and will be able to better define our questions. Just as importantly, we will develop courage! Once our intellectual curiosity is working, we will forget about our fear. The further we get into our topics, the more we will *enjoy discussing them with others.* By the time we get to the Emerald City and share our results, we will look back on this part of the journey and smile.

Tin Man: Especially if it is a topic we really wonder and care about, and have developed ourselves . . . (*softly*) . . . with a little help from our friends.

Authors: Right you are. In fact, Tin Man, we are going to start this phase of our journey with *wonder,* with little wonders (I wonder how I could . . . ?) and curiosities (What if . . . ?). The action researchers whose case studies we present here will become travel companions as they share their curiosities and wonders which, in the next few chapters, develop into studies.

CASE STUDIES

Helping Jen Learn English as a Second Language

One day, the principal of Shawn's school arrived at the classroom door with an announcement: This second grade would be getting a new student. That wasn't the surprising part—new students come and go in any elementary classroom. Shawn's newest second grader would be a young girl from Korea.

Although Shawn was pleased to be getting a new student, she immediately wondered, How can I best teach her? Shawn knew little about English as a Second Language (ESL) issues or strategies, the child, or Korea. No one in the entire district spoke Korean. Undaunted, Shawn was committed to help each student, including Jen, to succeed.

Shawn accepted the challenge willingly as a valuable learning experience. She knew there would be support from the school ESL teacher and from the research mentor from the university program where she was completing a master's degree in reading. How would this child from a different country, immersed in a new language and culture, fare? She wondered, How can I facilitate Jen's becoming comfortable in the new classroom community? How would Jen learn English, and how would this process proceed? How would Jen's need to learn English have an impact on her growth in other subjects? Shawn's many questions fueled the desire which led to a case study of Jen.

The Literature Circle's Study

Jan and Terry are veteran teachers who share an interest in improving the teaching of reading with 10- and 11-year-old students. Terry taught in a school that insisted upon *tracking* or "ability-grouping" classes (in spite of the fact that considerable research demonstrates the negative effects of tracking—see Oakes, 1985; Slavin, 1988; Wheelock, 1994), and had been given all the lowest-achieving fifth-grade students and least proficient readers, according to standardized tests. In fact, Terry's school labeled these readers "at-risk," based on below-average reading-level test scores. Since Jan was on sabbatical and did not have her own classroom, the two teachers decided to team up in Terry's classroom. They wondered, "What can we do to improve matters for these children?"

In the past, the readers assigned to Terry's class had received instruction limited to district-adopted basal readers and accompanying workbooks. Terry's concerns about the lack of choice, excitement, and high-quality literature in this program resulted in her seeking alternatives. Terry felt strongly that the monotony of the reading program was failing to enthuse students about reading. Both teachers were committed to their students having exemplary instruction—instruction that would be consistent with the current theory and practice that they were studying in their master's degree program. So, these two teachers asked: Would "at-risk" readers become excited about reading and improve their abilities if the teachers implemented a literature-based approach with the use of trade books, literature response journals, and meaningful discussions about literature in place of the mundane diet of basal readers and workbooks?

The S.T.A.R. Club Study

"I just don't get it!" Andy exclaimed to his fellow special education teacher. "I know these [regular education] kids have been with our students in *inclusion* classes in the past, but they act like they've never seen a student from special education. I thought inclusion worked well at the elementary school, but it isn't working here!" The rationale for including Andy's students with multiple handicaps in some regular education classes was for these students to gain acceptance from their "typical" peers. But what he observed in the hallways, in the lunchroom, and in classes where his students were integrated with "typical" students was limited conversation, limited interaction, and often the shunning of students in special education. Was this because it was not "cool" to hang around with kids who were "different"? With this sense of frustration and desire to understand and change the situation, Andy, a veteran middle school special educator, wondered what he could do. He looked for insights and solutions to this vexing problem.

The Democratic Classroom Study

Rosie was a student teacher in a ninth-grade civics class who thought it ironic, even disturbing, that students were learning about democracy but not practicing it in their classrooms. Research on the teaching of social studies bore out her own observations over the years—that social studies was not living up to its potential as a learning ground for participatory democracy. Mindful of the important role schools can play in developing informed and active citizens, Rosie found that her question revolved around this issue: How can I create a democratic civics classroom? Rosie wanted to transform the course students described as "boring" and "irrelevant" to one in which they would all become immersed participants in the complexities of the democratic process. Rosie's own activist spirit fueled this commitment.

Dorothy: That's quite a diversity of things to wonder about.

Authors: Yes, action research projects can cover a range of interests and settings. In our cases here; they cover English as a second language, reading, special education, and democracy in the classroom. These action researchers have in common the wish to improve their own practice, school conditions, and learning of their students. What they are not yet aware of is how *they* will change as well. What will enable these teachers to do so? The next chapter will offer suggestions for ways to begin this part of the journey.

From Curiosity to Research Questions

Curiosity is more than a starting point—it is fuel to sustain us for the journey. It is light, it carries energy, and it compels us in ways that force can only envy. When you are curious, you poke around a bit. You explore. Together with its two best friends, wonder and creativity, and used in the service of AR, curiosity is a powerful force for learning. Propelled by our commitment to live out our belief in the possibilities of democratic schooling for social change, we will find our explorations sustained through even the most difficult of challenges.

Let's look for a few minutes at these common words: *curiosity, wonder, creativity*. We will see what we can learn from *Roget's Thesaurus* (1980) and the *Merriam-Webster Dictionary* (1974). What does it mean to be in the presence of a curiosity? To be curious? To wonder? To create?

Curiosity: Interest, marvel, celebrity, prying, wonder, inquisitiveness, interrogativeness, phenomenon, oddity, rarity (Roget, 1980, p. 94).

Curious: Inquisitive, odd, inquiring, recondite, meddling, unique, questioning, scrutinizing, rare, prying, peering, searching, peeping, singular (Roget, 1980, p. 94).

Wonder: Miracle, surprise, awe, puzzlement, fascination, phenomenon, admiration, marvel, sign, surprise, prodigy (Roget, 1980, p. 488).

Create: To bring into being; to exist; make; produce (Merriam-Webster, 1974, p. 176); frame, construct, shape, mold, form (Roget, 1980, p. 90).

Sounds like fun, eh? Being curious, wondering, and creating are often pleasant states. There are other reasons to cultivate them during our journey, especially at the start. In addition to providing fuel for our work, they can turn much of our work into play. Yes, *play.* Long disparaged, play is one of the supreme accomplishments in adult life. In fact, at least one notable scholar of human development, Ashley Montagu, in *Growing Young* (1989), writes about this. He points out that adults need to take clues from children and adopt many of the *children's* characteristics and qualities, most notably play, wonder, curiosity, and openness to experience.

When we are able to take what we know, suspend judgment, and enter into a playful state with an idea or object, then new ideas, conceptions, and uses can present themselves. There is room for them. When we stop relentlessly trying too hard, sometimes a magic synthesis takes place. This magic synthesis *is* creativity (Arieti, 1976). When we are crowded with *shoulds* and *oughts* and *rules* and concerned with knowing it all, there is no room for play and the kinds of discovery and invention that play makes possible. AR is more concerned with what-if than with rules.

Piaget said that too much assimilation was boring, and too much accommodation was overwhelming. To grow, we need a balance of both—the equilibrium we talked about earlier. The comfortable way we feel when we understand enough about something (assimilation) to play with it enables us to walk off the edge of our known worlds into something new (accommodation). We create something new and therefore create *more* of ourselves as well. We learn. We enlarge our repertoire. Each time we do this, Piaget found, we have the same reaction and good feelings that babies do. We may display it differently—we don't usually wiggle, gurgle, and chuckle—but we, too, feel good inside and find pleasure in practicing our new found abilities, whether they are mental (discovering a new computer tool) or physical (discovering how to stop while skating). A *playground* is a place to recreate. When we play, we re-create. And we frolic.

Dorothy: So, why are these qualities and characteristics important to action researchers?

Authors: Good question. They are important to all of us, researchers or not. But they are especially important to action researchers. Take a minute to think about this. Go back to our definitions of curiosity, wonder, creativity, and play, and think about action research. Now what do you think?

Dorothy: I think I wouldn't normally think of the words *play* and *research* in the same sentence!

Authors: Action researchers are . . . meddlers! They are searchers who inquire into their own experience. They meddle into what they did not question before. When they try something different, they upset their routines. To do that, they have to be inquisitive, interested in what is going on. To search means to look at something from different points of view. Action researchers are creative. They ask themselves, What is going on here? and What if I try this out? In a sense, action researchers have to be able to turn experiences inside out and to pose and entertain possibilities. And that takes a sense of wonder and curiosity, an openness to surprise, because you don't know what you will find. Yes, action researchers construct new ways of doing things and of framing and portraying these things to others.

Often we get too busy to remember the value of keeping these things alive within us. The sparks that drive us get covered over, and our senses are dulled. Action research is a way to rediscover and cultivate these qualities and to enhance our capacities for further questing. By paying attention to the conversations in our heads about our practice, to the feelings that take hold of us, and to the ideals we hold as possibilities for our students, our schools, and ourselves, we will define questions that transform us into scholars and our classrooms into learning communities.

How Do Questions Evolve?

Many fruitful questions begin with a sense of curiosity. You want to know how something might work. Or you may wish to better understand your students: Perhaps you wonder what it is like to be a child with a hearing disability in your classroom. Perhaps you have attended a workshop on multiage grouping, and you wonder what it would be like to teach in such a setting. Perhaps you are dissatisfied with how long it takes to do routine tasks and wonder if there is a more efficient way. Or you want to study an aspect of your practice that you feel needs some attention, for example, testing and the time you devote to it (preparing for tests, administering tests, communicating with parents about tests, changing schedules to accommodate tests). And you also want to hold it up to a critical light: Is this time well spent? Importantly, what do the tests measure? Who designs them and for what purposes? Whom do tests "advantage" and whom do they "disadvantage"? You may or may not have an opinion at the beginning of your inquiry, but by following up on your curiosity, you will find yourself making more informed decisions based on this critical kind of reflection.

These types of questions emerge from the three domains of knowledge that Habermas (1972) described: technical interest in how things work, a practical need to understand, and a critical sense of the social, cultural, political, and economic realities that form the context of our teaching. They also illustrate the many ways in which curiosity works to fuel our explorations. It is

- A *wish to understand* ("I wonder why inclusion isn't working?").
- A *dissatisfaction* ("We don't *live* democratically in this classroom!").
- A *concern* ("This is an improverished reading program. I wonder what . . . ?").
- A *challenge* or *problem* ("How can I help Jen to learn?").
- An *issue* ("What are the consequences of the testing program at my school on our first graders?"). Issues have multiple and conflicting perspectives. They may be highly controversial, such as imposed testing, student privacy rights, dropout rates, year-round schooling, bilingual education, and school uniforms. *Issues* are the basis of questions that often get coverage in the media.

The stance we take toward our topic is important. If we maintain a sense of wonder and curiosity as opposed to one of judgment, we may be able to view the topic from multiple perspectives, rather than just one perspective. Viewing the topic (question) as a problem or a possibility, an issue or a concern, will influence the design, conduct, and consequences of our study. Maintaining curiosity throughout the research process is almost a guarantee of success.

Questions evolve over *time.* While many action researchers enter an AR class knowing exactly what they want to study and how, more often, they enter with vague and general questions. They may have a hunch or an uneasy feeling about a topic. Although refining our thinking to define a question can be a lengthy process, often it is not. Just as Dorothy quickly found the Yellow Brick Road, so, too, can we, once we know our direction. If you have a fuzzy question right now, that's fine. By the end of the chapter, with its exercises, you will likely shape your question into one that can be researched.

Lenses for Inquiry: Zooming In, Zooming Out

Questions can evolve as we work with them over time. There is a process of thinking about a question and shaping it as we ponder responses to the questions we posed earlier: What is my research interest? What is my question? What do I already know? What do others know? What do I expect to find? Our focus can become clearer as new aspects of the topic come to mind, as we sort out key elements: background, foreground, main events, and processes. Noticing one element and its relationship to other elements makes us more aware of our focus and the context within which it sits. The process is not unlike an inquisitive meddler poking around with a zoom lense; inspecting this; zooming over there, up and down, and all around; visually taking things apart and putting them back together, just to see how they work.

Many travelers, especially photographers, pack camera equipment for their journeys so that they can capture a wide-angle view of a region as well as a close-up of a rare insect, flying monkey, or flower (microcosm). Just as photographers do, action researchers need multiple lenses to study different aspects of their topics. As we conduct our inquiries, we need the flexibility to zoom in and out between and among different perspectives. This is a continuous process. We need a wide-angle lens (macrocosm) to view the phenomenon from larger contexts (the big picture). We need both a narrower lens to focus on the immediate context and the ability to zoom in for a close-up of specific phenomena. From snapshots at these different levels, we get much more detailed and comprehensive pictures of our topics, and we can use these to construct an album or portfolio for others to view and discuss our work with us.

We may choose to focus on an individual student or group of students, a classroom, a school, district, state or province. Whatever we select as our focus, we will need to zoom in and out, alternating between perspectives: the child, the classroom, the schools, the child, the community. Figure 8.1 displays these lenses as concentric circles, with a pie-shaped cutout to show questions that cut across all lenses.

Focusing on one student.   Action research can be focused on one child or on a small group of children. Perhaps we wonder about *an individual student* (the innermost circle in Fig. 8.1). Perhaps a student looks tired, disinterested, or unengaged in lessons. Perhaps, as in Shawn's case, a child needs special attention. What is the best way to meet Jen's needs?

Lesley, a kindergarten teacher, had a child in class who was delightful, confident, and amusing, but performed academically and socially like a much younger child. Timmy better fits with a class of preschoolers than with a group of 5- and 6-year-olds, this teacher thought. His delightful personality frequently made him the center of attention. Yet, as others in the class began to develop more advanced lit-

FIGURE 8.1 *Areas of Concern*

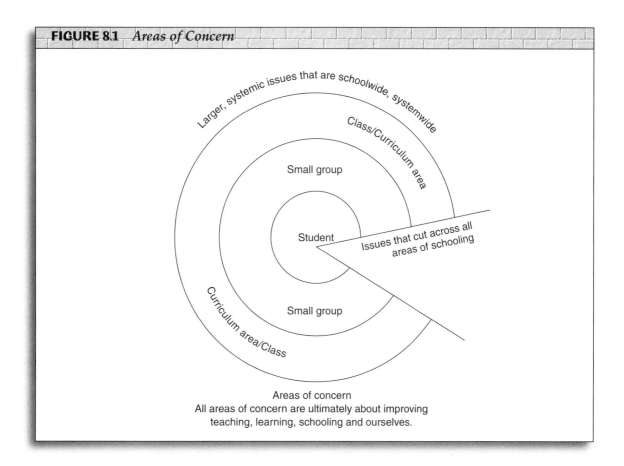

Areas of concern
All areas of concern are ultimately about improving
teaching, learning, schooling and ourselves.

eracy behaviors, Timmy, smaller than his classmates, was not yet ready for academic work suitable for his classmates. Some investigation revealed a thick folder in a school office. Timmy had been born prematurely and spent his first months in a neonatal ward. His family had received many social services since that time. Lesley investigated characteristics of premature babies and found that his behavior was, in fact, typical of such youngsters. What was perceived as "premature" could more accurately have been applied to the curriculum he was (unsuccessfully) being forced into! A push to make him function at a higher level than his development was as nonsensical as expecting a flower to bloom without a stem. The teacher's action research enabled her to be an informed advocate for the child. She aimed to prevent decision making that could be damaging to the child.

Another action researcher conducted an in-depth study of a man who couldn't read or write. The man was attending evening classes at an adult education facility where the researcher worked. The researcher's intent was to understand this individual and his issues about learning and literacy, and to find ways to help him.

Studies like Leslie's and Shawn's often result in single-subject designs, which are discussed in Section 5. When our focus is on our teaching of a single student, a single-subject design can be useful.

Studying a small group of students.   A small group of students who raise similar concerns may be the topic you want to tackle in your action research (still the innermost circle in Fig. 8.1). You may have several students who do not thrive in spite of your best efforts, and the efforts of support services. We know many teachers who design studies around small groups of students who present the greatest challenges to them as professionals.

A kindergarten teacher studied the six youngest children in the class to delve more deeply into their perceptions and their needs. Realizing that the range in most kindergarten classes is diverse, the researcher knew that better understanding of the needs of the youngest children would also benefit future students. At the other end of the developmental scale, one researcher felt that the program in which he taught was inadequate for the most advanced students. A nagging sense that these students could be more academically challenged led to finding new and better ways to meet their needs. Similarly, another teacher designed a study around a handful of second-language students, much as Shawn did with Jen. In this case, they didn't speak the same home language, but shared the need to learn English and to become members of new classroom communities.

Studying a curriculum area.   At times, a curriculum issue is the focus of research. The issue can effect the entire *class* or classes that you teach (the middle circle in Fig. 8.1). It could be the way spelling is taught, the reading program that is used, the lack of critical thinking, or the didactic teaching of science or social studies. Perhaps we have observed a lack of student enthusiasm or the ineffectiveness of a program. Terry and Jan were veteran teachers concerned with a curriculum problem that was affecting the entire class. In some ways the problem was a result of school policy with which they did not agree—the ability grouping of entire classes for teaching (tracking). Those practices ran contrary to their values (and much research). They wanted to implement more effective practices in the curriculum—and they were committed to students labeled *at risk.* They felt that students considered to be less proficient than others were systematically denied opportunities provided to more advanced students for critical thinking and creativity, which meant that "low" students would likely stay "low" through no fault of their own.

Jonathan, a middle school math teacher, initially thought that the use of math journals would be beneficial to students, by raising their grades on pupil progress reports. Bonnie, a French teacher, thought foreign language teaching needed an overhaul when she noticed that none of the techniques and strategies she'd been learning about first-language literacy were applied to communication and literacy in a second language. She decided to try the same type of dialogue journals (Fulwiler, 1987) with French I students that she saw English teachers using with success.

Margie, who taught in an urban school with mostly African-American students, wondered if third graders would spell more conventionally if they increased their journal writing. Kelly knew that students disliked her English class. In this vocational high school, students viewed English class as a distraction in their day filled with the vocational classes they so enjoyed. But, Kelly wondered, would students respond more enthusiastically to reading and other literacy-related activities if she used the daily newspaper instead of the existing, somewhat mundane materials? Her students seemed quite interested in current events.

Maureen, a teacher of 11-year-olds, taught students identified as gifted and talented. Feeling that her curriculum wasn't engaging, she began to think that she could bring new life into her class by applying Gardner's theory of multiple intelligences (H. Gardner, 1993). Her focus on curriculum would cut across all areas of study; it would serve to help her identify student strengths, to better know herself as a teacher, and to explore new ways of teaching to student strengths.

Studying a larger issue.   No matter what the focus of a study, there is a larger context or arena within which it takes place (the outer circle in Fig. 8.1). Kyle, a student teacher in a middle school, was concerned when it became apparent that students enrolled in music appreciation weren't learning anything about the appreciation of music. These students spent most of their music time in what was essentially a study hall, because the priorities and resources for music education were devoted to students specializing in music performance through chorales, the school band, or orchestra for the school. The "average" student, it seemed to Kyle, was shortchanged with this method of allocation. This posed a challenge, a chance to create something and make a difference. Kyle wondered what could happen if, in fact, music appreciation were to become a reality during the study hall. This was a complex issue because it involved addressing a school district and community's priority for performance over appreciation and exploration. Middle school philosophy, on the other hand, advocates student exploration and appreciation of a wealth of curriculum and career options.

Jan's and Terry's desire to change the curriculum for "at-risk" readers also had roots in a systemic issue. Their district, as a matter of policy, grouped classrooms by ability without questioning the practice, in spite of the plethora of published literature and research against the practice, often called *tracking* (Oakes, 1985; Slavin, 1988; Wheelock, 1994). This district practice had long been unquestioned, and would be difficult to change. Consequently, Jan and Terry fit their concerns into what they could control—the manner in which those "low ability" readers were taught. Both teachers harbored the hope that they could prove a point to their colleagues and their district—that children labeled *low ability* will respond to exciting literature and excellent teaching as their more successful peers do, and, in the end, will look less and less like low-ability students. Ultimately, the teachers might even begin to see all children as unique and worthy of the best conditions for learning.

In doing AR, many teachers find that their concerns challenge district, state, or national mandates, policies, or traditions which have an impact on education as a system of interrelated rules and practices. Kallie's study of how to help vocational students pass the writing proficiency test led her to ask many questions: Why did the school assume that these students were incompetent? Why were teachers and administrators at the school not permitted to judge the suitability of this test? Furthermore, what was the value of a test that would reinforce students' feelings of failure and further encourage them to drop out of school?

Kallie learned to question the *system* and the mandates. Presenting the results of her study, Kallie threw her notes down in frustration, saying, "I don't care anymore about whether or not my students passed this test!" What Kallie learned while implementing a comprehensive writing program for these students was that they *needed* to write because they had important things to say, that writing was a valuable form of expression. Once she enabled them to write, which was difficult at first, floods of heart-wrenching stories pored out onto paper. She got to know the students. Kallie's study, like many action research studies, turned out very differently from the original plan. The study led her to be more politically aware and active, and thus to influence local and regional educational policy.

Studying social issues in a classroom.   Social issues can cut across ages, disciplines, regions, and boundaries (the pie-shaped cutout in Fig. 8.1). Some aspects of the implicit curriculum, such as unspoken cultural norms of behavior, are critically important to educational success. Learning is a socially constructed process, and schools present unique contexts with their own structures, features, and governing relationships. These types of issues are possible topics for action research.

Toni's story provides a good example. As a middle school health teacher, Toni was concerned about how disrespectfully students in health class in the urban, low-income neighborhood treated one another. Toni's question touched on not only the content of the teaching, but also the idea of bringing harmony to the group so that teaching and learning would be embedded in a more pleasant, open, accepting, and supportive community. Students did not appear to respect one another. They seemed to rejoice in each other's misfortunes; they engaged in name-calling and put-downs. While some students seemed to control the class dynamics, others were nonparticipants. With all these dynamics at play, very little productive work was being done. Toni wondered if, in one semester, this situation could be moved toward greater respect and a greater sense of community support. Toni would not be able to feel satisfied with the curriculum while such negative classroom dynamics persisted. What could Toni do to improve the situation?

It was soon evident to Tracy, a middle school social studies student teacher, that males dominated the class. Why was this so? Was it something about this age group? Was it related to how lessons were structured? Was female participation simply less overt? Tracy, like Toni, wondered if this situation could change so that student participation would become equitable between genders, and girls could be helped to feel comfortable and empowered to express their views and ideas. Tracy felt it was essential to have students profit equitably from class discussions and lessons.

Andy's S.T.A.R. (Students and Teachers Advancing Relationships) Club is another prime example of studying a social issue. Despite a functioning inclusion model (students with special needs integrated into regular classrooms), students with and without multiple handicapping conditions in Andy's school were not interacting with one another in meaningful ways. Andy's commitment to the "special" students and his willingness to try to achieve the long term goals of inclusion spurred the study which led to starting the S.T.A.R. Club.

CHAPTER SUMMARY

In summary, developing a curiosity into a question can begin with self-study: Why am I interested in this topic? Through self-study, we can awaken ourselves to our democratic commitments. By nurturing curiosity through creativity and playfulness, we move beyond asking, What *should* be, to asking, What *if*? By zooming in and out, constantly focusing and refocusing, we are able to gain new perspectives on our topic.

There is an important cautionary note in our efforts to frame a research question. While many researchers are able to pose a question that they follow through an entire study, others begin in one place and meander to a related question. We like to think that we are getting smarter in our wanderings. We call this process, of getting more focused and sure-footed in our direction, *progressive focusing*. It can be a natural part of the cycle of action research, although it often isn't.

For example, a science teacher may begin by asking, How can I motivate my science students through my own enthusiasm? And the teacher may decide after a while that even though a teacher's interest and enthusiasm for the subject matter are important, what is really of interest is to help students find ways to get engaged in subject matter by helping them find relationships to their own lives. The new question becomes, How can I help students find relationships between their own personal interests and the subject matter?

In the next chapter, we will explore our questions further by making problematic the taken-for-granted assumptions underlying our questions. To do this, we will explore not only what we already know about our topic, but also what others have to offer.

Exploring and Problematizing Our Practice

Teachers often begin with very large and broad questions because they understand the complexities of learning and classroom life. As we explore our questions and unwrap the issues that surround them, we often find them to be even more complex, yet at the same time simpler. This process of unwrapping the multiple layers in which our topic and curiosity are embedded is called *problematizing* our practice. We focus on two sources of making our work problematic: inside sources (what we already know) and outside sources (what others know). We follow this with a brief look at the importance of keeping track of our expectations about how the project will go.

What Do I Already Know?

Taking into account what we already know about our topic is an important first step in defining our research interest. Often we doubt our own experiential and intuitive knowledge. These doubts are not surprising, for we are inundated with media from a variety of sources that discount what teachers know in favor of the promises of expert "wizards," who willingly provide easy, step-by-step remedies for all that ails our educational system. But as explorers of our own terrain and developing scholars of our own practice, we know that meaningful understanding and change demand a kind of wisdom that begins at home.

What do I already know about this child? Her family? How she learns? What gets in the way of her learning? What do I already know about how groups of students become engaged in subject matter? What are my students' attitudes toward learning, and what skills do they already possess? Some researchers call this knowledge *baseline data*, and it may be found in the observations we have noted in our journal or grade book, surveys we have administered, and student work and performances. This knowledge forms the hunches that we have already made about student potential, how they might respond to a particular curriculum, etc.

But to *explore* implies the unexpected, that we don't know what we might find. We follow up on a curiosity with the hope of discovering something we don't know. Further yet, to *problematize* is to explore with a *critical* stance. It requires that we become skeptical of familiar territory, that we "question the historical, social, economic, political, and cultural realities that shape our lives" (Leistyna, Woodrum, and Sherblom, 1996) and practice. It has been said that to problematize is to unwrap "professional routines" which "are, by definition, seldom, if ever challenged or consciously engaged" (Tripp, 1993). As we investigate, we can explore (and expose) our implicit assumptions and theories. By taking an interested and nonjudgmental approach to making the familiar unfamiliar, we can better weather the loss of the somnolence and comfort of our unexamined practices. So, not only do we want to rely on what we already know, we want to question that knowledge.

Dorothy: So we have a choice. We can simply say, "I know what works and what doesn't work. I have been a teacher for many years. I know!" Or we can try to wake up from our nice, comforting sleep in the poppy fields!

Authors: Yes. For only when we are fully awake can we explore our unquestioned assumptions and discover how they might prevent us from seeing in new ways. While the term *problematize* may be unfamiliar, to some degree we problematize everyday when we ask questions such as, Now where did that come from? Why do we do it that way? Is that the fairest way to do that? Who made that policy, and how was the decision made? Were other possibilities entertained?

Dorothy: What are some of the specific professional routines that comfort teachers?

Authors: We can revisit several routines which are common practices in many schools.

- Grouping students by "ability."
- Lining up students in rows.
- Forty-minute classes.
- Starting school at the crack of dawn and ending school in the early or middle afternoon.
- The ways in which we determine promotion and retention.
- Giving homework.
- Standardized testing.
- Teacher-led parent-teacher conferences.
- Orientation programs that prepare students for the next level of schooling.
- The way we organize levels of schooling.

We have plenty of unexamined routines in teacher education, too. Why do students begin their program with observing and end (until recently) with full-time teaching? Who dares to question these practices—despite the almost-universal comments by students that they "really start to learn" during their full-time teaching experience? We can become so entrenched in the details of our teaching lives that we rarely even *think* to question them, let alone have the courage to challenge the way things are "always" done and to question cultural norms.

And what questions would we ask? Let's take the example we mentioned earlier of Chuck, our daydreamer, and his teacher. Let's imagine that Chuck's teacher has asked a critical colleague to help her problematize her teaching.

Problematizing the Story of Chuck

Chuck's teacher: What an amazing occurrence! I have mixed emotions! Here Chuck is, seemingly oblivious to the class, while I am straining to explain a math concept in a way that the children can understand—I try to snap him out of his biological excursion, and instead he leads the class into understanding! How do you figure?!

Critical colleague: Yes, strange. You seemed pretty frustrated all right. Did you think he was daydreaming?

Chuck's teacher: Well, I didn't actually think he was daydreaming. I mean, he was so wrapped up in the squirrel and bird play going on outside the window that he didn't have time for daydreaming or for what was really important to me: math. And, yes, I was frustrated. I pulled out every trick in the book, and I couldn't seem to help the children make the connections they needed to. And then zap! Chuck did it!

Critical colleague: What, do you think, was going on?

Chuck's teacher: Now that I can look back on it, I realize that he already knew the math I was trying to teach. I also know that my method of teaching wasn't working—but I knew that before!

Critical colleague: Tell me more about your method of teaching. What did you assume about teaching and learning with the methods you were using?

Chuck's teacher: That's an interesting question. I was caught between two worlds with my teaching. I hadn't thought about it consciously until you asked, but I was trying to teach the way I think children learn, with manipulatives and having the children work in small groups. But I was also trying to have a whole class discussion when I realized that most of the children weren't getting the concept as quickly as I thought they would. So I went back to the way I was taught, the lecture.

Critical colleague: Were you caught between "encouraging their exploration" and "direct teaching?" Did you think you had to do one *or* the other?

Chuck's teacher: Precisely. In a sense, I didn't trust the newer way of teaching, although that is really where my intuition tells me we ought to be moving. I slid back into the way I was taught, and it didn't work. I was frustrated with myself, although I didn't know it at the time. I had a whole lot of "shoulds" buzzing in my head: "They should be getting it faster! They won't be ready for the proficiency tests!" *"Do something!"* And in the *"do something"* voice, I was the font of all knowledge; and if not all eyes were on me, well, how could they possibly be learning?

Critical colleague: And Chuck wasn't helping, was he?

Chuck's teacher: No. He was like a match to gasoline! And now I see that match was just what *I* needed! I was part of the problem; Chuck was part of the solution!

Thanks for helping me to process this. It really helps to reflect on this with you. I don't feel that you are judging me, and I can hear my own words as I reflect honestly on my teaching and on what the children were telling me. Thanks!

Authors: We will add a few footnotes to the story. What if we told you that Chuck is now a well-respected biologist? Does that make any difference in how you interpret the story? Does that one piece of information enable you to see the whole situation from a different frame of reference? Might the scientific, logical mathematical gifts of this young child have enabled him to quickly grasp the concept *the way the teacher was teaching it,* and teach his classmates in a way that most other people, including the teacher, could not? Might his interest in the bird and squirrel have been what was *really* important and in his best interests, despite the belief of his teacher *at the time* that it wasn't?

Chuck's teacher is not alone in her frustration with trying new ways of teaching and reverting to the way she had been taught. Although the case in point took place 30 years ago, recent research in mathematics education bears out her belief that children learn mathematical concepts by working them through in concrete ways, by themselves and in small groups, not by working on abstract problems presented by the teacher (Rowan and Bourne, 1994). Why don't we more readily adopt the most current methods of teaching? A simple response is: It is harder than it looks! And often, it is "both" not "either-or."

In spite of a plethora of research studies that demonstrate the value of new ways to teach math, teachers continue to teach in ways reinforced by the dominant cultural norm—that students learn best when teachers talk to the whole group and students listen. Historically, that is the way it has been done. Students have been moved through the educational system like cars on an assembly line, each getting the same treatment and each being labeled as able or not. The lecture method has been considered to be the most efficient in terms of money and time (and politically it is wiser to do things the way those in power are accustomed to).

Dorothy: Considered to be most efficient *by whom?* Who are the experts in this case, especially since you say that researchers in mathematics education see things differently?

Authors: The so-called experts often promote the traditional ways of doing things as they are governed by cultural norms. That is where politics come in. We are talking about human and cultural change—both of which are resistant to change. AR challenges both. That's why we need it!

Scarecrow: It sounds as if these are two separate things: people and culture changing. Aren't they more interdependent than that?

Authors: Yes, of course they are. But it is sometimes easier to understand if you treat them separately.

Remember when we talked about Piaget and how we need to assimilate and accommodate and come to new ways of seeing and being through our own constructions of reality? This is as true for Chuck's teacher as it is for Chuck. (It is also true for cultural change.) Seeing and believing that a new way of teaching is more effective aren't enough to make it so. Chuck's teacher is going against much of what she was taught, and it can take time and critical incidents, such as with Chuck, to help her make a transition to more inclusive and effective ways of understanding and teaching mathematics.

By examining this story through *cultural, psychosocial, political, economic,* and *historical* lenses, we can begin to identify the underlying assumptions that govern so many routines. These unexamined assumptions serve as collective blindfolds. With the help of our critical colleagues, the possibility for growth occurs. And as this happens, we may see our questions in new ways. For example, if Chuck's teacher were investigating her teaching, we can imagine her initially asking, How can I keep my students on task? With her new insights, however, her question might become, How can I examine the way I structure learning in my class so that I can better understand how my students learn and what I can do to facilitate their learning?

At the risk of belaboring the point, let's use the dialogue between Chuck's teacher and her critical colleague as well as our cases (Shawn, Jan and Terry, and others) to construct some critical questions and examples that can help us practice problematizing. The questions will shift our focus to looking inward, looking methodically and contextually, and looking ahead.

A Scaffold for Problematizing

If you are developing a topic area or question for your action research study, you may want to work through these questions. The most challenging questions are usually the ones in which we look inside and converse honestly with ourselves about our practice. They may also make us a little uncomfortable.

What are my feelings? Chuck's teacher had a range of feelings about the episode: *hope* and *optimism* at new ways of teaching, *frustration* that it didn't seem to be working, and *anger* at Chuck who wasn't helping, and beneath this *fear* that the children would not be ready for the proficiency tests, and finally *surprise* and even *incredulity* at how Chuck saved the day! And she is still telling the story 30 years later! Rosie felt *frustration* about how students in her civics class treated one another, while Terry and Jan felt *anger* that their students were required to use inferior curriculum materials. Shawn was *excited* about having a new student, and Andy was *disappointed* with student interactions. First feeling our feelings, and then pondering what they might be trying to tell us, is one of the most important indicators that we are ready to learn something new. Bringing intelligent thought to areas that attract strong feelings can open many areas for growth.

What are my motives? What might have been Chuck's motives for looking out the window? In a critical event in Wendy's sixth-grade classroom, Wendy was moved to go to graduate school to learn more about reading. On one very ordinary day she told the class to "get ready for reading." Mickey, a sensitive child, said under his breath, "Yeah, but when do we get to *read?*" It seemed that in the frenzy of working with the school's new reading series and its slick accompanying pretests, skill lessons, posttests, reteaching skills lessons, retests, and its other workbook exercises, there was precious little time for enjoyment of the stories! Mickey knew it, and so did she.

What are my biases? We have biases in all directions. It may be easy for Jan and Terry to recognize that they have a constructivist bias to reading, but more difficult for them to recognize and admit that they feel more comfortable around some children and uncomfortable around others. It is difficult for most of us to realize and to act on the realization that race, social class, and gender are issues for us, too. Unearthing our biases is one of the most important aspects of our professional work.

How do I—and can I—visualize this? If Rosie were to close her eyes, relax, and summon an image of what a democratic civics classroom might look like, she might visualize a vibrant discussion among students. She might diagram or draw a picture with arrows from students who initiate discussion to show the range of engagements and interactions. Next she might think about the class as it currently functions and visualize a conversation in which only very few of the students are engaged. The quantity and quality of the conversation would be quite different in her two images. She could draw a picture with arrows from initiating students, but it would be mainly from the teacher and a few students. Another simple and powerful way to get an image of a situation is to let an image come in the form of a symbol. In Rosie's case the first image might be a growing pulsating organism; in the second a plant with only vestiges of green, the rest withering or dead.

One of the benefits of visualization is that we can focus on different aspects of the topic. Our emotions, motives, biases, and aims are culturally shaped and housed, so that the social and cultural contexts within which we conceptualize our work need equal attention. The following questions help us to focus methodically and contextually.

What are the elements of the topic, and how do they work? Many, if not all, topics can benefit from visualization and working with symbols to represent and explore dimensions of the topic, and to uncover implicit knowledge. Along with the synthesizing that takes place with visualization, we can benefit from analyzing elements or parts of a topic. We cite two examples. Amy, a second-grade teacher, was interested in integrating math and poetry. She read an inspiring article that pointed out how the two areas are both symbolic processes, and that one could support the other in curriculum development and teaching. Intrigued at the notion, she designed her AR around it. Her question has multiple parts. She'll have to understand the math and poetry areas and begin to make connections between the two.

Judy, a middle school teacher, wanted to know why so many eighth graders failed the newly mandated writing proficiency tests. Pursuing this question has several obvious parts: the test, the students, her roles and responsibilities as the teacher. Judy has to learn about the nature of the tests. What were students unable to do on these tests? What could she learn about the students and their needs?

What were their weak spots? This would give her an opportunity to critique the test in the process. She would have to get to know more about students who failed. Could she develop lessons and strategies as an intervention for students who'd be retaking the test in the near future?

Scarecrow: Wait a minute. If I understand the concept of problematizing, there is something amiss here. In the example you just gave, the young people (students, or "test takers") are the problem, and your solution is to find out more about the test and ways you can fix the students' gaps so that they can do better on the next test?

Authors: That is certainly one reading of what we just said.

Scarecrow: Why couldn't you make the *test* problematic instead of the *young people?* What were the biases of the test makers? What wasn't tested? What was tested? What are the assumptions underlying the test, how children learn, what is important to learn? Who does the test favor? Who does it disadvantage? What are the implicit messages in the way the test is constructed and the time and space within which it is administered? You could also get into the teacher's roles in all this! Why *should* she teach, or worse yet, *train,* to the test? What is gained and what is lost by doing so? Who should determine this?

Authors: Quite right! You have made this a more complex issue than was apparent before! The point is that there are many aspects or elements to explore, and in this case, the teacher's advocacy role for students was overshadowed by external factors.

How does my topic compare to something else? What might be learned from related experiences? For example, perhaps you have designed a curriculum project that flops. Remember the social studies curriculum project entitled "Man, a course of study," in which one of the finest teams of subject matter curriculum specialists put together an exemplary curriculum and it flopped because they didn't involve teachers and parents in the process? Might there be any lessons from this project to apply to yours? Rosie had this problem too and took it seriously. As she thinks about how she can help to foster a democratic classroom, she involves others, most importantly her students, in the process.

In what ways does time enter into the picture? Jan and Terry's fifth graders are labeled low-ability because according to *time* they are not performing at grade-level norms. They are "behind" the typical and expected time line. The time it takes second-language students to learn and adjust to a new language is considered as lost time. Successful bilingual programs exist in which "content" and language studies continue in a first language while students are gaining proficiency in the new language. With Shawn's student, this opportunity isn't available. Who *could* teach Jen social studies or science in her own language? Lesley, the kindergarten teacher with the child born prematurely, foresaw problems because the child could not meet district-articulated and developmentally inappropriate goals. He would be "behind" his age-mates *timewise.*

Time is an intriguing issue because we usually take it for granted and make unquestioned assumptions about its boundaries. Time is treated as a commodity in our culture (Bloome and Katz, 1997). We pay people based on *time* worked. We divide school days and the school year into time segments. We note "typical" benchmarks and measure our children's growth by time.

Time is a cultural construct. Indigenous peoples who were nontechnological in recent memory have no words in their native languages for clock-driven time. The cultural use of time (timed tests, assignments due dates, changing classes by a bell) is difficult for many students from nondominant cultures (Kasten, 1991). As we consider our research questions, *time* is an important variable to problematize.

In several chapters, we allude to constructivist and developmental theories and their implications for teaching and learning. How is time construed in these theories? Is a child premature, or is the judgment premature? Are we lacking knowledge and understanding of the child's and mother nature's time frame? Are Jan and Terry's students behind in their reading, or are our observations and the theories we use to understand growth and development inadequate to describe the students' realities?

What are the cultural and historical contexts? What is valued? If culture is composed of ways of thinking, valuing, and behaving (Heath, 1983), what are the norms and practices within which you will conduct your study? There is a model in sociology that uses the terms *high* and *low* culture to describe different cultural orientations (Hall, 1976). What is referred to as a high-context culture is where people are closely linked, more dependent and interdependent, work together, and are more long-term, family- and relationship-oriented. A low-context culture is characterized by use of technology, individualism, and independence. These are more highly valued, and relationships in general are tied to specific events, opportunities, and circumstances. The Amish culture, a group of people originally from Germany (many are now living in the Midwestern United States) who live much as they did in small farming communities 100 years ago, is a good example of high-context culture; the postmodern upper-middle-class suburbanite is an example of low-context culture. Images help to bring this concept out: Picture a family at home together after a day working on the farm, spending a leisurely hour or so together enjoying roast beef, mashed potatoes, cole slaw, and rhubarb pie. Contrast this with a person or two for 15 minutes at a drive-in for a Big Mac, fries, and soft-serve cone on the way to a soccer game after work.

Tin Man: What a minute! That sounds pretty stereotyped to me!

Authors: It is. We purposely did that to sharpen the contrast. High and low cultures can be that marked, but the distinctions also become muddier as cultures mix and change. The point is to begin to look at the different ways people live together, at their shared values, and see what this means for your work. History has a considerable impact on culture and thus on teaching and learning. What are people's beliefs about what is important? What are their ways of working, together and singly? How do some of these beliefs look in practice?

In Jan and Terry's school, for example, the staff is mature; they have been together for a long time, and no one has questioned the way children are grouped or the curriculum is "developed" and "delivered." It is a relatively low-context culture in which independence is valued as long as people conform to and respect school norms and policies. There are relatively few collaborative projects in which teachers, parents, students, and administrators work together in creative ways. Jan and Terry will take this into account as they move their study along. Andy may discover that the culture of segregating special students from other students has been in place for so long, and is so entrenched, that the effort to change may be met with resistance. Rosie's reading and personal life experiences as a student activist and mother of school-age children, as well as extensive reading in critical democracy, have prepared her to understand the culture of the school and to work with this knowledge in her project.

What forces are supportive of and resistant to change? Twenty years ago in the curriculum field a process called *forced field analysis* was popular. This is a way to assess and evaluate the possibilities for change in a cultural setting. Simply put, it entailed listing factors which were in support of change and factors which served as constraints to change. Let's see what Shawn might find.

Factors supporting the change

I am committed to teaching each child.
I can get info off the Web about Korea.
I can observe carefully and try things out.
The principal said she would help.
I can work with the ESL person.
Jen is bright and enthusiastic.
The children want to make friends.
I know quite a bit about child
   development.

Factors constraining the change

I know nothing about Korea!
I know almost nothing about Jen.
Jen doesn't speak *any* English.
No one I know speaks Korean!

For Rosie, trying to initiate a democratic classroom will go against tradition and the norms in her school. Some of her obstacles, then, are political. For those students who benefit from the traditional system, the new system could provide a rude demotion, and fallout. The force most powerful in supporting change is her commitment to do so, which comes from her conviction that a democratic system works.

For Terry and Jan, there were several forces that made change unlikely: a group which set policies for the district curriculum, past experience of teachers who had been "innovative" finding themselves unemployed, and a lack of resources and curriculum materials appropriate for their proposal. One of their strongest assets was that there were two of them. They each had considerable experience and confidence, and they were willing to make this a major project—planned, documented, and evaluated—with shared results. They were willing to put in the time to research and prepare a professional proposal for change and to communicate with all necessary parties.

As we look inwardly, outwardly, and contextually, we keep coming back to our purpose. Where are we heading? We'd best keep Oz (or Kansas) in mind, or we may end up in some remote place that is nice to visit, but where we are unlikely to find the Wizard (or Aunty Em)! These last two questions help us to frame our topic from the perspectives of long-term effects—ones that we may not be around to deal with. Decisions can be made with myopic vision, and if we are not mindful, short-term goals may jeopardize long-term goals and violate our vision for the future.

What are my long-term aims, and how do these fit with my short-term goals? Rosie believes that if her students live the democratic process in the classroom, they will understand and "own" it, and they will more likely take an active interest in community activities, voting, and the world around them. Jan and Terry want their "low-ability" readers to read, finish school, and continue to read. This team thinks that if they fall in love with books, there's a better shot at this. They are not alone in that belief.

Caught up in everyday issues and unquestioned assumptions and norms, we can easily lose sight of our larger aims. This is why it is important to formulate, publish, consult, refer to, and revise long-term aims and goals. When jointly negotiated, constructed, and used by various stakeholders (students, teachers, parents, the wider community), school cultures can and do evolve.

Goodlad (1984) asked more than 27,000 people how learning and long-term goals were served in their districts. Results were remarkably consistent. Most people wanted high academic standards and for school to be a humane and caring place. In general, parents and teachers have similar long-term goals: to have children grow into good citizens, communicators, problem solvers, critical consumers, and parents, and learn to live happy and fulfilling lives. Each community defines what is meant by *good,* but the categories are similar. While it is important to jointly determine aims and goals as a framework for planning (if we want all students to graduate from school, we need to anticipate practices and policies that may in fact hinder students from graduating), as problematizers, we also want to question goals that simply maintain the status quo at the expense of students and families who are not privileged by the current system.

What are the consequences of change, and for whom? At first glance, we might say that those people best served by maintaining the present circumstances will lose their benefits with that change, and that those most disadvantaged by present circumstances will benefit from changes that are in their best interests. However, this assumes that change must advantage and disadvantage some people. This may be so, or seem so, in the short term. However, by taking a longer-term perspective, it may be that *both* or, more accurately, *all* groups will be advantaged. Is the child who "shines above all others" in a competitive, stepped, "single-intelligence," hierarchical system really better off than he would be in a system where all children are enabled to grow and shine, where collaboration, multiple intelligences, and continuous progress (formative) were acknowledged, valued, and supported? Does not an inferior education for Jan and Terry's students affect the quality of education within the school, and thus the quality of education for all students?

Taking time to examine the consequences of change from both long- and short-term goal perspectives for all people involved is well worth the effort in terms of both individuals and communities.

While exploring and problematizing on our own are important, we are mindful of the need to work with colleagues to mutually expand our own knowledge and scholarship. How we can work with these colleagues is the subject of the next section.

What Do Others Know? Scholars and Colleagues as Resources

Think of the many resources available to us as we try to make informed decisions about our work: Other teachers, counselors, social workers, psychologists, parents, business and community partners, media specialists, friends, researchers, and theorists quickly come to mind. Talking over a cup of coffee to a teacher who has helped second-language learners might be a first stop in Shawn's exploration. E-mail list servers, chat rooms, and Internet sites instantaneously open up our world to distant colleagues. Libraries give us access to the scholarship of researchers, thinkers, and teacher-researchers who may have pondered the same questions that puzzle us. They have developed their own ideas and theories that can inform our thinking. We would be remiss in our research if we did not consult available resources. While we will focus on one resource—scholars who have written about a particular topic—we do so not to diminish the contributions of others, but to highlight the importance of scholarship in helping us expand our knowledge about our research interest.

Reviewing the Literature

Exploring the library and the Internet related to one's topic can be not only informative but also downright invigorating, as we discover more about the terrain we are traveling and the resources available to us. We can use relevant literature to help us shape our inquiry. In fact, a single article can change the way we think about a topic; it can act as a catalyst for our thinking and help us to define the study and our direction. An article or book can be a gold mine from which to draw much of our review. It may contain a list of references which, when reviewed carefully, can provide key sources for further investigation. *Using* the wheel, rather than reinventing it, may enable us to move further down the Yellow Brick Road.

One action researcher we know learned a related lesson the hard way. She was interested in *buddy reading* (children read back and forth to one another without teacher supervision). After several weeks of frustration with students' lack of interest, she went to the literature and found a wealth of research and materials which helped her to understand the process and how to proceed. "Ah, if only I had consulted the literature earlier!" she exclaimed.

Dorothy: Better late than never!

Authors: Yes indeed. There are many times when consulting the literature at the beginning of one's thinking about a topic is advisable, and there are times when it is advisable to conceptualize and begin the study, after which the literature may become useful. The traditional bias has been to do the former. With AR, however, it is often advisable to do the latter. There are studies in which the literature is not essential, or even necessary, even though the study itself may contribute to it! It all depends upon one's topic and purpose. By laying out some of the possible benefits and cautions in reviewing the literature, it will be easier to determine the best approach for our studies.

We have already listed some pretty compelling benefits, not the least of which is that such a review helps us to map out the terrain, locate resources, define and refine our topic and questions, and save time. The attendant dangers include: allowing the literature to shape our questions when we are in a better position to do so, getting sidetracked or distracted by other issues, and feeling the need to read beyond the point necessary to conceptualize one's study ("I need to read just one more book!"). One way around these potential problems is to read critically and to keep summarizing our thinking about our studies as we proceed through a limited body of literature.

We have learned from action researchers who have searched libraries and Internet sources for scholarship that helped them to develop their questions. We include a few of their ideas for your consideration:

Read broadly and generally at first, then read more narrowly. If you are interested in using cooperative learning, first you may want to read a book that describes all kinds of cooperative learning strategies. Then you may want to narrow in on articles, chapters, or books that focus on the particular approach that makes sense for you and your students. To read broadly, browse through catalogues and stacks to discover some general and useful information: Is the topic considered to be controversial? Is there agreement about the topic among professionals? Has information on the topic changed greatly over recent years? What are key works and key scholars concerning the topic? What do experts consider to be central issues and as yet unexamined? You may stumble on research syntheses that provide many different perspectives on the topic and a list of references leading you to specific works that will narrow your focus. See Figure 9.1 for sources to consider when browsing.

FIGURE 9.1 *Scholarly sources for reviewing literature.*

- **Journals from learned societies.** Publications sponsored by organizations central to a field of study are usually instrumental in setting national and/or regional standards for the field. Referred to as *juried, blind-reviewed,* or *refereed,* anything going in these journals, has been judged worthy by at least three readers to whom the authors are unknown. Thus the work has been judged on its merit and not on the fame or connections of the author. The purpose of refereed journals is the dissemination of knowledge. Writers and even editors are generally not compensated.

- **Online journals.** Many learned societies offer online journals which are refereed, like their paper counterparts. Web addresses are generally available in paper journals and from colleagues, media specialists, and society web pages. Some journals have access fees. Some online journals are free, but more typically they require subscriptions either through your Internet browser or through your academic institution. Be cautious about information obtained from the web when the source cannot be documented as scholarly or reputable. Anyone with minimal computer knowledge can post web information. When in doubt, consult a reference librarian. Some online sources are not intended for scholarly use, but are more like electronic encyclopedias with concise information for use by the general public.

- **Professional books.** The market for books to inform teachers and others is rich and exciting. Certain publishers cater to the needs of educators, and nearly any topic that has been around for a few years has a book on the subject. Consult reputable publishers in your discipline. Your action research mentor can assist you in finding out which publishers are appropriate. With a professional book, the credentials of the authors should be advertised, including their experience and affiliations. Professional books, like journals, have been reviewed throughout the publication process by others to ensure content and writing quality. Be cautious of books or other print materials that are self-published, or published by the author-owned company although they can be as reputable as known sources. Reference librarians have publishers' directories that include all legitimate publishers and information about their ownership.

- **Conferences.** While attending a local, regional, national, or international conference of educators, you may have the pleasure of hearing a notable speaker whose words or handouts you would like to use in your research. Publication manuals list rules for citing such sources. Be cautious to differentiate between conferences sponsored by scholarly, learned societies where proposals were reviewed by a proposal committee and commercial, for-profit conferences or workshops which are primarily a business enterprise (the quality nonetheless could be good), as the latter often lack checks and balances to ensure quality. Materials from the former are generally safe to use in a literature review. Consult your action researcher mentor for a recommendation on others.

When you are researching a novel topic that seems to have few resources, look for related topics and synthesize them. The first people who wanted to study children and computer use would have been unable to find information in professional journals on their topic! Instead, as they progressed in their inquiry, they found that literature on how children learn and on computer processing could be useful to their research. They became synthesizers of these two bodies of literature and brought them together in new ways. In these instances, the researchers make their maps as they go. The entire map becomes visible only in hindsight!

Consult primary sources where possible. When the first generation of babies born addicted to "crack" cocaine arrived in kindergartens around the United States, no one was prepared for the difficulties these children would have in school. A library search would not have been useful. But local hospitals and agencies that serve families of preschoolers were aware of some of the issues, had research studies in progress, and had reports and resource people prepared to share information. Getting information firsthand from those conducting the research and publishing their findings is to consult *primary sources* and is preferable to using *secondary sources* (those sources which build on, quote, and use other people's research). Having said this, we acknowledge that it is not possible to use only primary sources. The rule of thumb is to use as many primary sources as is possible and feasible, and to check secondary sources to make sure that the information quoted is accurate.

Ask for help. Sometimes information is difficult to find. The terminology or the databases you are searching may not be suited to the question. A few well-placed questions to a librarian, media specialist, and colleagues can be helpful in these instances.

Read enough to get started, but not so much that you become too exhausted to conduct your study! Those pursuing advanced degrees may want to read until they see ideas repeat themselves. Those whose interests are more immediate may simply read until ideas are framed in a context that makes sense for their purposes. To read everything on cooperative learning would be senseless if you discover that your primary interest is how to formulate groups of students.

As we read from a variety of sources, we read with a critical eye. Each of the questions we reviewed for problematizing can be posed to sources in our literature reviews. Other questions include these: What are the theories, assumptions, and frameworks of the authors and researchers? Are they plausible? Are they consistent with what you know? What theories, if expressed explicitly, undergird their work? What is explained? What is left for interpretation? What are the credentials of the author(s)? Do they take themselves into account as part of their study? The public theories that we read in the literature can enhance the development of our emerging private theories.

Figure 9.2 offers some suggestions for ways to keep track of your tools, your data, and other resources.

FIGURE 9.2 *Looking ahead: Considerations for managing information.*

- **Consider permissions.** To conduct your study, you may need clearance from the institutions involved. In addition, you may need permission from families of your participants. This is especially important if you plan to use audio recording, video recordings, student work, or photographs in your work and in your report or presentations. Consult your action research mentor as well as school district personnel for local guidelines.

- **Consider exploring baseline data.** Often teachers give assignments at the beginning of the year (such as writing or interviews about content knowledge) or surveys to parents about prospective students. Others take reading samples on audio tape, or videotape early school-year behavior. Also, schools maintain cumulative files with data from previous school years. Some of this information may be useful in your study design and analysis for identifying focus participants, for comparing growth in a subject area, or for making numerical comparisons from available test scores. Local policies may affect how and when these files are accessed and used.

- **Shop for supplies.** As smooth journeys most often require careful and compact packing, research requires organizational skills and procedures. Consider how you will keep track of readings. (Notebooks? Index cards?) How will you keep track of data? (File folders? Binders? Envelopes?) How will you keep track of what you have done and what you still need to do? Where will you store these things? Will they be on computer files? Where will you store backups? Sometimes colored labels, files, or highlighters can help separate different kinds of data.

- **Protect your baggage.** As you collect data, date and name every item. Photocopy written materials. Maintain backup files on your computer and on diskettes. Be careful transporting files between home and school. Don't leave important parts of your research in unsecured places. Carefully documenting can prevent a last-minute scramble for citations and page numbers. If, at the last minute, you discover one part of a citation is needed, a reference librarian can generally help retrieve the missing information.

- **Know your library and your librarians.** Take time to get to know your library and its services, especially interlibrary loans, online sources, and the magic library staff—the *reference* department. They are knowledgeable about finding and obtaining information. *Ask for their help.* Most academic libraries have a *reference desk.* Talk to a librarian knowledgeable about your area of interest.

What Do I Expect to Find?

Action researchers are continually mindful of their own thoughts, feelings, values, assumptions, and biases. We realize that only through self-reflection will we develop into professional scholars of our teaching. Being mindful of our own expectations for where our questions may lead us is also a way to keep track of how our own lenses filter the way we look at our journey.

CHAPTER SUMMARY

Problematizing our questions and our practice is perhaps the most challenging part of our action research journey. By beginning with what we already know and adding the wisdom and critique of colleagues (teachers, researchers, theorists, and others), we may be able to move beyond the confines of the Yellow Brick Road, to a little more dangerous but richer journey.

SECTION SUMMARY

We conclude this section by recalling the questions that the teachers in our case studies developed over the course of their action research projects. What can you learn from them?

1. How can I best teach a child who speaks a language different from that of the rest of the class?
   - How will Jen fare when immersed in a new language?
   - How will Jen learn English?
   - How will Jen's lack of English affect her learning and social relationships?
   - How will I learn about Jen's culture? How will that learning inform my teaching?
2. How do children who have had difficulty with reading respond to a rich literature-based approach with the use of trade books, literature response journals, and the opportunity for meaningful discussions of literature, when they have been used to reliance on basal readers?
3. How can I create a democratic classroom environment in my civics class?
4. "I just don't get it! I know these kids [students placed in regular education classes] have been with our students [students placed in special education classes] in inclusive classes in the past, but the regular education students act as if they have never seen a child with disabilities? Why isn't inclusion working?" Is it because it is not cool to hang around kids perceived to be "different"?

   In each case, the questions are related to personal values and commitments:
   - A desire to help a child who speaks another language feel included and an eagerness to learn about the child's culture.

- A belief that learning to read requires a variety of rich and interesting resources and meaningful discussions with peers and adults.
- The idea that it is important to model a democratic classroom if we expect students to become active citizens.
- A belief that all students need to be and feel included.

Their beliefs form the commitments which, combined with curiosity, fuel their desire to know.

Questions that lead to illuminating studies are fueled by curiosity and commitment to a set of values. They focus on interpreting and critiquing one's own practice and center on matters of consequence to the researcher. Although the results of such studies may be useful to others, their purpose is not to generalize.

The beginnings of journeys are usually rich with potential but they can also seem rough and dangerous for lack of knowing exactly where our interests may take us, how our journey will unfold, and what the journey may teach us about ourselves. It must still seem a long way to the Emerald City. To move closer to the Emerald City let's take time to make use of what we have just explored and further frame our research questions in "Exploring the Forest."

Exploring the Forest
From Curiosity to Research Topic and Questions

In these chapters, we offered many suggestions to begin to define and shape a study topic and questions. These explorations and exercises are designed to assist you in being the educational conductor of your own professional work. They will help you to develop professional judgment. As you proceed, you may choose to change your idea anywhere along the way, as you acquire new information and make it part of your developing reportoire. Give yourself a few minutes for each exercise. Just write, don't think. You can always return and expand on your ideas, if you decide that would be beneficial. Do a free-write for the first four items which follow.

1. What are three things that you are curious about related to professional practice?
2. What are three concerns you have about being a caring and committed teacher?
3. What three problems (or dissatisfactions) do you have, or foresee, with your teaching and professional work?

Now, look at what you have—look at the nine things you have listed.

4. What larger issues come to mind? Are any of these related to others on the list? Can you find an issue related to each curiosity, concern, and problem? What different perspectives or viewpoints are inherent in each? What (if anything) is controversial or contestable in each? Take one issue that holds promise as a research topic, and do a free-write about it. You might choose to focus on your thoughts, ideas, experiences, and questions related to this possible topic.
5. Take the issue you wrote about in item 4, and turn it into a statement of the problem (curiosity) you (tentatively) will investigate. Then pose a question or two or three that go to the heart of what you think is the problem. Limit yourself to one page.

Do you notice anything about what you have just done? What connections did you make as a result of writing? What thoughts and feelings did you have as you did this, and about the process itself? You now have a tentative topic and questions for a study. You have also generated ideas that you can take through the same process and develop into an area for investigation, perhaps an action research project. The next section will take you further into thinking critically (problematizing) about teaching, learning, and curriculum development.

6. Make a list of several teaching or instructional practices in your field of study. For example, you might list the practice of students expanding their vocabularies by looking up words from a list in the dictionary and then using the words in a sentence. Some other common practices might be writing spelling words for practice; answering questions in science or social studies at the end of the chapter; conjugating verbs in a foreign language; memorizing multiplication tables in math; diagramming sentences in English grammar; or asking students to identify and copy the elements of art in well-known paintings. Ask yourself, and a few colleagues, questions about the practice and the assumptions that seem to underlie it. This is a good activity to do in a small group. Although we cannot be sure of what someone else assumes unless we ask them, we can think through what seems to follow logically from the activity. Here are some questions to frame assumptions.
   a. What might be assumed about how learning takes place in this activity? What might be assumed about how children learn? Adolescents? Adults? What might be assumed about students' roles and responsibilities in this learning?
   What might be the assumptions about the teacher's roles and responsibilities in this teaching and learning?
   b. What is assumed related to the student's overall education? Might we assume that this will make the student a "better" or "more educated" person?

7. Select several issues of a prominent journal in your field or discipline. In small groups, select several articles and read only the literature reviews. The literature review will be easy to locate—it will summarize many studies. Have each group member read the same two or three literature reviews. Then, as a group, decide how to describe the literature review and the role it plays in the article. How do the literature reviews vary? What do they have in common? How might the article be different without this section? Share your findings with the group or class as a whole. These literature reviews may serve as useful examples later, if you need to write one. Keep in mind the references you make in your own study may be used sparingly—just enough to get you started on your journey.

8. Write a draft of an introduction to your project. You many find that you can use this again later as an introduction to your report. Include the following in your introduction:
   • What is my research interest?
   • Why am I interested? (What are my values and beliefs?)
   • What is my question?
   • What do I already know?

- What do others know? (These are things you have learned from the literature, from other professionals, from family, from the community, and from technological sources.)
- What do I expect to find?

Limit this draft to a page or two. Be concise and stick to the topic. It is appropriate to write in the first person ("I"). Trade drafts with critical colleagues or classmates, asking them to react to your idea and your writing. Ask them to tell you, in their own words, what they believe you said.

9. Select an issue or controversy in your school or in the news (school uniforms, year-round schooling, multiage classes, national teacher testing, national standards, etc.). Using the chart based on the three orientations of Habermas in Chapter 4, frame an argument either for or against this issue or practice: one from the *technical* orientation, one from the *practical* orientation, one from the critical or *emancipatory* orientation. For example, the issue of out-of-school suspension has many aspects that can be debated. From a technical point of view, how efficient is out-of-school suspension in punishing students? Do students return to school with a better attitude toward learning? Are they less of a threat to other students? From a practical point of view, we may want to know if out-of-school suspension allows us to better understand these students. From a critical perspective, we may want to know which students are suspended. Is any ethnic or socioeconomic group overrepresented? Here are some issues to try out with this exercise. Try these or generate your own:
   - As a teacher, you notice that your "nonmajority" students continually score lower than the group as a whole on the standardized test used by your district. You are considering this as a research question.
   - Your state or region is talking seriously about retaining all eighth graders who do not pass a local mandated proficiency test, preventing them from proceeding to the next grade level. You and your colleagues are concerned about this policy.
   - You have been teaching vocabulary in your high school the same way for years—separate from the context of literature. You are bored with it, and the students are bored with it. The parents highly value the fact that vocabulary is taught this way, as they believe it will help their adolescents score higher on college entrance examinations.
10. Using the list of questions for problematizing in this chapter, examine the issue or practice you just explored in exercise 9. Or, your may want to revisit the vignette about Chuck, the child who wasn't paying attention to his teacher during a math lesson. Or you may want to take the research topic and question that you are considering for your own action research project. Ask a critical colleague or a group of colleagues to think with you so that you can clarify for yourself what your research interest is. Let them know that while you value their advice, this is not an advice-giving session. Rather, you want them to ask you questions, questions such as those listed in this chapter in the section on

problematizing, that will help you clarify the situation or problem or interest. You may want to begin by writing a few sentences that describe your research interest or problem. Then read them out loud to your colleagues. Next the questions begin. Close the session by asking one of your colleagues to reflect on what she or he heard and saw and felt about you and the way the process went. Many researchers have found this kind of "think with me" reflection to be one of the most beneficial parts of beginning an action research study. Finally, reflect on what you have learned through this process. Were you able to see things from perspectives that were not apparent to you before? Do you have any new insights into the research interest or into yourself? What are the ways in which you are involved in the situation? In what ways might you play a part in the problem?

Designing and Planning an Action Research Study

T his adventure [with monstrous beasts] made the travelers more anxious than ever to get out of the forest, and they walked so fast that Dorothy became tired. . . . To their great joy, the trees became thinner the further they advanced . . . suddenly they came upon a broad river . . . on the other side of the water they could see the road of yellow brick running through a beautiful country . . .

"How shall we cross the river?" asked Dorothy.

"That is easily done," replied the Scarecrow. "The Tin Woodman must build us a raft so we can float to the other side."

. . . When they reached the shore . . . they knew the stream had carried them a long way past the road of yellow brick. . .

"What shall we do now?" asked the Woodman.

"We must get back to the road in some way," said Dorothy.

"The best plan will be to walk along the river bank until we come to the road again," remarked the Lion.

The Wonderful Wizard of Oz
L. Frank Baum (1900)

Authors: Bravo! Figuring out how to cross the river to get back on the Yellow Brick Road took some ingenuity, Scarecrow!

Scarecrow: Geez. . . . It was nothing.

Authors: Sure it was. You have *all* used ingenuity and creativity and courage in facing adventures and obstacles. This journey certainly does not follow a straight and narrow path!

Dorothy: Now that our questions are taking shape, we want more than ever to get to Oz—no matter the route! No matter how many changes we have to make in our itinerary.

Tin Man: It helps to have one another. I wouldn't have thought about building a raft—I don't much like water.

Authors: That is quite understandable. Let's see, now. We need to use a little mind (reasoning and ingenuity), plus a lot of heart (the will to get there with our companions), plus the courage to face challenges and not turn back.

Lion: No siree. We won't turn back!

Authors: Those three things help us to figure out creative ways to cross rivers that seem so wide when we first see them.

Dorothy: This reminds me of those fancy terms you used before—*cognitive complexity, moral-ethical commitment,* and *psychological maturity.*

Authors: Yep. Mind. Heart. Courage. That's what helps us to make professional judgments.

In this section, we will explore how professionals address their questions by carefully planning a road map. We will explore the kinds of data that professionals produce and evaluate to make adjustments in even the best laid plans. By the end of this section, you will have designed a thoughtful study to address your questions. Helpful hints in boxes called *Stepping Stones* and exercises in "Exploring the Forest" at the end of the section are provided to guide the design of your study.

Dorothy: This sounds like "on-the-job" training for a lifetime of exploration!

Authors: Right! Now let's take a look at the plans that our teachers have developed to address the questions they posed in Section 4.

CASE STUDIES

Helping Jen Learn English as a Second Language

Shawn knew having a child who spoke Korean in an English-speaking classroom would be a challenging experience. Shawn's respect for Jen as a learner from a different culture provided the impetus for the study. After deciding to make this into an action research study, Shawn had to decide how to proceed. Because Jen was the focus of the study, a single-subject case study approach certainly made sense. Shawn immediately began keeping a researcher log where she noted observations about Jen. In the beginning, Shawn wasn't sure what to write in the logbook, but was confident that as time went on, interesting and informative anecdotes would need to be recorded about Jen's development.

Reading, language, and socialization were of primary concern, as these would influence nearly all other learning for Jen. The literature on English as a second language (ESL) offered many suggestions for ways to enrich the language learning of ESL students as well as all students in a classroom. Shawn's plan for Jen included working with a self-selected buddy, hands-on activities, modified written work, drawing and labeling of pictures, a picture journal, and independent computer work. An integral part of the study was for Shawn to learn about Korean culture.

With each new strategy, Shawn decided to save Jen's journals and analyze her progress. Shawn planned to conduct interviews with the ESL teacher in the school both to become more informed about strategies to use with Jen and to collect the other teacher's insights on her progress. Shawn systematically saved all Jen's written classroom work for later analysis to look for progress in literacy and language development. Finally, Shawn decided to give three periodic quizzes of commonly used words for second graders to assess Jen's progress in knowledge of common but vital vocabulary. These four data sources would provide multiple ways of looking at her progress.

As in many action research projects, Shawn was uncertain exactly how the study should proceed. One thing was certain—a number of things would have to be tried out. Shawn would observe Jen's responses, note changes in a researcher log, keep tabs on progress as evidenced in the student's journal, and adjust teaching as things were learned along the way. One of the members of Shawn's university research class agreed to be a critical colleague.

Shawn knew that the report would be presented in the university action research class for which this study was being conducted, so permission was obtained from the university Human Subjects Review Board prior to actual data collection. In addition, Shawn obtained written permission from Jen's parents, who were eager to participate in any way they could. The principal of Shawn's school had suggested that a brief presentation at a faculty meeting would be beneficial to staff.

The Literature Circle's Study

Jan and Terry decided to conduct their study with a class of 20 fifth graders tracked as the lowest-ability fifth-grade readers in the school. All these students were labeled *at risk* by their school. Within this class, literature circles were selected for special focus. The goal was to help students become enthused, engaged, and excited about reading in hopes that they would become lifelong readers. Specifically, the goal was to help students become self-confident in reading and language and develop critical thinking skills.

The teachers decided to implement literature circles (Daniels, 1994; Kasten, 1995) in which groups of five students would meet daily for approximately a 5-week unit to read award-winning juvenile novels, keep written responses to their reading, and conduct student-led discussions. The literature circles would replace the basal reading program, put in place by the district, which consisted of anthologies of short stories, questions about each story, and workbook exercises of skills that were decontextualized from the stories.

The "Reader Self-Perception Scale" (Henk and Melnick, 1995) was to be administered to the class at the beginning and end of the semester as pre- and posttest measures of student attitudes toward themselves as readers. Student journals would be collected, and one group's journals would be analyzed for evidence of higher-level critical thinking. Jan and Terry designed a form for students to self-assess their participation, their contribution to the group, and their understanding of the literature. Selected student discussions would be audio-taped for evidence of critical thinking and level of engagement with the story. The teachers also planned to take anecdotal notes about students and group process skills. A close look at student responses on the attitude scale, the content of the student journals, and their own researcher logs would hopefully reveal some patterns that would help them make some good decisions about how best to use literature circles to develop student interest in reading and student critical thinking.

Because of their review of the literature, Jan and Terry were aware of some kinds of expected written and oral responses and planned to look for those plus other kinds of responses that might emerge from all these data sources. In the back of their minds, they were thinking of how to demonstrate student progress at the end of the one-semester study to other teachers. They suspected that they would find that "at-risk" readers can respond to literature in engaging ways. It was not necessary to obtain written parental permission for this study because blanket permission for action research studies was obtained through the principal's office at the beginning of the school year. However, Jan and Terry did write a letter to parents informing them about the plans, hoping that they would encourage their children to talk about their selected books at home.

The S.T.A.R. Club Study

Andy's study focused on creating situations in which "typical" middle school students would be more accepting of the 16 students in two multiple handicapped (MH) classes. The 16 students had been diagnosed with Down's syndrome, cerebral palsy, language disorders, vision impairments, and autism.

Andy considered several alternative actions before deciding on a *peer club* as an extracurricular activity. The sole purpose of the club would be to increase the time for social interaction between "typical" students and students with multiple handicaps. This option was appealing for two reasons. First, it addressed the social needs of both groups of students. Second, it supported the middle school philosophy of providing choices for all students to participate in the life of the school. The group would be called the *S.T.A.R. (Students and Teachers Advancing Relationships) Club*. Interested students could sign up with a friend and be paired with a peer with special needs.

During first semester, Andy would organize the club: find interested peers and teachers, pair them up, and think of club activities. During the second semester, the club would sponsor one activity per month. Andy thought activities like a pizza party would be fun for everyone involved and would be a natural way to increase social interaction, and hopefully acceptance.

To triangulate the data, Andy decided to use a personal journal to keep track of observations and personal reflections, a before-and-after survey of student attitudes toward peers with disabilities, and a focus group interview of S.T.A.R. club members to probe more deeply into their attitudes. An advisory group of teachers would be consulted for feedback, and emerging hypotheses would be tested for disconfirming data. Data would be analyzed in relation to the literature on inclusion and Andy's personal experiences of working with students with special needs. Administrators, teachers, and parents would be informed about the results of the study. Because Andy was interested in seeing if the S.T.A.R. Club would make a difference in social interaction and acceptance, the study used a before-and-after design which also looked at feelings and activities *during* the year.

The Democratic Classroom Study

Rosie gave some serious thought to ways she could address her question. She wanted to help her ninth-grade civics students develop knowledge, skills, and characteristics that she felt were necessary for active, involved citizenship in a democracy. Her goal was to develop a sense of community among the students in three of her college preparatory civics classes, something she saw lacking during her practicum observations. Drawing on readings about community development in classrooms, she decided to start out by focusing on building a collaborative ethos. She brainstormed ways to enhance collaboration between teachers and students and between students and their peers. Her ideas ranged from student choice, to group work, to discussion of controversial issues, and to a classroom compact.

Rosie realized that she would need to collect evidence to determine the consequences of her efforts. She considered this evidence to be *formative evaluation* of progress toward the development of a sense of community in her classroom. She also knew that she would have to verify that the results of her study would hold up to the judgment of others—her mentor, her university advisers, and fellow student teachers when she made a presentation to them at the end of the term. So as she decided on data collection strategies, she kept these things in mind. In an effort to save time, rather than interview all her students individually, she decided to survey students about their sense of community, both at the beginning of her student teaching and toward the end. Rather than develop a survey of her own, she was able to obtain one from a journal article recommended by her research adviser. This, too, saved some time. She would also collect student work and student journals. The journal would be a source of information about student attitudes about collaborative work. Her own journal would be a source of private reflection on how the study was progressing and what she was learning. Here she could record her hunches and thoughts about issues that were emerging. She decided the best time for her to write would be in the evening after she put her children to bed. Observations by herself, her mentor, and her university action research adviser would provide information about student group work and participation. She knew that she would need their continued support as critical colleagues in order to carry through her plans.

With all these perspectives, she felt that any conclusions drawn would be fair and reasonable. Before she drew conclusions, however, she planned to examine her data closely, looking specifically for things that contradicted her own hunches. She planned to interpret her findings in light of experience (her own and that of other teachers) as well as the reading she planned to do. Next steps would come as the study evolved. Before administering the first survey, she told her students about the study and gained written parent permission and support.

Let's briefly reflect on the journey of the teachers in our cases as they explore their options and develop their plans of action. The English as a Second Language Study and the Literature Circle's Study are conducted by veteran teachers aware of the detours and obstacles that may redirect their journey. For this reason, they plan tentatively. The S.T.A.R. Club Study and the Democratic Classroom Study are conducted by student teachers whose limited teaching experience is both wonderful and problematic. Strong commitments and ideals motivate their work, but like their more veteran counterparts, they must work within existing classroom and school structures that moderate their plans. All these detours and obstacles (classroom and peer culture, school or district, mentor and student "agendas") inform the professional judgments made by our teachers.

Each of these studies is based on a strong commitment to understanding the self as teacher, the setting, and students, and to action that is consistent with a vision for teaching and learning. In this section, we explore specific tools of inquiry that will provide "data" for the professional journal. In the following section, we will see not only how the stories unfold, but how these teachers develop professional judgment that relies on both careful analysis of data *and* intuition (and ingenuity) that leaps beyond the immediate and concrete evidence.

From Research Questions to Planning a Study

If you have developed a question in the previous section that you would like to carry out as an action research study, this chapter can be used to help you quickly design a "trial" study. Or you may want to develop a sample question and use this chapter to design a study for practice. The ideas that we introduce here are developed further in the next chapters.

What Is Design?

Design is a plan. It is a personalized road map that we create to address the questions and curiosities we have about our teaching. If the idea of designing a study seems a little foreign, we want to assure you that design is part of our everyday lives. Selecting the clothes we wear to create a certain image or feeling, choosing and arranging furniture to create a special kind of living space, and customizing a car for safety, comfort, or utility are all examples of how we design our everyday lives.

Action research involves designing our teaching lives with our students. To plan and develop a curriculum requires that we take an active part in designing our teaching and our relationships with students. Just as Dorothy and her friends deal creatively with obstacles (flying monkeys, witches, the illusive Yellow Brick Road), action researchers face seemingly unsurmountable obstacles (such as standardized tests for students, checklists for teacher evaluation, and bureaucracy) that stifle creativity. Internal obstacles are just as difficult to overcome: Unexamined personal and professional assumptions about the way things *ought* to be can easily become our own roadblocks. It takes creative energy and thoughtfulness to design a journey that will enable us, with our students, to learn and develop.

Why create a plan? Planning a study in advance may be the glue that holds the research together when things do not go smoothly. It is a starting point, not a rigid, step-by-step guide for what must happen. Planning necessitates stepping back and thinking about where we want to go, knowing full well that we will make changes in response to what we learn along the way. Many teachers plan for action research before school begins so that they have an idea of how to carry out their studies before students arrive and the thousand details of the school year demand their attention. For student teachers unfamiliar with the classrooms in which they will teach, planning ahead might seem difficult. To ease into their studies, our students spend time in their classrooms prior to student teaching. They make observations, read research, talk with teachers, and reflect in their journals and in seminars about what interests them. If this is not possible, the first weeks of student teaching can be spent trying to formulate questions. Small inquiry groups can be formed based on the common interests of student teachers. The written plan usually comes *after* time is spent in teaching and in reflection on how we want our classrooms to be. As a general rule, start by designing a short, easily manageable study. Beginning one's research with a complex, multidimensional, 2-year study can easily be an exercise in frustration!

Designing a Quick Practice Study

Think of something you did recently in your teaching that didn't work. Perhaps it worked previously, or it has come up for the first time and you had to figure out how to make it work. Now jot down some notes about it in your journal.

The following example illustrates how one teacher thought about her teaching. Kathy, an experienced kindergarten teacher, started to question the value of "letter of the week," a practice for reading that she had carried out consistently as "a firm believer" for many years.

> As I continued to use the letter of the week, I noticed my enthusiasm for teaching the alphabet began to lessen. I was no longer excited or enthused about activities. I noticed the children felt the same way. There seemed to be an overall attitude of "I will do this because I have to, not because I want to do it." I also noticed that the children who functioned at a lower level were not learning sounds and the letters in isolation. As I began to seriously take a look at what I was doing, I asked myself, Does teaching the letter of the week really suit the children's needs? . . . The thing that bothered me the most, though, is that I have always been a strong advocate for a developmentally appropriate curriculum and thought that I was really teaching one! But as I looked at my classroom practice, I really began to question whether I was actually providing a developmentally appropriate curriculum for my children. I began to search for other ways . . .

What did *you* do as a result of *your* situation? Jot it down in your journal. Now see what Kathy did.

> I began to read, and I attended a conference and came away with new ideas and enthusiasm . . . a better understanding of phonemic awareness. With the help of Dr. Bruneau and numerous resources, I implemented [a more comprehensive] phonemic awareness [program] in my classroom. This simple change in my teaching has given me a whole new enthusiasm for teaching. I am really pleased

with what is happening in my classroom and have documentation through an action research project to prove that it works!

(Kathy, Journal excerpt)

Louise, a teacher unknown to Kathy struggled with a similar problem. Let's look into her journal reflections:

In looking back at my journey, I discovered that teaching in isolation does not work for every child. I began my study by focusing on phonemic awareness and letter sounds. I thought that by teaching these concepts children would be able to see and/or hear a word and have the ability to segment the word by letters. I believed that the children would then be able to read and write the sounds they heard and/or saw. I assumed that because the children would be taught the skills, the enthusiasm, the enjoyment and the understanding of literature would come with it automatically. I was wrong. I was able to teach the letter sounds and phonemics awareness, but there was something missing. The children were not enjoying the literacy experience as much as I had anticipated.

(Louise, journal excerpt)

By thinking about something that didn't work and what you might try differently, and then actually trying out ways to make it work, you were engaging in an initial cycle of action research. To remind you of this cycle, we have included Figure 10.1.

Now, let's design a study. Quickly answer the following design questions:

1. Describe a hitch in your practice—something you would like to improve. Select something that might take a week or so to try out some different actions.
2. What can you try out?
3. How will you document the process?
4. How will you report and discuss it with others?
5. How will it make life better?

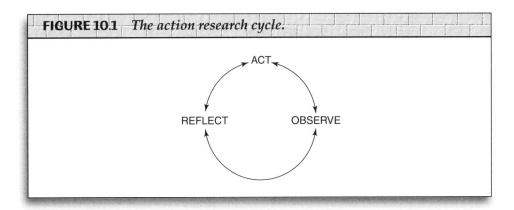

FIGURE 10.1 *The action research cycle.*

In thinking about your hitch in practice, you were reflecting. By trying out some alternative actions, you were acting. By documenting the process, you were observing the consequences of your actions. By reporting and discussing it with others, you were engaging in collaborative reflection. By thinking about how these actions would make life better and planning for your next steps, you were again reflecting on the consequences of your actions and moving toward more action.

In research terms, you have just designed a brief proposal for a study, complete with research questions (How can I improve?) and methodology (What can I try out? How will I document the process? How will I report it to others?). You have also given some serious consideration to your own value commitments when you reflected on how it would make life better. It's called a *proposal* because of the tentative nature of design—it needs to be responsive to events and ideas as they unfold.

To be action research, the design (proposal) needs to reflect the characteristics of action research. It is based on (1) ethical commitment to improvement, (2) a cycle of reflective practice, (3) collaborative work, and (4) making our work public for others to examine and critique. Figure 10.2 shows the research language that is used to describe the cycle of action research in the beginning stages of design. As the design process proceeds, we will add ideas to the research cycle which can be used in planning to assess our teaching.

In the next chapters, we will expand on this brief proposal, adding some questions. Even though you may not be ready to tackle all the questions, you will at least be aware of them.

FIGURE 10.2   *What researchers do in the action research cycle.*

Carry out the Design

ACT

Design the Study   REFLECT   OBSERVE   Document the Process

CHAPTER SUMMARY

The questions you addressed in the practice study form the framework of your design. They are the elements of designing an action research study. In the next chapters, we fill out that framework with additional questions and practical suggestions.

1. What is my research interest? (Chapters 8 and 9)
2. What will I try out in order to improve my practice? (Chapter 11) (McNiff et al., 1996)
3. How will I document the process? (Chapter 11)
4. How will I verify that my judgments are trustworthy and credible? (Chapter 12)
5. How will I interpret the data? (Chapter 13)
6. How will I portray what I have learned and make it public? (Chapters 15, 16, 17, 18)
7. How will these actions make life better? What will I do next? (Chapter 14)
8. What are the ethical considerations? Are permissions needed? Who will my critical colleagues be? And the cycle continues. . . .

Elements of Design: Planning and Documenting the Action

In this chapter we think through the actions that might be taken to address research questions. As researchers, we carefully monitor our actions and document the consequences. Documenting the consequences can be a useful way to think about evaluation and assessment to inform change. We try something out and assess the outcomes, both the ones that we predict and the unexpected ones.

What Will I Try Out in Order to Improve My Practice?

What kinds of strategies can we carry out in our classrooms to address our questions? What will help us to come closer to realizing our dreams and commitments? Answering the questions concerning who, what, when, where, how, and why will guide this part of the design. Let's look at the Democratic Classroom Study to see how Rosie described her design plans. See Figure 11.1.

Who. The participants, or *who* of a study, are determined by the purpose of the study and the amount of time and energy available. Some teachers want to study an aspect of *all* their classes and *all* their students. Progressively they begin to focus their attention on a few classes or a few students. The Literature Circle's Study is an example of this focus—what we affectionately call the "big data–little data" design. In this design, data are collected for all students, but analyzed for only some. Or after collecting data for the whole group at the beginning of a study, we narrow our focus to a smaller group. We may be drawn to study a group of students who resist our efforts, or who excel in spite of our hunches that they will not do well. As our questions become more focused, so, too, might our samples. In other situations, such as the case of Jen, a case study design of an individual is most appropriate right from the beginning. If we are tutoring students, we may, for example, want to conduct an action research study with them. In summary, we can start with a wide-angle lens and progressively focus, or start with a zoom lens and pan

FIGURE 11.1	*Who, what, when, where, how, and why in the Democratic Classroom Study*
Who:	Ninth graders in three college-preparatory civics classes.
What:	Community-building activities focusing on collaboration between teachers and students and between students and their peers.
When:	A variety of activities tried out and analyzed throughout the 12 weeks of student teaching. Activities will last from a few days to a few weeks.
Where:	A large comprehensive high school in a middle- to upper-middle-class, predominantly white suburban community. There is dissension among students, put-downs, lack of respect.
How:	Group work (learning pairs, jigsaw, and chapter talks), student choice in selecting groups and topics, and preparation for playing a variety of group roles. Work with mentor in observing and making decisions.
Why:	These activities were chosen for their potential to build a democratic community in my class and model democratic principles that are the foundation of the civics curriculum.

out. No matter the size of the sample, in keeping with our ethical commitment to benefit all our students, we readily put to work whatever we learn for *all* our students in *all* our classes. Our new knowledge becomes a part of our teaching.

We can describe participants in a variety of ways, as individuals or as members of a larger group. For individuals, we can describe what we know about them, how they respond in class, what we know of their knowledge, how they interact with other children, family context, etc. We can provide a rich description of our students and classrooms based on our observations and insights. For example, Rosie wrote in her proposal: "My cooperating teacher and I noted that the students in the civics classes rarely participated in class discussion. . . . a few students tended to dominate, opinions were rarely supported by evidence, and there was little interest in civics as a course of study." We can also include available demographic information that describes students as members of a larger group, information such as ethnic background, gender, and academic achievement. This is sometimes referred to as *objective* or *face sheet data*. If appropriate, we can also include test scores, inventories, or other information gathered from a counselor, social worker, special education teacher, tutor, etc. as part of a larger evaluation process.

We use the term *participants* rather than *subjects*, the term typically used in many types of research. Participants can take roles in planning, directing, analyzing, and interpreting, whereas the term subject implies a more passive role. Students, parents, community members, other teachers, and administrators can be fully involved members of your research team.

FIGURE 11.2 Excerpts from Rosie's schedule for the Democratic Classroom Study			
Date to start	**What will happen?**	**For how long? How often?**	**Who will be involved?**
February 10	Pretest: Classroom community survey	15 minutes	All 86 students in three civics classes
February 11	Bill-of-Rights Project—students choose topic, group members, due date.	Every day for 2 weeks 10 weeks	All 86 students
February 12	Weekly student reflection journals	Students write twice a week and turn in on Fridays	All 86 students
March 25	Classroom compact activity	3 days	All 86 students
April 5	Posttest: Classroom community survey	15 minutes	All 86 students

What and How. Before deciding on *what* to do and *how* to do it, action researchers consider a variety of alternative actions. Brainstorming strategies that we have mined from the literature, our colleagues, and our own experiences are an effective starting point. By keeping in mind the purpose of our study, the criteria by which we will judge the outcomes, and the time, effort, and resources that will be required, we select strategies that we feel will help us to accomplish the task. It is easy to select an approach or strategy. Without careful thought, however, we may select a plan of action that has little potential to help us reach our goals.

Shawn wanted ESL strategies and practices that would benefit all students' language development and additional strategies that could be applied to helping Jen in language, reading, and socialization. A larger vocabulary was one criterion for success, so a periodic vocabulary quiz was a specific strategy selected to accomplish this. Shawn also monitored Jen's daily journal for evidence of Jen's developing use of written English.

When. *When* refers to a time period and schedule of activities. When will the study start? How often will a particular strategy be used? For how long each time? For how long will data be collected? Which participants will be involved at what time? When will the study conclude? By developing a schedule that breaks the study down into a sequence of steps, we make what may seem overwhelming, more manageable. Figure 11.2 is a schedule for Rosie's Democratic Classroom Study.

Where. The *where* of a study is the social and cultural context. We might describe a school building as old but comfortable, in a neighborhood of small, tidy homes.

Or we might describe a school building as a massive three-story brick building with a leaky roof, a maze of darkened hallways, chipped metal bars over the windows in a neighborhood forgotten by municipal services. Some of us have little knowledge about the overall student population we serve or the family and community context in which they live. To know our students involves knowing about the communities in which they live. While our own classroom, team, or school provides an immediate context, our district, state, province, and country also shape our lives and the lives of our students. School districts provide demographic data (ethnic composition, social class) and ways in which students are categorized for services (gifted, limited English proficiency) and percentages of students in those categories. The location of the school (urban, rural, suburban, small town) can be a useful descriptor.

Why.   *Why* this strategy, this approach? Are there other reasonable ways to approach this? How will this approach enable me to create the kind of just and empowering classroom community that I envision as best for learning? Each time we hitch our practices to our dreams, we create energy in ourselves. When we hitch our dreams to the dreams of our students, we create energy in our classrooms. When we hitch our mutual dreams to a collective wish for a better life, we create schools with the potential to enhance the quality of life for many students and their teachers.

How Will I Document the Process?

The reflective teaching process necessitates ongoing documentation. In general, we need to document our experiences so that we can reflect on them and learn from them. That is what a scholar does: *learns from experience.* We will talk about many ways to document experience in this chapter and ways to "house" those data in an organized fashion so that we can draw evidence from them in order to interpret them and make public our new understandings.

As we talk about documentation in this section, our assumption is that you will use your journal as a place to both reflect and store the different forms of data that you decide to use in your study. Although we each must develop our own ways of organizing and making sense of our data, you may want to section off the journal so that you can easily maneuver between data sources: a general section for daily recording and another section for autobiographical writing, such as we did in Chapter 6, and then sections for interviews, observations, and documents collected along the way. If a word processor is used to create the journal, separate files for each section may create an easy way to locate, add to, modify, and analyze data.

In documenting the process of AR, noting the consequences is important. The term *consequences* is a useful one because it alerts us to the importance of paying attention to what happens to student learning, to ourselves, and to our situation when we try out something new or modify an existing practice.

Because we are inquiring into our teaching (actions) *and* the self (motives, assumptions) that teaches, data are often not separate from ourselves as is the case in some other forms of research. In traditional research, collecting data is a means of accumulating information (that becomes evidence). Explicitly or implicitly we may be trying to prove a point; for example, that one method of teaching is better than another. But in AR, our data are often *in* our teaching. Data are used to problematize the many assumptions we make about teaching and to redefine our relationships with one another (we shall soon see how a student's poem helps Rosie and her students to reconsider their relationships with one another). Data are collected to enhance our understanding of ourselves and others, the setting in which we work, and to increase our capacity to bring our actions into closer alignment with our values.

The term *consequences* is not to be confused with the way it is used in other types of research. As you might recall, in experimental studies researchers seek cause-effect relationships. If the teacher does X, then Y happens. Classroom life is much more complex than a one-way relationship between our actions and what happens to our students. We know, for example, that our assumptions "color" what is happening. (Recall the teacher on the Native American reservation who thought her students were not interested in books?) For this reason, action researchers build multiple sources of data into their studies and consider multiple points of view as they interpret the data. Not only must we be cautious in thinking that we *cause* specific things to happen, but also we must pay close attention to *how* we and others are constructing the situation.

The term *evidence* is an apt description of the information a teacher gathers related to the consequences of actions taken. Just as an explorer looks for evidence of cultural life in footprints, pottery, clothing, furniture, and written artifacts from ancient civilizations, good teachers look for evidence of the social, intellectual, and ethical consequences of our actions. In other words, we look for evidence of student learning, personal and professional growth, justice, equity, and respect. So a corollary question to How will I document the process? is What evidence will I collect to show the consequences of these actions?

Brought to critical colleagues and students, data provide an opportunity for debate about what is true. In the verifying of "truth," we as a community of scholars come to learn what values and beliefs we share. The rest of this chapter is about how groups come to verify particular data as evidence of growth, learning, justice, equity, and respect.

Dorothy: And how do teachers learn to examine data so that data become evidence?

Authors: That is a good question, Dorothy. It touches on a few other terms, too.

For example, we are bombarded everyday with lots of *information*. Some of it is useful, for example, the telephone number of a friend you want to call. Most of it is not. In order for information to be useful, it has to fit our purposes. That a student scores in the 25th percentile on a test of reading comprehension is information. What makes it data is our interest in this student's score as baseline before tutoring. As a researcher, you gather information and when (and if) you invest it with interest, it becomes *data*. Data may also become further differentiated into *evidence* if you use it to make a point in your study. Simplified, it might look something like this:

Information   →   Data   →   Evidence   →   Interpretation and portrayal

We continue to filter information related to our purposes. Finally, we interpret what it means in the context of our projects, and we portray it to share with others. The latter processes, interpretation and portrayal, are very important to the success of our efforts. We will talk about these in Chapter 13 and Section 7. What this process and all of the terms have in common is that they depend upon professional judgment. Harry Wolcott (1998), a well-respected ethnographer, places more emphasis on what you *do* with these data and evidence (interpretations and portrayal) than on what you gather in your fieldwork.

What we *do* (analyze, interpret, portray) with what we have depends, at least in part, on our professional judgment, and this takes us back to those domains of development we talked about earlier: cognitive, moral-ethical, and psychological. We grow toward cognitive complexity, moral-ethical commitments, and psychological maturity and health as we exercise our professional judgment. These qualities are inextricably linked to ongoing assessment of our students and ourselves. To conduct ongoing assessment or, more broadly termed, formative evaluation, we use different *methods of data collection, verification, and interpretation* (the latter two will be developed in greater depth in Chapter 13). And as explorers of our own worlds of teaching, we want to develop these tools throughout our careers.

Can you think of different ways to observe, interview, and study documents prepared by others? You probably already use many of these and have not considered them research techniques, but that is what they are. In Figure 11.3 we describe three major forms of data collection that we have adapted from Wolcott (1992). We have included specific techniques that can be used with each of these forms. Notice that there is some overlap in that one technique may seem to fit into several different forms of data collection. This list is not exhaustive, and you may want to add some of your own.

Each of these tools may be loosely or tightly structured, depending on where we are in the study and the purpose of our studies. Interviews can be as scheduled and standardized as reading from a prepared script, and they can be as casual and open-ended as playful discussion with Toto. So, too, it is with observations—they can be as open and expansive as the horizon, or as close and highly focused as observing the sounds of particles of sand slipping through the looking-glass.

Although we present each of the scholar's tools as discrete ways of describing our experience, they are often complementary and used together to study life in classrooms. For example, we may interview our students based on our observations of their work and/or analysis of their papers (artifacts). And then, as a result of our interviewing, we observe differently! We might also teach differently, and students' work may change as a result.

Dorothy: But doesn't this take time away from the regular responsibilities of teaching? Who has time to use the tools of scholarship when there are so many students and so many daily routines to attend to?

FIGURE 11.3 *The tools of professional scholarship: data collection*		
Observing	**Interviewing**	**Examining Documents and Other Data Sources**
Experiencing Through our Senses	*Inquiring into the Experiences and Thoughts of Others*	*Examining Documents and Artifacts Prepared by Others*
Note taking and field notes	Informal interview	Personal-experience methods
Shadow study	Formal interview	Student work
Anecdotal record	Questionnaire	Photographs and video and audio
Log, diary/video diary, journal	Attitude scale	Recording
Checklist	Checklist	Technology
Rating scale	Rating scale	Physical traces
	Critical incident interview	
	Sociogram	
	Projective technique	
	Creative visualization	
	Informal interview	
	Focus group interview	

Three categories are from Wolcott, 1992.

Authors: Trepidation about the time it takes to become scholars is natural. What we want to explore is how the scholar's way of *thinking* can become a part of our teaching. There are also some practical tips we can offer.

Next we will present each of the major forms of data collection used by action researchers. We have included a variety of examples of the work of action researchers as a starting point for thinking about data collection strategies you may want to develop.

Observing

Observation is foundational to all good research. Whether we decide to observe at a distance (intervening as little as possible into what is observed) or to become a full-fledged *participant-observer* (engaging to different degrees with the observed person or activity), or anything in between, knowing what to look for, how to apprehend it, and how to describe it for later reflection is a key element of the evolving repertoire of scholars.

Scarecrow: And by scholar you mean us, don't you?

Authors: Indeed we do. You may be surprised to find that a key element of being an observant scholar is intuition. Although we may think that research is a strictly procedural process, intuition is as important to observation as the techniques we will share with you in this section. In fact, many of us, including Albert Einstein, think that intuition and its bedfellow, imagination, are more important than knowledge. If you could develop only one of these, then let it be intuition! Thankfully we can work on both, which are really part of a single process.

Dorothy: There you go with riddles again!

Authors: Intuition is based in part on experience and points us toward certain kinds of information which can lead to knowledge. At the same time, knowledge can make certain kinds of intuition possible. In "Exploring the Forest" at the conclusion of this chapter, we will help you to make use of your intuition. In this chapter, we will deal with gathering information that can provide a database from which understanding can be derived. How we describe what we see is as important as what we see, for when we describe a phenomenon, we open the possibility of seeing it differently. The richer the description, the fuller the observation will be—and the richer the eyes that behold!

While it may be easy to look into our classrooms, it is much harder—and much more fun and profitable—to *see* into them. Looking is an act; seeing is an accomplishment (Eisner, 1985). John Moffit has written a poem that makes this point very well.

To Look at Any Thing

To look at any thing,
If you would know that thing,
You must look at it long;
to look at this green and say
'I have seen spring in these
Woods,' will not do—you must
Be the thing you see:
You must be the dark snakes of
Stems and ferny plumes of leaves,
You must enter in
To the small silences between
The leaves,
You must take your time
and touch the very peace
They issue from.

Source: Dunning et al. (1966, p. 21).

We develop the ability to see by looking with intent; by practicing conscious looking and seeing. This is part of what it means to be a scholar—to develop our abilities and capacities to see. We have also used the terms *educational connoisseurs* and *critics.* This is what Kathy did when she started to see what was going on in her classroom. She started to develop her ability to see as she focused more carefully on her children's responses to the letter of the week. And she did it by paying attention to her own feelings. They told her something wasn't right, and she heard them and did something as a result. The results were a product of her courage to take action!

Scarecrow: *Informed* action.

Yes. Our aim in observing is to develop understanding and empathy. We can do this, in part, by writing what is often called *thick description.* It is the difference between describing the reeds in the pond as tall green grass and as "dark snakes of stems and ferny plumes of leaves" where you "enter into the small silences between the leaves"!

Because we are so immersed in our classroom life, we as teachers "know" a great deal about what is going on. But in order for us to be action researchers, we must step back from our intense involvement and become more *self-conscious* of our roles as participant-observers. This may require us to give up some of the beliefs that we hold about what is going on, because these beliefs may blind us to other ways of seeing and may limit us to only a small part of the picture.

In the early stages of research our observations tend to be broadly focused. Who is here? What is going on? What are the emotions that are being expressed (our own included)? When are things occurring? How long do they last? How is space being used? In other words, we make general observations about who, what, when, where, and how, taking into account participants, activities, goals, emotions, time, and space (Spradley, 1980).

As we describe our observations and record hunches, these may in turn shape the focus of new observations. Like photographers, we might survey the broad landscape and then zoom in on specific views and then out again to broader views. In this way we can see events, things, and people in context. This process of zooming in and out enables us to better ground our observations and interpretations.

A story will illustrate our point. Franki, a third/fourth-grade multiage teacher, schedules the first hour of each day as exploratory learning time in which students choose activities, alone or with partners, that appeal to a wide range of interests. One pair of boys, Franki observed with worry, did the same thing each day. One of the pair constructed a building from some Lego-type building toys, and the other constructed a vehicle from the same materials. At the end of the exploratory hour, the boys staged a huge crash, destroying both structures. Franki's initial judgment was that the pair was acting out violent and aggressive behavior. She held back and observed for weeks, debating whether to intervene. Finally, she decided to query the boys as to their project. They explained carefully and articulately how after each crash, they studied the weak points in their respective structures. Each day, they tried to engineer a modification to their respective structures that would better withstand impact. Franki's first assumptions didn't come close to understanding the sophistication and complexity of what was going on. By observing and reflecting on repeated observations, Franki illustrates the kind of professional judgment used by "complex thinkers" (Yeah, Scarecrow!), "socially responsible feelers" (Yeah, Tin Man!) and "emotionally mature adults" (Yeah, Lion!).

At other times we might miss a great deal if we wait too long to make judgments. By making tentative hypotheses early on, we can then produce and examine data to confirm or disconfirm those hunches.

Another consideration in using observational methods is whether to focus on an individual, on a group, or on both. Most often we use a combination, perhaps starting with a group and then zooming in to an individual or vice versa.

Note taking and field notes.   Recording notes about observations (as well as interviews, artifacts, and documents) is the most common method used by the action researcher to describe what is occurring. Field notes are direct observations of what is being said and done as well as impressions or hunches of the observer. They are called *field* notes because they are taken in the field—the classroom or school setting. In the shadow study, the notes taken in the space provided in the chart would be called field notes.

Writing down our observations and reflecting on them helps us to become aware of the point of view from which we observe. *We are never neutral in our observations.* We observe with a limited eye, both informed and constrained by our cultural lenses, and without sufficient understanding to make sense of many of our observations. We may observe with a sympathetic eye because we have ourselves been in such a situation. We may observe with a critical eye for the injustices we see in the way students are treated. We may observe with an eye toward seeing how efficiently things can be done, or an eye toward understanding the perspective of the other. Being fully present and open to experiences around us allows us to see and understand more of the complexity of our classrooms. Recording that complexity through rich detail will help us as we try to analyze and synthesize what we have observed. In Chapter 15 we will further explore the possibilities of writing down our observations. And you may want to turn to those beginning pages of Chapter 15 on *writing up, writing down,* and *writing about* before you proceed with a further reading of this chapter. They may inspire you in your note-taking adventures!

There are a variety of types of field notes:

- Running record—recording regularly occurring events such as attendance.
- Time intervals—recording what is happening at regular intervals, such as quickly "sweeping" the classroom every 5 minutes to see what kinds of conversations students are having during computer time.
- Specified events—recording every time a specified event occurs, such as students asking questions of their peers during discussion (as opposed to asking the teacher).

- Critical incident—recording moments that seem to be pivotal points in a study, such as the moment a teacher realizes that it is only the male students who are objecting to reading a particular novel, not the entire class.
- Anecdotal record—recording incidents that show growth over time (more on this later).

Teacher action researchers have used a variety of time-saving approaches in their studies. Recording the date, time, and focus of observations helps later on when you are trying to locate data and verify findings. When you are recording multiple events or students are creating a form with multiple columns, one for each category is useful. However, at other times, keeping a wide right-hand margin for impressions and hunches is preferable. Either way encourages the researcher to begin analyzing data early on, which may lead to focusing the question. Ongoing analysis may also lead to a change in research strategy. For example, by reading over field notes, a researcher might decide to write in the margins that note taking during interviews detracts from the ability to listen to what students are saying, hence the decision to get permission to tape-record. (While this may seem an easy solution, keep in mind that for every 7 minutes of tape recording, it takes about 1 hour to transcribe it!) While we typically associate note taking with a pen or pencil and paper, technology can be helpful, too. Laptop computers and even handheld "palm" computers may speed up note taking and increase accuracy. Suggestions for note taking are presented in Stepping Stones 11.1, Note Taking.

Several observational techniques are useful to action researchers. These techniques allow us to focus on individuals, groups, classrooms, and larger contexts. We will begin with techniques for gaining appreciation and empathy for the experiences of our students.

Shadow study.   A shadow study of an individual student is an exercise that is good practice at focusing our observations, and it can help us to derive insights from firsthand experience of what it is like to be a student. When we immerse ourselves in the life of another, we can develop an understanding of how that person makes sense of school, knowledge that is of critical importance for understanding how we can negotiate our own roles as teachers (Bullough and Gitlin, 1995).

Although there are many different ways to conduct a shadow study, we will outline some strategies that our students have found helpful.

1. Select a student whose experience of school is considerably different from your own experience. Gain written permission from the parent and verbal permission from the student to spend an entire day shadowing the student.
2. Record information about the student that is readily observable or available, for example, grade level, gender, ethnicity. At 5- to 7-minute intervals, record the specific behaviors your student is engaged in. In separate columns record information about the environment of the classroom, study hall, hallway, etc.,

STEPPING STONES 11.1

Note Taking

Keeping field notes can be time-consuming. There are a few shortcuts that inventive teachers have designed to make the task more efficient and less disruptive to teaching. Power (1996) suggests the following:

1. Set goals for each note-taking session.
2. Establish a routine—if outside of the classroom, find a favorite place, a favorite pen, favorite music, a set time with a "Do Not Disturb" sign.
3. Experiment with different times (during or after the fact) and different places.
4. Experiment with different tools—index cards or address labels for anecdotal records that later can be arranged in a way that makes sense; project planner paper with two columns, one for student records of the day's events and one for teacher comments; a computer; a transcribing machine; loose-leaf paper; carbon paper, saving the time of going to a copy machine; a large notebook to store tools.
5. Develop personal shorthand codes, such as T for teacher or S for student. This will help to speed up writing.

and any impressions, hunches about what is going on, ideas, and personal feelings.

3. At some point during the day, conduct an informal interview with the student to check out emerging hypotheses or to gain further insight into the student's perception of school. For example, you might ask: Is there an adult at this school in whom you can confide? What is your favorite class? Your least favorite? What do you like most/least about this school?

Figure 11.4 presents excerpts from a shadow study conducted by Rick in the weeks just prior to student teaching. Rick, whose own high school experiences were in the college-bound accelerated mathematics program, spent the day with a more relaxed, vocational student named Joe. The example illustrates several ideas: the importance of separating our opinions (to the extent that we are able) from observable facts; the way in which hunches propel our observations to test out those hunches; and the way in which we can use observations to zoom in and out from individual to group, to larger context.

Notice how in the columns for behavior and environment Rick describes the actions of Joe and the classroom environment without interjecting personal opinions

FIGURE 11.4 *Excerpts from shadow study of Joe*

Student Pseudonym Joe   Grade 11   Age 16   Gender Male

Racial/Ethnic Group Caucasian   Regular/Special Education/Ability Group/Track Vocational

Date Nov. 19   Starting Time 7:50 a.m.   Ending Time 2:45 p.m.

Observer Rick

Time	Specific Student Behavior at 5- to 7-Minute Intervals	Environment (what is happening in class, halls; teacher, room arrangement, sounds . . .)	Impressions, Hunches, Ideas
7:50 a.m.	Fidgeting, looking up and around	First period social studies. Older, white male teacher. Quiz on Spanish-American war. Twenty-six students seated in rows.	Student forgot to meet me in hall. I went into class without him. Body language is telling me that he is uncertain about answers.
7:55 a.m.	Raised hand and told teacher that he would only be in class for 10 minutes the following day because of his involvement in the play.	Teacher writes in grade book; turns out lights and starts movie on Spanish-American War.	
8:00 a.m.	Holds his head while watching movie.	Teacher grades papers; handful of students looking drowsy; movie sounds coming from next door.	"The Indians would never rise again. . . ." This violent cartoon version of conflict with native people was too simplistic.
8:05 a.m.	Watching, holds up head; looks at nails.	Teacher grades papers; interjects, Remember this information; students are fidgety	"With leaders like Roosevelt, we had to find new worlds to conquer" is such an imperialistic attitude—this movie bugs me.
8:10 a.m.	Watching, holds up head, looks at nails; yawns.	Eight students have heads on desks.	Students have no opportunity for engagement in learning during movie, which seems so stereotypical and removed from their experiences.

Later that day

(continued)

FIGURE 11.4 *Excerpts from shadow study of Joe, Continued*

Time	Specific Student Behavior at 5- to 7-Minute Intervals	Environment (what is happening in class, halls; teacher, room arrangement, sounds . . .)	Impressions, Hunches, Ideas
10:28 a.m.	Operating cash register in school restaurant. Taking orders, ringing them up, bantering with students and teachers.	Fourth period, culinary arts. Teacher is absent so restaurant is closed except for carry-out. Phone continues to ring with orders.	Hectic atmosphere, but Joe seems to enjoy it. This would be exciting for me if I did this. No such experience for me as a college-preparatory high school student.
10:35 a.m.	"Out of $5? Is that $4.25 or $3.75?"	Cash register clicking out bills. Students standing in line, some poking each other.	I just sit and watch, hungry, but should I order lunch? I decide to just be an observer, though my stomach is growling.
10:40 a.m.	"Did you come to bother me? I don't have time for this!. . . I don't care what he said. She loves me cause I was born on Walt Disney's birthday." Gets a little flushed when teacher discusses change for order. Takes a minute to figure it out.	Hectic. Ten students waiting for orders.	Seems to have settled into the pattern. Getting past the hectic time. Gets more talkative. He takes things in stride and seems to juggle work and play.
Later that day			
1:57 p.m.	"It's the gingerbread man," Joe announces himself to the class.	Eighth period, geometry. Teacher walks around to check homework. Students settle down.	In between classes Joe said he dislikes most classes except English and culinary arts. He doesn't mention anything about geometry—probably because he knows that I am a practicum student for the geometry teacher. Even though he seems open, there is that subtle student reservation around me as a teacher—I don't like this!

		FIGURE 11.4	Continued

Time	Specific Student Behavior at 5- to 7-Minute Intervals	Environment (what is happening in class, halls; teacher, room arrangement, sounds . . .)	Impressions, Hunches, Ideas
2:00 p.m.	Yawns and looks at nails and writes something down.	Says, "We'll go over homework for the next 20 minutes."	Most of day seems to value intellectual work over physical work. Are these classist notions of work? I must remember to do some more reading in this area.

or feelings? In the column labeled "Impressions, hunches, ideas," however, we learn a great deal about what Rick is thinking and feeling. In this column are included hunches, personal feelings, and ways to change the methods used to conduct the shadow study.

Rick's use of the final column illustrates the development of his emerging theory about student engagement. As teachers, we often have our own ideas about what student engagement means, and we observe students to see if they are raising their hands, responding to questions, doing their assignments, and participating in activities. But Rick begins to pay attention to the quality of the *opportunities* to engage in meaningful learning and hypothesizes that we do not always provide these opportunities for students. Rick's concern that schools reinforce classist stereotypes (for college-bound "upper-class" students, schools emphasize the importance of the intellect whereas for vocational students the physical is emphasized) is one that will require investigation beyond this brief study. This hunch, however, is rooted in careful observations which problematize the concept of engagement.

Rick's decision to forgo lunch and remain an observer was a methodological decision. By reflecting on and noting changes we make in our studies (changes in planned activities), we are making important decisions about methodology. These changes are *not* mistakes. They are informed decisions. Keeping a record of these changes can help us to become more professional and confident in our decisions.

Finally, we may want to record experiences from our personal lives that may shape how we observe and how we act. Moods, prior experiences, and mental and physical health all influence our teaching and our observations. Rick's negative attitude toward what he perceives to be a shallow, imperialistic portrayal of Native Americans in the movie is important to keep separate from Joe's attitudes. Joe may or may not share those feelings.

Often the student being shadowed will request to look at the notes. Share them! If you want to record personal commentary, not appropriate for a student to see, record it in a separate place. (This piece of advice applies to any type of data collection activity. Many teachers keep separate journals at home for private reflections that helps them make sense of their school life.)

Occasionally prospective teachers are uncomfortable with the idea of shadowing a student. Their concerns center on invading privacy. This issue should be taken seriously. If you decide that the conditions are favorable to the student, proceed. Feelings of discomfort are natural; they tend to diminish as the day goes on. Students who agree to participate in shadow studies typically welcome the interest of another person. One resource that has been helpful to those hesitant to undertake such a study is Fine and Sandstrom's (1988) *Knowing Children: Participant Observation with Minors.*

Anecdotal record.   Anecdotal records are factual descriptions of incidents a teacher observes. They are useful in recording changes over time, particularly when they include a separate interpretation of the incident. Piaget used anecdotal records when studying children's cognitive development.

Joanne recorded anecdotal entries as part of a study of students' use of journals in a graduate course. One incident involved Terry, a student in her middle forties who was returning to school for the first time in 20 years. Figure 11.5 is an anecdotal record and interpretation written by Joanne. By filing anecdotal records on index cards, adhesive labels, or in the computer, the action researcher can easily organize and reorganize them for later data analysis.

Log, diary, journal.   As we discussed in "Exploring the Forest" in Section 1, there are many different types of personal written documents and, depending on the discipline, there are slightly different definitions of terms. Some people use diary and journal interchangeably, while others use journal and researcher log as equivalent. On our journey together we use journals as the evolving and reflective professional document which holds our perceptions, plans, descriptions, explorations, and exercises, as well as our trepidations and interpretations. They contain diary and log-type writing and become richer as we continue to develop. As our research evolves, we will use the journal in more specific and complex ways. We will return to our descriptive data to interpret and make sense of them from different perspectives. Logs and diaries, case records, field and dialogue journals, and many other kinds of documents can be used as data sources to record and study observations.

1. *Log.* Do you watch Star Trek? The Captain's Log, like other ships' logs can contain considerable detail and be important in establishing events and circumstances. Simply put, a log is a running record of transactions. Incidents

FIGURE 11.5 *Anecdotal record and interpretation from Joanne's master's degree class*

Class: Curriculum and Organization in the Middle Grades

Date: July 17   **Student:** Terry

Place: College of Education   **Observer:** Joanne

As students filed out of class after picking up their journals, I asked Terry if I could speak with her. She looked terrified. "Have I said something wrong in my journal?" she asked.

"I am just concerned about several comments you made in your journal that my expectations of you are too high, particularly in your journal writing," I replied. I assured her that her work was exemplary. "Are you feeling overwhelmed by all the requirements in a 5-week summer session? Do your ideas differ from mine about the purpose of a journal? [I had asked them to reflect on readings and class activities, and her writing was more of a summary.] Or do you truly feel that my expectations of you are too high?"

Tears welled in her eyes as she haltingly said, "I just lack confidence. It has been so long that I have been in school, and your enthusiasm for what we are learning is somewhat intimidating. I am not sure I can be as excited as you are for what you want us to do. I also think that a journal is a place to say whatever we want to say, and I resent having to do the kind of reflection you want us to do."

Interpretation

Terry's work was always very creative and thorough. But when it came to the journal, she did not reflect on readings and class activities as I had asked. I asked students to use their journals as a place to reflect on *academic* matters because I myself did not like to write personal reflections to be read by an instructor whom I hardly knew. When asked to do so, I revealed very little about how I really felt. By structuring the journal in this way, I sought to minimize the invasion of privacy which I assumed everyone would feel. I still need to explore how journals can be used by students (and myself) in academic settings. I think that we overuse them, and sometimes it can turn to abuse.

such as phone conversations with parents and daily attendance while simpler than a ship's log, can provide useful information for the researcher and are here referred to as researcher logs. Figure 11.6 shows how Rosie's log was used to keep track of the various activities designed to create a more democratic classroom. Each activity was carefully developed to respond to situations that arose in the classroom. Another type of researcher log can be found in Figure 11.8 where Andy uses detail in a functional, concise, and highly focused way.

2. *Diary/video/audio diary.* A diary is a personal, unedited account of feelings and thoughts. For example, you might keep a diary of personal conversations related to your research, to return to later. Videotaping might be preferable for those who enjoy verbally and visually recording personal reflections. Videotaping oneself at regular, convenient intervals such as in the evening after dinner, Saturday mornings, or during lunchtime may provide clues, for example, to understanding one's development as a teacher.

As a personal document, the journal is a potent tool to collect, analyze, and interpret data. A journal can take many forms. Perhaps you can add to this list.

FIGURE 11.6 *Rosie's researcher log of classroom activities*	
Date	**Community-Building Activities**
2/11	Jigsaw discussions—to emphasize importance of participation.
2/17	Presentations on Bill of Rights—to emphasize the importance of rights.
3/5	Class compact—to encourage students to examine values and build agreement.
4/15	Show movie "Rigoletto," film about prejudice based on physical appearance.
5/4	Personal values project—students demonstrate a deeply held personal value.

3. *Dialogue journal.* A dialogue journal is used to converse with someone else about thoughts, feelings, and incidents. It may be used by both teachers and students to describe, interpret, reflect, and evaluate. In a dialogue journal, teachers respond to the writer's questions, concerns, and thinking on topics chosen by both students and teachers. These interactive journals allow writers (students, colleagues) the opportunity for a one-on-one tutorial and provide teachers with curriculum ideas to extend and enrich development. The journals also give students and teachers the chance to evaluate their curriculum experiences. A traveling journal is an ongoing conversation between a student teacher, mentor teacher, and university mentor that travels between these three people.

4. *Researcher journal.* A researcher journal is a place to record issues that arise related to research, such as research methods; hypotheses; evolving research questions; reminders to ourselves to follow up on things, such as books to read, people to consult, and additional data to collect related to hypotheses; and analytic memos (ongoing analyses and interpretation). Shawn's researcher journal was a comprehensive recording of the development of Jen's literacy. A few entries shown in Figure 11.7 illustrate the dramatic leaps in learning that occurred in a very short time.

   Shawn's journal entries note the daily observations as well as periodic benchmarks. The growth in Jen's vocabulary from February 24 to March 14 is one source of evidence that her language development and literacy are both proceeding rapidly.

   Andy's researcher journal contained systematic observations of the social interactions of students with multiple handicaps and their "typical" peers—in the hallways, cafeteria, and classrooms. Several journal entries (see Figure 11.8) show the development of Andy's hunch that there was little interaction between the students in his class and other students. He used this hunch to focus observations.

   Noting the pattern of alienation that occurred repeatedly during the week, Andy concluded: "Somehow the relationships that inclusion was supposed to be fostering were just not happening" (November 24, Andy's journal).

FIGURE 11.7   Shawn's researcher journal of Jen's literacy development

1/27 (first entry)

I have been working with Jen on a one-to-one, daily basis. We are keeping a journal and labeling pictures that she has drawn. I am having her form "sentences" about the picture. She seems to be good at writing and labeling the things that she knows. She has a hard time sounding out the names of unfamiliar things. She is not aware of the text that she is creating.

2/24

Today I quizzed Jen on basic sight words commonly used by second graders. Out of 108 words, she recognized 47 words. She was able to correctly use 30 of the 47 words in a sentence or phrase. I could see that she was understanding the meaning of the words.

3/14

I quizzed Jen on basic sight word flash cards. Out of 100 words, she was able to correctly read 79 words and use 68 of them in phrases or show me what the word meant.

FIGURE 11.8   Andy's researcher log

Log for Week of November 17

Observer: Andy

Note: Students with multiple handicaps are referred to as students A, B, C, D.

Wood fabrication (inclusion class):   Student A came into the classroom, and no typical student talked to him or paid attention to him. A typical student said "hi" to student B as he walked into the classroom. Student C initiated a conversation with a nonhandicapped peer by asking, "Do you like the car I made?" The typical student answered, "Yes."

Cafeteria: Typical students move from a table where their peers with disabilities are eating lunch.

Hallway: A typical student waved and said, "Hi, how's it going?" to student D. (They went to elementary school together.)

Home economics (inclusion class):   One of the typical students did not even talk to her own cousin, a "special" student integrated in home economics.

Andy used the data to problematize a belief held by district advocates of inclusion—that it would naturally foster the social acceptance of students labeled *special education students.* Based on these focused observations and years of experience, Andy decided to start the S.T.A.R. Club.

5. *Multiple text journals.* A multiple text journal (such as the one used in the shadow study) is a type of journal which allows the researcher to record different kinds of observations and reflections. Forming columns is one way to organize the data.

In addition to the information we have provided, there are several useful sources on logs, journals, and diaries. They include Holly's (1989) *Writing to Grow: A Personal Professional Journal;* Connelly and Clandinin's (1988) *Teachers as Curriculum Planners: Narratives of Experience;* and Grumet's (1990) "Retrospective: Autobiography and the Analysis of Educational Experience."

Checklist.   The checklist is a structured observation instrument. It is "a list of points to notice in direct observation [and] used to focus the observer's attention to the presence, absence, or frequency of occurrence of each point of the prepared list as indicated by check marks" (Hopkins and Antes, 1985, p. 467). Checklists may include data that remain the same, such as ethnicity/race, gender, and time, and data that describe attributes that may change, such as *withdrawn* or *extroverted*. A checklist might simply list the relevant points and ask, "Yes or no?" Points on the checklist need to be related to the goal of the study, and as many action researchers have found, using a checklist developed by someone else may be confusing if the points are not directly related to the study. For that reason, many action researchers, such as Jan and Terry in their Literature Circle's Study, prefer to create their own checklists. They created a checklist indicating student preparation for literature circles and participated in group activities (Figure 11.9) to look for when their students met in literature circles.

Rating scale.   Another structured observation instrument is a rating scale used by an action researcher or student to evaluate a particular behavior or activity along a continuum. McKernan (1996) suggests that they are particularly useful in observing social and personal development in areas such as cooperativeness, in-

---

FIGURE 11.9   *Checklist of Literature Circle indicators showing participation and preparation*

Student_____   Date_____   Y = yes, N = no

Brought materials to class	_____
Participated in discussion	_____
Worked cooperatively	_____
Completed assignment	_____
Took notes	_____
Made predictions	_____
Used context to understand	_____

dustriousness, tolerance for difference, enthusiasm, and group skills, among others. We present four types:

1. *Category rating scale.* The rater selects the category which best describes what is being rated.

   How often does the student participate in discussion?

   Never ___ Seldom ___ Occasionally ___ Frequently ___ Always ___

2. *Numeric rating scale.* Rating on a numbered scale from 1 to 5 (or any number up to 10) lends itself to later statistical analysis.

   Student explains problem situation

   (1) Very clearly, . . . , (5)Very unclearly

3. *Graphic rating scale.* The rater places a check mark along a lined continuum. The advantage is that the rater is not restricted to a particular category or number. It is widely used.

   During literature circle discussions, the student participates:

Always	Frequently	Occasionally	Seldom	Never
1	2	3	4	5

4. *Pictorial rating scale.* This can be used by teachers to rate observations and provide feedback on student work. Students are often asked to express their attitudes about something by using a humorous cartoon-type rating scale. For example, the smiley faces in Figure 11.10 have been used with young children.

In constructing a rating scale, we suggest that it rate substantive as opposed to trivial activities; that the scale use no less than three and no more than seven points; that more than one rater be used; that it avoid putting personal biases into the wording of the question, avoid double negatives, and keep the items short, rating one item at a time. It is also important, as with other types of structured observation instruments, to test it first with a small sample to work out the kinks.

We have found several useful resources for the construction of observation instruments. They include Borich's (1999) *Observation Skills for Effective Teaching,* Hubbard and Power's (1999) *Living the Questions: A Guide for Teacher Researchers,* and McKernan's (1996) *Curriculum Action Research.*

FIGURE 11.10 *Pictorial rating scale*

How I feel about doing math journals

Careful observation and thoughtful description are especially important in the beginning stages of research because they help us to develop a context, focus our research interests, and gain appreciation for others' perceptions. Because of its valuable role in evaluation, many teachers are now building observation time into their schedules. Based on observations and the questions and hypotheses that emerge from them, action researchers can follow up observations with interviews to create a richer picture of what is happening.

Interviewing

In trying to understand the perspectives of students, teachers can conduct interviews, both formal and informal, as a regular part of teaching. The interview may be as informal as Shawn asking Jen to label pictures of things commonly found in the classroom, Jan and Terry asking a literature circle to tell them how the group went that day and what was the most valuable part of being in a literature circle, talking with a student during an editing meeting, or asking a mathematics student how she or he solved a particular problem. In each of these cases, the teacher is trying to *understand* what the student is thinking or doing and how that person views the world.

On the other hand, an interview can be as formal as Rosie's Democratic Classroom Survey, adapted from a survey she found in a journal and administered at the beginning and end of her student teaching. Or, an interview can be as formal as evaluation instruments that we ask our students to complete at the end of a course. Formal interview instruments are typically designed to enable the researcher to explain a pattern of student responses. Interview questions and answers can be written, drawn, or verbal, or a mixture of these. Questions can be opened-ended, eliciting responses without shaping them, or closed, thus limiting the responses to the choices provided. And even though we provide examples of teacher-led interviews, the interviews can be conducted by students, parents, administrators, and other outside observers.

Informal interview. The aim of the informal interview (or as some might say, a *purposeful conversation*) is to understand the perspective of the student (or parent, etc.). The interviewer poses a question related to the research interest, then uses the responses as a lead for the next question. As in the following example, extraordinary revelations are made in what might start out as a very ordinary moment. Jimmy, a child born with fetal alcohol syndrome, was a constant challenge in Danny's first-grade classroom. Jimmy had spent the last year watching his mother drink herself to death. His erratic behavior in school paralleled the erratic support he received at home from his father, who also had a problem with alcohol. Frustrated with the father's unresponsiveness to a variety of initiatives, Danny finally got the father to come in for a conference. What follows (in Figure 11.11) is a summary of the conference (informal interview) as recorded in Danny's journal.

The lines of communication opened because Danny cared enough about Jimmy to engage his father in an authentic conversation characterized by give and take,

---

FIGURE 11.11 *Danny's informal interview with Jimmy's father*

At this first conference, I wanted to know how Jimmy's father thought he could help his son succeed in school. But I didn't ask him specifically about how he helped his son with homework, or whether he checked his son's backpack after school each day. Nor did I ask him why the forms were never signed and returned. Rather, I spoke from my heart to his heart. I asked him if he knew how much Jimmy desperately needed a father—someone to play an active role in his education. Then the floodgates opened. He expressed doubts about being able to do this as a single person, and I assured him that he could be a good father and that I would support his efforts. He shared his grief, his fears, and his tears. Then *he* asked what he could do, and we talked about different ideas. It was at this conference that the lines of communication opened.

April 4, Danny's Journal

---

openness, and empathy. Danny gained the father's trust. For most of us, the rules of formal interviewing simply don't apply: Techniques such as maintaining objectivity, withholding opinions, and consistently asking the same prepared questions are inadequate for our desire to establish the trust we need in our everyday relationships. When we speak authentically, from the heart, these techniques become less important if not irrelevant or counterproductive. As one feminist researcher pointed out, there is "no intimacy without reciprocity" (Oakley, 1981). Reciprocity is at the heart of action research. The action researcher learns from her or his students and parents as well as the other way round. Reciprocity is a moral and ethical cornerstone of action researchers, not merely a methodological concern.

Formal interview.   Sometimes referred to as structured interviews, formal interviews have set, standard questions that are asked of all interviewees and are often recorded using a predesigned coding scheme. All interviewees receive the same questions in the same order. In the case of verbal interviewing, the interviewer does not give his or her opinion, does not interpret or modify the question, but is attentive and shows interest in responses that help the student to feel comfortable. The formal interview techniques we will discuss are questionnaires, attitudes scales, critical incidents, sociograms, and projective techniques which can be administered orally or in writing. This is followed by a discussion of group interviews.

Questionnaire.   When it is not possible to interview everyone, the action researcher may want to use *questionnaires* (or attitude surveys or group interviews, discussed in the next sections). Questionnaires are written questions requiring responses about facts, attitudes, or values. Rosie adapted a questionnaire from Schaps et al. (1996) to measure classroom community, and we have excerpted it in Figure 11.12.

FIGURE 11.12   *Excerpts from the Classroom Community Questionnaire*

For this set of questions, use this scale:

1—Disagree a lot

2—Disagree a little

3—Don't agree or disagree

4—Agree a little

5—Agree a lot

_____ Students in my class are willing to go out of their way to help someone.

_____ My classmates care about my work just as much as their own.

_____ Class is like a family.

_____ The students in my class don't really care about one another.

_____ A lot of students in my class like to put others down.

_____ Students in my class work together to solve problems.

Adapted from Schaps et al., 1996.

In constructing the questionnaire, Rosie asked the same question in several ways, some worded positively and others negatively. She tried to make her questions neutral so that students could not guess how she felt about the class. These are *closed* questions because they force a response from a list of possibilities. Because responses are numerical, it will be easy for Rosie to average the scores of each student and look for trends across students.

What Rosie learned from her survey (which she gave at the beginning of student teaching and near the end) was that the fifth-period civics students rated their sense of community the lowest of all her classes. In fact, she found that as she poured her efforts into *creating* a sense of community, the amount of disrespect among students actually increased in *all* classes, even the ones that had a fairly high sense of community at the beginning! Notice how Rosie uses multiple sources to examine classroom community: what students say (on surveys and in interviews), what her mentor says (in the classroom profile and follow-up conference), and what Rosie suspects (and records in her journal).

An open-ended questionnaire, on the other hand, allows students to respond in their own words. For example:

What communities do you belong to? What makes each a community?
In what ways is our classroom like a community?
In what ways is it not like a community?

Although open-ended questions are more time-consuming to analyze, they also can yield more specific and meaningful data. Many times it is most useful to use a combination of forced-choice and open-ended questions in a questionnaire.

Attitude scale.   Attitude scales are designed to measure the strength of an attitude or opinion to get at underlying beliefs. By numbering each item on the scale, for example, from 1 (strongly agree) to 4 (strongly disagree) with a 0 for uncertain, the range of attitudes within a group can be studied. In Andy's study of inclusion students, the question was "typical" students felt about special education students. Andy asked the typical students to circle the words that best describe their attitude on a Likert-type scale.

> I would be interested in spending more time being a friend to a student with special needs.

> Strongly agree   Agree   Disagree   Strongly disagree   Uncertain

It is not necessary to scale or measure attitudes to explain how students feel. On another section of the survey, Andy had this question:

> Circle the words that describe your feelings about this statement:

> Students labeled as students with special needs make me feel

> Sad   OK   Pity   Happy   Nothing

> Upset   Fine   Friendly   Like helping them   Other _____

Checklists and rating scales, discussed in the section "Observing" may also be appropriate as a means of collecting interview data.

Critical-incident interview.   *Critical incidents* are events that are turning points or especially revealing moments that, when uncovered, provide insights for both interviewer and interviewee. For example, in a study of primary-grade student attitudes toward learning in a multiage classroom, researchers asked each child to recall a critical incident:

> Think of a time in school when you really learned a lot and enjoyed what you were doing. Tell me about it—What did you do? Whom did you work with? How did it go? What did you do first, second, . . . What did you learn? What did you like about it?

Because multiple researchers conducted the interviews in several classrooms, it was important that each interviewer ask the same questions. Rather than perform numerical analysis, the researchers will later look for concepts that emerge as consistent patterns in student responses and incidents that illustrate the patterns.

A major problem in formal interviews is that students will often give socially desirable responses to please the interviewer. Sam's middle school science students, for example, were reluctant to reveal negative attitudes toward "environmentalists" because their teacher was a "nature lover." Sam had to figure out another way to get at their attitudes before constructing a unit on the environment. Students may not want to reveal their opinions, or are too shy or embarrassed to reveal their thinking. Other more indirect and nonthreatening ways of interviewing students, such as sociograms, projective techniques, and focus groups (as well as observations, documents, and artifacts), may be helpful.

Sociogram.   A sociogram is a technique for studying peer networks and relationships to determine a student's position within the social structure of a classroom. It is a way to identify those students who are revered by peers or who stand out in some way. It may also help identify people who are isolated and in need of extra social support. It has been used by teachers to help in understanding discipline problems and student preference for curriculum and groupings. Hubbard and Power (1993) have developed a useful protocol for this type of interview:

> You meet with each child and say, "I want you to give me first, second, and third choices in response to this question." Then you give the sociogram question. . . . You might ask, "If you could work with anyone in the class whom would you work with?" or "If you could play with anyone in the class, whom would you play with?" (p. 39)

Figure 11.13 is an example of a sociogram that describes sixth grade girls' first and second choices of partners for a field trip.

The sociogram suggests that Cheryl, Jan, and Kathy are a tight group, popular, and other students desire to get to know them. Sally and Elizabeth appear to have found a friendship in each other, although they would like to be associated with the three most popular girls. Melinda does not choose one of the popular girls. Betsy is chosen by no one and is generally observed working and playing alone in school.

FIGURE 11.13   *Sociogram of sixth-grade girls' preferences for field trip partners*

Projective technique.   A projective technique is an open-ended type of self-report interview in which the interviewee "projects" her or his feelings, attitudes, beliefs, and values by answering open-ended questions. It is like an ink blot test. One method is to present a hypothetical situation. If, for example, we wanted to know how student teachers really felt about doing action research, we might say:

> There are some faculty members and former students who have concerns about action research being a requirement of student teaching. If you were responsible for the student teaching seminar, how would you handle the action research component?

The distance established by using the hypothetical situation may enable some students to be more honest than if they were asked the question directly.

The incomplete sentence is another way to help interviewees project themselves. Sentences may be presented verbally or in writing. For example,

The best thing about math journals is . . .
The worst thing about math journals is . . .
I am happiest as a teacher when . . .
The thing that I am most worried about as I begin student teaching is . . .

Incomplete sentences are a useful diagnostic as well as evaluative tool.

Creative visualization.   Asking people to use their imaginations in creative ways can yield rich data. One technique is guided reflection, sometimes called *creative visualization*, in which you ask the person or group to close their eyes and to visualize how something might be or was. You ask them to take themselves there— to that time and place—and to engage their senses. Then they can tell you what they see, or they can draw or write about it. In some of our classes we do all three. Students, for example, are asked to take themselves back to childhood and to recall an incident in school. Perhaps it is the first day of school. Who is there? How do you feel? What do you see? Do you see yourself? What are you doing? What do you smell? What do you want to do? After students have drawn their visualizations (skill in drawing is beside the point—in fact, sometimes we have them draw with their nondominant hands so that they forget about "I can't draw"), they turn them over and do free-writes describing the experience in words. Finally, we discuss these in class and include them in our journals.

Focus group interview.   As we mentioned earlier, students can be reluctant to open up and speak honestly during individual interviews. Their reluctance is with good reason as people have too often been exploited or punished for being honest. This puts a considerable burden on the researcher to come from an ethical base that honors the respondents, regardless of their responses. Students may not want to participate, or they want to please the teacher with the "correct" answer, or may simply be too shy to talk privately with someone in authority, no matter how much we may try to establish trust and to diminish status differences. Sam, the middle school teacher and environmentalist, had to figure out another way to get at their attitudes before constructing a unit on the environmental education that would address their prior conceptions and stretch their thinking. The focus group turned out to be just the right technique.

A *focus group interview* is a group discussion addressing a particular topic or issue. Before breaking into groups, Sam lead a brainstorming session in which students generated topics, questions, and issues related to the environment. One of them was, What do we think of environmentalists? The class was then divided into groups of five students. They moved to round tables, all of which had tape recorders except one. Students who did not want to have their discussion recorded selected the table without a recorder. A student at each table was elected to facilitate, and the discussion began, focusing on the topics they had brainstormed. Sam walked around the room, but didn't stay at any table for more than a minute. After listening to the tapes and transcribing them, Sam found the terms *nerd* and *tree hugger* as well as descriptions such as "They don't bathe very often" when students referred to environmentalists.

No wonder they didn't want to reveal their attitudes in the whole-class discussion to their "tree-hugging" science teacher! Sam knew that any unit on environmental education would have to address these negative attitudes.

Suggestions for using focus groups are developed in Stepping Stones 11.2, Focus Groups.

The advantages of a group interview over the individual interview are that it encourages elaboration, it aids in recall, and it is stimulating to have multiple respondents interact. When the teacher plays only a minor role, focus groups also provide leadership opportunities for students. On the other hand, one person may dominate the group discussion, and the group culture may dominate individual speech with "group think" as the result. When students are prepared for facilitation roles, the potential hazards are lessened.

We hope that our discussion and examples demonstrate the potential of the interview to democratize the research process (Carspecken, 1996). The interview

STEPPING STONES 11.2

Focus Groups

The following suggestions for conducting a focus group are adapted from Tripp (1996, p. 23–24):

- Form groups of three to six.
- Students elect a facilitator or a teacher facilitates, keeping in mind that questions are to be directed to the group, not individuals.
- The topics for discussion can be the teacher's, the students', or a combination.
- Time limits encourage coverage of the topics.

STEPPING STONES 11.3

Interviewing

1. Select the interview approach that is most comfortable for you. Start with informal interviews during routine parts of the lesson—an editing conference or an after-class tutoring session provides the kind of comfortable structure that will ease you into the process. If you are open to hearing what your students are telling you, and you care about what they have to say, your relationship will be an authentic one. The rest will come with practice.

2. Ask questions to fit your purpose. Different questions get at different things. We have summarized the kinds of questions McKernan (1996, pp. 130–1) suggests for action research interviews:

Why questions encourage greater depth and detail.
Should questions get at values and beliefs.
Affect questions get at feelings, for example, How do you feel about . . .?
Leading questions help to explore a new area of inquiry: What do you think about the problem of teachers not having the time to do research?
Recall questions aid in remembering events, information, etc.
Comparative questions may yield new insights.
Experience/behavior questions elicit what the interviewee can do or has done.
Demographic questions help to find out how the interviewee describes herself or himself.

does more than build on the rich descriptions created through observation. By inviting students (and parents) to have more of a voice in the classroom and a chance to challenge our understandings and actions, we are establishing conditions that encourage reciprocity out of which genuine understanding can grow.

Suggestions for conducting interviews are included in Stepping Stones 11.3, Interviewing. We have found a section called "Student Feedback" in Tripp's (1996) *The Scope Program* and the classic by Spradley (1979), *The Ethnographic Interview*, to be helpful for various approaches to interviewing.

Documents and Artifacts: Studying Materials Prepared by Others

Artifacts and documents provide descriptive records that can enable the researcher to derive insights different from those provided by observations and interviews. Through observations we see with our own eyes. Through interviews we inquire into other peoples' perspectives. Just as clothing, jewelry, furniture, and stoneware of ancient civilizations tell us a great deal about the beliefs and practices of long-ago cultures, examination of records, texts, and products of work provides *physical traces* of the culture of students, classrooms, and schools.

Examining documents and artifacts is an unobtrusive way of collecting data that is becoming more common for classroom researchers. Portfolios, for example, provide physical evidence of what students (and we ourselves) know, believe, and have accomplished. Teaching portfolios might include video clips, student records, awards, statements of our philosophy, lesson plans, and articles we have written. When rubrics based on either internal or external criteria are used to examine the pieces in a portfolio, for example, rubrics based on the standards developed for scientific literacy or classroom environment, we call the design an *evaluation study.*

As he was doing his dissertation, Sam wanted to become more aware of the beliefs and potential biases he brought to his qualitative study. So he examined documents he had created throughout his doctoral program: comprehensive examination, pilot studies, and papers for courses. Each formed a part of his story of scholarship. They provided a database from which he could derive insights into his beliefs about middle school science.

Personal experience methods.   In Chapters 6 and 7 we outlined many techniques that we as action researchers can use to explore the beliefs, values, and identities that form our own personal-professional road map. Among them are self-talk, examining personal artifacts, interviewing family and friends, recalling significant others, generating metaphors, recalling critical incidents, and creating a time line of incidents and people.

Each of these techniques can also be used to gather data from students about their own personal experiences. Student experiences, as John Dewey and many since him have told us, are central to learning. School learning occurs when students are able to link their own experiences and purposes to academic content. Personal experience methods play an important role in helping students to make these connections. Thus, gathering data about student experiences can be helpful to students and teachers as we work together to construct our own learning. Jo's story provides an illustration of how a teacher's assignment can draw on students' personal experiences. These student experiences can, in turn, help students make connections to subject matter.

An initial questionnaire in Jo's middle school Spanish class indicated the presence of many cultural stereotypes by students. The study's purpose became to help students gain a deeper appreciation and acceptance of cultural practices in Spanish-speaking communities. Through a series of individual and group activities, students were asked to make connections between their own experiences and the experiences of Marta, a female Mexican protagonist in the movie "Sweet 15." In their final essay, in which students were to compare their own struggles to the struggles of Marta, Jo noted a shift in their thinking. Examples from student essays (see Figure 11.14) illustrate this development.

The ethical dimensions of using personal experience methods requires serious consideration of who we are in our student's stories (Clandinin and Connelly,

---

FIGURE 11.14 *Exerpts from student essays about Marta*

Marta showed her responsibility by helping her father become a U.S. citizen. Marta and I also must show some independence and trust. We have to show that we are able to do things by ourselves to gain our parents' trust.

Marta's parents didn't believe that she was an adult yet. My parents feel the same way about me. They don't understand how much having adults accept you as one of them means to us.

I think I am very lucky to live the life that I lead. Marta's life as a teenager is not as easy as most people's, including mine . . . she was a Mexican in an Anglo-dominated society.

1998). When we enter into a research relationship with participants and ask them to share their stories with us, there is the potential to shape their stories as well as our own. We must also pay attention to what happens after the research. Helping students deal emotionally with revelations they uncover in personal stories becomes part of the ethical responsibilities of action researchers who use these methods. Reminding students that stories told in class must remain there, maintaining anonymity and using pseudonyms, are ways to protect the privacy of participants. On the other hand, privacy and anonymity become less important if we seek full participation of students and colleagues.

Student work.   Student essays, poetry, problem-solving, work, musical compositions, journals, and the many types of performances that students use to demonstrate their understanding and appreciations are ways to document student learning. A good source of ways to document student work is Barrell's (1995) *Teaching for Thoughtfulness: Classroom Strategies to Enhance Intellectual Development*. Working with students to document their growth in portfolios also helps us as teachers to understand how we might address issues in our own teaching.

Shawn saved Jen's computer-generated work to keep track of her literacy development and to illustrate and make visible Jen's remarkable progress over a 4-month period. Jen's progress was traced by examining illustrated stories she developed with a computer program. See Figures 11.15 and 11.16.

By examining Jen's entries for overall number of words, words spelled conventionally, increased vocabulary, and change in sentence structure, Shawn noted significant changes in Jen's writing.

Photographs and video and audio recordings.   Photographs and audio and video recordings may get at evidence of spiritual, aesthetic, and religious sensibilities and experiences that go beyond what is available through written work. Photographs and video recordings, found or researcher-produced, are underused data that can create powerful images. They also allow the researcher to relook at what

FIGURE 11.15   *What Jen and her family did over spring vacation—April 15*

happened. Whether the photographs were taken in the past (such as in the case of the student teacher who documented her transformation through photographs of herself as an overweight kid hiding behind others to a newly "blonded" cheer-leader and prom queen) or are taken by the researcher for the purpose of telling a story, photographs and video can become powerful evidence. Since they can elicit emotions and record objects, people, or events, we must be careful to provide the context in which they are taken. We need to keep in mind that what we select to frame in a photograph or video represents our own understanding of the subject.

One researcher ran a video recorder in a center area in one part of her class-room. Her primary-aged children soon ignored the presence of the camcorder on a tripod. What the tapes revealed about interstudent conversations and lan-guage among these ethnically diverse students identified as severely "language-impaired" was fascinating and revealing. Analyzed segments demonstrated the role of language in the social construction of knowledge. One picture can tell 1,000 stories. It can be interpreted differently by each observer! Remember those multiple selves we explored in Chapter 6?

A vocal music student teacher made and shared audio recordings of her young adolescent male students to help them through the period when their voices were changing. (After listening to the recordings, our class had a far greater appreciation for vocal music teachers who want to be inclusive rather than exclusive in select-ing students for their programs.) An elementary teacher, eager to attempt student-led group discussions of books but curious about whether discussion would be productive, placed audio recorders on each student table. She listened to them in her car tapedeck on the way home and later categorized their responses.

Technology.   Technology provides new and rich sources of data to help us un-derstand our students. One teacher was working with her students on a project and using the Internet as a resource. She wanted to see what sites the students used and how long they stayed there when browsing the web for information. She used the

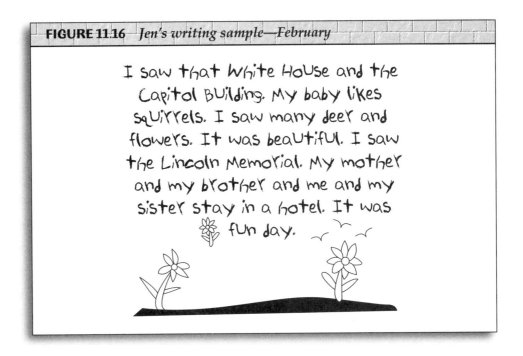

FIGURE 11.16 *Jen's writing sample—February*

> I saw that White House and the Capitol Building. My baby likes squirrels. I saw many deer and flowers. It was beautiful. I saw the Lincoln Memorial. My mother and my brother and me and my sister stay in a hotel. It was fun day.

history file from the browser. This file indicated the first and last time they visited a particular site and how many times they visited it. She then went to each site and bookmarked it. At the end of the students' project the teacher determined whether their search for information progressed to the use of more complex materials, if they stayed longer at the sites, and if they incorporated the material in their reports.

Another teacher took advantage of the school system's networked computer system. He and colleagues from across the country set up a virtual project for students in their social studies classes. The teachers noted how students' communication differed when they used chat and e-mail correspondence as opposed to regular classroom conversation. They began to collect e-mail and chat logs, comparing them to the quality of the discussion within the classroom.

Technology offers a whole new world of opportunities for student learning. Just as with other methods, researchers need to be mindful of the ways in which they protect student privacy and anonymity.

Physical traces. Evidence of learning and development may be found in some unexpected places. A sixth-grade social studies teacher learned through a survey that her students hated social studies. She asked the school media specialist to provide her with a printout of circulation records just before and during the time she introduced historical fiction to increase student enthusiasm and involvement with social studies. By examining student choices, she could document whether there was an increase in the number of historical novels or social studies–related books checked out by her students. An art teacher counted fingerprints on glass cases after a field trip to an art museum to determine which kinds of art and sculpture were most appealing to students. And a technology teacher monitored interest in his homework web page by recording the number of hits made every evening. Webb et al. (1966) call the buildup of physical traces *accretion*.

Erosion, on the other hand, is the wearing away of physical traces. A quick look at the wear and tear of student textbooks indicates the extent to which they are being used. Popular paperbacks often have no remaining covers at all! Another researcher studied teaching styles by the types of supplies teachers used up over a school year. Gathering artifacts and documents with accretion and erosion in mind may lead to some very creative research designs!

Suggestions about what documents and artifacts to save and how to organize them are presented in Stepping Stones 11.4 and Stepping Stones 11.5.

We have made a chart of the numerous possible situations the action researcher might find herself or himself in and ways to collect data in those situations. Can you find your emerging study in this chart? See Figure 11.17.

Finally, while most of this chapter is devoted to data that the action researcher creates in context, we must not overlook the wealth of "data" that are available outside of our classrooms. Other people, theories, empirical studies, electronic resources, and philosophical inquiries are valuable resources that we have highlighted in earlier chapters. Moving between these sources enables us to gain multiple perspectives and deeper insights.

STEPPING STONES 11.4

What Documents and Artifacts to Save

Saving the following kinds of things may be useful for your study:

- *Samples of work produced over time*—journals, math problems, laboratory experiments, artwork, writing samples, audio or video recordings.
- *Correspondence*—notes, memos, journal, diary, field notes.
- *Records*—attendance, grades, certificates, minutes of meetings, library records.
- *Currciulum materials*—lesson plans, textbooks, CD ROMs, Internet sites.
- *Accounts*—newspaper clippings, journal articles, video clips about classroom or larger work context.
- *Accretion and erosion* of any of the above.

Identifying work by labeling and dating needs to be a routine part of our work. If students forget to date their work, a student can be assigned the task of stamping the date as work is turned in. Labeling work by describing the assignment and identifying the author by name, which can later be removed to protect privacy, or by some other method such as numbers or letters can be done either directly on the work itself or by attaching an adhesive note.

FIGURE 11.17 *What do I want to know? How do I get at my question?*

If. . .	Then. . .
I want to know how students perceive something or feel about something	I probably need feedback from interviews, surveys, or questionnaires.
I want to know how their attitudes or perceptions about something *change*	I probably need to collect feedback at least twice, whether it's a survey, interview, questionnaire (pretest, posttest).
I want to know something about parents, their ideas, perceptions, input about their children, etc.	I probably need to survey or interview them, in person, by letter, by phone, etc.
I want to see if what I'm doing impacts quality or quantity of student work in some way	I probably need to collect examples of related student work at intervals (once a week, once a month, etc.) or study selected students' work over time in some depth.
I want to know how my students make use of something existing or introduced (like a library center, particular books, study aid, etc.)	I probably need an observation instrument that is a checklist, log, anecdotes, audiotape, etc.
I want to know how students use consumable items or collections	I may need to track the use of the items or depletion of the supplies related to the topic.
I want to know how students use something new I'm teaching them	I may need to track their use of the thing, or strategy in a desired context.
I want to see if one intervention works	I need to decide what signals "working" and track the progress in observation, or artifacts, or student comments or feedback.
I want to compare more than one intervention	I need to document each intervention through student work and/or student opinions and/or observation.
I am studying one learner in great depth for whatever reason	I probably need a comprehensive and regular researcher log in addition to interviews with the student, about the student with others, and collect things the student has done related to my topic.
I want to know if what I'm doing influences something students do outside my classroom	I'll need to collect data outside my classroom from parents, librarians, other teachers, etc. or wherever I want the influence to be.
(Self-assessment) I want to assess *my* effectiveness at something I'm doing with my students	I might examine artifacts to see if I'm getting what I want; I might directly ask students. I might ask them to write about their understanding; I might interview them about it. I might listen to related comments, nonverbal comments.

STEPPING STONES 11.5

Getting Organized

Systematically and coherently managing the large amount of data that accumulates in an AR study is of critical importance in data collection, storage and retrieval. Because data management is so closely connected to data analysis, the subject of the next chapter, we will mention here only those things that will help the action researcher before the data collection even starts.

1. If we know what the categories are that form the rubric for a study, then simply filing data in those categories is the most logical way to organize data. A portfolio with standardized categories for evaluating teachers and students is one such example. As additional categories emerge from preliminary and ongoing data analysis, the portfolio can be expanded to include them. Organizing by types of data, such as interviews, artifacts, documents, field notes, journal will make it easier to add to and retrieve the data.

2. Numbering pages, developing a table of contents, summarizing contents, labeling documents and artifacts with relevant information such as date, time, length, place, type of data, e.g. interview, preserving original student work, and filing them on a regular basis are strategies that will prevent the task from getting out of hand. Notebooks, index cards, colored file folders, storage boxes or file drawers, and computer software that were described in chapter 6 are the typical tools of data management.

CHAPTER SUMMARY

Trying out a variety of actions and documenting those actions strengthens our awareness of the consequences of what we often take for granted in our teaching. Most of us are constantly trying out new ways to better reach out to students. We are now learning the tools that can help us make *informed* decisions. In the next chapter, we will look briefly at some of the other elements of design that strengthen our decision-making powers.

Elements of Design: Verification, Interpretation, and Portrayal

In addition to planning and documenting the action, other important elements of design need to be taken into consideration prior to launching a full-blown study or at least in the early stages of a study. Verification, interpretation, portrayal, action planning for next steps, and ethical considerations are dealt with briefly in this chapter and developed more fully in chapters to come.

How Will I Verify that My Judgments Are Trustworthy, Credible, and Respectful?

As we design our studies, we want to build in assurances for ourselves and for others that our professional judgments are trustworthy, credible, respectful, and reflective of our values. A fuller discussion and examples of verification are included in Chapter 13, so you may want to skim that section right now if you are designing your study. In Chapter 13 we present suggestions such as the use of multiple perspectives, application of indicators (both internal ones developed by the researcher and other participants and external ones developed by professionals in our respective fields), presentation of raw data in the form of student quotes, stories of occurrences, frequencies, descriptive accounts, and dialogue with colleagues.

A simple way to enhance the verification process is to plan ways to triangulate the data by using observations, interviews, and other data sources. What do I observe? What do students say? What do I see in student work?

These are the kinds of questions you can build into your study and data collection. While we want to be systematic in data collection and make sure we look into our classrooms from multiple perspectives, we also want to use our feelings and intuitions to guide us in the data collection process.

How Will I Interpret the Data?

While interpretation (making sense of the data) is the focus of Section 6, planning how we will interpret the data is part of designing a study. Because analysis and interpretation are an ongoing part of the action research process (e.g., we check on student progress throughout a unit of study, not just at the end), we want to consider how we will make sense of the data. When will I read over my journal entries? How often and when will I collect and assess student work? What will I look for in the data? What indicators will I use to determine the quality of work? Are there any theories that I can use to guide my understanding of student learning and my own growth as a professional? (We often write about those theories in the "What is my research interest?" section of the proposal.) Researchers are often fearful of what they will do once they have collected all their data. By anticipating *how* we will make sense of these data, the task of analysis and interpretation becomes more manageable.

How Will I Portray What I Have Learned and Make It Public?

Even as we begin designing our studies, we need to be aware of the possible ways to portray and make public what we have learned. Will we use critical incidents? Photographs? Will we create aesthetic representations through music, art, sculpture, dance, drama, or poetry? Video or audio tape recordings? Student work?

Who are potential audiences? In other words, with whom will my research be shared? Parents? Colleagues at school, university or professional conferences or elsewhere, such as on a listserve? Students? School board members? How will our collaborators participate in sharing what we have learned? Will it be formal or informal? As we collect data, we want to keep in mind these audiences and the kind of evidence they will most appreciate and value. In Section 7 we will explore the many options open to action researchers, some traditional to research and others in emerging forms.

How Will These Actions Make Life Better? What Will I Do Next?

Action research requires that we examine critically the consequences of our work. So often important professional judgments are made without consideration of the consequences of our actions and how those consequences relate to our values.

Dorothy: Isn't the word *better* kind of subjective? What is better to you may not be better to me! So how can we judge the quality of the consequences of our work if we mean different things?

Authors: When we speak of making life better, we have in mind the professional commitments that we discussed in the first three chapters of this book: collaboration, community based on justice and equity, participation of those with whom we work, authentic communication as a way of building strong relationships, etc. Commitment to these qualities as well as to our own professional growth is the cornerstone of what we mean by *better.* For example, if we believe in collaborative and participatory education, then an element of design we will want to consider is how we might involve our students and parents in designing our study. To what extent should students and parents become involved in raising the questions, developing alternative actions, and documenting the study?

What Ethical Considerations Need to Be Made?

When we speak of making life better, we are considering not only the consequences of our actions, but the research process as well. Earlier in the book we said that to teach well is to inquire well. Yet action research involves a wider audience than does traditional teaching. As a result, ethical dilemmas may arise. These dilemmas revolve around procedural issues (e.g., how, when, and from whom to gain permission); legal and institutional issues (e.g., compliance with Human Subjects Review Board regulations, turning over documents such as journals to legal authorities in cases of child abuse and neglect, etc.); relational issues (e.g., building trust, using data to build up the community as opposed to using data only to further one's career); and role confusion (e.g., According to Zeni (1999), multiple responsibilities of action researchers to research, to students, and to parents).

Zeni (1998) argues that the dilemmas that arise are related to underlying issues:

1. *Representation*—how students and the school are represented to others. Is it accurate? How do others feel about the way they are represented? How open

is the communication between researcher and participants, so that differences of opinion can be taken into account?

2. *Ownership*—who owns the data? The student, the teacher, the school, legal authorities?

3. *Responsibilities*—our primary responsibility as action researchers is to our students. How is potential abuse, of those over whom we have power and whose trust we have gained, minimized?

These considerations relate to the values of action research. We can think these through with others affected by our study. The following are ethical guidelines to be used as new situations arise. See Figure 12.1.

FIGURE 12.1 *Ethical guidelines for teacher action researchers*

Obtain permissions: Let your students and their parents know what you are doing. Obtain written permission to conduct the study from parents and oral or written permission from students. If the study is conducted through a university, appropriate Human Subjects Review Board permission is often required. The school or district may also have guidelines for research. Reciprocity between a school district and a university is preferable so that the researcher does not have to file separate applications. If students can be identified (through the use of video, audio, or photographs), special permissions are needed indicating this fact. If private records are needed, gain school permission to use them. When possible, obtain permission to use quotes and student work, negotiating with participants how they are represented to others.

The process of obtaining informed consent involves written permission from parents and oral permission from children. In each case the researcher provides the following:

1. Topic.

2. Purpose.

3. Brief description of study and how participants will be involved.

4. Description of potential risks and benefits (risks are usually minimal, but if there are any that the researcher is aware of, they need to be stated).

5. Procedures for anonymity/confidentiality (except in the event that participants opt to waive this requirement because of the cooperative nature of the study).

6. Students' option to stop participation (except if it is regular course work) without fear of reprisal.

7. Phone number of researcher (and research adviser or university researcher officer) and invitation to contact one of them with questions.

8. Space for agreement. For example,

I agree to (take part/let my child take part) in this project. I know what (I/she/he) will have to do and that (I/she/he) can stop at any time.

_____   _____

Signature   Date

FIGURE 12.1 *Continued*

Involve participants: Encourage the full participation of those who will be affected by the study, and give them credit for their work. Encourage participants to help with design, data collection, and interpretation. Be willing to extend or clarify accounts for the purpose of enhancing fairness, relevancy, and accuracy. Share your progress with those involved, and seek their ideas. Seek out the points of view of those involved, even if those points of view differ from yours. Then include their points of view in your report, along with yours, so that the readers or audience members can form their own judgments.

Ensure confidentiality: Building a classroom environment based on respect is the first ingredient of ensuring confidentiality. Students and other participants need to trust that what they say in private will remain private, particularly in their journals and diaries, and that their thoughts and feelings will not be used against them. However, students need also to be aware that in the event that they reveal information leading the researcher to believe that the student is suffering from some sort of abuse or neglect or is engaged in illegal activities, it is the responsibility of the researcher to report this information to the proper authorities.

Ensure anonymity: Generally, anonymity is preserved through use of pseudonyms or the exclusion of student names from any documents or examples used in a report. It is difficult in most classroom situations to hide the identity of students when making reports to parents, colleagues, administrators, or school board members. Zeni (1998) suggests alternatives to pseudonyms: composite rather than individual portraits; interchanging physical description, grade level, gender; etc. There are times when we do not want to keep identities anonymous, particularly when our students are coparticipants in our study and the report will be presented to larger audiences.

Inform participants of the right to withdraw: Students need to know that they may withdraw from the study at any time without fear of negative consequences. In most cases, if the study includes teaching activities and curriculum that are part of the regular teaching process, withdrawing is not an issue. For example, if all students were participating in small group work related to a topic in social studies, they would not withdraw from the study. They might, however, choose not to participate in a survey about how they felt about the group work or their partners.

Build relationships of trust: Open communication, trust, and reciprocity are the cornerstones of action research. Whether we like to admit it or not, as teachers we are in positions of power, and we may intimidate students into complying with our research agenda and interpretations by virtue of our status. We need to consider how we will continue to justify the trust that students and parents have in us.

Be self-reflective: Include self-reflection as an integral part of the study. How does this research fit with your values? Consider ways in which you as a researcher influence or do not influence what happens in your classroom, so that you will interpret and portray the evidence you have gathered with honesty, respect, fairness, and accuracy.

These guidelines reflect several sources: our own experience as teacher action researchers, application for approval to use human subjects in research (Kent State University), Zeni's (1998) article entitled "A Guide to Ethical Issues and Action Research," and Hopkins's (1993) book, entitled *A Teacher's Guide to Classroom Research.*

CHAPTER SUMMARY

Keeping in mind the elements of design presented in this chapter and the dilemmas that planning and documenting action may pose can help you to increase the power of your design and get you off to a good start. While modifications are usually made along the way, planning for the journey may prevent or alleviate detours and delays.

SECTION SUMMARY

Design is tentative. It provides a roadmap that can change and evolve as we gather data and reflect on what we are learning. Where we end up can bear little resemblance to where we thought we would end up. There is no definitive time to start developing a design. Often it begins after much data collection has already occurred, data that provide evidence that we need to address a particular aspect of our teaching. Toni, for example, had been studying math journals for a year before realizing that two students with special-needs were having the same difficulty with solving equations, thus motivating Toni to launch a case study of these two students.

Thus, we return to the cycle of action research. To the basic cycle of reflect, act, and observe, we have added the research layer of design, carrying out the design, and documenting the process. This blending of teaching and research becomes the mark of the scholar as we continuously assess where we are, modify practice based on informed decisions, and describe what we are learning. See Figure 12.2.

In Figure 12.2 we summarize how the elements of design fit together as a basis for developing a proposal for an action research study whose goal is to develop professional judgment and improve classroom practice. A proposal is simply a way of getting our thoughts organized. It is a way of saying (to ourselves, our colleagues, our students, and others), "This is what I plan to do to address my questions and concerns." (See Figure 12.3.)

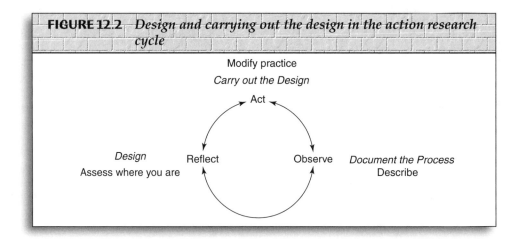

FIGURE 12.2 *Design and carrying out the design in the action research cycle*

Modify practice
Carry out the Design

Act

Design   Reflect   Observe   *Document the Process*
Assess where you are   Describe

FIGURE 12.3 Designing an action research study

Questions	Methodology: How to address the question					Consequences
What is my research interest?	*What will I try out in order to improve my practice?*	*How will I document the process?*	*How will I verify that my judgments are trustworthy, credible, and respectful?*	*How will I interpret the data?*	*How will I portray what I have learned and make it public?*	*How will these actions make life better? And what will I do next?*
What is my question? (How can I . . . ?) Why am I interested? (values, beliefs) What do I already know? (through my experience) What do others know? (literature review) What do I expect to find? (my hunches)	Who? What? When? Where? How? Why? Develop a schedule.	Data are collected to give evidence that shows the consequences of actions. Data are gathered by: • Observing • Interviewing • Examining artifacts and documents Continue reading and consulting with others. Gain permissions	Verification is process of making interpretations and judgments by: • Making your standpoint clear • Using multiple perspectives • Applying indicators • Providing raw data • Writing descriptively • Being systematic • Being reflective	Interpretation is an interactive process of giving meaning to data by: • *Analyzing:* What are the parts? • *Synthesizing:* How are the parts related? • *Theorizing and making assertions:* What do I/we make of all this (with reference to personal and public theory)?	Portrayal is . . . • A presentation • Written report • Listserv • Video/audio • Art work • Drama Made public to . . . • Faculty • Parents • School board • Community • Students • University classroom	The "so what"? How will changes in myself, my students, and my situation foster equality and community? What might I try out after the first phase of my study?
Criterion *Significant to self and others*	**Criterion** *Doable process which addresses the question or issue in a potent way*	**Criterion** *Provides for rich description and multiple perspectives*	**Criterion** *Trustworthy and credible*	**Criterion** *Given the evidence, our intuition and experience, our interpretation makes sense.*	**Criteria** *Captures essence and illustrates* *Authenticity for audience*	**Criterion** *Based on critical reflection and democratic values.*

Values: Ethical commitment to equality and community through collaboration, participation, and reflective practice

There are several useful resources on design in qualitative research that provide a good overview of methods and issues: Marshall and Rossman's (1999) *Designing Qualitative Research*; Creswell's (1997) *Qualitative Inquiry and Research Design: Choosing among Five Traditions*; and Stake's (1995) *The Art of Case Study Research*. An excellent resource for data collection is Denzin and Lincoln's (1998) *Collecting and Interpreting Qualitative Materials*. For design related specifically to action research, see selected chapters and cases from Carson and Sumara's (1997) *Action Research as Living Practice*; Kemmis and McTaggert's (1988) *The Action Research Planner*; and the book by Atweh et al. (1998), *Action Research in Practice: Partnership for Social Justice in Education*.

In Section 4 we focused on questions and how to develop them. In Section 5 we have focused on the actions we can try out and the data we can collect to document the consequences of those actions. In Section 6 we will offer suggestions for analyzing, verifying, and interpreting the data we have collected. In Section 7 we will look at ways to portray for others what we have learned, so that they can learn from our actions and critique the claims we make. The *substance* of each of these chapters, however, goes beyond methods and techniques and is concerned with how to make our classrooms and schools more democratic and just places.

Dorothy: We have come a long way! The beasts, the rivers, the fields of poppies that have detoured our journey are really a part of the process of finding our way. They are more than methods. They are the way we figure things out.

I am curious to see what we make of these encounters (or data) we have met along the way. And I assume that is what we will do next? So it's on to analysis and interpretation!

Authors: Yes. But first, let's explore the forest for a little while.

Exploring the Forest
Designing an Action Research Study and Doing Fieldwork

In Section 5, we devoted our attention to designing a study. In these exercises you will conduct fieldwork in your classroom or school by observing, interviewing, and examining artifacts and documents—in other words, collecting data for your study. By completing these exercises, you will be designing your study.

Design

1. If you have not yet designed a *practice* study, now is a good time to do so. By answering the following design questions and then carrying out your plan for about a week or so, you will get a good feel for the action research process.
   a. Describe a hitch in *practice*, something you would like to improve. Select something that might take a week or so to try out some different actions.
   b. What can you try out?
   c. How will you document the process?
   d. How will you report it to others?
   e. How will it make life better?

   Share your plan with a critical colleague, someone you feel has insights about teaching that would be helpful to you. In a week or so, check back with the colleague with a progress report. If you need help in documenting the process of your action, invite the colleague to collect and examine the data.

2. Now that you have designed a practice study, select a question you would like to pursue in your action research project. It might be the one you selected in Section 4 or the one in the practice study. Or it may be something that occurred to you while you were reading Section 5. Write out your question. Have you already collected some information about the topic? If not, you might interview knowledgeable people, search the Internet, and read articles, chapters, or books on your topic, paying attention to different ways you can address the question.

3. Now comes the fun. Think of possible actions to address your question. Based on the information you have gathered and your own personal experiences, brainstorm possible actions. Think of at least five.

In brainstorming, allow ideas to flow freely without editing them. Free-writing is a good technique for this. Have a critical colleague and/or your students brainstorm with you.

After you have a list of ideas, categorize them. Are some related to the same idea? Perhaps an even better idea will come to you by this clustering. From all these ideas, which ones seem to fit your beliefs about teaching and learning and life in your classroom? Which ones seem most like you? Which ones could you commit to working on for awhile? Which ones seem most achievable in your classroom? Which ones seem right at this time (or do they require something else to be done first)? Which ones hold the greatest potential for the amount of effort you plan to expend? Which ones best match resources? Which ones fit with the ethical commitments of action research, a commitment to the improvement of yourself, your practice, and the larger community through the principles of equal relations, shared leadership, authentic communication, inclusive involvement, and active participation? Are there any other criteria that come to mind?

Now, using the criteria that make most sense from the previous exercise, select an idea you would like to start with, saving others that meet your criteria for another cycle. Write down *why* you selected this approach and what you will do.

4. Answer the questions concerning who, what, when, where, why, and how about your proposed action. Be as specific or general as you would like knowing that you will develop each more fully in your final draft. Look back into Section 5 for details about the kinds of information you can gather to answer each question.

5. Develop a schedule for your action. This is much like an action plan. It will make the plan much more real and doable when a list of activities, times, and participants is laid out. You might want to use the chart in Figure 12.4 as a guide. Share your schedule with a critical colleague. Ask what he or she thinks about it.

6. Before you try out your plan, think about how you will collect data to show the consequences of your actions. What do I think is going on? And how do I know? By using multiple sources of data, you will be in a better position to respond to both questions. You might want to use the format presented in Figure 12.5 to help you triangulate.

FIGURE 12.4 *Schedule for action research proposal*			
Date to start	What will happen?	For how long? How often?	Who will be involved?

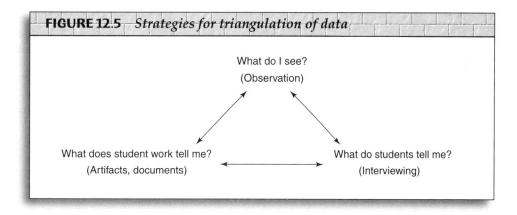

FIGURE 12.5   *Strategies for triangulation of data*

What do I see?
(Observation)

What does student work tell me?
(Artifacts, documents)

What do students tell me?
(Interviewing)

7. What will you look for in the data (as evidence that your values or goals are being realized)?
8. What do you expect to find? Stating your hypotheses (hunches) based on experience, intuition, and other resources is important because as you test your hypotheses you may adjust or formulate new ones.
9. Complete the data collection plan in Figure 12.6 as a starting point for your design.
10. With whom will you collaborate? Who will your critical colleague(s) be? In what ways will full participation of your students (and others) be encouraged?
11. What permissions are needed, and how will you get them?
12. In the following chapters, we will explore other important design questions: How will I verify that my judgments are trustworthy and credible? How will I interpret the data? How will I portray what I have learned and make it public? How will these actions make life better? And what will I do next? You may or may not want to fully address these questions until you have read Sections 6 and 7, but by thinking about them now, you will anticipate what these chapters (and your study) hold in store for you.

Practicing Data Collection

13. Try out your action and practice your observation skills. In your journal, label a section "Field Notes." Develop a format for your field notes that makes sense to you. Remember to leave wide margins on either the left- or right-hand side of notebook paper for your hunches, methodological decisions, and personal notes. At the top of the note paper, write your name, the setting of the observation, the date, and the focus of the observation (if you have one). For example, in your first observation of your students during an activity, you might want to look at *who* is doing what? Describe. *Where* is the activity taking place? Drawing a picture might help with later recall. *When* do things occur? Is there some regularity? Now write for 10 minutes.

FIGURE 12.6 *Data collection plan*

Topic: Problem Solving	Research Question: How can I improve student problem solving in science class?

What are you trying to accomplish?

Improve student problem solving through direct teaching of the scientific method.

Your plan:

What will you try out?

1. Present a series of four problems throughout the semester and guide students through the scientific method.
2. Provide additional opportunities for students to solve problems.

What data will you collect to provide evidence of the consequences of your actions? How will you gain multiple perspectives?

1. Student written responses to four problems using a scoring rubric to keep track of how they are doing.
2. Mentor observations of student problem solving during laboratory time recorded in a log.
3. Informal interview with students as they are presented with problems during laboratory time.

What will you look for in the data?

1. Clear statement of problem.
2. Increasing number of alternative solutions.
3. Selection of alternative solution with greatest likelihood of success.
4. Willingness to try out solutions.

What do you expect to find?

I expect that students will become better problem solvers when I am more direct in my teaching of problem solving and use the rubric to assess their problem-solving abilities. I then will modify my teaching based on what I learn.

Read over your notes and insert information that enhances or extends the description. Add hunches, impressions, methodological decisions, and ideas that come to mind.

14. Select someone, a group, or your whole class to interview. What will you try to learn in the interview? How does the interview relate to your research question? How will you design the interview? What will you use, a survey, questionnaire, informal interview, or a formal interview? Does a focus group interview make sense? Develop your interview questions or survey in such a

way that it will be easy to analyze. For example, a Likert-scale from (1) highly agree to (5) highly disagree is easy to score, but it does not have the richness of an open-ended interview. During an informal interview, take notes, and get direct quotes where possible. As soon after the interview as possible, go back to your notes and fill in details.

15. Examine artifacts or documents produced by your students. Make sure that names are written clearly on the work and that the work is dated. Ask the students if you may keep the original; or if they are keeping it in a portfolio, ask that the portfolio be kept where you can retrieve the works you want to examine. Begin by examining them. What do they tell you about the student? About what they are learning? About the assignment? What else could you note in your journal?

Getting Organized

16. Begin to develop a data management plan that will work for you and the space that you have, be it a drawer, a shelf, a file cabinet, a box, or a binder. Make sure that everything you save is labeled, named, and dated. How will you organize the interview and observational notes and artifacts? Ask your colleagues for suggestions about how they organize their offices, their homes, and their student work. Share your plan with your critical colleague.

Writing a Proposal

17. Use the chart "Designing an Action Research Study" (see Figure 12.3). Examine the criteria for each section of the proposal. Write a proposal for an AR study, labeling each section. For example, the first section is "What is my research interest?" Write a few paragraphs, using the questions and criteria from the chart as a guide. Your proposal can be written in an informal, first-person narrative style. The length is up to you, but it is not usually more that five to eight double-spaced pages. Include a reference list for works that you have cited in your literature review. You may want to review Andy's proposal in Appendix A to see how one student designed a study.

Analyzing and Interpreting Data: Playing with What We've Got and Making Sense of It

The four travelers walked up to the great gate of the Emerald City and rang the bell . . . [They] passed a sleepless night [waiting for Oz to see them], each thinking of the gift Oz had promised to bestow.

The Wonderful Wizard of Oz
L. Frank Baum (1900)

Dorothy: Such excitement and trepidation. The moment we have journeyed for. And now we will learn what the end of our journey has in store for us. Home cannot be very far away!

Lion: Dorothy? Do I have the courage to learn what awaits me when the Wizard grants my wish? Those poppy fields were something else! I still smell danger.

Dorothy: Oh, I think so, Lion.

Authors: Ah yes. There are still dangers lurking, but none beyond your prowess! One danger is that as we play with our data, trying to make sense of it, we will get lost in the details and forget to pay attention to how they might all fit together. That once we take the data apart, we will lose the "whole." But never fear! We are prepared for this. We will walk back and forth between broad and narrow views of our data, keeping in mind all the while where we are going.

Scarecrow: It will take intelligence and courage to understand what we are about to hear.

Authors: Indeed, it will. The Wizard may be helpful, but as we look at our data from different points of view and begin to make connections and see relationships. We may not need as much help as we might think.

Tin Man: I can feel my heart pounding with anticipation—as if I already had one!

Authors: Yes, feel it! Conserve some of that precious energy.

You have already sensed what is ahead! We offer many ways of exploring data and some of the "Aha's" will probably come from putting together small, over-looked puzzle pieces in our minds. Not only BIG pieces and patterns make our hearts THUMP! YES! EUREKA!

You, dear Scarecrow, are picking up on the other side of Lion's sense of danger. Piero Ferrucci (1982, p. 24), an Italian educator, said it well: "The moment we see the range of possibilities opening in front of us, we are filled with a sense of wonder and enthusiasm. But we should also beware lest this enthusiasm lead us astray; certain distortions and consequent dangers are . . . widespread." He goes on to say, "Perhaps the most fundamental distortion is the belief that the technique itself is the main transforming agent, rather than the way in which it is used." (p. 24)

So, you see, we need it all: intelligence, courage, and heart, as we move through the gate. Ferrucci is suggesting that an all-important factor in our journey is the *attitude* with which we use our research tools: "We can use them with attention and patience as tools to transform . . . Or we can use them mechanically . . . and just waste our time. We can make use of them what we want; in themselves they hold no guarantees." (p. 24)

We have been so diligent in laying out our path and carefully monitoring our actions. Are we ready to open that door—to learn through critical reflection what insights we may derive from the data? Our case studies will take us through the gates into the land of Oz, where Dorothy and her companions hope to find answers to their questions. As *we* all know, Oz holds some surprises for them.

In Section 5 we showed how action researchers monitored and kept track of their actions and how information becomes data through the filter of our questions. In Section 6 we will *transform* data to evidence, using our creative and analytic powers. Then, examining the evidence from many perspectives (with heart, and mind, and courage), we will interpret and make sense of that evidence. Finally, these interpretations will guide our actions in ways that further the development of just and caring classroom communities. Transformation is the key!

CASE STUDIES

Helping Jen Learn English as a Second Language

Shawn's classroom already had an integrated focus, using only a few texts and mostly authentic assessments. With a balance of small and large group lessons, Shawn would have to decide for each lesson and activity the extent to which Jen could participate, or how to include her in the activity.

Jen's progress would be monitored through several means. First, Shawn was keeping a daily and fairly detailed researcher log. At times, Shawn would do some preliminary data analysis by writing what might be called an "analytic memo." Through these memos, Shawn gained a different perspective on things that would not be perceptible on a daily basis. A log of entries detailed the flow of the lesson and how Jen fared during a particular kind of activity.

Second, Shawn kept and dated all Jen's writings, from the earliest ones that were mostly drawings, to her first attempts at written English, to her fully developed sentences and stories. Shawn also designed a quiz of common English words that would be important for a second grader to know. Three times during the study Shawn administered the exact same test, which asked Jen to read and define common words. In addition, Shawn interviewed the ESL teacher during the study.

Shawn logged Jen's quiz scores as evidence of her increasing use of common English words and examined her journal in detail to look for changes, which, as it turned out, were large and easy to describe. Jen's last journal entry during the data collection period was a written entry about a trip Jen had taken with her family. It consisted of 45 English words, and seven syntactically and semantically appropriate sentences. Only one sentence contained a syntactical miscue with incorrect verb tense.

The Literature Circle's Study

Jan and Terry carried out their plan for a literature-based program for all students in Terry's fifth-grade class. They decided to study six students in depth. All students had completed a "Reader Self-Perception Scale," known as the RSPC, at the beginning and end of the study. Jan and Terry also analyzed the written responses of students, collected as part of the strategy, and an instrument which included a checklist that tracked activity of all group members in terms of their role and participation in the groups. Each student also completed a written self-assessment of his or her role and feelings about participating in the book groups. In spite of the short duration of this study, many students began to see themselves as better readers. They also wrote more substantive entries in literature response journals as a result of their reading.

The S.T.A.R. Club Study

Sensing that "typical" students had negative attitudes toward students with disabilities and feeling curious about their survey responses, Andy immediately analyzed the data collected at the beginning of the study. He categorized the kinds of feelings students expressed about their peers with disabilities and arranged them on a continuum. Their attitudes ranged from "sad" and "pity" to "fine" and "like to help them." Next, he tallied the number of responses in each category. He found that the responses were more positive than negative—43 responses indicated that students were "fine/OK," "comfortable," or "happy" or would "like to help," while 31 responses indicated discomfort, sadness, or pity. But what he thought really interesting was that while all 30 students had classroom experiences with special needs students, only 13 chose to have lunch with a student with special needs and only 13 were interested in spending more time being a friend to a student with special needs. The remaining 17 did not want to develop such relationships.

He reread observations recorded in his log. What stood out was the absence of meaningful interactions between typical students and students with disabilities. He conducted a focus group interview with typical students who also indicated relatively positive feelings about students with disabilities but had relatively few social experiences with them. Putting this all together made him even more committed to taking some action. He wondered whether increasing social interaction outside the classroom would encourage the desire for friendships. Would typical students choose to have lunch with their peers with disabilities? He journaled regularly during the S.T.A.R. Club activities, noting that typical students began to show interest in their peers with disabilities. He repeated the final survey and found some heartening results.

The Democratic Classroom Study

Rosie did not wait until the end of student teaching to carefully examine her data. She planned each of her actions based on the unfolding story that her data opened to her. Right from the start of her study she recorded observations of her students' participation. Conferences with her mentor supported her hunch that only a few students participated in discussion. Then, in order to understand the student perspective on citizenship and what it entailed, she administered a Citizenship Survey. When she found that students thought that participation and knowledge of government were unimportant to citizenship, she planned activities to encourage collaborative and participatory work.

Another way she tracked student perceptions of community was through the Classroom Community Survey, which students took near the beginning and near the end of her student teaching. Analyzing the results of the "before" survey confirmed her hypothesis that fifth period had a lower sense of community than her other classes. Her teaching would have to address this problem. She continued to monitor her activities and carefully reflect on them throughout student teaching, verifying her own interpretations by consulting with her mentor, and her students. She kept in mind her goal of encouraging strong student-teacher collaboration and student-student collaboration as a means of creating a classroom community that would ultimately result in students showing more care and respect for one another.

In spite of her efforts, things seemed to be getting worse—lack of respect among students, particularly those in fifth period, seemed to be increasing rather than decreasing. One student's poetry reading taught the students (and Rosie) a lesson they would not soon forget.

Unraveling and Putting Together the Stories

Let's focus on Rosie's study to illustrate how interpretation works. As her study unfolded, Rosie noted several important events recorded in her journal that seemed to be directly related to her research question:

- Two groups of boys create classroom compacts that use put-downs about "dirties." When it comes time to select one of the pacts from those developed by all the groups, students did not vote for the ones developed by those boys.
- The democratic classroom survey reveals that fifth period is less collaborative and more disrespectful than the other periods.
- One of the "dirties" reads a powerful poem to class about an outcast who learns to be invisible. The class reacts with complete silence, and then breaks into applause: "Give her an 'A'"!

These are pieces of data that drew Rosie's attention and begged for reflection. Taken together, they became the *issue* that drove her to make sense of what was happening: As Rosie struggled to create a democratic environment for learning, some of her students were becoming tyrannical! To make sense of the irony of this situation, Rosie had relied on both her sense of intuition *and* her power of analytical and logical thinking. While logic would tell her that she was doing everything "right," at least according to what she was reading about classroom community, her intuition and the data told her that something was very amiss. Somehow her intentions were being subverted!

In some cases, we rely on our intuition totally, and bypass the logical part of our analytical brain to make immediate sense out of situations. Andy, for example, saw two cousins sitting next to each other in an inclusion, home economics class. One was a student with disabilities, and the other was not. The "typical" student did not even acknowledge his cousin's existence in spite of repeated attempts to make conversation! Andy *knew* that something was wrong. Analysis might uncover some details related to the relationship between these two cousins, but instinct says "something is amiss."

Interpretation is a process used to explain, to give meaning, to make sense of the many disparate events and ideas that we encounter as teachers. In some cases, we take data apart (analyze), put them back together in new ways (synthesize), and make assertions (theorize) that propel us to action, all the

185

while seeking verification. We proceed systematically, using our logical and analytical powers to make inferences and draw conclusions about what actions we should take. At other times, one instance serves to make its point to us—we need go no further to interpret what is going on and that something does or does not need to be done. Our common sense, experiences, insights, and intuition we hope, can come to our rescue. If we think critically *and* relax, the spaces between the logic of the stones beneath our feet might quietly fill with understanding. Taken together, logic and intuition and artistry can be brought together to help us to transform our classrooms and ourselves to the possibilities we imagine.

We visualize this transformative process of interpretation (and action) as an interactive one. (See Figure 13.1). We analyze and *intuit* to inform our actions. The analysis also helps us to synthesize—to get a better picture of the whole. We synthesize and go back to the parts to check out our hunches, and we create a whole upon which we can base our assertions, which leads to action, and so on.

In the remainder of the chapter, we will provide ideas and additional resources for analysis, interpretation, and verification of judgments made based on the data collected. There are many paths to take in this process. We will cover some commonly used ones.

Ongoing Interpretation

Interpretation (making sense of the data) is not a separate part of action research that comes at the end of a cycle. After all, as teachers, we constantly try to understand our students, their work, and their world *and* ourselves. Interpretation is an ongoing process that begins as soon as we decide to study our own practice. Thus it includes everything from making sense of baseline data we collect at the beginning of the study, to making sense of selected pieces of data even as we write up the report. The meaning we attach to the data depends on how we look at it—on our circumstances, on our motives and hopes, and on what we expect to see.

We have some suggestions for interpreting data *while* your study is in progress.

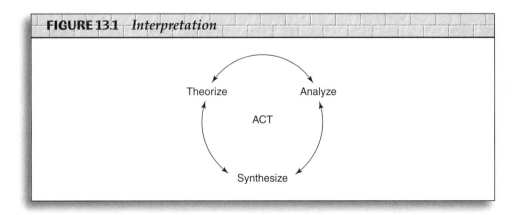

FIGURE 13.1 *Interpretation*

1. *Continually narrow the focus of your study.* Think of the narrowing process as a funnel—wide at the top and narrower as your study progresses. This process will also narrow the scope of the data you collect. For many of us, the action research process is simply one of focusing and narrowing until at the end of our study we are actually beginning to get a sense of what is important to study—and the cycle begins again. This may mean focusing on fewer students, or selecting only 3 of the 10 questions on a survey for analysis because they now seem the most important or relevant to your question.

   At the beginning of the study you had some broad questions that may change and develop as you learn more about your students. At first Rosie was interested in knowing how to create a democratic classroom. While this remained her general question, she began to look more carefully at how she could increase tolerance and respect among students. Her data led her to these new questions and issues. This process is called *progressive focusing.*

Scarecrow: That sounds too simple!

Authors: Yes, it is. Many, if not most times, we narrow and broaden back and forth many times in a study. The movement is not all in the narrowing direction.

2. *Use what you learn from your data to plan further data collection and action.* Ask yourself, What have I learned here that will help me and my students? How will I document what is happening next? Perhaps Rosie could focus her next observations on those students who are the most intolerant. Andy might spend more time observing those two cousins to learn more about the nature of their relationship. Jan and Terry might focus on their most successful group to learn what makes this group successful and use that new knowledge to help the less effective groups.

3. *Record your own thoughts and feelings.* To keep track of how you are thinking, write personal comments about methods, hunches, ideas that occur to you in your field notes, interview notes, on sticky pads that can be attached to student work, etc. When patterns seem to emerge, make note of them. You may want to label them O.C. (observer comments). For example, Rosie wrote in her personal journal:

   O.C.: I am beginning to think that I should have done the Classroom Compact at the beginning of our class rather than wait until the middle. It might have provided the kind of common commitment to one another and to learning that seems to be missing.

4. *Write analytic memos.* After several days or weeks of data collection, it may be useful to read through all the data you have collected and write a memo to yourself about what you see emerging as *patterns of behavior, words, key ideas, events.* Analytic memos are also a way to record *methodological dilemmas*—what to try next, given that the things already tried do not seem to be working, and *hunches* about what is happening. They can *remind* us of what we need to do next, based on what we have learned through our reflections. Perhaps we need

to read something about our topic, or talk to our critical colleagues or to a student's guidance counselor. It can remind us to look for something in our next observation, or to develop a particular idea or theme in our next journal entry. Shawn, for example, began to note changes in Jen that were separate from the research questions about her development as a speaker of English. Since Shawn was actively studying Korean culture, she realized Jen's behaviors were considered disrespectful in the home culture. It seemed that

---

FIGURE 13.2   *Analytic memo written by Rosie for her democratic classroom study*

Week 12

Analytic Memo

I was anxious to look at the results of the "after" Classroom Community Survey. I wanted to compare student responses to the "before" survey. I arranged the data in a chart so that I could look carefully at the questions that related to teacher-student collaboration (questions 1, 2, 3) and student-student collaboration (questions 4, 5). Here is my chart:

A comparison of means on the before and after Classroom Community Survey

Class periods	Question 1		Question 2		Question 3		Question 4		Question 5	
	Before	After	Before	After	Before	After	Before	After	Before	After
4th	3.2	3.5	2.7	3.7	3.6	4.0	1.9	2.5	3.8	3.5
5th	3.1	3.5	2.2	3.1	3.3	3.7	3.0	3.4	2.7	2.1
8th	3.0	3.6	2.5	3.5	3.3	3.7	3.0	3.4	3.0	2.7

What I noticed is that in all three classes in the six weeks between the first and second surveys, students sensed an increase in teacher-student collaboration as evidenced by responses to questions 1 (Students make decisions about what is going on), 2 (Teacher involves students in decision making), and 3 (Students in my class work together on solving problems). On the other hand, I noticed that there was an increase in disrespect in all classes and particularly in fifth-period, as evidenced by a decrease in the mean scores of students on questions related to student-student collaboration: questions 4 (A lot of students in my class like to put others down) and 5 (Students in my class treat each other with respect) where the higher the average, the less the respect. Something isn't working! I wonder what is going on? I suspected all along that my fifth-period class was not showing respect toward one another. When we did the classroom compact, the boys in those two groups made so many put-downs about the "dirties" that many of the students in class were visibly upset. Thank goodness the rest of the class had better sense and voted on a classroom compact that was more respectful of others. I am going to have to address respect and tolerance for others more seriously between now and the end of student teaching. I think I'll have them watch Rigolleto, so that they can explore the theme of tolerance. I may also give them time to work on a final project in which they can express their own ideas about democracy.

This is so discouraging. I wonder if I am cut out for teaching!

Jen was "testing" the limits and rules in her new surroundings. Shawn had to react to Jen's behavior as well.

Analytic memos are personal field notes to ourselves, helping us to notice things that we did not notice before. Written periodically during data collection, analytic memos can help us to look carefully at our data. They can also be incorporated into the final report. Here is an example of an analytic memo written by Rosie for her Democratic Classroom Study. (See Figure 13.2.)

5. *Make creative comparisons.* So often we become bogged down in the concrete particulars of our data that we cannot see the possibilities they hold for us. By asking ourselves, What is this similar to? or Is this idea like another concept that I am familiar with? we may unleash some powerful insights into our data. Mary Lou was stumped about how to think about a teacher in one of her studies. He seemed to have everything going for him, the right educational background, the right words to use in describing his classroom and students, . . . but something was not right. She thought to herself, What does he remind me of? And it came to her in an instant—a "tarnished spoon." By letting her mind range freely, Mary Lou came to have a clearer understanding of this teacher. After this flash she wrote about why the image fit so well. She included details and evidence which enabled her to create other visual images. With considerable talent, the teacher was, at the time, not able to shine, and only later realized how difficult a time his tarnished period had been.

6. *Visualize ideas.* If you like to doodle, you may be a natural at creating pictures that show relationships or organize ideas. Visual devices can be used anywhere during the action research process. Circles and arrows, lists, charts, graphs, diagrams, or even sketches of people or classroom space are ways to both break data down into parts and then put them back together.

7. *Check out your insights with participants.* What do they think about how you are interpreting the event or conversation? Are you on target or completely off-base?

To give you a concrete example of how Rosie's analysis proceeds while she is teaching and collecting data, we have included a table that shows what she planned to do week by week. (See Figure 13.3.)

We have summarized suggestions for ongoing data analysis in Stepping Stones 13.1.

Rosie constantly compared one set of data with another to make decisions about what to do next. When she found that things were not going as she had expected, she looked in different directions, especially in her own private reflections of experience. She examined her own assumptions about participation and the political process and began to reflect on her students' understandings of community.

Ongoing interpretation, exemplified by Rosie's thinking, relies on our ability to use three important research tools—comparing, asking questions, and speculating.

1. *Comparing.* We compare one piece of data to another. For example, "So many of the students in this morning class are saying the same thing as my afternoon class. Both classes are saying they just don't get the point I am trying to make!"

FIGURE 13.3 *Excerpts from the time line Rosie used in analyzing her data*

Week	Activity	Data Collection Strategy	Analysis
1	Collect baseline data about student perceptions of "citizenship."	Citizenship survey. Bi-weekly researcher journal.	Compute means. Discussion with mentor. Look for patterns in journal.
2	Read literature on collaboration. Conduct community-building exercises.	Informal interview with research adviser. Classroom Community Survey. Researcher journal. Student journal.	Discussion with action research group. Compute means. Read journals.
3–4	Bill of Rights project.	Student projects. Student journal. Researcher journal.	Use rubric to evaluate projects. Read journals. Write analytical memo.
12–13	Assess student collaboration. Classroom Compact.	Classroom Community Survey. Student compacts. Researcher journal. Student journal. What can we do to create a community?	Compute means and compare with "before" survey. Look for patterns in journals. Write analytical memo. Discuss patterns with mentor.
14–15	Personal values project.	Student projects and presentations. Researcher journal. Student journal.	Use rubric to evaluate a project. Analytical memo.

2. *Asking questions.* As we compare, we ask questions of the data, look for key ideas, categories, issues and patterns of behavior, thinking, and ideas. For example, "Why can't the students in my comparison group answer a simple question, Who is your favorite author? Kids in the other class did."

3. *Speculating.* We make educated guesses about what might be happening, basing those guesses on hunches, critical self-reflection, and dialogue with others. We think critically about what we have in front of us and what we still need to know. We conjecture. For example, Wendy asked students in different settings, "What was an assignment the teacher gave from which you learned the most? The least?" Wendy noted that with the exception of students from a small island in an English-speaking country, most students responded that

STEPPING STONES 13.1

Ongoing Data Analysis

1. Narrow the focus of your study as needed.
2. Use what you learn from your data to plan further data collection and action.
3. Record your thoughts and feelings.
4. Write analytic memos.
5. Make creative comparisons with data.
6. Visualize.
7. Check out your insights with participants.

they learned when they had choices. The students from the island were all unable or unwilling to answer the question. Wendy then had to speculate about why. Was the phrasing of the question unclear? Did these students think that they were being asked to critique their teacher and their school? And if so, were they unable for some reason to do this? Another word for this process of conjecturing is *hypothesizing*. Hypotheses are formed from careful analysis *and* from making creative leaps. We talk more about that later.

We will now go into greater detail about the process of *interpretation—analysis, synthesis,* and *theorizing* which allows us to make *assertions*—that helps us to make decisions that are not only logical and intuitive and artistic, but also ethical in their commitments to creating a just and caring environment for learning. While we present it as a linear process, it is, in fact, cyclical, interactive, and spontaneous, as we will shortly see.

Analysis

Analysis means taking things apart. We use analysis to "get it right" (Wolcott, 1994). To get it right, we carefully look at data, identify the parts, and develop them. But getting it right also means looking for the holes, the patterns, the secrets, the mysteries, for what is in between the stones, the hidden assumptions, the disguises that we find when we follow the path that wanders off almost silently into the forest where the Yellow Brick Road disappears. It takes courage to work in a systematic, intuitive, and creative way with existing data and data that have not yet been mined, working with them in such a way that they yield insights that are dependable, accurate, reliable, *and* irrationally right!

For example, Meridith, a student teacher interested in how her "reluctant" readers would respond to young adult literature, was disturbed by responses to *The House on Mango Street* by Sandra Cisneros (1991), a story narrated by a young Latino girl, alienated from U.S. culture. Comments such as "Yeah, and they really are that way—those Spics" confirmed her suspicion that her students were being racist. When students sneered and called her a feminist when she asked them to consider the portrayal and treatment of Hispanic women, her observation that they were being sexist was confirmed. Comments such as "I hate this book!" and "This is stupid!" made her question her original hunch about the potential of young adult literature to turn on these kids to reading. Their comments left her discouraged that their racism and sexism would interfere with their experience with young adult literature. Had she ended her inquiry at this point, it is easy to see the conclusions she would have drawn about her students and the potential of young adult literature. But she noted the silence of the female students. When she asked students to write down their reactions to the novel, the female students resonated with the perspective of the female protagonist. Perhaps their silence was the result of enculturation into a world of male "voices."

The tools we present for data analysis will help us to get at the systematic, the intuitive, and the creative aspects of data. While we present them in a numerical order, actual analysis may not be so orderly and discrete.

1. *Get ready.* Assemble the data informally and conduct an inventory: What data do you have? (Researcher log, diary, student journal, student work, interviews, questionnaires, analytical memo.) Is it complete? Are there missing responses on some surveys? If it is too late to have students fill in missing data, you will have to adjust your calculation to take this into account. Is everything labeled and dated? Is there some order to the piles, folders, index cards, etc.? For example, are all the interviews together, either on successive word processing files or in a folder or binder with pages numbered? Likewise, is student work organized in some way that makes sense to you?

   If you are working with numbers, such as calculating averages to compare student scores on different surveys, tests, or rubrics, now is the time to do some initial processing. Although much of what you want to do can be done manually or with a calculator, you may want to explore the option of using a spreadsheet, which is often part of a software package that came with your computer. Either way, you will be "entering your data" into some sort of matrix or table and calculating means, percentages, or in some cases correlations, making the data ready for you to examine more closely to see what they tell you. We have included examples or graphs and simple calculations of means, median, and mode in Appendix B.

   Remind yourself of what you are going to look for in the data: What is the research question? What issues concern you? What hunches do you have about what you might find? Keep your eyes and mind open to seeing things that you do *not* expect to find. Find a comfortable, quiet place and some uninterrupted time when you can spread out the data in front of you. Take a deep breath and . . .

2. *Read and reread.* Immerse yourself in your data. What is going on here? Who? When? Where? How much? Why? What is *not* going on here? What jumps out

at you by its presence? Or by its absence? In wide margins of your notes or on adhesive note paper, write down your impressions, your questions, your speculations. Read for evidence related to your question and your issues.

Andy reads his own journal entries and researcher log, looking for evidence of improved student attitudes toward children with disabilities, examining observations of student body language and communication, and reflecting on what others have observed as well. What strikes him, even shocks him, is the absence of interaction. Rosie looks for evidence of community—the kind of community that she wants to see—in exchanges between students and between students and herself, in survey responses, in comments made by her mentor. What angers her is the lack of peer respect. In searching for ways to include Jen in the classroom, Shawn looks for evidence of language development and notices huge leaps. Jan and Terry, wanting to create a holistic literacy learning environment, look through student journals and survey results for evidence of reading development related to literature circles; and they begin to notice a move toward critical thinking and more positive attitudes toward reading.

When reading over surveys, questionnaires, or interviews, we often find that some questions are more relevant and illuminating than others. Since we cast a wide net at the beginning of a study, we may want to later select only those questions for analysis that now seem important. Here is an example of what one action researcher did. On a survey about reading habits and preferences, one pair of researchers asked students whether they visit their neighborhood library. After they read the set of responses, it was clear that many students were unfamiliar with their public library. On further thought, the researchers realized that the neighborhood where the respondents lived was very far from a library branch and that most families in this neighborhood had limited access to cars. This question, then, did not reflect anything that the child as a developing reader could control. The researchers decided against using it in their analysis. On the other hand, you may find that responses to one or two questions offer very important clues—analyzing those questions, while keeping the others in the back of your mind, may lead to some important insights. One researcher developed a student attitude instrument with 10 questions and discovered that one question was so informative that its response would predict the results of the rest of the questions. A one-question instrument would have been just as valuable. Sometimes we word questions awkwardly or unclearly. It is not surprising that these questions later prove of little value to us, serving to remind us of the importance of trying out questions on a small sample of students before giving them to the entire class.

Finally, make time to walk away from the data, to talk them over with others. To sleep on them—maybe even to dream about them! And then . . .

3. *Look for the parts.* Skimming the data, look for words, phrases, behaviors, ways of thinking, events that seem to repeat themselves. Look for parts related to the issues and questions that most concern you in this study. Look for things that jump out to you as well as the subtleties. Look for patterns, or lack of them.

a. Grouping these ideas together is a process of *categorizing*. Categories can be ideas, issues, themes, dilemmas. Make a list of these categories. Open a file in your computer for each of those categories, and write about each. Include quotes, descriptions, critical incidents, and your own thoughts. As your study continues, look for data to add to each file. (Files can be in your computer, on index cards, in your journal, wherever it makes sense to you.) Also, be open to the possibility that the categories (like your questions) may change. While it is preferable to develop your own categories so that they accurately reflect what is happening in your situation, action researchers sometimes use categories developed by other researchers or theorists. Here are some examples of both kinds of categories from our case studies. (See Figure 13.4.)

In some studies the categories are more like issues or dilemmas or tensions. In a study that Joanne conducted with her graduate students, she felt student resistance to course content was a major issue. She decided to look for the points of resistance to understand the dynamics of power that were in play in her classroom. The forms of resistance she noted are listed in Figure 13.5.

FIGURE 13.4   *Categories developed by Andy, Shawn, Jan, and Terry*

Andy's categories, developed from the focus group interviews, describing student attitudes toward children with disabilities (the S.T.A.R. Club Study).

- Comfortable
- Empathic
- Uneasy

Shawn's categories describing Jen's progress (helping Jen learn English as a second language):

- Vocabulary
- Word recognition
- Written expression
- Social adjustment

Jan and Terry selected these categories from Daniels (1994) to describe reader progress (the Literature Circle's Study):

D/C   Drawing conclusions

P   Predicting

S   Summarizing

E   Enthusiasm

Q   Questioning

C   Connecting

I   Illustrating

In another study, this time a study of the first year of a newly formed professional development middle school, Joanne and her teacher-researcher colleagues noted several dilemmas in their study of multiple perceptions of the new school. (See Figure 13.6.)

This is how the process of categorizing worked for one action researcher. Jennifer made audiotapes of oral discussion at each table in her elementary classroom where literature groups were meeting. She listened to the tapes every night on her commute home. After playing each tape several times, she began to invent labels to express what was taking place in those discussions. With her list of labels, she relistened to the tapes and coded each for the type of response and the frequency of each type of response.

Certain discussions were harder to code than others, so she asked a critical colleague to listen to them. This collaborative process helped. Jennifer ended up with 12 categories of oral responses from simple ones like *predicting* what would happen next in the story or *clarifying* story

---

FIGURE 13.5   *Forms of resistance to power*

- Emotional resistance to power—doctoral students reacted strongly (both favorably and unfavorably) when they were asked to critique their own fields of inquiry because they are so committed to them.

- Conceptual resistance to power—doctoral students found it difficult to make assertions about power relations in their own fields.

- Political resistance to power—doctoral students openly critiqued the power vested in the position of professors who claimed to have the authority of knowledge in their respective fields.

- Moral resistance to power—doctoral students questioned the moral authority of Foucault's challenge to the existence of absolutes or moral truths.

- Ethical resistance to power—doctoral students felt that studying Foucault's notions of power made them question the ethics of things that they had previously found acceptable. This questioning made them uncomfortable.

FIGURE 13.6   *Dilemmas faced by teachers, students, parents and other school professionals in a newly formed professional development middle school*

- The dilemma of discipline: We want students to be self-directed, and we want to impose discipline.

- The dilemma of involvement: We want involvement, but we are frustrated by it.

- The dilemma of the orderly school: The ideal school is both orderly and caring.

details to more sophisticated ones such as *judging character's actions* and even *judging author's choices and writing.*

The categories that emerge often come from the theoretical perspectives of the researcher. A constructivist-oriented researcher will most likely develop a different set of categories than a behaviorist-oriented researcher. Joanne's categories, for example, related to resistance, emerged in a context of a class that was studying power and its effect on teachers and teaching.

We find that for beginning researchers, it is often helpful to have a set of *possible* ways to categorize data. The following "prompts" are adapted from Bogdan and Biklen (1992). (See Figure 13.7.)

To make it easy to locate these categories in the data, researchers devise different ways of organizing and coding their data:

- Color-code each category with a different color (highlight positive responses with green, etc.).
- Develop a code for each category through numbers, symbols, abbreviations, letters, etc. For example, P indicates the reading strategy of *predicting;* the computer symbol :-) indicates a positive attitude toward children with disabilities.
- Sort data into piles, into file folders, into boxes, into word processing files.
- Using the search function in a word processor, retrieve words that relate to the concept that is emerging. Or you might want to use the word count available when you do a spell check. There are many data analysis software packages on the market, some fairly sophisticated and probably not necessary for the typical teacher researcher. (If you enjoy making your study more systematic, however, you might want to explore a software package

---

FIGURE 13.7 *"Prompts" for categorizing data*

- *Setting* includes school demographics, location, per-pupil expenditure, classroom arrangement, and classroom environment.

- *Definitions* include how students and teachers define key concepts such as *discipline, engagement,* or *good student* and what political, religious, socioeconomic orientation shapes their perspective.

- *Rules and norms*—the ways in which things are routinely done, such as reviewing math homework at the beginning of each class—are often expressions of underlying rules, values, and beliefs.

- *Roles and relationships*—roles such as mother, caretaker, and police officer and relationships such as mother-child, nurse-patient, police officer-criminal, leader-follower, and boss-worker—often emerge as important ways to understand how people do or do not see themselves.

- *Processes*—time periods, steps, chronology, turning points, benchmarks, transitions—are ways to organize data to show changes and growth.

Source: Adapted from Bogdan and Biklen (1992).

called Ethnograph or one called N.U.D.I.S.T., which allow you to code text. For example, you might want to type all your own journal entries and format them with numbered lines that tally any part of or all the categories.)

b. The next task is to see whether the *categories selected really fit the data.* Does the label need to be changed to more adequately and powerfully reflect what we are finding in our data? Are categories overlapping, so that a list of 10 categories might be reduced to 5?

c. We also want to *develop these categories* by defining them. Definitions provide specificity about the category. For example, Shawn sees Jen's *social adjustment* as *participation* which included *speaking* in discussions, *sharing* her work with other children, and *volunteering* to take a nonspeaking part in a play. He also notes that sometimes she participates in a *quiet* and *shy* way and sometimes in a more *assertive* way. These italicized words are descriptors of what it means to "adjust socially."

Developing and understanding the categories is a major task of analysis. And researchers often find useful ways of organizing their work to facilitate the development process. Jan and Terry did exactly that. After combing through student responses for categories, they developed a table and tallied the number of times they saw evidence of predicting, summarizing, etc., in student journal entries. Figure 13.8 presents the analysis of one student's journal entries. The tally sheets on Sam, one of the focus students, revealed that as time went on, he moved past the simpler skill of summarizing to skills such as connecting and questioning, skills associated with critical thinking. But using a table to tally the recurrence of a particular skill or concept is only one way to organize and use categories. See Appendix B for a variety of visual displays.

Synthesis

Synthesis is the process of combining parts to make a whole. Once we have taken things apart in our analysis, we need to put them back together and ask ourselves, How do the parts relate to one another?

Synthesis is a creative process. In fact, one expert on creativity, Silvano Areti (1976), calls creativity the *magic synthesis.* While it might sound as if you simply take all your data apart and make sense of the parts (analysis), and then make sense of the whole by reassembling the parts and putting them all back together (synthesis), that isn't what really happens. We have separated the two processes because we feel it will be easier to understand them this way.

Dorothy: So what really happens?

Authors: They work together. As you take something apart, you see possibilities—you create connections and integrate things in your head.

Dorothy: That's the Aha! So this is how that works!

Authors: Yes. Analysis and synthesis are constantly working together. And, as in most of the processes taking place in our heads, we are not normally aware that they are taking place.

FIGURE 13.8 *Analysis of Sam's student response journal entries following literature circle discussion*

D/C = Drawing conclusions   P = Predicting   S = Summarizing
Q = Questioning   C = Connecting   I = Illustrating   E = Enthusiasm

Date	Words	D/C	P	S	Q	C	I	E
8/31	27		|	|		|		|
9/18	50		||	|		|		
9/23	13	|						
9/24	56	|				||		|
9/25	41		||			|		
9/26	17	|		|				
9/28	30			|	|			|
10/1	49				|||||			
10/2	61		||	||				
10/3	28		||					
10/28	52		|	|		|		
10/29	67	||		||				|
10/30	61	|	|	||				
11/4	38	|	|			|		
11/5	32		|	|		|		
11/6	49		||	||				
11/7	43			||		|		
11/11	56			|		||		
11/12	78	|		||		||		|
11/13	84			|	||	|||		
11/14	64	|			|||	|		|
11/15	32	|			|			|
Total		10	15	20	12	17	0	7

Dorothy: This may be pushing it a bit, but when you said that, I got a picture in my head of a person being taught to breathe by only exhaling!

Authors: That's an interesting picture. In a way, taking in data is like inhaling. And analysis and syntheses are much like exhaling. For the uninitiated, what takes place between the two parts of breathing is magic! In our case studies we got a good look at some of the parts that were analyzed in different studies, and as we continue, we will see what our scholars make of these—the products of their synthesizing.

Dorothy: And most important of all—we will do some magic synthesizing ourselves!

Authors: That you will. We will talk more about that in the next chapter when we talk about narratives. Narratives are the product of synthesizing—you synthesize as you write. For now, let's look at how we can encourage synthesis and holistic thinking.

1. *Find patterns.* Learning is change as a result of experience. Finding patterns in experience facilitates learning. Noticing patterns in experience, from the simplest to the most complex, enables us to draw our data together in new ways. As researchers, we keep our questions and issues in mind and look for the ways in which the parts relate to one another. Does one part always occur when another part occurs? Does one part happen more often than others? Does each part happen simultaneously? What are the conditions under which this or that happens? What is the role of power? What happens when the data are "disaggregated" by gender, race, ethnicity, ability, social class, achievement level, time, or age? As action researchers, we look for changes in thinking, behavior, feelings—for developments in ourselves and our students—that are consequences of our actions.

   To determine whether changes were occurring in student collaboration, Rosie arrayed the "before" and "after" survey data in a table. In her analytic memo shown earlier, you can see how she displayed these data. Were students becoming collaborative? Was one class more collaborative than another? If so, in what ways? When examining her own journal, she looked for clues to her own frustration: What is my contribution to the disrespect my students show toward one another?

   Andy noted that instances of uneasiness decreased over the course of the year. Neutral and negative attitudes were replaced by more positive, helpful attitudes in which typical students expressed interest in becoming more engaged with their peers with disabilities. She asked, When did this occur? And she noted that after S.T.A.R. Club activities had been going on for some time, typical students asked her for information about students with disabilities. They began to sit together at lunchtime.

   Shawn noted that Jen gradually changed from being a shy, reserved, and physically passive student to one who volunteered to participate in class. Shawn's analysis of data found that this change happened in a context of peer support. Jan and Terry noted that over time, students in the literature circles summarized ideas less and moved to more substantive responses including raising questions, judging characters, evaluating the author's style, and relating events and actions to their own lives. These teachers knew from their literature review that these changes are associated with increased critical thinking.

   We may want to look at the conditions and contexts surrounding these thoughts, behaviors, and feelings—these patterns. We can do this by asking questions of our data. What are possible causes? What are possible consequences?

We most often think of patterns in terms of frequency. How many times do students participate, or look bored, or sign books out of the library, or complete their homework, or score an A on a test? But this is only one type of pattern. In Figure 13.9 we illustrate the rich list of possible patterns that can be found in data and examples of each. We have adapted this from David Tripp's SCOPE Program (1997).

Because frequency of occurrence is an often used and important pattern, we have included information about how to calculate the mean, median, and mode in Appendix B along with an example of how to construct a means table. Each pattern that we notice becomes the basis for making sense of the data. However, many relationships are unimportant, and we need not follow up on them. Key questions to ask about any pattern are, So what? and What does this mean?

2. *Look for confirming and disconfirming data.* While we have made the point that it is important to continually look for evidence in the data that confirms our hunches about patterns we see emerging, we must also look for disconfirming evidence—evidence that does not fit into our emerging understanding of what is going on. Disconfirming data can be *very important* to understanding what is going on. Joy, a shy, attentive, gentle, and generally slow in movement and response second grader was out of character on Thursdays. Mary Lou, who was one of the teachers, recorded in her notes that instead of taking care of the younger children in the class, Joy would become bossy and agitated. When exploring this further, Mary Lou discovered that on Wednesday evenings, the entire family went to a long church service—Joy would not get to bed until after 11:00 p.m. When Mary Lou shared with Joy's parents what was happening on Thursdays, the parents made arrangements to get Joy home earlier from the church service. We may find important secrets in those instances that just don't seem to fit into the dominant pattern. In this case, a pattern in Joy's classroom behavior was disrupted, and through data collection and analysis, another pattern was noted—Thursdays!

Theorizing and Making Assertions

So what? What do I make of all this? What does it mean in light of my original question and my new question? What does it mean in the context of my study? How do I explain the patterns? What do others make of all this? What assertions can I make based on what I have learned? These questions we can ask when we are theorizing about our teaching.

Assertions can be statements that direct action. When Rosie says, "My own experiences in politics and my understanding of the Bill of Rights should have warned me that a democracy that relies too heavily on rights cannot create a safe community." She is making an assertion. It is not new knowledge, but knowledge that is tacit and given new meaning in the context of her teaching. The potential for her teaching is clear—emphasize both rights and responsibilities.

FIGURE 13.9 *Patterns in data*

Patterns	Questions	Examples
Frequencies	How often does this occur? How often does "this" occur in comparison to "that"? Does it occur constantly and evenly? Does it occur periodically and in waves?	How often do children visit book corner during free-choice playtime? How may French vocabulary words taught in class appear in the journal writing of French I students? How often do girls and boys seek help during science lab?
Times	What things occur simultaneously? Do the similar things occur during similar periods, or at similar times of the lesson, day, week, year? What things occur in a sequence?	Who arrives first in class each day and who leaves last? During what time during the lesson do my students seem most engaged?
Spaces	How are things connected in space? Close or distant? Above or below? Beside or opposite? Crossing or parallel? Inside or outside? On or off? Over or under?	Where do the boys sit in class? The girls? The academically successful students? The academically unsuccessful students? Who stays inside for lunch? How does room arrangement enhance or frustrate learning?
Interactions	What is this acting on? What is this reacting to? Who is interacting with whom?	To what are students responding when I ask them to write a journal entry about what we have learned today? Do they respond to what they think I want to hear, or to what they are reading? Or to something else?
Causes	What are the possible causes of this? What does this cause?	Why do some students do better on tests when they study in groups and others do not? What are some of the possible causes of student misbehavior in my classroom?
Effects	Is the effect of this to increase or decrease that? To balance or unbalance that? To change or maintain that?	What are the effects of student participation in school decision making on their sense of autonomy? What are the effects of interdisciplinary teaming on students' sense of belonging?
Conditions	Is this a necessary condition for that to happen as it does? Under what circumstances does this occur?	What kinds of control do adolescents need over their environment to feel that their work is meaningful? What are the effects on children, if any, when the teacher engages in sustained silent reading with them? When black, white, and Latino middle school students participate in a multicultural awareness workshop, what are the effects on the ways they socialize in and out of school?
Speeds	Does this happen as fast as that?	Do children who are taught holistically develop at the same speed on reading tests as those taught with phonics only? Does one method of word processing instruction produce faster typists than others?

Assertions can also be claims to new knowledge. Andy's concluding remarks exemplify this: "My original impressions about the "typical" student and their interest in students in special classes were erroneous. These middle school students had mostly positive attitudes about those with disabilities. The problem was that they no longer had the same opportunities to socialize as they did in the elementary classroom." In each case, assertions are made with forcefulness and understanding.

Our assertions are often based less on recently acquired facts than on our own personal frameworks of seeing the world. Rosie is immersed in political science and critical theory. Andy's thinking is shaped by experience as an elementary school teacher where inclusion worked by virtue of the extended time students spent together in self-contained classrooms. Shawn, Jan, and Terry are enrolled in a master's degree program which describes itself as constructivist. Students are encouraged to be change agents, creating classrooms that are more holistic and constructivist in their orientation. Rethinking our personal frameworks can be accomplished with the help of our friends.

The point of interpretation is to generate many possible hypotheses. The richer the range of possibilities, the more complete the interpretation can be. Here are some examples of ways to generate multiple hypotheses to stretch your thinking.

Assume the *role* of an interested party. How might a frustrated parent view the patterns? A struggling student? An accountability-minded principal? A budget-minded community member? A contentious colleague? A novice? An expert? We are trying to stretch our thinking, to move away from our taken-for-granted view of ourselves, our students, and our situation by taking the perspective of someone else. The point is to "take the attitude of the other" (Mead, 1934) and develop empathy for that person's position. Our assertions need to be made in interaction with others. Interpretation is thus a "catalyst for mutuality and reciprocity" (Brennan and Noffke, 1997, p. 25).

There are times when our theorizing and assertions are blocked. We have too much data. We are too close to the situation. We have too much conflicting information. At times like this, it might be best to stand back, relax, and allow the spaces between these facts to open up to our creative powers. Metaphorical thinking is a valuable tool. How are these students' lives like a tapestry? How is my classroom like music?

Theorizing also draws ideas from the larger body of literature and the public theories that have been developed by researchers and thinkers relevant to your field of inquiry. In this way we join an ongoing community of scholars which, over time, adds new ideas and modifies existing theories.

And finally, assertions are made in a context. We are not generalizing to all students, or all teachers, or all classrooms. Rather, we are making statements that seem to apply in our own situations. Andy's assertion that inclusion is not working is made in the context of a middle school in which students move from class to class, as opposed to an elementary school in which students become more connected to one another in the self-contained classroom.

The process of analysis, synthesis, and making assertions is illustrated by the work of Mary Schwartz, a fifth- and sixth-grade teacher who decided to invite parents and members of the community to present their ideas at a math workshop. She showed students the connection between classroom math and the real world by presenting their ideas. Part of the data collection was a letter students were asked to write, telling Mary how they felt about the math workshop. To analyze the data, she first read over all the letters, noting the ideas that continually appeared: *relevance, enjoy, motivation, organized, confidence,* and the role of the *teacher.* She then reread the student letters and wrote codes in the margins (R for relevance, E for enjoy, M for motivation, O for organized, C for confidence, and T for teacher). See Figure 13.10.

Next, she opened files in her word processor for each of the categories and added the words or phrases from each student letter that fit into that category. See Figure 13.11.

Based on this analysis, she created a concept map that synthesized the emerging connections between the categories: When students see the relevance of math in everyday life, their confidence seems to grow. See Figure 13.12.

With this assertion about the relationship between the categories, she wrote assertions about each individual category and developed each assertion with student quotes to illustrate her points. She incorporated the resulting paragraphs into the section of her report called "What have I learned?" For an example, see Figure 13.13.

FIGURE 13.10 *Coding data*

Dear Mrs. Schwartz,

Thank you for creating the Math workshop. I thought it was pretty cool. I learned a lot about math from Mrs. Lungu, Mr. Patrick, Mr Zizzo, and

(R) Mr. Peaslee. I didn't know that a lot of jobs use math. I liked the math

(E) workshop because it was exciting and I learned something at the same time. I learned chemistry, (I didn't know it involved science) sports statistics, how Mr. Peaslee uses math to help people that have an injury, and how math is used in our culture. This was a great idea because it also shows how important math is in the world. I think this

(M) helped me to love math more than before!!! I learned so many new and cools things from these parents. I hope we can do this next year.

(T) Thanks Mrs. Schwartz and parents for making math fun.

From your student,

Nadine Masagara ☺

FIGURE 13.11 *Categories of student responses to the math workshop*

Relevance	Enjoy/fun	Motivation	Confidence	Important role of teacher
"How Mr. Peaslee used math to help people with a sports injury."	"It has been the most fun thing in school."	"I want to get a good job using math."	"I now know I can get it [math]."	"When teacher is motivated and excited, it spills over to students."
"I realize I need math no matter what I do."	"I liked the math workshop because it was exciting and I learned something at the same time."	"I think this helped me to love math more than before!!!"	"I feel stronger in practicing my math."	"You make it fun."
"I do math around the house."		"I will put more effort into math."	"I know how to learn."	"You show us the relevance of math."
"I used to not care, but now I see the impact on people's lives."		"I want to be a really good student."		

FIGURE 13.12 *Synthesizing and showing relationships*

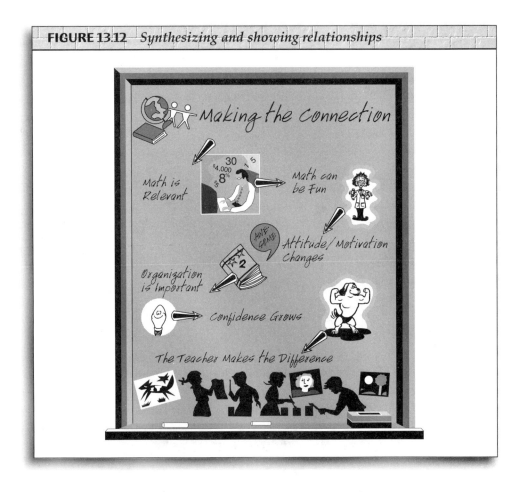

FIGURE 13.13   *Developing the category of relevance for the written report*
Relevance
I had hoped that the Real World Math Workshops would help the students see the relevance of their classroom math. The student letters evaluating the workshops revealed that the students had indeed made the connection. Their comments included phrases like "I realize I need math, no matter what I want to do" and "I used to not care, but now I see the impact on people's lives." They also said, "I know how grownups use it," particularly "how Mr. Peaslee used math to help people with a sports injury." "It is something more than what we do in school." "I do math around the house!" One fifth grader said that now when her family goes to dinner and to the movies, she calculates how much it will cost for the family. These sample comments show that students now recognize the importance of math in their daily lives.

Verification

Dorothy: But how do we know if we have gotten it right?

Authors: Now *that* is a very good question. We have tried to show how interpretation is a systematic, intuitive, artistic (playfully so, we hope), and ethical process. And if that sounds a bit contradictory, you will find our discussion of what constitutes "right" even more paradoxical!

Dorothy: Here we go again!

Authors: How do we ensure that the judgments we make (based on the data we have collected, our experience, and our intuition) will lead to action that is "right"? For action researchers, *right* has a special meaning. As you may recall, we defined action research as an ethical commitment to improving society (that is, become more just), improving ourselves (that we may become more conscious of our responsibility as members of a democratic society), and ultimately improving our lives together (building community).

When Andy interprets the indifference of regular education students toward special education students as a result of lack of positive interaction rather than a lack of caring, his interpretation is based on carefully collected data and a growing body of literature on inclusion. Rosie's interpretation of the growing disrespect among students (in spite of her direct actions to create harmony and respect) is placed in a larger context of political life. She recalls from her own studies that "a democracy that relies too heavily on rights cannot create a safe community." Her self-reflections lead her to understand how she herself is involved in creating conditions that undermined her teaching goals. Blame, prejudice, anger at students, and a desire to be a "savior" were feelings she sought to temper with empathy, equanimity, understanding, and acceptance of her own limitations as a person and teacher. Rosie's interpretations are thus made within her multiple commitments to justice, self, and community.

As action researchers, we want to verify that our professional judgments are trustworthy, credible, respectful, and reflective of our values. There are several aspects of verification that we might consider:

1. Our judgments are made from a particular standpoint. We are environmentalists, liberals, feminists, conservatives, critical thinkers. Understanding and clarifying our positions and values is important information to share with others. Carspecken in his book *Critical Ethnography in Educational Research* (1996) argues that *all* research is political because "all researchers seek some form of self-empowerment through their work, just as all people in everyday settings seek recognition and dignity" (p. 170). He goes on to say that all research claims are made in complex social and cultural situations in which power relations are naturally present. Critical researchers argue that the more we reduce power differences so that participants have an equal "say" with researchers, the closer we come to making valid statements. The action orientation of critical researchers is not, however, without pain. By opening up the research process in a way that gives equal say to all participants, we open ourselves to being "wounded" (McLaren, 1992). Rosie can certainly attest to that, as can any teacher-researcher who really listens to students. We can be hurt by student responses. But by being open to our students through our commitment to equity, we (and our students) may grow personally and professionally.

2. Critical researchers also argue that validity and truthfulness lie within consensus among participants. Stringer (1996) reminds us that "we are not looking for the 'best' or most 'correct' explanation, but one that makes sense or can be accommodated by all of the stakeholders" (p. 93). From this perspective, how groups come to verify particular data as evidence is more important than overcoming the "threats" to validity, such as adequate sample size, randomization, history and maturation. For teacher action researchers, then, claims of "truth" are developed and tested within a group. Using this line of thinking, winning broad consent may allow us to generalize.

3. To find the truth, we need to seek out the voices of our participants, and ensure that even the most quiet or most contrary will be heard.

4. Self-reflection and self-awareness are an integral part of making claims to knowledge. As we try to transform our classrooms, we also need to become aware of ways in which we need to transform ourselves.

5. Reciprocity in relationships characterized by mutual trust, caring, and awareness will help us to shape judgments respectful of others involved in and represented in our research.

6. Commitment to justice, respect, and the dignity of our participants and a desire to improve the lives of our students will influence our interpretations and claims to knowledge.

Lincoln (1997, p. 66) says that making quality judgments is about "how we can trust each other and the things we write, and how we can translate our inquiries into meaningful, purposeful individual and collective social action. The image of a triangle is offered by interpretive researchers as a means to get closer to a truth. We build triangulation into our studies by using multiple sources of data, multiple methods, even multiple theories to develop diverse perspectives. If and when these perspectives converge (and sometimes the points of view that are brought to a study are vastly different), we are encouraged to believe that the *findings* of a study are credible and trustworthy. But can we be sure that three different perspectives will find a fixed point on the horizon in the same way that sailors use the stars to triangulate their location?

Truth is elusive. What is right in one context may be wrong in another. We have found that Richardson's (1998) image of the crystal to be a more robust way to approach the world. Rather than a three-sided, fixed triangle, a crystal is multidimensional and changeable. It reflects the external world, but it also refracts within itself, "creating different colors, patterns, arrays" as it casts off light in different directions. "What we see depends on our angle of repose" (p. 358). The image of the crystal breaks down the notion of validity as the search for a single or ultimate truth. It reflects the possibility that there is no single truth and that the data we study (such as writing, oral communication, body language, photographs, drawings, music) have multiple meanings and validity. Rather than finding the complete truth, we find that truth is partial and culturally constructed. And although we feel that our knowledge is growing because of the complexity we begin to see, we are left with doubts about what we know.

Dorothy: Those doubts, the lack of certainty about where we are headed and what we will find, have made us less surefooted than we had hoped. Yet as our path veers off and we meander with hesitation into the forest, we have found some wonderful and terrifying surprises!

Authors: There are several methods that action researchers use to verify the claims they make. The methods we suggest aim for trustworthiness, credibility, and respectfulness. Here are some suggestions for maintaining veracity in the inferences we make from our data:

1. *Make your standpoint clear,* to the extent that you are able. Let others know your values and positions on relevant topics.
2. *Use multiple perspectives* of various people, theories, and methods. They offer a rich array of possible ways to transform and crystallize data into evidence related to our questions. There are several ways to gain these multiple perspectives:
   - *Triangulation and crystallization*—of people, methods, theories—is a way to cross-check data sources and open up, for argumentation, the veracity of possible interpretations. To triangulate with people, we might select students, a colleague, and a mentor to observe our classrooms and provide feedback. To triangulate with methods, we might use observations,

interviews, and documents produced by others. To triangulate with theories, we might approach the data we have analyzed from the perspective of a developmentalist, a behaviorist, a constructivist, or a critical theorist. While triangulation suggests three sources of data, two or more than three might be appropriate. The concept of crystallization suggests that using multiple sources is not a search for truth, but rather a search for clarity on the perspective we each bring to data and its analysis.

- *Revisiting data*—by oneself or with a group—can open up possibilities of uncovering meanings that did not appear the first time around. Sometimes we are too close to our situations to stand back from data; we can't see the forest for the trees. But revisiting data, a week, a month, even a year later, may help us see things in a new light. Focus group interviews or informal group discussions with colleagues or other interested stakeholders may open up the data to the "mind-constructions" (Brennan and Noffke, 1997, p. 39) of others.

- *Member checking*—means taking data or interpretations back to the people most affected by it to ascertain their perspectives on what you have found. It is a valuable way to gain understanding, clarity—and veracity. Member checking can point out potentially valuable omissions or errors. It can also send the researcher back into the forest to rethink the data, or the research question that prompted the study. Member checking serves to democratize the research process by equalizing power relations between researcher and participants; it values the perspectives of others. Member checking can be accomplished through an interview or a discussion or by simply writing up what you have learned and giving it to participants to read. This can take courage. What happens if a student disagrees with an action researcher's interpretation of the data? Such disagreement can lead to a productive discussion and to mutuality. By including both interpretations, the reader or audience members can make sense of both perspectives.

3. *Applying indicators* to the data can add legitimacy to the interpretation. Indicators are criteria that can be used to judge the quality, or worth, or adequacy, or completeness, of data and interpretations. Involve community (students, parents, professional groups) in developing indicators that will be applied. For example, Trish wanted to document students' problem-solving skills over time, so she developed a list of indicators of what a good problem solver actually does. The list included exploration of the problem situation before writing a problem statement and willingness to generate alternative strategies for addressing the problem. Based on these indicators, she then developed a rubric to study a series of four problems that students were given over the course of the semester. In addition to researcher-developed indicators, action researchers may choose to use externally derived indicators. Standards and rubrics developed by testing companies, professional teaching associations such as the National Council of Teachers

of English, and state or provincial Departments of Education provide indicators for accountability. Teachers often use external indicators as one *source* for their own personally developed list.

4. *Provide raw data* so that readers can make their own interpretations.

5. *Write descriptively* so that the reader can imagine what you saw or heard or felt or smelled. When readers resonate with what you have said because they can imagine a similar experience, your situation becomes plausible.

6. *Be systematic.* By carrying out research in a systematic way and making our research processes transparent, we make our interpretations and explanations more credible. It means checking out our emerging hypotheses in a systematic way by discovering categories and patterns of behavior, and looking for confirming and disconfirming evidence of our hunches. But being systematic is not as linear as it may appear. It is an evolving process that relies on judgment all along the way. You may be more systematic in the telling of what you did than is obvious to you during the process. Following a hunch may lead you away from your original plan but have a coherence when you reflect back on the process. Describing how you carried out your study helps the reader make judgments about your inferences.

7. *Be self-reflective.* Is your interpretation based on knowledge of your role in the situation? Is it based on mutual trust and caring?

The action researchers from our cases have used a variety of methods to ensure the veracity of their interpretations. One example will serve to illustrate the power of these approaches. Had Rosie relied only on her understanding of students' disrespectful behavior, she would have failed to see her contributions to the problem. Without revisiting those data, she might have continued to lay complete blame for student misbehavior on students. Without consulting critical colleagues and friends, she might have overemphasized her perceived failure.

CHAPTER SUMMARY

In this chapter we explored the process of transforming data to evidence about the consequences of our actions. We discussed evidence and found that it can be based on method, intuition, artistry, and ethical commitments. Transforming data involves taking things apart (analysis), putting the parts back together in new and creative ways (synthesis), making assertions (theorizing), and assuring ourselves and others that what we have learned is credible and trustworthy (verification). Interpretation also relies on our ethical commitments—our personal frameworks, experience, and insights. It is both method and artistry.

This could be an overwhelming task. Categorizing all our data would prevent us from ever being able to take action! So we sift through our data, looking for the most relevant incidents, interviews, and observations, and set aside the rest. We often make interpretations without categorizing and looking for patterns.

We try to glean the essence of our data and to provide a context for that essence. We focus our evolving questions and issues to narrow the scope of what we will examine.

You may want to read Section 7 on report writing, and then come back to Chapter 13. The ways of writing up a report and portraying what you are learning in multiple formats may yield insights both for how data are collected and how they are analyzed. For example, if we know that our audience is a school board, we may want to consider presenting a videotape of student study participants. Putting together the videotape is a process of analysis and synthesis. Since action research is cyclical and rarely a linear process, you may find yourself going back and forth in this book many times throughout your study.

CHAPTER FOURTEEN

Taking Action—What Will I Do Next? And How Will It Make Life Better?

The purpose of interpretation is to make sense of our data so that we can better understand our practice and our students' learning. Interpretation is to help us to make decisions about actions we might take in our classrooms. Others can give us advice about what course of action to take, but the systematic yet intuitive process of action research with its emphasis on multiple perspectives and collaboration gives us the confidence and credibility to make sound judgments *and* to plan for next steps.

Without action, there is no action research. An easy way to think about this is to list all the things that we have learned about ourselves, our students, and our situation, and to think about what we will do next as a consequence of what we have learned. We think about how these next steps will make life better.

Rosie's reflections about next steps will help us to see how she turned what she learned into actions to direct her teaching and her thoughts about herself as a teacher. Figure 14.1 contains excerpts from her action plan.

As in Rosie's situation, we often realize that we need to reevaluate our position and our values. Her savior spirit, one that she had prized throughout her life, did not serve her well as a teacher. It got in the way of helping her students take responsibility for their own actions.

Action research is a process of professional development. Rosie plans to use her knowledge about creating a democratic classroom in her social studies classroom. She has decided that she really wants the challenge of working with early adolescents. Andy is already planning his next S.T.A.R. Club program. Shawn is making plans to become certified as an English as a Second Language (ESL) teacher. Since their study, Jan and Terry conducted Literature Circle's workshops for other teachers.

Each teacher has in some way transformed understanding of her or his practice toward the kinds of ethical commitments we have outlined in this book. Frequently, we use our insights and interpretations to begin another cycle of action research.

While this book focuses on individual classroom action research by teachers, we want to acknowledge that the same process of action planning

FIGURE 14.1 *Rosie's action plan*		
What have I learned?	**What will I do as a consequence of what I have learned?**	**How will this make life better?**
A democracy that relies too heavily on rights cannot create a safe community.	I will create a classroom compact earlier on, at the beginning of class. Then, when students act in disrespectful ways, I will bring them back to the compact and remind them of agreements they had made.	We will establish a common ground of the responsibilities that democracy entails.
I have always wanted to be a type of "savior," wanting to stop the war in Vietnam, wanting to reverse the ills of society in the civil rights movement, and now trying to create a type of classroom that champions the rights of students.	I need to temper my savior spirit. I will keep reminding myself (with a little help from my friends) that I can easily burn out as a teacher if I take everything too seriously. I think that my journal will be my lifelong companion.	I will be more realistic about what I am able to do while maintaining the ideals that shape my commitment to teaching. I hope that I can remain in teaching for the rest of my career.

may extend to a team or an entire school. In cases such as these, a more elaborate action plan may be required that lists the who, what, when, where, how, and why that we illustrated in the section on designing a study. For further information about action planning, you may want to consult resources such as Geoffrey Mills's *Action Research: A Guide for the Teacher Researcher.*

We also want to acknowledge the multiple and overlapping barriers to action and change that daily present themselves to classroom teachers trying to improve their practice. Hargreaves et al. (1996) summarize a large body of literature on the difficulty of educational change in their book *Schooling for Change: Reinventing Education for Early Adolescents.*

Change is a technical process of managerial efficiency that requires special planning, design, and structural alignment. If not all elements of the system, from the district level to the classroom level, support the change, teachers are likely to feel frustration at their individual efforts.

Change is a cultural process that requires building effective collaborative and consultative relationships in an environment that encourages individuality. It is a process that requires understanding and involvement.

Finally, change is a political and paradoxical process. Not only do people fear change because it presents something new and uncertain, but also educational change is a contested one. Formal education often is a gatekeeper to opportunity and a powerful distributor of life chances. In a socially divided and culturally diverse society, what education is and how it is defined, tends to favor some groups and interests over others. So attempts to change education in fundamental ways are ultimately political acts. They are attempts to redistribute power and opportunity within the wider culture.

Zemelman et al. (1998) offer suggestions for supporting the kind of evolution in teaching that is needed to make classrooms the centers of collaborative inquiry based on principles of developmentalism and constructivism. We outline them here and refer you to their book *Best Practice: New Standards for Teaching and Learning in America's Schools* for further elaboration.

- Teachers need regular time together.
- Teachers' change efforts must be supported by collaborative, social experiences and extensive open discussion of issues.
- Significant change needs leadership from the top, even while the support itself emphasizes teachers' decision making and initiative.
- Schools and staff development programs must support and strengthen teachers' latent professionalism.
- Staff development should be built around experiential activities, rather than theoretical lectures.
- Teachers need to reflect, to analyze, to compare—to build knowledge and theoretical understandings about their work (pp. 226–228).

We would like to argue that action research, by its very nature and definition, fulfills many of the conditions presented by Zemelman et al. Critical colleagues and making knowledge public, two important parts of action research, provide the collaborative and social experiences necessary to support change. Action research recognizes the teacher as a professional and the contributions that teachers make to the evolving professional knowledge bases for teaching. Action research acknowledges the importance of teachers' experiences as a starting point for development as well as theoretical (public) knowledge. Reflection, analysis, and comparison are the essential features of the action research cycle.

Administrators and teachers need to argue for time and recognition of the importance of the reflective work that has been outlined in this book. Teachers need to become involved in what Blase (1988) calls *positive politics* in which power is used *with* other people rather than *over* them. Blase suggests several strategies that teachers can use to benefit their students: Understand the micropolitics of your school; act as political agents (use influence, diplomacy, etc.) to gain the support and resources that you need; empower students, parents, and colleagues so that they will commit their energy and become more competent; celebrate conflict as a condition of change; and speak clearly and understandably (rather than use educational jargon) to parents, the public, and your students about your ideas for teaching. Rather than avoid the political as something self-serving and distasteful, embrace it on behalf of your students and their learning.

THE TENSION BETWEEN DEMOCRACY AND CONTROL IN EDUCATIONAL CHANGE

In taking action and planning for next steps as we discussed here, the tension between democracy and social engineering is often evident. The scenarios we are about to describe involve classroom teachers and teacher educators.

The democratic impulse is evident in many action research arenas:

- Helping teachers participate in change—evident in the school-based curriculum development projects in the United Kingdom in the 1960s and the "process" approach to teaching writing in the United States today.
- Equalizing relationships in the classroom—evident in the many efforts to give students a voice in classroom decisions.
- An explicitly emancipatory project—evident in the studies of ways to end discrimination toward Aboriginal students in Australia and efforts toward ethnic and gender equity in classrooms.

While we may act in democratic ways, we also may be complicit in acts of social engineering by:

- Helping teachers adapt to change, instead of (or simultaneously) encouraging their empowerment to shape change.
- Working toward changing teachers' attitudes toward research. ("If you hate most kinds of research, I promise you will really like AR.")
- Developing hypothesis about the ways teachers develop, that is, studying teacher development as an action research project instead of (or simultaneously with) supporting collegial development.
- Working toward changing students' attitudes toward school, instead of (or simultaneously with) working to change the conditions of schooling that make it undemocratic.

CHAPTER SUMMARY

While we have just touched on the surface of the issues that emerge when we contemplate changing our practice to be more in line with the democratic impulses we have outlined in earlier chapters, we encourage you to think about your own situation and the paradoxes and conflicts that may arise with the changes you propose. Involve others in thinking through issues. This can be the first step in securing support to accomplish even small goals.

SECTION SUMMARY

The process of interpretation is presented in Figure 14.2. It shows our conception of the cyclical process of the search for meaning in which we transform data into evidence. To make sense of experience, we analyze (take things apart), synthesize (put parts together), and theorize (make assertions). This is a natural part of reflective teaching used by professional teachers to make informed judgments and decisions about how to act.

In this section, we presented the tools of interpretation used by action researchers. We summarize them in Figure 14.3.

FIGURE 14.2 *Interpretation and the search for meaning: transforming data into evidence*

Verification is an ongoing process

Make Assertions (Theorize)

ACT

Take apart (Analyze)

Put the parts together (Synthesize)

FIGURE 14.3 *Tools of interpretation*

	Tools of Interpretation
Analysis: What are the parts?	Get ready. Read and reread. Look for the parts—the categories (issues, concepts, dilemmas, themes). Check the categories to see if they fit the data. Develop the categories.
Synthesis: How do the parts relate to one another?	Find patterns. Look for confirming and disconfirming data.
Theorizing: What assertions can I make?	What does this mean to me? To you? In this context? Is it related to a "public" theory? How are my ethical commitments furthered or modified?
Verification: How do I know I am right, that the interpretations and judgments I make are trustworthy, credible, and respectful?	Make your standpoint clear. Use multiple perspectives. Involve community in developing indicators to be applied. Provide raw data. Write descriptively. Be systematic. Be self-reflective.
Action: What will I do with this knowledge? And how will it make life better?	How can I use what I have learned to improve myself, my situation, my students, my teaching, according to my values?

You may want to turn to Appendix C, for strategies that have been developed to help teachers analyze student writing and mathematical understanding. We focus on these two areas because of the attention they are receiving on local and national levels.

Dorothy: I can see that we need to use all our powers—our heads, our hearts, and our courage. We also may want to apply some special techniques. But even when we use those techniques, we may have to mess things all up again, as when we find those "outliers" that don't fit into our categories.

Authors: True enough. Now we"ll see about portraying and sharing what we have learned in a public forum. But first, let's develop our tools for interpretation in Exploring the Forest.

Exploring the Forest
Developing Tools of Interpretation

If you are conducting your study as you read these chapters, these exercises will help you to analyze and interpret your data. If you are conducting a mini action research study, you can use those data for these exercises. Or you can simply read the exercises and return to them later when you have an action research study underway. Create a section of your journal labeled *Analysis and Interpretation.*

1. Tracing our evolving questions is a key aspect of reflecting on our development as teachers. These questions become important tools of data analysis and interpretation because they guide us as we look into our data to see what secrets we can derive from them. Create a section in your journal for a log of questions that arise as your study unfolds.

2. Read through the data you have collected thus far, and write an analytic memo (a note to yourself about what you see emerging as categories and patterns of behavior, words, key ideas, and events) to place in your journal. The analytic memo is a way to record and solve methodological dilemmas about what to do next. Record hunches that point in new directions for actions and data collection. They serve as reminders about what to look at more closely. Write freely. When the data are still fresh in your mind, you will be surprised at the insights you may uncover. These memos may form part of your written report.

3. In Section 6 we discussed several processes that are part of interpretation:
   - Analysis: What are the parts?
   - Synthesis: How are the parts related?
   - Theorizing: What assertions can we make?

   Now we are going to practice using those tools in the brief case exercise. Briefcases often carry a very diverse array of things that may be quite revealing. The purpose of the activity is for a group of researchers to analyze the contents of the briefcase as if it were a set of data. The directions which follow are for leaders to use in instructing participants of the briefcase exercise.
   - *Ask questions and describe.* Prepare a briefcase, real or contrived, for every five- to six-member group. You may want to ask members of your group to share their briefcases.

- Using tables or the floor, instruct members of each group to empty the contents of a briefcase. Members of the group can take turns describing items—in rich detail. Looking at the contents as a whole, what question would they like the contents (data) to answer? Some possible questions include, How is this briefcase used? What can the contents of this briefcase suggest to us about its owner? What might be some of the issues in the owner's life? Group members can ask questions about each item and what it represents to the owner. Who is in this photograph? Why are you carrying it in your briefcase? How long has it been there? What does it mean to you?

- *Look for categories.* Keeping in mind the question that is being addressed, begin sorting the contents into categories. How many categories will you need? Each category will need a label ("office supplies"), a definition ("anything that is used in a part of work in an office setting"), and items that can serve as examples of that category (paper clips, index cards). To help organize the data into categories, you may want to use chart paper, a chalkboard or word processing table to create a chart such as the one in Figure 14.4.

  Next, check to see if the data fit the categories. If not, you may want to modify the labels for the categories until each of the pieces of data seem to fit into one. If there is an outlier that does not seem to fit anywhere, you might want to consider what that particular piece of data is all about.

- *Look for patterns.* Do certain words, items, behaviors, ideas repeat themselves? Are there categories? How does one category compare to another? In other words, what are the relationships, if any, between the categories? It is often helpful to create a visual display in order to identify relationships. Graphs, charts, and concept maps are useful devices. For example, if you want to see the frequency of items in each category, a bar graph might be useful—it would show which category had the most items and which the least. This information might be helpful in later interpretation. But frequency is only one pattern. You may want to refer to the list of patterns presented in Figure 13.9. For other types of patterns (or relationships), such as cause-effect, a flowchart or concept map might be better than a bar graph. See Appendix B for samples of visual display. This is where playfulness comes in! After you look at your visual display, do you have any hunches about what is going on or about what these categories reveal related to the research question? What issues seem to be emerging?

- *Revise the categories and patterns.* Now it is time to go back into the data to see if these preliminary categories and patterns still apply. What if one item doesn't seem to fit anywhere? What do you do with it? You may either adapt the category so that it will include that item, or you may want to create all new categories. Or you may keep the items that don't quite fit, (the outliers), separate and look at them again when you interpret the data.

FIGURE 14.4 *Organizing data into categories*		
Issue 1/Category 1	**Issue 2/Category 2**	**Issue 3/Category 3**
Include quotes from interviews; observations recorded in field notes, on charts, in a journal; excerpts from documents you have saved. For example, from the Briefcase exercise: *Category 1: Work-related items* Scissors Diskettes Manuscript Textbook Calendar		

- *Synthesize.* After taking things apart during analysis, we need to put things back together—this time in a way that we perhaps have not thought of before. Again, visualizing data is a powerful tool to see data in a new way. Charts, graphs, concept maps, flowcharts, drawings—these are the tools of synthesis! We take our categories and arrange them in ways that will help give meaning to them.
- *Make assertions.* Finally! The point of analysis and synthesis is interpretation—making sense of what we have. *What does all this mean?* If the work-related category is much larger than the others, can we interpret that to mean that for the briefcase owner work may be more important than leisure? Or, that the "stuff" of work simply requires more concrete objects, or . . . ? *What dilemmas or issues emerge?* Do the categories reveal a person who may be struggling to achieve some sort of balance in her or his life, balance between work and play and family? *What are the perspectives of others?* What if another group doing the same exercise comes up with entirely different categories and interpretations? That is fine. It is even to be expected. That is why multiple perspectives are important. If several groups conduct the analysis with the same items and come up with different interpretations, it might be worthwhile to discuss those differences and go back to the data with new questions. Action researchers connect emerging theories to experience and imagine conditions where life could be lived differently. *What assertions can you make?* What statements can you make about what you have learned? For example, "The contents of this briefcase reveal a person who struggles between balancing multiple personal interests with work commitments." Remember that these are only possible interpretations that require further study. The fact that a briefcase is full may lead some to believe that the owner is very busy. What are other explanations? Might the briefcase just be in need of a good cleaning out? The presence of things such as a crossword puzzle book, a pocket video game, and a novel may lead one to assume this person works to balance his or her personal and professional lives. But there my be another explanation. This briefcase may serve as an airline carry-on and serve as a storage place for idle-time activities. Make a list of new questions that the data bring up for you. Why does this person travel? Does she or he have children, or might those crayons be used for something else? Discuss how one might find answers to such questions. What types of data would be needed and how can those data be obtained (interviewing, observing, etc.)?

Discuss insights about the research process gained through this activity. What further questions do you have about data analysis and how this process can be applied to your data?

4. Now it is time to analyze and interpret your data. Try using the process we have outlined in item 3. Invite a critical colleague to join you in the process as

you are doing it, or after you have completed it. Does the critical colleague interpret the data in the same way you do? Does the critical colleague introduce new interpretations? Is the possible interpretation richer for your two perspectives?

5. While there are many frameworks for interpretation, we suggest that examining your data from the lens of adult and professional development may be a fruitful approach. This lens provides a framework for exploring and learning from data. See Figure 14.5.

   For example, is what I am learning about the situation in my classroom, informed by my ethical responsibilities to create a more humane and participative environment? Am I able to view my students in more complex ways, using my tools of inquiry, rather than looking for easy solutions to difficult problems? When confronted with obstacles, am I able to use the courage of my convictions to make the changes that I believe are necessary? Am I able to accept the limitations of my study without feeling inadequate?

   Reflect on these kinds of questions as part of your data interpretation and include them in your journal. They will be a valuable part of the "What I have learned" section of your paper.

6. Create an action plan based on what you have learned through your study. Reflect on what you will do next with respect to yourself, your students, and your situation. Reflect on how this will make life better. Examine your values. Are there any shifts or changes? Use the chart presented in Figure 14.6 if you feel it will be helpful.

FIGURE 14.5 *Frameworks for interpretation*

Frameworks for Interpretation: Three Domains of Adult and Professional Development

	Cognitive and Conceptual Complexity	Moral, Ethical, and Social Responsibility	Psychological and Emotional Maturity
What am I learning about myself?			
What am I learning about my situation?			
What am I learning about my students?			

FIGURE 14.6 Examining the consequences		
What have I learned?	What will I do as a consequence of that I have learned?	How will this make life better?

Writing and Sharing the Research Story

"That is a long story," answered the King (of the flying monkeys) with a
  laugh; "But as we have a long journey before us, I will pass the time
  by telling you about it if you wish."

"I shall be glad to hear it," she replied.

The Wonderful Wizard of Oz
L. Frank Baum (1900)

Tin Man: You "shall be *glad* to hear *it*?" Forgive me, Dorothy dear, but how many
  reports of research have you listened to recently? Hardly exciting reading, eh?

Dorothy: Well, yes, er, I mean *no*. If it's just another one of those boring research
  reports, I *will not be glad* to hear it. But I *want* to hear about what happens to
  our researchers. What happens to Jen? And to the fifth graders doing the
  literature circles? The students in Andy's club. And the students my age
  learning about a democratic classroom!

Scarecrow: What happens in the democratic classroom? I sure hope that story
  isn't like most research reports I have heard about!

Lion: Or we might suddenly find ourselves back in the poppy fields—sleeping!

Authors: The purpose of this chapter is to make sure that our research is
  communicated and that our reports are *not* like the reports you remember
  with such dread! No sirree. That doesn't mean that a report has to be a
  riveting read (sorry, Tin Man, nothing personal), but it is likely to get a wider
  audience if it doesn't put people to sleep.

Dorothy: I'll bet these kinds of reports are a lot more fun to write, too.

Authors: That is probably true. At least, that's our experience. Part of the reason
  that our reports will be good reading and telling is the way we approach the
  process of communicating. Writing is an integral part of the gathering,
  analysis, and interpretation of our data, as well as portrayal. Read on . . .

Zip! Zluuuuononkk!

Wizard: Hi there! Sounds like you might want some wizardly words of wisdom on this part of your journey. Is that true? As a postmodernist—I am a master of illusion—and certainly not tied to convention. I anticipate some exploration here. Mind if I come along?

Dorothy, Lion, Tin Man, Scarecrow: Oh MY! NO, of course not, come along.

Authors: Please do. After all, we have come such a very long way to meet you. Come along with us and see what is happening with our teacher researcher colleagues.

CASE STUDIES

Shawn's student from Korea

(excerpts from Shawn's report)

The results from this case study have shown significant growth in all areas. Jen has shown a vast development in her sight word recognition and vocabulary. At the beginning of the study, she recognized 47 out of 100 words. She was able to use 30 of the 47 words in a phrase or sentence that made sense. I tested her again about a month later using the same word list, and Jen recognized 79 out of 100 words and was able to use 68 of those in a phrase or sentence that made sense.

I have also seen a change in Jen's social adjustment. When I began observing her in January, she was somewhat reserved. She often did not share during our weekly "show and tell" sessions. She did not volunteer to answer questions. Slowly, I saw a great change.

* * * * * * *

I enjoyed this study very much. Not only did I learn many new strategies to teach all the children in my classroom, but also I discovered another aspect of teaching that I thoroughly enjoy. . . . I have also let my school principal know how much I have enjoyed this challenge and have expressed great interest in having more ESL students in my class in the future.

* * * * * * *

I chose a topic that really interested me and I have thoroughly enjoyed every aspect of completing this case study. Even the literature review, which I thought was going to be the worst part of this paper, was an enjoyable learning experience. . . . I feel very proud of this accomplishment.

The Literature Circle's Study

These are excerpts from Jan and Terry's study:

During this time, Mrs. S (Terry) had been reading the response journals, looking for signs of progress toward more critical thinking. Specifically, she was looking for drawing conclusions, questioning, predicting, and illustrating using pictures or graphic organizers. To keep track of the growth and give concrete evidence to students' growth, she developed a tally sheet. In initial responses, students focused more on summarizing and predicting. As they became more comfortable and practiced with literature circles, the responses became more expansive with an increase in questioning, connecting, and drawing conclusions.

* * * * * * *

The results of the study were encouraging. We were able to abandon the basal and use authentic literature successfully with students at-risk. A definite move toward more critical thinking was observed. We expect this progress to continue as we expose these students to more authentic texts.

* * * * * * *

We have noticed a marked increase in motivation and enthusiasm as well as an increase in self-esteem for these children. With this in mind, we have met our goal in providing all students with open membership into the "literacy club."

* * * * * * *

As other teachers in the building have heard us discussing our study, many have shown an interest in what we've been doing. One teacher went so far as to "borrow" a misplaced evaluation sheet left on the copy machine. Several teachers have stopped by the classroom to watch the literature circles in action. We plan to present our findings and share strategies to implement literature circles at a future staff meeting.

The S.T.A.R. Club Study

These are excerpts from Andy's report:

My original impressions about the "typical" students and their interest in students in special classes were erroneous. These middle school students had mostly positive attitudes about those with disabilities. The main problem was that they no longer had the same opportunities or time to socialize with one another as they did in the elementary classroom. Their schedule did not allow them to stay in one classroom and get comfortable in one environment. Each time they switched to another class, they were with new students. What I perceived as a lack of interest was largely a lack of opportunity.

* * * * * * *

I found the research process interesting, thought-provoking, and sometimes staggering. As a special education teacher, I was usually accustomed to planning and implementing activities for 16 students. This research project compelled me to organize approximately 70 students for various social events. The commitment to the research, the activities, and the club members could be exhausting, but I felt it renewed my devotion to teaching.

The Democratic Classroom Study

These are excerpts from Rosie's report:

Everywhere people bemoan the state of U.S. society and the destruction of democracy. Pundits argue that civility has declined, aggression has increased, and U.S. citizens grow more cynical about the political process. Fewer and fewer people register to vote; not all those who register, vote. Fewer and fewer people write letters to the editor, wear campaign buttons, try to convince others about an issue or a candidate, or donate money to a campaign. Those who are concerned about these developments say that people are too willing to give up control over the decisions that affect their lives, thereby giving too much power to too few and leaving the citizenry vulnerable to manipulation.

* * * * * * *

How does this become the problem of the classroom? I believe that rehabilitating democracy requires citizens to challenge the status quo. . . . Such people can be nurtured in democratic classrooms.

Dorothy: Look what is happening to Jen! Shawn certainly has a lot to show for the AR project. I like to see that the children participating in literature circles are more enthusiastic about reading.

Scarecrow: Rosie's report about the democratic classroom sounds good enough to argue before the City Council!

Authors: Yes, and as we can see from Andy's report, he learned some surprising things.

Now that we have revisited our teacher colleagues and their work, let's look at how *we* can write and share ours. In this section we will talk more about the processes and products of writing. We start out by discussing the process of *writing as a research process* and revisit a question we posed earlier: *Whose eyes can see what?* We will extend our discussions on *writing down, writing up,* and *writing about* our work to share it with colleagues and others. We will discuss some of the many options for point of view, voice, and form in report writing, and we will provide general and specific information about preparing research reports. Part of the mystery surrounding research can be dispelled by understanding the importance and meaning of language, style, and the points of view in reporting research. Finally, we will discuss ways to share what we have found, both to strengthen our findings and to spread the work and contribute to an evolving library of professional knowledge. In "Exploring the Forest," we will try out some different kinds of writing for our studies.

Writing as a Research Process: Whose Eyes Can See (and Tell) What?

Writing is a powerful process for learning; for describing, synthesizing, analyzing, and interpreting experience; for coming to terms with what we know, how we know it, and why it is important—if it is—to know. This last part, the value of what we know, depends upon our points of view. And that brings us to our eyes (and hearts and courage!)—and what they *can* see and *want* to see, for these are usually related.

Those exploring writing in the late 1970s and early 1980s talked about writing as thinking, as cognition. Their thesis outlined how writing is, in itself, a most complex and engaging process that is multifaceted and contains many subprocesses, such as planning, analysis, synthesis, and sequencing, to name a few, making writing a heuristic process (Emig, 1977, 1982; Flower, 1981; Flower and Hayes, 1980; Perl, 1980, 1981).

Writing is not only a cognitive process, but also a political process. We observe and write from a point of view, actually from many points of view. Since we are normally unaware of these processes, we don't perceive the options we have for conceptualizing and portraying research.

Scarecrow: So, *if* we perceive options, we have them!

Authors: Yes. As we explore options in this chapter, you can begin to perceive some of the possibilities—and the responsibilities—that come with consciousness and knowledge. For example, as we try to live out our values in our teaching, we have the responsibility to make that value position known. *What* we select to focus on and *how* we record it will determine to a large extent the data we have to analyze and interpret. It also matters what we decide *not* to focus on or record, and what does not enter into our consciousness. Writing is not an automatic or inconsequential act!

Follow this process one more step into consciousness, and we find that "Representation . . . is always self-presentation . . . The Other presented in the text is always a version of the researcher's self"

(Denzin and Lincoln 1998, p. 319). This means, at the most basic level, that our studies tell as much about us as they do about others. Because there are almost an infinite number of ways to represent experience (Brady, 1991, p. 5), and each of these ways carries its own interpretive lenses, the reader, as well as the author, needs to think critically about what is recorded, analyzed, and interpreted.

Each of the paradigms and theories that we discussed in Section 2 has its own orientation. A person from a constructivist orientation, for example, will ask different questions, collect different kinds of data, interpret them in different ways, and portray the data differently than a person with a behaviorist or feminist orientation. Even if by some unlikely twist of fate these three groups had the same data and research questions, they would still write very different reports.

Let's make this even more complicated—

Dorothy: Thanks a lot.

Authors: Ah, but you might like this part. Not only do we choose our perspective, we can select a way to portray what we have learned. We may want to choose a very concise, scientific type of report, or we may want to write a more conversational, narrative account. We may choose to discuss informally what we have learned with a teacher research group (in person or through the Internet) or present our study at a conference. It may also be a source of relief to realize that whatever format we choose, we are simply giving an account of a phenomenon at one time rather than a definitive study of a topic.

Dorothy: If that means that we can play a little and not worry about getting it right for always . . .

Authors: Yes. You needn't be concerned about "getting it right for always." The writer Henry Miller once said that "writing is a voyage of discovery." The personal and professional discovery that AR makes possible, happens throughout the research process: from capturing and writing down data, to writing up our results, to writing about our work in ways that lead to further discovery with others. We will explore specific options for writing, but first let's revisit and extend our discussion of the process of writing.

Writing Down, Writing Up, and Writing About

Recall from Section 5 that *observation* is key to all good research, and as we can surmise from what we just discussed, observation is always from a point of view. We develop our observation skills as we observe and as we put what we observe into words. This is how we develop as connoisseurs and critics (Eisner, 1985).

Dorothy: What does that have to do with writing *down* and *up* and *about?*

Authors: Plenty. Connoisseurs appreciate the significance of the topics they choose to study. Careful observation makes it possible to document and record (*writing down*) what you see so that you can return to it later, analyze and play with it, and put it into a form that makes sense of the pieces, that shows relationships of one aspect of the data (or data sets) to others. That is what we call *writing up* the results of a study. Once you have written up your report, you have a base from which to *write about* the study for presentation to others in the form of publication or presentation. When writing about your study, your options in terms of audience, form, and style are more than accouterments: They carry the meaning of the story. As critics make their keen observations public, so, too, do action researchers.

The richer the database from writing down, the stronger the foundation for analysis and interpretation, and for writing up and about the research later on. This means documenting and snooping, probing around corners, asking challenging questions of what you see, to get different angles and perspectives on it to record.

Wizard: Yes. The idea is that the more work you put in early on, collecting the information, the better. Did you tell them that the more comprehensive and organized the proposal, the easier it will be to conduct the study?

Scarecrow: Oh my, yes. We worked hard on that and reaped the benefits in our analysis.

Wizard: Ha Ha! That is true *sometimes*—and *sometimes not!*

Dorothy: Another riddle! Whatever do you mean?

Wizard: I mean that some people start with less "well-developed" or "comprehensive" proposals and do marvelous studies in less time than other people, who prepare very thorough proposals and find themselves so stuck to their plans that they miss the main event, or clues that will take them to it! They do not see what is in front of them if it doesn't fit "the plan." Sometimes researchers follow their instincts without much fanfare, and it works. Some of our greatest discoveries happen in that way. They *aren't* laborious! They *flow.*

Authors: That is not to discourage carefully prepared proposals. The Wizard is only pointing out that good ideas come in many ways. Some come in flashes, others in uneven tempo, and we need to be open to our intuition and visits from parts of ourselves that may know more than the rational parts. For example, an author of a delightful, award-winning children's book wrote it in less than a day! The ideas had been growing inside since her childhood when she lived the story the first time. What happened was a magic synthesis. And that can happen to each of us. Had she labored at it, she may have lost the pulse and we might have been deprived of this treasure.

Writing in its many forms—from free-writing possible ideas for research, to writing about research for publication—is a powerful tool. Since we have been writing in different forms all through our journey, perhaps it is time to stand back and put a simple framework around writing and a few of the many forms it takes in carrying out research. (See Figure 15.1.) Although the forms may be seen as progressive, one leading to the next, and indeed this can be the case, it is also true that these forms take place throughout the research. Free-writing, for example, can be useful no matter what stage or part of the action research cycle one is in. Ideas for *writing about* can occur to one at any time, and can be noted in one's journal for future use.

Dorothy: I'm beginning to look at writing differently. It isn't the simple process I thought it was.

Authors: That is true, Dorothy. The kind of writing we are talking about here is professional writing. It helps a professional to be just that. We have done quite a bit of free-writing, and we have written our proposals. So let's extend a few ideas that we sprouted in the last two chapters related to the last three terms.

Writing down is the process of recording observations. As we discussed in Section 5, there are many ways to take notes and make records. Sometimes we record the landscape and take a broad sweep; at other times we focus more narrowly, carefully (and for the Wizard's adventurous postmodern mind, **creatively**), with a connoisseur's eye for detail. Remember the "dark snakes of stems and ferny plumes of leaves" from John Moffit's poem "To Look at Any Thing" in Chapter 11. This is an example of the rich detail we are aiming for in recording our observations. We are acutely aware and fully present. What do we see with our ears? (Silence in Moffit's poem.) What do we see with our eyes? Detail. What do we see with our noses? Dampness and green. This is the opportunity to be the young child who literally sinks into what she sees, Dorothy. The clearer our vision, the richer the database for description and later interpretation. Some researchers capture the essence of what they see in lines and phrases to use as they write up their observations.

FIGURE 15.1   *Writing related to research*

Free-writing: writing without taking time to think about it, to edit (either internally or externally), or to labor over our writing; giving the creative parts of our minds free reign. There is usually no audience for free-writing other than the author.

Proposal writing: focused and disciplined writing often informed by ideas from free-writing with the purpose of proposing a study.

Writing down: developing the art of observation and data collection; capturing rich, detailed information. The audience may be oneself, a professor, colleague, funding agency or others.

Writing up: analyzing and synthesizing the results of our observations and data in writing; refers to rendering our considered observations and interpretations in written form (portraits, case studies, research reports). This is usually available for outside audiences; it is part of making research public.

Writing about: taking our reports and creating products from these to share; usually moving beyond the report in rendering it in other forms (presentations, articles). This is usually prepared for presentation with an outside audience in mind.

Mary Oliver, a Pulitzer Prize-winning poet, provides a good example of each of these points: *careful focusing* by *being fully present* with *all senses open for engagement*, with a *childlike sinking into experiences,* and *capturing, in sentences and phrases,* material from which to write up in a story or poem. In *Blue Pastures* (1995) Oliver gives us a glimpse into her work and provides a good illustration of these points. She carries a notebook with her and captures phrases and ideas as they occur. Following are four examples from *Blue Pastures:*

- Little myrtle warblers kissing the air
- You there, like a red fist under my ribs—be reasonable.
- Just at the edge of the sea, a dolphin's skull. Recent, but perfectly clean. And entirely beautiful. I held it in my hands, I was so excited I was breathless. What will I do?
- Something totally unexpected, like a barking cat.

Can you see and feel, smell, and hear these? Do these words and their images transport you there?

From a research perspective, Mary Oliver is collecting data, *rich* data. Once she has written down these rich data, she will make sense of them as she *writes them up* in another form.

Authors: (*to travelers*) We can read on your faces "But I can't do this! She is a prize-winning poet!" Ah, but you can. We all can. We can accept the invitation into a connoisseur's world to cultivate the powers of our senses! Does the child in your room *walk, bound, saunter, shuffle,* or *vault* to the drinking fountain?

Because we have long written up our research according to canons seeded centuries ago, "value-free" and modeled on science, we have few examples in education to draw upon. From the 17th century on, for example, the world of writing was divided into two streams: *literary* (fiction, narrative) and *scientific* (nonfiction, expository).

"Fiction was unfortunately considered to be 'false' because it invented reality, unlike science, which was considered 'true' because it simply 'reported' 'objective' reality in a single, unambiguous voice" (Richardson, 1998, p. 350). Today, since fiction is defined as human experience in narrative form, we would not call fiction false. In our own time, what has been called *realism* with its "objective, precise, unambiguous, noncontextual, nonmetaphoric" scientific voice was so strong that for a time even poets and novelists tried to adhere to realism's guidelines. "By the late nineteenth century, 'realism' dominated both science and fiction" (Clough, 1992, in Richardson, 1998, p. 350), and its effects can still be felt. In postmodern times, neither scientific nor literary writing is in a higher position. Today, no one can "know all" with realism's precision, but each can "know something" (Richardson, 1998, p. 350).

Scarecrow: Oh my, all this knowing . . .

Wizard: I see that straw face drooping, scarecrow! But never fear! Not knowing everything is a not a bad thing. People *never knew it all,* but they *didn't know* *that they didn't know it all!* With postmodern thinking we are free to know what we know and to question that knowledge as well as what we don't know. We can provide evidence for our claims, but we don't have to pretend that we have discovered truth or to know more than we do. This is very freeing!

Recall that writing up is drawing upon what you have written down and interpreting and developing it further. Mary Oliver makes poems out of her notes. As you draw on your data, trying to make sense of it, making connections, noting patterns and findings, and synthesizing elements of the study, you begin to write up your cogitations, too. Writing up detailed description, all by itself, can easily seem to be "enough" analysis—after all, we are taking something that *wasn't* obvious to us before and making it visible in new ways. But for AR, this isn't enough. Since issues usually undergird our research (fairness, etc.), the careful presentation of data, as creative and suggestive as it might be, is not usually sufficient. We must probe and develop our results so that we, and our readers, can contemplate the "So what?"of our research. What does this finding mean related to the underlying issues that frame my research? What do these results mean to my classroom?

"When I began observing her [Jen] in January, she was reserved. She often did not . . .". Here, Shawn writes up her analysis of the data. Often in writing up results, the researcher makes a statement about the data and provides examples as evidence to support the statement. Such evidence might include "plays with other children, takes part in recess activities, and works in collaboration with her science group." In writing up the results of their Literature Circle's study, Terry and Jan wrote, "In initial responses, the students focused more on summarizing and predicting. As they became more comfortable and practiced with Literature Circles, responses became more extensive with an increase in questioning, connecting, and drawing conclusions." Examples, such as: "Myron, Abbey, and Gerald's group spent four times the amount of time questioning the text, and five times the amount of time discussing their conclusions and what these meant to them, than they did three weeks ago," lend credibility and clarity to the findings. The use of time in this case need not necessarily show growth, but as an indicator, it can point in that direction, especially when combined with further evidence, such as "Whereas during the first few weeks of the study Myron dominated the discussion, providing 'answers' to questions he had before the other children were able to grasp the ideas and pose their own questions. By the end of the study each of the children contributed to the discussion and Myron made certain that each of the children had the opportunity to contribute." What the teachers found, simply put, was growing and consistent evidence of higher-level thinking skills; the children moved from literal questions (Who is the main character? What did she like to do?) to higher levels of thinking (posing questions, making judgments, thinking critically). Their next step could well be to relate these findings back to the larger context or issue: "So what do these results and related examples suggest for enabling the children to think critically and creatively? What can *we* do differently in the classroom to encourage further growth in critical and creative thinking?"

Scarecrow: Another way would be to write up examples first, and *then* make a general statement. Then readers could conjure up their *own* ideas.

Authors: Yes. That is the way it often happens both for readers *and* writers. As researchers write up the examples, they begin to discover the importance and relationship of one example to another. In a real sense as researchers, we *write into understanding.*

Writing about your study after you have presented a preliminary report can be fun—regardless of your paradigm. Think about *writing about* as if you are an artist who has just completed a pencil drawing of a landscape. You have the landscape, now you can make something else out of it: Paint it, zero in on one part of the painting and blow it up large, combine a few parts of the painting to make another painting. Perhaps you can use multimedia to emphasize different aspects of the painting. Writing about your study, once you have prepared a report, leaves you open to many of these options, some of which will be influenced by those to whom you want to present your work. Writing up includes literally *writing,* as in a form for publication or other forms of distribution, and *presenting* or telling about your study from alternative perspectives. Later in this chapter we will talk about audience.

Wizard: [SMILE]. Ah! This is where I come in. This is the time for true wizardry! This is the time for magic and sorcery! And witchcraft!

Wicked Witch of the West: HARRUMPPPPppph!! *It's about time you remembered me!* **I can add fire!** HEH HEH

Authors: That is true enough. What you both say is true. And we can use it all to communicate our work in robust ways.

Scarecrow: Eeeeck! Fine friends you guys are! I have a very personal concern about fire. Fire can lead to *ashes*!

Authors: Ah, and that's a cause for fear. But, dear Scarecrow, in your case, if you face the fear (with magic!), you can use it to your advantage. The fire you fear has tremendous energy that you can use to generate light and to melt away—

Wicked Witch of the West: **AHHHHhhhh!**

Authors: Its unseemly and dangerous aspects.

Kind Witch Glinda: **Whhiisssssssssssssht!** What you say is true. This takes courage.

Lion: I knew it! I knew it!

Authors: As long as you remain aware of your commitment, of the reason why you are on this journey—

Tin Man: And know it in your heart—

Authors: Yes, and knowing it in your heart, you will be able to use the energy that would otherwise have been wasted in fear. The energy is the same: What you use it for makes all the difference. How, for example, might you write about your study in ways that enable you to see it differently? What forms might you create to share your work with others? What different stories might you tell? This leads us into the whole idea of narrative, or story. We have been using narrative (and writing it) all along our journey.

CHAPTER SUMMARY

In this chapter we discussed writing as a vital part of the research process. The quality of our observations as we record them reflects a point of view and provides the material for analysis and interpretation. We termed this gathering-of-data process *writing down.* After we have the data, we write up our findings, providing analysis and interpretation. The third general type of action research writing is writing about our study to communicate with others. This is often overlooked and yet is an important way to share our research and through the process to further develop the ideas embodied in the report. In Chapter 16 we discuss narrative writing and some ways that we can tell our research stories.

Narrative Writing

It is hard to conceive of a report without narrative, so it is important for us all to give narrative writing some thought. With the rise in the use of qualitative methods to study educational issues, there has been a concomitant increase in the use of qualitative, or *narrative,* reports, which often are longer than more traditional reports. They are different in nature. Just what is narrative, and what is a narrative report? Why would we want to write a narrative report?

Narrative Defined: A General Term, a Process, and a Product

According to Donald Polkinghorne (1988), who has studied narrative, "The most inclusive meaning of 'narrative' refers to any spoken or written presentation" (p. 13). In common usage we often think of narrative as the parts of a document that are words and sentences in contrast to the parts that are numbers, tables, and figures. The same can be said for an oral presentation of narrative research. Narratives, whether written or spoken, are the explanatory commentary of a report. In qualitative research, which much of action research is, narrative reports are those that take the reader to the data in personal and highly descriptive ways. Narrative, as Polkinghorne uses the term, stands for both the process and the results. We use the term *narrative* in these two ways here, as the process of narration and as the product, a narrative. Here, we are talking about a narrative report.

"'[S]tory' is equivalent to 'narrative'" (p. 13), according to Polkingham. Although there are a few qualifications to keep in mind when referring to our research writing as a story, we find that "story" has more benefits than liabilities. Figure 16.1 contains a few of each that you can add to.

Dorothy: It seems to me that if people are more likely to read it—that alone is reason enough to try using narrative when writing!

Wizard: Yes. Storytelling is perhaps the *oldest* method of teaching. Long before there was even the term *research,* let alone "methods" of it, there was story, a way to pass along culture from one generation to the next. Long before our brains were as highly developed as they are today, we

FIGURE 16.1 *Benefits and liabilities of using story*	
Benefits of using story	**Liabilities of using story**
Easy to understand;	Easy to dismiss its importance because most people associate "research" with traditional reports;
We think in stories rather than linear ways;	
Aids understanding on multiple levels;	Data may not easily "fit" into story line;
Reader less resistant to considering results;	If reader is looking for traditional research report categories, main point may be missed;
More inviting to read;	
Connects with reader on a human level;	Story calls on participation and non-linear processing of reader;
Uses story conventions in creative ways;	
Reader brings imagination and intuition to the text.	Findings may not be as clear and unequivocal as in a traditionally structured research report.

responded to life and made sense of experience through stories. Story, then, speaks to us on multiple levels, including the primitive level, and conveys meaning in ways that more rational (seemingly more pointed and straightforward) approaches are unable to convey. Story speaks to us in a tempo and form that allow us to entertain information that we would not otherwise consider. Direct presentations can be threatening and perceived as irrelevant, so that much that they might have to impart never reaches consciousness.

Authors: It is rather like Ken Macrorie's (1980) suggestion to "show, don't tell" in writing and teaching. Stories show. While there are those who think "No pain, no gain!" and scoff at the idea of research engaging the audience in creative and playful ways, we can learn much through story—and often happily so.

We have all sorts of ways in which we protect ourselves from new ways of thinking. And for those steeped in traditional forms of research, narrative methods can be disconcerting, or more likely, dismissed. There are conventions of narrative writing just as there are for more expository and scientific writing—the data are no less important, and the engagement of the researcher with the data is no less rigorous. As Denzin and Lincoln (1998) point out, researcher's narrative stories are "couched and framed within specific story telling traditions" (p. 4).

Think of narration as the way you describe and make sense of your experience. Narrative is the story that you weave in order to make sense of your life and world; it is the glue that holds experience together in a coherent way. As we narrate, we link, synthesize, integrate, connect, and make meaning of our experiences.

Because action research is rarely as neat, tidy, and sequential as suggested by report formulas familiar to many of us (purpose, rationale, research question, hypotheses, literature review, methodology, results, conclusions, discussion, references, and appendices), we may choose to use different ways to write up what we have learned.

Writer Perspectives

The narrative report can be written from many different perspectives. We have drawn from the work of Robert Stake (1995), John Van Maanen (1988), Thomas Mallon (1984), and Eliot Eisner (1985) to compile a list of possible perspectives from which the author can write.

- The *chronicler, biographer,* or *historian* narrates the story, giving the reader an event-by-event accounting of the historical case as it develops, focusing on key components (Mallon, Stake).
- The *researcher* or *experiential authority* tells the story of developing the research, what it looks like from this person's point of view, methodologically and substantively (results and meaning of results) (Stake, Van Maanen).
- The *describer* or *connoisseur* offers rich, thick description of major components of the research (Stake, Eisner).
- The *documenter* or *journalist* or *traveler* puts you there as the story unwinds, privy to details that stand for typical behaviors, patterns, places (Van Maanen; Mallon).
- The *culture member* tells the story from the perspective of the member of the cultural group that is being studied, using her or his own accounts, quotations, language, cliches (Van Maanen).
- The *confessor* engages in truth telling beyond what is needed or wanted, including more about the field worker than about the study; what is key to the reader and to the author is muddled (Van Maanen, Mallon).
- The *impressionist* offers personalized interpretations of selected elements of the research and does so in a dramatic form (Van Maanen).
- The *ecologist* tells the story from many vantage points and dimensions (Mallon).
- The *pilgrim* comes from a point of view and values that are obvious to the reader; the story is told explicitly from this point of view (Mallon).
- The *apologists* "wish to explain, to justify, to plead the case before history . . . at least to get their versions on the record" (Mallon).
- The *creators* create the story as they go; interpretations and images are rich and thought-provoking. The creators sometimes explain the detail and its meaning, sometimes not. The story can be a collage, either with a clear beginning and ending, or not.
- The *prisoners* escape into writing; they come alive through writing and are far braver in this form of communication than in direct conversation, which is a surprise to people who think they know them well (Mallon)!

Dorothy: These don't sound like the perspectives of reports I have read in school! Aren't we supposed to be neutral and *objective?*

Wizard: Well, you probably have read reports from a few of these perspectives. Schools are pretty eager to present experiential authority and have more than a few chroniclers who want to share their stories. With this list in mind, you may find other research accounts in which a particular perspective is embedded. Now, let me throw you a sticky wicket! How can one be an insider (one who writes the point of view of a person inside the culture studied) and yet look at the data as an outsider (able to gain distance and look at the phenomenon under investigation with a stranger's fresh new perspective)? It *is* possible!

Authors: Being an insider or an outsider in relation to the data and participants is a discussion still being carried out among modern and postmodern researchers. The insider/outsider perspective is a paradox of sorts, seeming to be a contradiction with some truth in it. Once, it was believed that if a researcher got too involved or too close to the data, the study was contaminated. As you may recall from Section 2, others, from a more qualitative orientation, argue that there is no such thing as objectivity. We construct meaning from who we are, our experiences, our gender, our world views. Recording data, its analysis, synthesis and interpretation enables one to return to it, to bracket it, and to critique it from alternative perspectives. One can record as an insider, and along with others step outside the data to critique it as an outsider. This is by no means inevitable, but for many researchers, it is possible.

    Another issue involved with the current insider/outsider debate concerns the researcher's rights, responsibilities, and capabilities to write other people's stories with or without their corroboration or comment. Whose story is it? For what purpose is it written? So, the first issue is, can a researcher write from insider and outsider perspectives, while the second issue is, **should** and **can** the researcher write from alternative perspectives?

Scarecrow: What does this have to do with reports?

Authors: Whereas once reports were viewed as simply writing up objective results of the study, we now realize that there are many issues to consider and that our insider's eyes shape all forms of writing—down, up, and about as we make connections, analyze, and synthesize and come to new understandings.

    The underlying element in all these perspectives is the telling of the story, which, according to Jean Clandinin and Michael Connelly, is "the closest we can come to experience" (1998, p. 155). Our experiences are "the stories we live" and in the telling of them, we "reaffirm them, modify them, and create new ones . . ." (1998, p. 155). We will soon present some different kinds of report formats, but before we do that, let's entertain a few of the ways that we can create new ones and thus enlarge our understanding in the process.

    We present a few newer forms of writing, what Laurel Richardson (1998) calls "evocative forms of telling," which necessitate relating to the data differently and thus coming to know data from alternative perspectives and angles. We plant these here as seeds, as new ways of thinking, not to provide comprehensive descriptions or ways to proceed. Richardson charts a path into new forms of telling, and we can travel with her for a few minutes.

Wizard: These are snippets to snuffle around a bit with.

Evocative forms of telling include:

- *Narrative of the self.* "This is a highly personalized, revealing text in which the author tells stories about his or her own lived experience." They use the writing techniques of fiction rather than those of traditional ethnography, and they are therefore not concerned with accuracy, but with the "literary criteria of coherence, verisimilitude, and interest" (Richardson, 1998, p. 356). The narrative of the self might easily be the culture member's story.

- *Ethnographic fictional representations.* These are products of the imagination where the author is "seeking a format in which to tell a 'good story.' " The story can be about the author but is more generally about the people or culture studied. Techniques such as "flashback, flash forward, alternative points of view, deep characterizations, tone shifts, synecdoche, dialogue, interior monologue, and, sometimes, even the omniscient narrator" are used (Richardson, 1998, p. 356). The chronicler could well adopt ethnographic fictional representations and its techniques to enliven the research story.

- *Poetic representations.* Poetic writing is often closer to how people actually talk than is the typical style of most academic writing. Writing up an interview in a poetic form can come closer to the reality of what was said than a verbatim transcript or a summary of it might convey. "Settling words together in new configurations lets us hear, see and feel the world in new dimensions. Poetry is thus a *practical* and *powerful* method for analyzing social worlds" (Richardson, 1998, p. 357). The connoisseur might find poetic representations the most meaningful way to portray and convey research.

- *Ethnographic drama.* "Drama is a way of shaping experience without losing the experience." Drama can incorporate many different forms of representation and technique, poetry, visual and oral arts, literature, and thus make multiple ways of appreciating the "text" possible. Importantly, drama can be used to "give voice to what is unspoken, but present" (Richardson, 1998, p. 357). The impressionist might select ethnographic drama to tell the tale.

- *Mixed genres.* Mixed genres give perhaps the most creative license to present one's work. The author can draw upon "literary, artistic and scientific genres, often breaking the boundaries of each of those as well" (Richardson, 1998, p. 357). Looking at a study from these multiple points of view enables a wealth of possibilities for portrayal and understanding. Creators and prisoners would find a wealth within mixed genres to tell their respective research stories.

You may want to experiment with some of these newer kinds of portrayal, as they will give you more options for your writing. There are two other forms of writing used in narrative reports which can be used in most of, if not all, the possibilities we just explored, from chroniclers and pilgrims to ethnographic drama. These are *portraits* and *vignettes.*

Portraits, Portraiture, and Vignettes

A portrait presents a likeness of a person, place, time, event, or circumstance. "The portraitist takes liberties and artistic licence to create the sense or essence of the [portrayed]" (Holly, 1989, p. 105). Robert Coles, a well-respected child psychiatrist, used portraiture to call attention to the inside stories of children's lives (a Pulitzer Prize-winning series entitled *Children of Crisis,* 1967, is a good example) and of men and women over the years. Coles is a qualitative researcher who argues persuasively for the use of stories. In fact, his book *The Call of Stories* (1989) makes the case for stories by presenting stories of telling stories in teaching, therapy, and research. The research from which his stories come is based on an immersion into the setting in which he observes, interviews, collects artifacts, and documents what he sees and hears and experiences. Each of Cole's books offers the student of portraiture and qualitative methods a feast, not only from the stories themselves, but also from his discussions of his research. Of portraiture, he says:

> The essential thrust is toward a reasonably accessible and suggestive "reading" of a given person's life. The writers become mediators; through them another life reaches toward the reader, and if the work has been successful, stays with the reader as a guest, a "spirit," whose mind and heart and soul have been registered upon the consciousness of distant strangers. (Coles and Coles, 1980, p. 4)

Portraiture is now considered to be a "genre of inquiry and representation that seeks to join science and art . . . [It] is a method of qualitative research that blurs the boundaries of aesthetics and empiricism in an effort to capture the complexity, dynamics, and subtlety of human experience . . ." (Lawrence-Lightfoot and Davis, 1997, p. xv).

Vignettes.   Vignettes and portraits are representations of life on paper. Vignettes are "small literary sketches of life that often fade gradually into larger pictures; they are segments that begin a story, and they are the smaller stories within a story; small centers of interest within a landscape or a painting or a life" (Holly, 1989, p. 105). Vignettes can stand by themselves. They provide mental images and pictures of past and current actions. Life histories are often constructed using biographical or autobiographical vignettes, which, when integrated, can form patterns and themes and provide the materials for the construction of portraits.

A critical incident is a type of vignette that captures a turning point in the story. The point may turn on a sudden insight—the moment Rosie realized that students need to be given responsibilities along with freedom. Or, from a more critical perspective, that she herself may have fed into the problem by taking shortcuts on her way to building a classroom community. In Rosie's case, she made these incidents critical during her process of reflecting on what she had learned through her study. Weaving incidents together may help us see our own development as critical researchers and to help readers understand how knowledge is and can be constructed.

Here is a vignette that is part of a larger portrait constructed by Robert Coles in *The Political Life of Children* (1986). The first paragraph is a small part of the portrait of Kate, who lives in Dublin, Ireland. This paragraph leads into the vignette that follows it in the second paragraph.

> She was, at twelve, tall for her age, with lanky legs and utterly straight brown hair, with a touch of red. The hair came down almost to her shoulders. When she got anxious or angry, she put her hands through her hair repeatedly, or lowered her head abruptly, so that her hair suddenly all came forward, covering much of her face. She wore a crucifix on a chain around her neck, and often played with it, sometimes stopping to look down intently at it. She was "deeply religious," the sisters told me: "Kate might become one of us when she's older, for all we know. She may have a vocation. She may!"

With this information, we have a context for the vignette in which Kate speaks for herself:

> As for Kate's idea, at twelve, of her vocation, it went like this: "If I could choose what I'd be, I'd be a surgeon! I'd be in a hospital someplace in Belfast, and I could help take care of our men, who get hurt. If I went with them, to fight the Brits, I could sew anyone up, who got hurt. If I saw a Brit, and he needed to be sewed up, I'd just walk away. I'd never give any of them help! They look down on us, and they never listen to what we say. If I could *really* have my choice, I'd be a soldier! I'd be in the Irish Army and we'd cross the border and fight the Brits and beat them. Then we could tell the Oranges: Stay here, and we'll be nice to you—nicer than you've been to us—or go back to your Scotland, if it means all that much to you! They've taken me in for being a 'public tease' to their soldiers, but if I was a soldier, I'd not get upset when some kid, a girl like me, starts saying what I said. I'd stop and listen to her! I'd ask my friends to listen."

Notice the pacing and shape of the text. Where do we go next? The pacing and intensity of the vignette are broken as there is a shift in both. The text is pulled back as Kate "pulls back." Very simply, Coles invites us, too, to contemplate what has just been said in the vignette.

> She stops there. She has begun to notice my incredulity—and maybe her own. She pulls back somewhat, acknowledges that it would be an exceptional soldier who would be that honest and open—even to a child. Anyway, she admits, she isn't exactly a child: "The Brits say we're all grown up—that's what they say when they arrest us! They told me I'd go to jail the next time . . ." (Coles, 1986, p. 119).

When writing vignettes and portraits, authors often include direct quotations from the people they portray. Coles makes extensive use of the language of the persons portrayed. At the other end of the scale, some authors use such quotations sparingly. In general, the trick is to be judicious in using quotations. Coles probably uses a small portion of his data in his books; but since he has more data than most to draw from, he is better able to use them! If a quotation is important to the story and the person says it best—use it. Scholars such as Robert Coles and Sarah Lawrence-Lightfoot (*The Good High School,* 1983, provides excellent portraits of very different "good" high schools) can weave magic with the language of the portrayed. In their writing, a book can be read as if it were the story told by the portrayed. In our experience this is not easy to do—but it is a highly effective way to report scholarship, when done well.

Scarecrow: Here we go again—more prize-winning authors. Excuse me, but we are *not* experienced. Who are *we* to tell a story our own way, create our own vignettes and portraits, and all that? We're not experts. We might get it wrong.

Wizard: Is this not your own journey? Are you not the one who experienced it? Does this not make you an expert on your own life? And besides, you are not alone. You have each other and these good witches and critical colleagues to assist you. Telling *your* story is not a matter of being *right* or *wrong.* It is a matter of being *authentic.* Was Kate right or wrong, or is it more fruitful to ask if she was telling her truth? Tell *your* story! And change it if you need to. Dorothy, Tin Man, Scarecrow, Lion, ask yourselves this: You have all come on the same journey. Did you all have the same experience?

Dorothy: Yes, of course, we were together all the time.

Scarecrow: But we had different purposes and questions along the way.

Lion: So I guess our journeys are . . . different.

Tin Man: My journey is a journey of the heart.

Lion: Mine is a journey of courage.

Scarecrow: And mine is all about brains.

Dorothy: I just want to get back to Kansas. Hmm. I guess that what we have learned may have some things in common, but what and how we share it with others will not necessarily be the same. Yet, we have been on the *same* trip.

Authors: You each have your own unique and valuable story to tell about this same adventure.

CHAPTER SUMMARY

In this chapter we defined narrative as "any spoken or written presentation." We use the term *narrative* as equivalent to *story*. We discussed several perspectives from which a narrative can be written, including that of the historian, the creator, and the ecologist. There are new forms of writing termed by Richardson (1998) *evocative forms of telling* which include ethnographic fiction and drama, poetic representation, and mixed genres. We concluded with examples of portraits and vignettes which can be used in many of these different types of writing. How we tell the story influences what people can derive from our scholarship, what they can see, hear, and apprehend. Now, in Chapter 17, we look at the commonalities that cut across the many different ways to write up what we have learned through our journeys.

Report Formats

There are a variety of ways to organize a report. In this chapter we present three for your perusal: a "traditional" report (Figure 17.1), a more issues-oriented narrative report (Figure 17.2), and a report based on the proposal format we presented in Section 5 (Figure 17.3). We include a column for estimated number of pages for each section, but only you will know what fits for your study.

The traditional report is typical of standard research reports. To make it more suitable for action research, we have added a section called "changes" to show how the study may have been modified from the initial proposal and a section called "reflection." You might want to weave the changes throughout the methodology and the reflections throughout the report. Modify Figure 17.3 to suit your study.

The second format we present, Figure 17.2, is an adaptation of a way to organize a case study report presented by Robert Stake in *The Art of Case Study Research* (1995). One of the reasons we recommend this type of format, and the way that Stake organizes his framework, is that it enables the action researcher to develop the *issues* indicated in the study. Especially in action research, with its overt agenda, the "questions, the contexts, the history, the case itself need more than to be described, they need to be developed" (p. 123).

The third type of report format, presented in Figure 17.3, is the one we have detailed in previous chapters. See Appendix D for an example: Rosie's report of the democratic classroom.

Use these possible frameworks as catalysts to think about what may be a suitable format for your study. You may want to take a few minutes now to jot down some ideas on how you might organize your report. The section which follows is designed to help you to further refine your thinking about your report.

FIGURE 17.1	*Outline for a traditional report*	
Abstract	Composed at the conclusion of the study, this is a concise, encapsulated summary of researcher questions, purposes, methods and findings/outcome(s).	50–100 words
Introduction	This personal section tells why and how the study came about, including personal motivation, rationale, need for study. It usually concludes with a statement about what researchers hope to learn.	$1-1\frac{1}{2}$ pages
Review of literature	This section summarizes what other researchers and theorists have learned about the topic of your study. Tell readers how review is organized. Present what you've learned in chunks, depending on how things fit together, complete with a summative statement, paragraph, or bridge to design section.	3–5 pages
Design and methodology	Indicate the who (participants), what (what you tried), when (how often, how long), where (setting), why (why you chose this approach and not some other approach).	3–5 pages
Changes	Few AR studies proceed exactly as planned. Save a section to write whatever changed in your study from your original plans.	Whatever needed
Results	These include findings, results of analyses (tallies, frequencies), tables, graphs, graphics, and your theorizing and thinking about all these. It can be divided into subsections if needed.	4–8 pages
Reflections	What would you do differently next time? Do you have new questions? What was your journey like? How do you feel about what you have done? What have you learned about action research? What have you learned about yourself, your situation, and your students?	1–3 pages
References	Include all the sources referred to in your paper.	1–3 pages
Appendices	Include copies of survey (sample only), interviews, artifacts, permission letters, excerpted research log, and whatever else is pertinent.	Varies by study

FIGURE 17.2 *Outline for an issues-oriented narrative report*

Abstract or story	Start with a brief summary or story that incorporates the main ideas of the study.	50–150 words
Vignette or anecdote	A short descriptive or suggestive scene can be used to introduce the study: poetry, dialogue, brief story within the study.	1–3 paragraphs
Researcher's perspective, issues, purpose, method	Invite reader to delve into the perspective of the researcher, why the interest in this study, the issues, purposes, and methods used.	3–6 pages
Defining the study and its context	Give an extensive description of the context, database, and related research.	3–6 pages
Development of the issues	Drawing on other research and data, more fully develop the issues mentioned earlier, which will lead into the data analysis and interpretation in the next section.	3–6 pages
Presentation of data: descriptive detail, vignettes, quotations, triangulation of data	According to Stake (1995), this is "the place for experiential data" including what the researcher does to confirm and disconfirm her or his observations (p. 123); it can provide a portrait which presents data but refrains as much as possible from interpretation.	2–4 pages
Assertions	Here, Stake (1988) suggests providing information that "allows the readers to reconsider their knowledge of the case," and presents a summary of what he thinks he understands about the case, and how these may have changed during the study (p. 123). These assertions are based on the researcher's interpretation.	2–4 pages
Closing vignette	A vignette or story serves to point a direction, or leaves the reader with an issue or sense of the main idea (if there is one), or opens out into another question. It can be thought provoking and end the report.	A paragraph.
Appendices	Include selective data and other materials useful to interpreting the study, its context, and issues	Variable.

Category ideas adapted from Robert Stake (1995), *The Art of Case Study Research*. Thousand Oaks, California: Sage Publications.

FIGURE 17.3   *Outline for a report that is based on the proposal format outlined in Section 5*

Abstract	Composed at the conclusion of your study, it is a concise, summary of study including major learning related to the research question.	50–100 words
What is my research interest?	What are the issues, concerns, problems, curiosities? What is my question? (How can I . . .?) Why am I interested? (Values, beliefs) What do I already know (through my experience)? What do others know? (Literature, colleagues) What are my hunches? What do I expect to find?	2–3 pages *Criterion:* Question is significant to self and to others.
What did I try out in order to improve my practice? What problems arose and how did I respond?	Who are the participants? What did I try out? When did the activities take place? (Time line) Where did the study take place? How did the action unfold? Why did I try these particular things and not others? What changes occurred in my plans as a result of what I was learning?	3–6 pages *Criterion:* Actions related to values addresses research question or evolving question.
How did I document the process (as I monitored my actions)?	How did I record observations? What did I observe? How did I conduct interviews? What kind of interview format did I use? Whom did I interview? What documents and artifacts did I save? What literature did I read, or what people did I consult with? How did I get permission from students and parents to collect and share data?	1–2 pages *Criterion:* Rich description of observations, critical reflections on actions, multiple perspectives.
How did I interpret the data?	How did I analyze data? How did I synthesize the parts into a whole? How did I formulate my theories? Did I use public theories to help me? Did I make assertions? Include charts, tables, pictures, and other processed data, but refrain, as much as possible, from interpretation.	1 page *Criterion:* Interpretation allows for reasoned thinking, intuition, and creativity.
How have I verified that my judgments are trustworthy and credible?	Researcher's perspective is clearly stated. Multiple perspectives are drawn upon. Indicators (internal/external) are applied. Raw data are provided (transcripts, student work, survey results). Hunches are confirmed and/or disconfirmed. Researcher reflects on self and on action.	1 page *Criterion:* Judgments are based on insights gained from several verification processes.

FIGURE 17.3 *Continued*		
What have I learned and what is the basis of making those interpretations? (Results and analysis)	Include assertions related to research question and the basis of those assertions.	3–6 pages *Criterion:* Interpretation captures the essence and illustrates (rather than tells). Given the evidence, the assertions make sense.
How will these actions make life better? What will I do next?	What are the consequences of these actions for • Myself and my values? • My students? • My situation? What are the implications for my practice? What have I learned about the action research process and becoming a scholar of my own teaching? What further questions do I have?	2–3 pages *Criterion:* Do actions relate to values of equality and democracy in my classroom?
References	List all sources used in paper.	1–3 pages
Appendices	Copies of surveys (sample only), interview transcripts, artifacts, permission letters, excerpted researcher log, etc., should be included.	Varies by study.

General Questions and Information about Writing and Sharing

There are several things to consider in preparing most reports. Depending on the kind of report you decide to prepare, different questions will carry different weight. Think about the following questions in light of the kind of report you will prepare. There are two sections of questions and information: *foundational questions* that might apply to any study and *questions related to sections of the report* and presentation.

Foundational Questions to Consider

The following seven questions relate to conceptualizing your study and therefore come before writing up the report.

1. *What is the purpose of my study and my report?* The purpose of a study and report (whether written or oral) is the foundation for all that follows; it is the touchstone that keeps the study and report focused. Ask yourself: Am I

keeping the purpose of my study in mind as I write? What literature relates to my purpose? Is my purpose evident in the design and analysis of data, in how I interpret the data? Has the purpose of my study changed as my study evolved? If so, how and when do I inform the reader?

Is the purpose of your report to fulfill a course requirement? To sell something to others? To inform? To fuel discussion? To enable others to benefit from what you have learned? To effect change in school policy or curriculum?

2. *Who is the intended audience?* The audience is closely tied to the purpose. Is the report written for a colleague, professor, your staff, the local board of education, a committee, parents, students, a professional community of teachers, or teacher researchers? Knowing the audience will enable you to decide on the amount of detail to include, the format (e.g., concise report or dramatic presentation), tone of voice, and level of formality. Picture a variety of audiences. How might your writing differ or be the same for each group? No matter who the audience is, strive to be *clear* and *succinct*.

3. *What voice, point of view, and writing style are most appropriate to my purpose and audience?* Voice, point of view, and style are what makes our written and spoken journeys unique. If our journey is governed and told by the heart, then the tale of our hearts will weave itself into the pages of our text. This tale may be that of the pilgrim. If it is governed by the mind, the researcher or experiential authority may tell the tale, and the intellect will be dominant. If the story is of inordinate courage, then tests of bravery may frame the narrative. The journalist may take you there, using ethnographic drama. Can you imagine the unique styles that our Oz companions can develop?

As to audience, a report to the board of education may well be argued in a crisp, expository style of the experiential authority or researcher with ample evidence from the research literature and one's own scholarship; whereas a report to teacher colleagues may usefully include the connoisseur's extended vignettes and examples of the students' work. Then again, your board of education may be more attentive to an illustrated story! Length, too, varies with the purpose and audience: short and concise for audience members who have little time to enjoy the vignettes you have crafted; longer for audience members who want to fully appreciate the nuances you have uncovered.

Whatever your perspective, *own your voice;* make it obvious to the reader. Where are you, the researcher, in this study? What are the values and commitments that prompted your study? What are your beliefs about teaching, learning, the purpose of schooling? Present your point of view so that audience members can interpret, question, and come to their own points of view. This is what developing professional judgment is all about—critiquing and forming one's own grounded opinions.

A technical aspect of owning one's voice concerns whether to write in the first person. Many of us were forbidden to use first-person point of view in report writing. Today, however, professionals work to make their writing invitational. They work to make their point of view known, their claims, methodology, and findings clear. First person can help them do this. Journal editors often encourage first-person styles, and oral presentation can be ever so much more engaging in the first person.

In this next section, we'd like to provide some thoughts on writing various parts of the manuscript. While there are many ways to write up a report, there are certain conventions that are followed in many accounts.

4. *What guidelines or rules govern style and the technical parts of writing?* Different fields use different "style" manuals, such as the *Publication Manual of the American Psychological Association* (American Psychological Association, 1994), that of the Modern Language Association, or the *Chicago Manual of Style* (University of Chicago Press, 1993). *Action Research for Teachers: Traveling the Yellow Brick Road* is prepared using American Psychological Association (APA) style for referencing and citations. If you are taking a course or writing an article for publication, consult with the instructor or journal's editorial guidelines for directions about which manual to use. Consult a *current* manual for style and mechanical questions. These manuals will provide information about the parts of the manuscript (abstract, introduction, etc.), grammar, editorial style related to punctuation, spelling, use of quotations, citing references in the text, tables, figures, reference lists, appendices, etc. Therefore, we will not provide details on these technical aspects of writing, but we will address one frequently asked question. What about verb tense?

   The APA manual suggests that the literature review and results are best written in past tense. However, using present tense to discuss the project, findings, or reflections on the work will invite the reader to join you in your deliberations about the work (American Psychological Association, 1994, p. 25).

5. *How do I get started?* There is no universal best way to get started in report writing or in presentation preparation. Some of us can hardly wait to put pen to paper or fingertips to keyboard. We have a beginning vignette in mind, and it sets the tone. Others of us would rather wash dishes, clean the garage, visit the dentist, or do income taxes than confront a blank page or computer screen. Our minds jump over the vast landscape of possibilities, and a hopeless, overwhelmed feeling descends upon us. If you are one of the former jump-right-into-it people, go to it! If you are one of the latter, never fear, for there are ways to conquer the malaise. Here are a few ideas.

   • Sift through all that you have saved. Look for patterns, critical incidents, descriptions, details, or moments that capture the essence of what you feel is important to convey. Now, just sit down and start writing.

   • Make a detailed outline, or a graphic organizer (like a flowchart or a web). Now, start anywhere on it, and proceed to other parts as they seem most relevant. Start writing a section that attracts your energy, a key finding or insight, or a powerful vignette or issue.

   • Robert Stake (1995) argues that topical outlines may give too much license to the writer to continue writing beyond what is necessary: "When each line in the outline has been handsomely developed, the 4 pages originally intended have become 8 or 12" (p. 124). Instead of using a topical outline,

Stake uses a tentative table of contents and allocates the number of pages per section he will write, making him "ruthlessly winnow and sift" (p. 124). Try it.

6. *How can I introduce the report?* No matter what form of writing or oral presentation we choose, whether it is storytelling, poetry, drama, or expository writing, we want to portray our research interest. Think briefly through these questions:
   - What are the issues, concerns, problems, and curiosities?
   - What is my question? How can I . . . ?
   - Why am I interested?
   - What do I already know (through my own experience)?
   - What do others know (other scholars, colleagues, parents, students)?
   - What do I expect to find (hunches, hypotheses)?
   - What do I hope to learn?

The exercises in Section 5 were designed to help you to develop the proposal which incorporated responses to many of these questions. Refer to your proposal when writing up your report, and make changes when needed. You may have used progressive focusing to identify your original questions. Did your questions change during the course of the study? In what ways did they change? Did you develop additional questions?

Use the introduction to bring your reader into the study and your purposes. Vickie Tapp, a teacher we know, does this by starting with a narrative that invites us to understand her desire to study the process of using math journals to help students construct mathematical meanings. This is how she began her report:

> In 1964, a blond, pixielike, third-grade girl skips home from school and runs upstairs to her room. She unloads her bookbag, opens the top drawer to her dresser, and quickly stuffs the math book under the clothes in the top drawer. She changes into her play clothes and goes downstairs. Her unwitting mother supervises her homework and sends her out to play. The next day, it is math time and the teacher announces, "We are going to play a game today. It is called 'Around the World' and we will use flash cards." All the children cheer. Well, almost all. This one little girl is frozen in terror. "I won't know the answer, I don't get math . . . I'll be so embarrassed." Too soon, it is her turn. Oh oh . . . too late! Lost again.
>
> Later in the same math period, the teacher gives out a computation worksheet. This little girl stares at the problems. Numbers dance in front of her eyes. She makes hashmarks on the side of the paper, then hides her hands under the desk and counts up on her fingers. Hot tears slowly trickle down her face, and she finds she is the only one not finished. The teacher takes her paper. Oh well, they were probably all wrong anyway. A few weeks later it is report card time. Our little girl is on pins and needles. Finally, she receives her

brown envelope. She slowly opens the flap and peers inside. An *A* in reading, *A* in spelling, *A* in language. So far, so good. An *A* in social studies. Oh no, an *F* in math. How could that be? An *A* in all other subjects and an *F* in math. What is she going to do? How will she tell Mom and Dad? School is no fun. Her attitude begins to change. Soon her mother has trouble getting her to go to school. She loses herself in reading, getting book after book from the library. Soon, she decides she is good at everything except math, so it is no use trying.

That little girl was me. An intelligent, capable child who for some reason got turned off to math. As a teacher, I have seen many students who are going through similar experiences with math. Some have a very negative attitude. Others have difficulty understanding the mathematical language. I have often wondered if there was some less traditional way of teaching math that might enable these students to use their language and communication skills to help change negative attitudes and bring them to a better understanding of mathematical concepts.

Vickie then discusses her growing understanding of the cognitive nature of the writing process, writing across the curriculum, and her desire to see if the use of writing in math will reduce math anxiety and foster better mathematical understanding among her students.

Jan and Terry begin their paper with a creative overview, inviting the reader to look into classrooms:

Down the hall another day is starting in Mrs. W's first-grade classroom. Seatwork is being assigned so that reading groups may begin. Students will spend 90 minutes on worksheets and workbooks as they cycle through ability-based reading groups using basal readers. This cycle is repeated in many first-, second-, third-, and fourth-grade classrooms up and down the hall, but in some rooms, this cycle is changing. Peek into Ms. S's fifth-grade classroom. No longer do we see the three distinct groups, but the whole class is receiving instruction that revolves on authentic literature and response. After a quick briefing on the day's discussion, students break away into their literature circles. By school policy, all fifth-grade students are homogeneously ability-grouped into four classrooms for reading. Ms. S has the readers who are struggling. Because of this, many of these children have been limited to the "basics." The focus of their instruction up to now has been skill-based basal instruction with few opportunities for what many refer to as enrichment literature activities. Since many of these children have not been members of the "literacy club" (Smith, 1988) in previous years of reading instruction, they have little enthusiasm or motivation to join a club that has excluded them from membership.

Our goal is to open membership in the literacy club to all these children. How can we motivate these children at-risk to take ownership of their reading and want to be members of the club? By using literature circles with authentic text and student-led discussion, we hope to ignite their desire to read. What strategies will best suit their needs—response journals, discussion, prompts, graphic organizers, role play, or cooperative projects? What management techniques have proved successful in other classrooms, and what adaptations of these techniques will be needed for success of literature circles in our classroom? We hope to see these children move from teacher-led activities to student-directed learning.

Jan and Terry cite Smith's idea about student exclusion from the literacy club as a way to confirm their own feelings and commitments.

7. *When, with whom, and how should I share during the writing process? Why* do you want to share? Do you seek a sounding board, serious feedback, confirmation? Do you want a witness to your explorations? Your responses to these questions form the basis for who to share with and how to do so. Do you have a critical colleague whose opinions or expertise you trust and value? How much and in what ways do you want her or his participation? What you seek from others, and who you seek it from, will vary with the time and task. In a period of incubation, where ideas are getting warm and coalescing, you may want a friendly witness, not another opinion. At another time, you may want challenging dialogue.

Report writing and planning presentations present great opportunities to invite collegial discussion. Professional writers rely on others. We can, too. Colleagues and family members can provide reactions and suggestions dealing with content, mechanics, and proofreading, and with audience response to your presentation ideas. Ask someone to read aloud what you have written. Read aloud to yourself and hear the syntax, the rhythm. Freeman (1995) advocates this for writers of all ages. The argument is that since we have often read fiction out loud in our schooling, we have developed an ear for the story, its cadence and rhythm. In writing this text, for example, the characters—

Scarecrow: Do they mean *us?*

Dorothy: I think so.

Authors: Sorry, that does put you into a box, doesn't it? Our point is not to be demeaning by lumping you all together. In fact it is the opposite, because you each have a unique voice, personality, and point of view. We could *hear* your voice when you wanted to speak as we typed our manuscript.

Using our *ears* helps us to edit our text. How does it sound? Do others respond with an understanding we think we intended? Are the main ideas fairly clear? Is there any critical information missing?

After you find a critic to provide you with feedback, tell the person specifically what you would like her or him to do. "I want to see if I did what I started out to do. Do my purpose and findings relate to each other in a coherent way? What do you think?" "Please read through my recommendations and see if they follow from my data." "Please read through the interview with Jen and see what conclusions you come up with." "Am I giving a fair treatment to all the students in my report? What is missing?" "Is this argument persuasive?"

Questions Related to Sections of the Report

Although your report may not have traditional sections as we have organized six of them here, we hope that thinking through them will call attention to what might usefully be included.

1. **Literature review.** *What will you include, and where will you include it in the report?* There are two main ways in which literature related to your study can be particularly useful to the reader. The first way is the grounding that a theoretical perspective can provide in the way of context and lenses from which to understand your study. Literature usually informs your way of thinking about the topic at hand, and how you will study it. This could be called your theoretical basis or foundation. Normally we function from our own theories of how life and teaching and learning work, and as we discussed early in the book, these can be referred to as private theories, which, when we look into them, are usually informed by public theories (i.e., constructivist and structuralist theories, behaviorism, theories of language, or psychosocial or cognitive development). Are there theoretical bases for your study? If so, share them with your readers and let them know how those bases will be used for interpretation.

The second way in which literature is useful to both you and your readers is in positioning your study in a larger context. Where does your study fit within a larger arena? Often there are one or more studies that are quite relevant to your study, and citing important aspects of these can be instructive. Action researchers read and cite literature that supports and challenges their thinking, and provides ideas to try out. As critical readers, we read with a skeptical eye. By reviewing this literature we synthesize multiple dimensions of our topic and deepen our understanding of the contexts of our own research.

Many action researchers refer to relevant literature throughout their reports: in the introduction, design, or interpretation sections. Their references to literature are informal and interspersed throughout the text whenever the literature speaks to a point the researcher is trying to make. Other action researchers organize the literature review systematically in a separate section of the report and label it "Literature review." The degree of formality and organization depends on your purposes. For example, a thesis or dissertation will most likely require a literature review section.

The literature review presents what you have learned about your topic. You may want to begin with an introductory sentence or paragraph describing how the literature review is organized. Try presenting the literature one aspect of the research area at a time. You might end the review with a summary of key points and a sentence connecting to what follows.

Figure 17.4 presents an organizer for a literature review. The topic was students' perceptions of school learning tasks. A group of action researchers was interested in making assignments more appealing to students. To gather baseline data, they planned to interview students about assignments from which they learned the most and the least, and one thing they might recommend to improve schooling. They also wanted to examine what others said about this topic. They found several big ideas through their reading.

Several sources (Alvermann, et. al., 1996; Eisner, 1991; Erickson and Shultz, 1992; Kotter, 1996) provided a rationale for conducting the study. These ideas included the belief that students are key informants about education. Some suggest that students are the consumers of education and for that reason should be consulted. Others, among them action researchers, suggest that student experiences *should* be at the center of attention of all research that affects students.

Another pair of studies involved middle school students, and so clustering these two studies was logical (Taylor and Roselli, 1993; Wasserman, 1995). Other studies revealed attitudes of students toward schooling and curriculum in general (Fouts and Myers, 1992; Maroufi, 1989; Shug et. al., 1984). The final idea that emerged was based on two different studies in which students were interviewed about their expectations of "good teachers" (McCabe, 1995; McDowell and McDowell, 1986). The researchers organized their outline as follows:

- Rationale for interviewing students.
- What middle school students like about school.
- Student attitudes about schooling.
- Student opinions about what makes good teachers.

Stepping Stone 17.1 presents suggestions for organizing the literature review and for citing references within the report.

2. The design and methodology.   What will you include about **how** the study was conducted? You will recognize the following questions from the chapters on designing your study.

- What did I try out in order to improve my practice? What problems arose and how did I respond? (Who are the participants? What did I try out? When did the actions occur? Where? How? Why did I try this and not that?)
- How did I document the process? (Observations, interviews, materials prepared by others)
- How did I interpret the data? (Analysis, synthesis, theories and assertions)
- How have I verified that my judgments are trustworthy and credible? (Is my standpoint clear? Multiple perspectives? Indicators? Raw data? Rich description? Systematic? Self-reflective?)

FIGURE 17.4 *Graphic organizer for literature review*

Rationale for study citations (present first)
*Young et al., 1996
*Eisner, 1991
*Erickson and Shultz, 1992
*Kotter, 1996

Present next:

Studies done on middle school students
*Taylor and Roselli, 1993
*Wasserman, 1995

Then:

Student attitudes about school and curriculum
*Fouts and Myers, 1992
*Maroufi, 1989
*Shug et al., 1984

Finish with:

Student perceptions of teachers
*McCabe, 1995
*McDowell and McDowell, 1986

In this part of the report, provide information to the reader about *how* the study was conducted—*not* what was learned. For example, we include how our theories and assertions are made, *not* what our theories and assertions are. Refer to Sections 5 and 6, and Chapter 15, where we discussed writing down and writing up, for details of the sections as needed.

When instruments are used as part of the data collection, explain each briefly in the design section. If the test, checklist, or observation instrument has been borrowed from another researcher, mention and cite the source of the instrument. If the instrument was teacher-created but similar to one found in someone else's study, cite it as one's own based on the work of so-and-so. If you create the instrument for this study, note your last name and the year on the bottom of the instrument. This makes it officially copyrighted as your own; or use the copyright symbol, year, and person's surname (*The Chicago Manual of Style,* 1993, p. 133).

Note changes in the study. We often change planned activities. For example, Rosie modified her activities considerably as she realized that students were becoming less tolerant and respectful of one another. Note extenuating circumstances

STEPPING STONE 17.1

Organizing a Literature Review

1. Look for commonalities in the findings of research studies, and make a statement that summarizes the commonality. Then cite the authors who have jointly made this point, for example, "Many authors talk of the pitfalls of ability grouping and its negative effects on student performance over long periods of time (James and Roberts, 1990; Johnson, 1991; Jones, 1990; Smith, 1989)." Another way to write this is to incorporate the citations within the sentence that summarizes their idea, for example, "Smith (1989), Jones (1990), James and Roberts (1990), and Johnson (1991) all state that ability grouping is generally detrimental to long-term student achievement and motivation."

2. When you are paraphrasing, page numbers are not needed. When you are using direct quotes, provide page numbers.

3. Index cards and chart paper are two supplies you may want to use when trying to find the main ideas for a literature review. By noting bibliographic information and main ideas on index cards as you read, you can simply refer to these cards to look for commonalities when you are organizing the literature review. Then use the chart paper to list the main ideas and the authors you will want to cite in support of the ideas. You may also want to create a graphic organizer (a concept map or outline) to organize the key ideas you will develop in the report.

that influenced the research. Perhaps you had difficulty interviewing students when a flu epidemic hit the school, or when students were preparing for a test. These obstacles are real and part of the story. *Whatever happens is the research.* And the things that happen that are unanticipated are just as important to what we learn as those things that we carefully plan.

3. Reporting what we have learned, and our bases for interpretation (results and analysis).   *What will you tell about? What have you learned and how will you share it with others?* In this part of the report, tell what you learned related to your research question. Robert Stake (1995), whom we mentioned earlier, is a well-respected scholar whose pioneering of qualitative methods of research have opened up new possibilities in data collection, analysis, and portrayal. He might describe your primary task at this point (and into the next section) as one of coming to understand the case(s), to tease out relationships between issues and participants, to probe issues, and to search for patterns (or lack of them), consistencies, and inconsistencies within certain conditions. Report writing "must winnow and sift for the forest's sake" (p. 121). You make sense of your results *as* you report them.

One way to formulate our learning is to make assertions. These statements are claims to knowledge. Rosie asserts: "It is not good enough to just encourage participants. I had to push for respect." What is the basis of this claim? Rosie goes on to argue that some students were so wounded by the classroom compact and teaching that she as a teacher had to intervene. She also provides a larger context for this assertion: "My own experiences in the political arena and my understanding of the Bill of Rights should have warned me that a democracy that relies too heavily on rights cannot create a safe community." Thus, Rosie relies both on her experience as a teacher and a political activist, as well as the larger framework of the Bill of Rights to make her claim. In Rosie's report, she portrays the teasing and taunts aimed toward one another in such a way that we who have experienced similar situations can identify with Rosie's situation and will resonate with her assertion.

We want to *show* (rather than tell) the reader what happened (the consequences of your actions), and then speculate about why these consequences occurred (assertions). This is the process of theorizing described in Section 6. You might also want to make reference to the public theories that inform your own thinking or to critique those well-established theories if they run counter to your own emerging understandings, grounded in evidence that *you* have amassed.

We want to provide evidence in the form of data to support any claims that we make. But we may also want to move beyond the evidence in making assertions. There are many things we *know* to be "true" that lay beyond the statistics or interview quotes or grades or written documents produced by our students, or any patterns that we carefully and systematically note in our data analysis. Our intuition, as a kind of peripheral vision, can unlock mysteries that all the coded data in the world cannot reveal to us!

To help us to consider our evidence and the quality of the claims to knowledge that we make, we will want to consider these questions:

- Whose story are we telling? (How much is insider/outsider information, and how is it presented, as insider or outsider?)
- On what basis do I make my claims and assertions? (What is the context within which I claim and assert?)

There are questions related to the technical aspects of supporting our assertions and claims to knowledge:

- What data should be included in the report?
- What form should those data take?

Include charts, tables, and other graphics only when they can clarify or otherwise enhance the reader's understanding of the text. Sometimes, in trying to make meaning with the data, we construct tables or charts only to discover they aren't informative or compelling, or, even if useful to the researcher, are not necessary to the report. For example, if the research includes a survey with responses that can be quantified, a table showing the mean score on the responses to each of the questions will allow the reader to see how you interpreted the data. It also allows the reader to interpret the data for herself or himself. In this section, we may also refer the reader to transcripts of interviews, journal entries, documents, and artifacts. We let the reader know that they are available in the appendix and invite the reader to examine them.

Dorothy: What if the researcher interviewed 23 students? Should all 23 interviews be included in the appendices?

Although it depends on the study, the answer is generally no. Include the interview questions and blank survey instrument, and sample responses that are typical of responses or that illustrate the point you are trying to make. If the data can be quantified, tables showing means, standard deviations, correlations, and other more advanced statistical analyses can be included. Within the text of the report, provide a brief description of these items and refer the reader to the appendix where they are included.

Finally, a graphic organizer can help the reader (as well as the author) to see how the study flowed, the context for decisions that were made, and subsequent learning that took place. Refer to Appendix B to see examples of flowcharts and "snake" charts that summarize the overall studies of several action researchers.

4. Reflections and consequences.   *How will you reflect on the consequences of your actions?* Since this is the topic of our concluding chapter, we touch on it here briefly and ask you to defer further cogitations until then. Reflecting on what we have learned, intentionally and unintentionally, is an important part of the report. Reflecting on the consequences of our actions (the so what?) has implications for future action. Since the ultimate aim of action research is to improve our professional practice, time engaged in planning how we can use our findings to improve our practice, our students' learning, and foster equality and community, is time well spent.

5. The references.   *How will you acknowledge the authors and researchers referred to in your study?* Include all the references cited in the report in a separate section. Follow the guidelines provided in the style manual you have chosen for your study.

6. The appendices.   *How and what will you include that enables the reader to see for herself or himself the artifacts of your study?* The appendices offer more detailed information to readers than can be written easily into the prose. Examples of instruments, student work, handouts during the project, rubrics, or other evaluation tools are all included for reader reference. Each appendix is labeled with a letter, Appendix A, Appendix B, and so on. There are no rules as to what goes first or second or last in the appendices except as it makes sense with the study. If a pretest was used, for example, it makes sense to have that appear earlier than the posttest (if there is one). After that, the order of the appendices generally correlates with the order in which they are mentioned in the report. Each appendix needs a succinct but descriptive title (*APA Manual*, pp. 166–167).

CHAPTER SUMMARY

In this chapter we looked into three formats for writing a report: traditional, issues-oriented, and a report that builds on the design presented in Sections 5 and 6. We discussed general questions about report writing (purpose of report, audience, voice, guidelines, how to get started, introductions, when to share and with whom) and specific questions about report writing (review of the literature, presentation of what was learned, reflections, and consequences, as well as references and appendices). In Chapter 18 we go one step further and discuss ways to share our research, in both paper and presentation forms.

Building Learning Communities: Sharing Our Research

In Chapter 1 we talked about learning communities and the value these can have for the profession and for our personal and collaborative growth. Action research is rooted in community. The first reason to share our work, then, is to contribute to the community within which we practice, and to strengthen and be strengthened through the process. These communities can be local, disciplinary, and, thanks to technology, connect various locations across the planet. With our abilities to archive and make information available, we have the resources to build a shared and evolving knowledge base for educational practice. The key is to make our scholarship public; to tell our stories.

Dorothy: I like that. This is *my* story, *our* story, and I can tell it.

Authors: That's right.

Dorothy: If I don't share my thinking, who will challenge it? Who will offer me critique? Who will help me to see in new ways?

Authors: We can all use help to protect us from insularity. Writing and telling our stories can bring thoughts and ideas together in powerful ways, and those powerful ways can bring us together in scholarly communities. Telling the story is as important as writing it. Both whom we tell it to and how we make it available to others have consequences for all who have an interest.

At our university, we keep action research (AR) reports and make them available to others. These reports provide examples for other action researchers for critique and discussion. They can provide guidance, ideas, models, and inspiration. Can you envision sharing your work at a faculty meeting, committee meeting, action research or other conference at the regional, state, and even international levels?

Lion: "Envision?" Pardon me, but I think I am going to faint.

Authors: Sorry, Lion. We're not asking this to scare you. As you complete your project, we predict that you, like Dorothy, will *want* to share it. You will realize what you have to share, and you will want to discuss it with others, especially if you have taken the creative route and stepped into new territory in preparation of your report.

Just as there are many voices and ways to write, so, too, are there many ways to share: writing, speaking, and using various forms of technology and media. We will mention a few common forms here: creation of a paper for publication, professional presentations, and poster sessions. We will conclude with a few technological avenues and a summary of the chapter.

Creating a Paper for Publication

Have you thought about writing about your study for publication? Imagine an account that colleagues or others may find of interest. Consider the options for publication: a newsletter, a newspaper, a magazine, a book, or a journal. Each may be viable. We will address the journal possibility here. Once you identify a potential journal, a quick analysis of its contents can provide useful information. This analysis may include the following:

- *What can you learn from the table of contents?* Discern the types of articles and topics consistent with the journal's mission. Are there articles in your area of interest? How long are the published articles?
- *Read several recent articles.* Can you envision your paper among these?
- *What can you learn from the directions for authors?* In the front matter, or on the back or inside covers, you will find information about submitting manuscripts: addresses where manuscripts are to be sent, number of copies required, style manual to consult, the mission and audience for the journal, and the kind of submissions the journal hopes to secure. Is there any indication of how long it takes for a response? Will the journal send reviewer critiques? Where can you write or call for further information?
- *Have you considered contacting the editor(s)?* Most editors encourage conversation about potential journal contributions. Is your paper appropriate for the journal? What is the likelihood of the journal's giving your paper fair consideration? Consider calling or sending electronic mail to someone on the editorial staff.

Consider collaborating on your first submission with an interested colleague, perhaps one with some experience, even if the colleague was not your co-researcher. Can you decide in advance how to share responsibilities for writing, manuscript preparation, and submission of the manuscript? Will your contributions be equal or unequal? Do you each have talents suited to different tasks? Typically, the person who drafts the copy becomes first author, while other author(s) contribute to rewriting, writing designated sections, preparing figures and graphics, editing, proofreading, and doing other parts of manuscript preparation.

Frequently, manuscripts are not accepted the first time, at least not without a request for revisions. Most experienced writers get requests to revise and resubmit. Reviewer comments and suggestions provide valuable opportunities for learning. Not all suggestions (even if more than one reviewer makes the same suggestion) are useful, or what's best for your paper. Do the suggestions seem reasonable and constructive? If so, give them serious consideration. Do the suggestions seem to miss the point? The reviewer may have misinterpreted or simply disagreed with your stance or premise, in which case you may choose to "stick to your guns" and not make changes. (Madeleine L'Engle, noted author of juvenile, young adult, and adult novels, enjoys sharing how *A Wrinkle in Time,* her Newbery Award novel, was rejected by 22 publishers before publication, most saying it simply "would not sell.") It pays to have confidence, courage, and persistence!

Professional Presentations

Many of us grew up when pupils were expected to be quiet and in their seats. "Talking out of turn" was considered bad behavior. We learned to be obedient and quiet. Oral presentations were "telling," even when they were showing and telling. *Engaging* others in related discussion was conspicuously absent. To present one's work as a way to start discussion would have been thought odd. If these are our only experiences in presenting our work outside our classrooms, the process can be difficult and anxiety-producing, in spite of the fact that we present ideas and material to our students everyday.

There are many ways to make an oral presentation. You can present a key idea and engage others in discussion of the issues involved. You can make a formal presentation and engage others in both active ways (pose questions for them to respond to or discuss during the session) and silent ways (pose questions to think about individually) depending upon what you say and how you frame it. *Invite* engagement with your ideas. How about starting with a question or a provocative vignette? You could end with a question or a provocative vignette. Change the pace midway into your presentation and pose a provocative question. Present a key idea and discuss it, present another key idea, and so forth. What can you do for a conclusion? Seed a discussion to take place *after* the presentation is over.

Dorothy: This is another "learning experience," isn't it? I can feel it.

Authors: Indeed, it is. Over the years, we have learned much from presenting our work, from the successes, and especially from the times when something flops. Humor is a great teacher! Figure 18.1 lists tips for making successful presentations.

Presenting your work can be an exhilarating experience, especially when you engage your audience, igniting sparks on both sides of the podium.

A presentation can take many forms: a chronicle of your study, in which you take the audience along on your evolving journey; a performance of "ethnographic fiction" in which different forms of telling or serendipitous audience involvement is included; or a well planned dramatic story, creating a feeling of being at a theatrical performance.

Many of the considerations and questions we raise in conjunction with poster sessions below can easily be applied to other types of presentations.

Poster sessions.   Teachers have long created bulletin boards to depict concepts, events, or projects. Poster sessions usually take place in large rooms where many movable bulletin boards, easels, or wall spaces have been segmented and designated for various researcher displays. Some poster sessions feature traditional displays where a researcher posts a title of the study, key charts or graphs or other

- **Who is your audience?** Know the expertise of your audience, the numbers involved, their interest in your topic. A presentation to teacher peers may differ from one for parents or school board members. The size of your audience can influence the kind of presentation and activity you can accomplish.

- **What is the physical context of your presentation?** The size and shape of the room, the acoustics, the ability to use equipment easily and readily, the need for a microphone, whether people are seated facing you or at round tables, whether you'll be able to move from a podium, whether the equipment you use will be managed during the presentation by you or by someone else—all these can influence your planning. Ask questions about the arrangement beforehand to minimize unwelcome surprises.

- **How can you be organized?** Will it be helpful to have the order of your presentation arranged by transparencies, note cards, or visuals? Be sure that transparencies or note cards are numbered or lettered for ease in finding them, and that all fonts are large enough for audience viewing. During presentations lights are often dimmed so the audience can see your transparencies, slides, or computer presentation. Be sure you can see what _you_ need to in low-light conditions. If you are using handouts, be sure to arrange for an adequate number. Have a sign-up sheet if the audience is larger than expected, so those desiring handouts can sign their names and addresses. Getting information out to others as soon as possible after the presentation will enable participants to keep the information fresh.

- **How will you reach out to your audience?** How will you introduce yourself? Making eye contact and beginning with an anecdote, personal related story, humor, or a poem, can establish rapport.

- **Speak clearly and at a moderate pace.** Many presenters speak too rapidly or slowly, or softly to be understood by everyone.

- **Will you use advanced organizers?** You may want to inform your audience, orally or with a graphic, of what your presentation will cover. This helps create a context for listening.

- **How will you use graphics to best effect?** If you display a table, graph, flowchart, photograph, etc., narrate it for audience members. They will need time to grasp what by now seems readily apparent to you. Explain symbols or abbreviations.

- **Will you share the text visually?** Teachers often wish to share examples of student work. A powerpoint presentation, transparencies, or handouts can be used. Large type and reading out loud can be useful.

- **Will you use video clips?** Is the video clip set in the right place and ready to go? Is the volume sufficient for the room size? Can all audience members see the monitor? Where are the room lights and who will dim and raise them? How will you prepare your audience? Are video clips brief and to the point?

- **How will you keep track of time and where you are?** It's easy to forget what you have said and what needs to be done. You may want to have an outline handy in large font for referral; or you may return to an overhead that gave your advance organizer, and remind people what is left at the same time. _Stick to your time constraints,_ especially if yours is one of several presentations. Remember the last long-winded speech you endured? A clock or a friend or both can tell you that you have 5 or 10 minutes left.

FIGURE 18.1 *Continued*

- **How will you conclude your remarks?** Often the tone you leave your audience with comes from your finale. Save a key piece of evidence, and issue an inspiring piece of student work, a story, an anecdote, or a related poem for your closing.

- **Will you build in time for audience questions?** Find out ahead of time if there is time allotted for audience questions. This can be one of the most valuable parts of the session. Respond to all questions honestly and respectfully (even if you covered the point in your talk several times), and redirect appropriate questions back to others in the audience. The nature of AR is dynamic, and discussing unanswered questions can be informative for all involved.

- **Do you want to offer a few summary statements?** These can include what you have learned at the session from others both in preparing and in presenting your work. Thank the audience?

- **How can you enjoy and learn from the experience?** Presenting your work can be exhilarating. If you are engaged, chances are that your audience will be, too.

graphics, and key learnings, conclusions, or implications in a concise, page-long narrative. Take your graphics as seriously—they convey important information and concepts. Your display will attract more attention and interest if it is as lively as your study.

Think of your poster (or presentation) as a composition with background, middle ground, and foreground. What are key aspects of each? What does the observer need to know about the context (background) to understand your work? What, then, are methodological considerations and data (middle ground) that bring you to your results (foreground)? Next comes the "so what" (centers of interest). What are the focal points of meaning along this research landscape? What is the main center (or centers) of interest? What do you want to convey to the observer, and how might you most succinctly and effectively do so? What attracts your energy about the study? How can you best portray and convey this in a parsimonious way? Preparing for a poster session (or presentation) enables you to sift and winnow one more time, but also to look at your study from new perspectives. Sit down and visualize your study. What symbols and artifacts come to mind? If your work were a painting, what would it look like? If you could select only one idea to develop, what would that one idea be? What metaphor, image or symbol captures the essence of what you have learned?

How might you present your research in such a way to engage others in discussion of the issues you bring out? Instead of a "telling" poster session, how might you invite conversation that engages others and takes you *beyond* your study? Two or three points with examples may be far more compelling than a longer and more comprehensive treatment. On the other hand, you may want to present your work as a collage, including the key aspects of the study and its evolution and consequences. Photographs, student artifacts, excerpts or intriguing quotations can capture a main idea. We are not advocating "show" in a decorative or glitzy way; rather we are advocating taking seriously and playfully the way others may be attracted to your work and how you can make it visually clear, strong, and inviting.

Technological avenues.   New avenues for sharing research and learning continue to arise. Figure 18.2 lists four popular methods of using technology. Ask for technical assistance from local media specialists, computer support personnel, and, in many cases, from children!

FIGURE 18.2 *Technological ways of sharing research*

Method	Description
Presentation software	Popular programs such as powerpoint, are readily available, a computerized multiscreen presentation can include text, photographs, charts and graphs, video clips, and even music or special effects. A storyboard, included in the presentation software, lets you plan each segment. Each segment can also be made into transparencies.
A web site	Create a (temporary or permanent) web site of your work. In addition to sharing findings, many web sites invite responses and can begin dialogues, and future collaborations.
E-Mail	E-mailing ideas emerging from our studies to colleagues may be the start of challenging dialogue.
Slide shows	Slide shows, both the old and the new electronic variety, can be effective for illustration.
E-mail discussion groups	The following is a sampling of the wide range of groups involved in teacher research. 1. Action Research Mailing List Subscribe (include subscribe arlist-1 firstname lastname) 2. Participatory Action Research Network Subscribe (include subscribe partalk-1 <your name>) 3. Teacher Researchers list Subscribe (include: subscribe xtar <your name>) 4. For a broader list of Qualitative Research Email Discussion Groups Contact: Judith Preissle Professor of Anthropology and Education Social Science Education Tucker Hall University of Georgia Athens, GA 30602-7014 Voice: 706-542-6489 Fax: 706-542-6506

CHAPTER SUMMARY

One of the most important parts of the action research process lies in making your study known to others, both for the process of public critique and for the contribution this makes to the learning community. Many of the same considerations we talked about in the previous chapters in this section apply to writing about the research and preparing it for presentation to others, for example, the voice, perspective, the form of the telling. To some people, the report can be presented without alterations; for others, the further development of the ideas in the report can be a most invigorating and creative process. If it is, it will be contagious.

Dorothy: And people will see that research doesn't have to be boring. Let people see the human side of scholarship and community.

SECTION SUMMARY

We have discussed two of the most important ingredients of action research in this section—the acts of *writing,* and of *sharing,* that is, of *making one's work public.* Both writing and sharing are key to critical practice. They, as we, are not neutral. In action research we observe, write, and speak from a point of view and a value system; and part of the presentation of our work is to make those perspectives known, to facilitate discussion with colleagues and others who have similar and differing points of view. The quality of what we open to discussion and critique is shaped by our observations and interpretations. As we shape our stories and continue to critique our own and others' action research, we stretch our capacities and fuel our scholarly communities; and not surprisingly, our ideas, practices, and professions grow. Our inner and outer worlds become more obviously part of the same world. From our evolving perspectives we find that Oz has much in common with Kansas and Kent and . . .

Perhaps at the beginning of this chapter, writing the report and presenting our work to others seemed a bit daunting.

Scarecrow: If *daunting* means intimidating, yes. But so did the beginning of our journey. The Munchkins would rather have faced the Wicked Witch of the West than face the journey to Oz and have to address the Wizard with *their* concerns! We've come on our journey together and found that each of us has valuable contributions to make. If you doubt the importance of each of us, just take a little side trip with L. Frank Baum, the original Wizard of Oz! By 1900 he had figured out that a brain, a heart, and courage were all part of the same person, and that growing takes all of them working together. Do you really think that teachers are any less fearful in taking *their* hearts and minds on an action research journey and presenting *their* works to the board of education a century later ? Why should *we* be any different?

Lion: Yeah. I've heard that more people would rather face death than speak in public.

Authors: Yes, many of us were fearful as we began our journey. We say *us* advisedly. For we had never written a book together, and when you guys popped up and invited yourselves along, how in the world were we to take *you* someplace over the rainbow when *we* had never been there either? Now that you have work to share, are you still anxious about presenting and discussing it?

Dorothy: No. It's different when you have something important to say. In analyzing and interpreting and writing, the importance of the ideas and actions take over; you find that you have something engaging to discuss with others.

Authors: Good. That is the point of this section, to help you to discover how much you have to say, and to help you to develop your voice and ways to communicate with it. We all have to face our fears and in so doing discover that we each have ruby slippers. (In case that realization hasn't yet dawned, we have one more chapter that will surely do the trick.) In this section we set out to discuss the writing process and to open up some possibilities for reporting your work. The weight of the past can be a heavy influence, and more than a few action researchers have tried to fit their work into traditional formats only to lose the study's vitality and coherence. You will know what kind of reports and sharing to do by the nature of your study. There is no one-size-fits-all. Once you develop a report in your own voice—whatever format you select or create—your colleagues and the profession will want to know of it.

Exploring the Forest

Portraying and Communicating

To get a feel for different ways to portray your work, we have put together several explorations and exercises for you to try. You might think of yourselves as artists and craftpersons who are trying out different kinds of media. The more media you try out, the larger your repertoire can become and the more choices you will have to render your work.

1. The four parts of this exercise will quickly take you into major aspects of your study:
    - Without taking much time to think about it, come up with an incident, finding, or quotation that might introduce your study to the reader. Write it up as an entry vignette. Now think about an incident, finding, or quotation and write it up as a vignette that will conclude your study. What, if anything, do these suggest for what comes in the middle?
    - Free-write. What *issue* or issues undergird your study? What have you learned in relationship to this issue from your research? What *actions* did you take in your study related to this issue?
    - In two paragraphs tell the story of *how* you studied what you studied.
    - In one paragraph, tell the "so what" of your study. What did you find out from what you did, and what does it mean?
2. In this exercise, we want you to try out four conventions for report writing that John Van Maanen identified. We won't write an entire report using one convention, but we will write up sections of our reports using different conventions to see how each might work with our studies.
    a. Write the preface (or introduction) to your report, using *experiential authority*. This means that you will establish your credibility as the researcher in this first part. Speak from your own point of view and in first person.
    b. Select one or two stories that you find to be most interesting within the material to be reported, some of the "parts" you studied, and write it (them) in a richly detailed vignette that could be used in your report. Write them up in a *documentary style*.

    c. Select a person who participated in your study, and write a portrait of this person, incorporating his or her language, thoughts, experience, and behavior. Although you put this material together, do not put yourself into the portrait directly—do not include your interpretations (although they will be part of what you select to tell). Keep the portrait brief, and try to portray the *culture member's point of view.*

    d. Write up the so-what of your study in a manner that conveys your *interpretive omnipotence.* This is a no-nonsense, no waffling, no humility, and no hint of insecurity kind of writing. Tell it as you see it—from your data and analysis.

    e. Now, cut and paste each of these together as a report. What do you need to add? How do these different parts and styles fit together? Which of the four conventions did you most enjoy using? Why? Which did you least enjoy using? Why? What did you learn about report writing from these different kinds of portrayal?

3. Work with a colleague or small group of colleagues. Take several issues of a respected journal in your area of interest. Locate at least three articles with literature reviews. Read these literature reviews with your partner(s). For each literature review, *read as a writer* and describe the review. How was it set up? How would you describe it? Did the author arrange it chronologically, by a raging controversy, or by several logically chunked subheadings? Compare your descriptions with others. No doubt, you will note that there are many ways to write a literature review. Perhaps you will find one that suits your study. Pay special attention to how the authors integrated many studies into a brief review.

4. After you complete a draft section of your report, invite a small group (three to four) of critical colleagues to read it, listen to it, or do both. Invite impressions and questions. Ask for written and verbal feedback. Each can yield valuable results. With written feedback, you get each person's perspective without the influence of one person on another. One person doesn't dominate and influence others' responses. Follow up on pertinent responses. However, if you would like to have their responses act as catalysts for group discussion, reading your work to them without the benefit of their having the written form might be more effective. Or, give them copies before you meet as a group, and ask for their responses so that when you meet as a group, each person can put forward her or his considered responses. To what would you like to have responses? What observations do they offer? Do they hear or see what you intended to convey? What else, if anything, do they hear or see? If you raise an issue, is it clear? Do they offer any suggestions? Note your thoughts as you begin sharing and after the process is completed.

5. Plan a presentation to a group in your school or institution.

    a. Decide on the group and why you would like to present your work. (Is it to inform, engage in discussion, help to bring about change, invite other perspectives?) State this as your aim. When you present your work, tell the group of your aim.

b. What three points would you like to convey?

c. Now, think "outside the box." How can you take these three points and invite others to ponder them? Think of three ways you could present or engage your group with them.

d. Mine your data—and your report. Where is the gold? What is hot, and what is not? Sift through your report. What attracts your energy? Go with it. Then think about why it attracts your energy. (What has the greatest potential to engage others in such a way that change is made possible?) Is there part of the insider story that you would like to tell?

e. Now, think about the bookends: How will you get the presentation off the ground? How might you conclude it?

f. Enjoy presenting your work. Now that you have ideas, use them to get started.

g. After you have "done it," what worked well and what were the results in terms of your aims? What else happened? What were the surprises? What did you learn? Where is your thinking related to your project now?

Lessons from Oz

66 But you have not yet told me how to get back to Kansas."

"Your silver shoes will carry you over the desert," replied Glinda. "If you had known their power you could have gone back to your Aunt Em the very first day you came to this country."

"But then I should not have had my wonderful brains!" cried the Scarecrow.

"And I should not have had my lovely heart," said the Tin Woodman.

"And I could have lived a coward forever," declared the Lion.

"This is all true," said Dorothy, "and I am glad I was of use to these good friends. But now that each of them has had what he most desired, and each is happy in having a kingdom to rule beside, I think I should like to go back to Kansas. 99

The Wonderful Wizard of Oz
L. Frank Baum (1900)

Are you ready to go now?

Dorothy: Almost. Here I am at the end of the journey. I have traveled the Yellow Brick Road, weathered flying monkeys and wicked witches, and found my way through apple-hurling trees, poppyfields, and hourglasses not in my favor—to the Emerald City, only to discover that the Wizard is just a scam artist without answers to my questions! And Glinda reveals that I have always had the power to get home! I need to think about all this. There are so many riddles!

Scarecrow: And puzzling paradoxes! But, you know, I think I'm beginning to understand. The journey itself, with all its riddles and paradoxes, was important, not just the destination.

Tin Man: My, that sounds erudite! And, it's true. I feel differently at the end of this journey. I guess it's sort of like . . . development.

Lion: Yep. Now, I can take on *anything* that comes my way! After all those poppies, monkeys, and witches, I'm rrrrready to stand by my values and act on their behalf no matter the obstacles! I'll grab those apples and use 'em, not just dodge 'em! I'll climb those apple trees and get to the bottom of my questions. No matter where my curiosity takes me and where I have to meddle, I'll go and I'll meddle!

Authors: It sounds as if we've all learned some valuable lessons. Let's follow up on some of those riddles and paradoxes you refer to. We can wander over to those tree stumps by the gates to the Emerald City and ponder our journey. Take a few minutes to come up with a riddle or paradox and we will come back to them soon.

Riddles, Paradoxes, and Contradictions

Most of us formally study teaching in a college or university, and after we begin a career, we realize that we have just *started* to learn the complex art of teaching. We find we have a continuous stream of questions about students, teaching, learning, education, and social issues. And we search for answers—from books, articles, courses, colleagues, and the web. These questions fuel our professional development and suggest more questions. We "finish" to "begin"! This is a paradox about becoming scholars.

Teaching presents a continuing stream of riddles and paradoxes necessitating the scholar's eye. Few things about teaching and learning are certain, predictable, or tidy. As we look for answers we find more questions. We want to help our students find answers, but only through helping them raise meaningful questions. The more we continue to learn, the more we question what we do. When we recognize, accept, and even celebrate this complexity, we are taking the scholar's journey.

The more we study our students and their learning, the more we can learn about *ourselves*. Teaching requires us to constantly examine ourselves as human beings committed to *teaching*. If we paid attention to what we already know (in our hearts, minds, and souls), and what our colleagues help us to understand, we would not have to journey far and wide to make teaching and learning better for ourselves and our students. But without that journey, we might not gain the wisdom, passion and courage that our teaching days require of us. That is one of the riddles that makes teaching and learning so complex and yet so simple. We cannot find our way home until we have gotten a little lost in the process of developing as professionals.

The story of Rosie's democratic classroom illustrates this point well. Her action research journey was taken to find ways to enact strongly held democratic ideals in her social studies classroom. Several students maintained *either-or* thinking and contradicted her plan by enacting their personal agendas. The dislike she began to feel for them reminded her even more of her responsibility to create and sustain democratic ideals in her classroom. She wondered if she had emphasized individual freedom without attending adequately to social responsibility. Had she inadvertently reinforced the belief that democracy could exist without responsibility, that we are EITHER free as individuals OR have social responsibility? For some students, this was a paradox.

As Parker Palmer writes in *The Courage to Teach* (1998), "In certain circumstances, truth is a paradoxical joining of apparent opposites, and if we want to know that truth, we must learn to embrace those opposites as one" (63). Part of teaching is helping others to think beyond what seems obvious and often this means accepting multiple perspectives and opposites. Yet, aspects of our culture work against a more integrated and ecological way of thinking. Where mind is separate from heart, we have cognitive objectives and affective objectives. Where one way of developing is separate from another way of developing we have gifted students and disabled students. Where theory is separate from practice we have experts and teachers. Where we have those who have attained great knowledge and those who are waiting to be filled with that knowledge, we have teachers and learners. Where we have those with power who try to control teaching and learning and those who carry out the will of those more powerful, we have accountability—for teachers only.

This kind of thinking is so embedded in our educational systems that we come to believe in these dichotomies, and base our practice on separation rather than on ecology and integration. The net result is that we typically regard teaching, learning, curriculum development, evaluation, educational research and professional development as separate and distinct educational processes. But as Elliott argues, "Action research unifies processes often regarded as quite disparate . . . teaching is conceived as a form of research aimed at understanding how to translate educational values into concrete forms of practice . . ." (1991, pp. 53-54).

Lessons from Home, Heart, Mind, and Courage

Here are a few lessons that action researchers have shared with us over the years. Their "lessons" are filled with paradoxes, not unlike those of our Oz travelers.

Maureen, for example, wrote, "The most important learning . . . was the realization that I should not want to control the outcome." She concluded:

> When I realized that research meant stepping back and allowing changes to take place without my input, I allowed myself to relax, let things flow, and wait. When I relaxed, I could almost hear a collective sigh from my students, and they began to make choices and decisions on their own which contributed to the results of my research. When I became aware of my apprehension about this, the true research began.

Maureen expresses one of the paradoxes many action researchers face. Part of becoming the teacher you want to be is achieved by stepping back and inviting students take the lead. By empowering students, we empower ourselves. The process of stepping back and letting go can be difficult. Yet, when we do, we find that we give up control, and we gain control. We give away power and we become powerful.

This theme of *power* can be manifested in expressions of confidence. As Maureen and Chris expressed it respectively, : "My view of myself has changed. I am more confident . . ." and ". . . the teacher as researcher process empowers me to be a better teacher and learner . . . I am using these skills in developing a new program . . ."

Patricia found that confidence can lead to courage: "I learned never to be content with the status quo." Similarly, Vicki resolved: "not to be afraid of experimenting and trying something new and different. I have already made my research project part of my curriculum."

Leann, a math teacher, wrote about the seeming contradiction that in order to understand matters of the mind, it takes *heart:* "I have learned the importance of research. In order to successfully teach and understand an educational concept, you need to get to the root of it. The only way that can be achieved is through heart-felt research."

We, Wendy, Joanne, and Mary Lou, worked through contradictions and paradoxes with this book and learned our own lessons in the process. For example, how might two seemingly opposing processes live within one person and project: the importance of, and need for, curiosity, imagination, creativity, and intuition *as well as* the skills, techniques and research methods necessary to a scholar? "Either-or" is easy; "Both" and "what-when" are harder to describe. How could we weave the elements of AR into a tapestry that would begin to do justice to this rich and evolving form of education? On the one hand we emphasized the need to be open and receptive to affective dimensions of the research process, and on the other hand, to adopt and cultivate specific rule-governed processes, where there is little or no room for creativity. We learned as we wrote and discussed our work. We found out how very different our experiences and perceptions were, one from another. We learned where our writing varied from the values we espoused.

And now, it's time to get back to our riddles.

The Riddles of Oz

Authors: Are you ready to share your riddles?

Dorothy: Yes. I am. I came all this way, through a land far away, and now, I understand home in new ways. I see it differently. It's not just a place called Kansas. It's me, becoming confident, comfortable with uncertainty, skeptical, and committed. Action research is a way to become more sure-footed. Mine is a journey of understanding the place I call home, and action research helped me to do just that, to understand.

Lion: Mine is easy. If I hadn't taken action and risks along the road and faced things that were scary, how would I have ever developed courage? Courage doesn't come to us when we are sitting around on the side of the road. Courage is related to acting on our beliefs, and when we do, we feel powerful. And when we work with others who share our commitments, that's real power! We are a team, after all.

Tin Man: That's similar to my paradox. I looked to the Wizard for a heart, as if it were a prize that he could give me. He couldn't give me one, but he could help me to see what I already had. This is just the beginning. I know that I won't get a heart all at once. I know I have one now, but my heart will expand as time goes on and as we continue on our journeys. I will see my heart grow as it is challenged, and I find it reflected back to me by good friends like you.

Scarecrow: And me, I looked for an answer only to find more questions! Now I know what it means to have a brain—not only for finding answers, but for asking thoughtful questions and reflecting critically upon them!

Wizard: Ah, my scholarly friends, while it's been said that necessity—whether for heart, courage, brain, home, or democratic classroom—is the mother of invention, let it also be a catalyst for that most splendid of the action researcher's resources, imagination. Let your stories evolve, and as you expand them, they "will become mirror and window both—reflecting back knowledge and understanding . . . for a widening circle . . . opening possibilities for all" (Ayers, 1992, p. 265).

Authors: Hmmm . . . "mirror and window both," wish we'd have said that. Put on those ruby slippers (they may be sneakers!). You will need them as we conclude our journey by . . .

FIGURE 18.3

Exploring the Forest

Constructing Lessons from Oz in a Portfolio

When Dorothy gets home and thinks about her journey and the forest she has just come through, her energy will still be there; and she can use this energy to take others with her, to *show* them highlights of her journey and the lessons she learned. Having completed that journey, she can reflect and create new perspectives, what we earlier referred to as *writing about* her research journey. The learning community that we have talked about throughout our time together is fueled by communication, and what better time to communicate than when you have something meaningful to say! This is what we will do together in our concluding exploration: We will reflect on our journey, we will decide what is most meaningful to say, and we will say it in a form that others can appreciate.

Reflecting on the Research Process

We offer several suggestions for reflecting on our journey, and, as is true of any party, you can accept the invitation or not! Select what suits you and come up with your own ideas.

1. Ask yourself: What were the *key aspects* of this journey for me? What were the *highlights* of the research process? What were the greatest *challenges?* What were the greatest *lessons* and *turning points* in the process? What were the *riddles* and the *paradoxes?* At what points did you call upon your *imagination?* Free-write about these.

2. Look back over your journal and the explorations and exercises you selected to complete. Skim them all. Now, write about what stands out in your mind about what you have completed. Free-write; don't think too much about it. Try to see the whole and the parts within, but do not get caught up in the parts (that's another adventure). Now that the wicked witch has finally been dissolved, and the monkeys are free from her control, they can offer assistance. Our purpose here is to bring the end into sight with the flying monkeys *helping* us to look down over the entire landscape we have traversed. Flying too low in any area could mean getting lost in its details. The monkeys can help to keep us at a safe distance.

3. If you were presenting a step-by-step story of your journey (from "What is AR?" to doing it, and completing the cycle), with a key aspect for each step, how would you describe the process? Take a few minutes to write about it.

4. Ask yourself the following questions. You may want to include your responses in the reflection section of your AR report.
   - What are the *consequences of my actions*—for myself, my students, my situation, my teaching?
   - What have I *learned about my students?* (How do they learn? How is their learning linked to the social, cultural, political, and economic contexts that frame their lives?)
   - What have I *learned about myself and my values?* (What have I learned about myself as a person, as a professional? Have I grown in any ways? Have my new understandings influenced others? Have I become firmer in my convictions? Have I modified my positions? Has my thinking become more inclusive, more complex, more differentiated?)
   - What have I *learned about my situation?* (What power do I have to influence my situation? What are the social, cultural, political, and economic factors that shape the context in which I teach?)

The ways in which we address these questions will help us to consider the next question:

- What are the *implications* of what I have learned (about the consequences of my actions) for what I will do next and in the future?

5. Finally, we will want to reflect on the *action research process itself.* We conceptualize teaching as a cycle of acting, observing, and reflecting—the work of scholars, best done with the help of critical colleagues. What lessons have we learned about the scholarship of teaching?
   - What have I learned about *documenting my work?*
   - What have I learned about *analyzing and interpreting data and verifying* what I have learned?
   - What have I learned about *working with critical colleague(s)?* How might we continue our work together?
   - What has been the most valuable part of this process? The least? The most difficult or challenging for me?
   - What lessons have I learned for future action research studies?
   - What will I need to do to continue this study or to start another one?

Let's take one last look at a few of Shawn's, Jan's and Terry's, Rosie's, and Andy's reflections on their work. Shawn's study had a major impact on her professional development and teaching career: "I am going to pursue a certification in teaching English as a Second Language. I have spoken to the current ESL teacher in my district, and she has directed me in what I need to do." About the researcher log, Shawn writes:

[It] was a valuable tool. I often went back and read what had gone on in the past week. I was . . . able to note some things about my teaching, for example, lessons that worked and those that did not. I made entries at least four times a week.

This seemed to keep me focused on the project. Jan and Terry reflect on the collaborative nature of their learning:

> Two heads are definitely better than one. Our strengths and weaknesses complemented each other . . . We had discussed the pros and cons of working together on this project at length before undertaking the study. This is not for everyone . . . Sharing a common philosophy of education has also made working together possible
>   . . . Just as the students keep learning, so do we.

Rosie writes about what she might have done: "I should have paid more attention to the results of the Citizenship Survey. Had I done so, I might have spent more time at the beginning of the class creating a common ground of the concrete details about what citizenship and a democratic community entailed." She also reflects on what she will do next: "I will . . . use some of the methods of documentation that I learned in action research. No matter what my teaching responsibilities might be . . . documenting the action and my thoughts and feelings . . . will help me to be more responsive to my students and more clear in my thinking." She goes on: "As far as tempering my 'savior' spirit, I'll keep reminding myself (with a little help from my friends) . . . my journal will be my life-long teaching companion."

Andy concludes his study with a narrative that shows the importance of his study and the direction it will take in the future:

Andy: 'Hey, are you going to do that club again this year?' a smiling eighth grader asks. 'Yes, as soon as I have my class up and running. Do you want to be involved?' I inquired.

Teacher: 'Oh yes,' she states. 'And my friends do too!' I chuckled for this is my third conversation like this today.

Kelly, another teacher, reflected on the process of AR, noting that "looking at all the data on one student was like opening a gift; I did not know what I was going to receive. I may have gotten some hints, but until all the data was assembled, I could only guess . . . I do not need constant tangible proof (a test, a work sheet, or discussion) that learning is taking place. I need to trust the process. Some of the superfluous proof I desired put brakes on my students. I am taking those brakes off . . ." Finally, Kelly learned that "perhaps my biggest revelation during the study is that my students and I are more similar than I thought."

The Researcher's Story of the Journey

Having reflected on the AR process, we will wrap up our journey by constructing a portfolio. Revisit *Exploring the Forest* in Chapter 2 for the portfolio section if you think this might be helpful. The portfolios we advocate here are narrated and illustrated. The portfolio is narrated by you, the researcher, and illustrated with examples. Engage readers; draw them into the story. Although you can prepare an action researcher portfolio for many different reasons (and from many different points of view!), here we will pose questions for a simple and straight forward portfolio.

You have been telling your story all along the way: to yourself, your colleagues and friends, and to your journal where you may have completed "Exploring the Forest" sections throughout the book. Having completed a few of the reflective explorations on previous pages, to get a picture of the "whole"of the journey and of some of the important aspects of the process and the results (at least some of which are processes), we are ready to construct a portfolio whose purpose is to tell the researcher's story of the journey.

- The journey, simply put, can be narrated by the author in a straightforward way, as the newspaper reporter or the historian might move through time, narrating the experiences of *doing the research* and of the *products of the doing*. It can be told from any of the perspectives we discussed in Chapter 7, as well as any others you may create and develop.
- Another way to reconstruct the journey is to find a theme or a few key aspects of the study and follow it or them through, not necessarily in chronological order. Incorporate the story and highlights of the study.
- How about selecting and even writing some vignettes and narrating them for the reader? Do you have any photographs? Take some of the responses you made to selected questions above, and use them to illustrate and tell your researcher's story. How does the tale begin? Where and how does it end? Or does it end? At least one author we know of, Walker Percy, ended his novel *The Last Gentleman* with a blank page! There you are, reading along, and as you turn the page . . . nothing! If you want to make your readers think, try something unusual.

Tin Man: So, this is the rainbow? Look at the colors!

Lion: All the colors together! I see it clearly, and, *it hasn't any end.*

Authors: So, there you have it. *We* have *all* become wizards, the colors are *ours* to use. As the rainbow brings colors together—the portfolio brings together our developing insights (just as this book, a portfolio or sorts, has done for us). We are now all part of the profession of wizards we talked about at the beginning of our journey. The magic is in you, not the wizard or the slippers or the authors . . .

Scarecrow: And, where do you think this rainbow leads?

Dorothy: I think its time for each of us to click our own heels and find out . . .

Glossary

Action research   (AR) A form of teaching; a form of reflective practice and professional learning founded on an ethical commitment to improving practice and realizing educational values. AR involvers individuals and groups identifying areas for improvement, generating ideas, and testing these ideas in practice. AR is characterized by cyclical, critical reflection and action, and collaboration. As research it is systematic, self-critical inquiry made public (after Stenhouse, 1975). AR "is an education process capable of fostering *educational outcomes*" and "developing the practitioners capacity for discrimination and judgement." (Elliott, 1991)

Applied research   Research that uses principles and theories but supplements them with informal discovery methods for the purpose of generating practical results.

Autobiographical inquiry   Inquiry into one's own history with the intent to grow as a person and as a professional.

Auto pilot   Act of doing something without thinking about it, often out of habit.

Basic research   A type of research in which knowledge is conceived of as separate from practice and can be discovered through the application of rigorous, experimental research methods. The goal of this type of research is the development of theories through the discovery of broad generalizations and principles. An example is Einstein's theory of relativity.

CARN   Collaborative Action Research Network is an international network of people who practice action research—this includes teachers, teacher educators, administrators, and others involved in education and social change. It has been active since the 1960s under the leadership of John Elliott, from the Centre for Applied Research in Education, University of East Anglia, Norwich, England. Publishers of the *Educational Action Research Journal* (*EARJ*).

Classroom action research   Action research that takes place within and is focused upon life and practices (teaching and learning) within classrooms and schools.

Classroom research   Any kind of research undertaken by a teacher, or teachers, or others, in and about classrooms.

Collaboration   Willing joint labor toward the same end by two or more people.

Collaborative action research   Action research undertaken by individuals or groups in concert with other individuals or groups.

Community   According to John Dewey, people "live in a community by virtue of the things which they hold in common; and communication is the way in which they come to possess things in common . . . aims, beliefs, aspirations, knowledge—a common understanding—likemindedness. . . " (Winn, 1959, p. 14, from *Democracy and Education*).

Constructivism   In essense, constructivism means that persons (and systems) constitute and construct their own reality. We are meaning-making beings. Learning is understood as a self-regulatory process of resolving inner conflicts that often become apparent through concrete experience, collaborative discourse, and reflection (Brooks and Brooks, 1993). A philosophical perspective, derived from the work of Immanuel Kant, which views reality as existing mainly in the mind, constructed or interpreted in terms of one's own perceptions. In this perspective, an individual's prior experiences, mental structures, and beliefs bear upon how experiences are interpreted. Constructivism focuses on the process of how knowledge is built rather than on its product or object (Harris and Hodges, 1995). The name most often associated with the study of how children and youth construct knowledge is Jean Piaget and his theory of cognitive development.

Critical methods, critical reflection, critical thinking, critical colleagues   Although the term *critical* is often used to mean "finding fault," it is used here to mean holding an emancipatory orientation to the world, and to exercise reasoned and careful judgment for socially constructive purposes. *Critical methods* are those methods that enable the researcher to examine false consciousness and to become aware of the dominant forces that have shaped us. Autobiographical and biographical inquiries are vehicles for reflection that can enable some of these forces to be identified and exposed. *Critical reflection* means the act of looking beneath the surfaces, asking questions, raising issues, exercising and judging merit based on an articulated value of social justice. Through *critical thinking* we question the social structures and practices which place people into their present circumstances, often in unequal and exploitative positions. A *critical colleague* is a person who presents a different perspective; one who helps us to question those things taken for granted, and helps us to view educationally related phenomena through socially and historically critical lenses.

Cycle of reflective practice   A continuous cycle of acting, observing, and reflecting which characterizes action research.

Developmentalism   Development is change over time. As Kegan explains, "Organic systems evolve through qualitatively different eras according to regular principles of stability and change" (1982, pp. 13–14). Although each individual is unique and varies from other individuals in her or his growth, and each is influenced by earlier environments and experiences, there are predictable patterns to development that can be useful for teaching and curriculum development. For example, what is appropriate for a 6-year-old may not be for a 9-year-old. Development is movement toward more complex, differentiated, and inclusive perspectives.

Diary   Often referred to as a *calendar;* a diary is a book in which personal descriptions, observations, and interpretations are written for one's own benefit and are rarely, if ever, for the eyes of outside observers. Diary-type writing is often a stream-of-consciousness type of writing; it can be creative, expressive, cathartic, and therapeutic. As noted in Section 5 on designing and planning an action research study, a diary is "a personal, unedited record of transactions and incidents."

Domains of professional development   Development is movement toward more complex, differentiated, and inclusive perspectives. Domains of professional development are the broad areas within which these take place.

Conceptual development   The developmental journey starts where a person is and moves toward greater complexity and simplicity, creates a larger repertoire from which to draw, and develops problem-solving, research abilities and capacities, and reflective processes.

Ethical, moral, and social development   Deepening consciousness and awareness, respect for diversity, and understanding of others. It promotes collaboration, community, and valuing others.

Psychological and emotional development   Movement from more closed, protective, defensive, rigid positions to more open, creative, and inclusive perspectives; toward higher self-esteem; and toward increasing capacity and ability to nurture these characteristics in others.

Educational learning   Learning that increases the capacity and desire for further learning toward socially worthwhile goals. For example, growing individual plants in the classroom leads to a community garden and environmental stewardship.

Educational research   A research experience that is educational in and of itself. It must, in John Dewey's terms, lead to further learning and democratic life.

Ethical commitment   A commitment to professional practice and to the democratic principles that undergird, and thus, support the foundation for any educational action research project.

Evocative forms of telling stories   A term used by Laurel Richardson (1998) to describe newer forms of writing to portray one's scholarship which include narrative of the self, ethnographic fictional representations, poetic representations, ethnographic drama, and mixed genres.

Experimental research and methods; quantitative research and methods   The terms *experimental* and *quantitative* are often used synonymously and have much in common, although research using quantitative methods of analysis is often not experimental. The principal methods of quantitative research are those which enable the researcher to quantify data and to manipulate these data for analysis. The researcher is looking for quantitative relationships in the data. The experimental researcher begins with hypotheses to be tested and controls variables in the hope of learning the effects of variables and generalizing these to similar phenomena. Experimental and quantitative research presume objectivity in the researcher. They are normally associated with basic research and with a technical and empirical orientation to research in which researchers use various methods of experimentation and observation of the empirical world. Hypotheses are tested, and variables are manipulated.

Free-writing   Writing freely, spontaneously, without forethought, or labor. Unedited.

General domains of development   Development is movement toward more complex, differentiated, and inclusive perspectives. Domains of development are the broad areas within which this development occurs.

Cognitive development   The term *cognitive* means "come to know." It incorporates all the various ways we come to know, including all the senses.

Physical and motor development   Changes related to physical development such as height, weight, muscle, and motor development, for example, dexterity in fine and large muscle control. Marked changes in this domain (sometimes referred to as growth spurts) are noted in early childhood and early adolescence.

Social and emotional development   Movement from reflexes and relatively undifferentiated feelings in the earliest stages of life to being able to distinguish between tears of laughter and sorrow and to engage in increasingly more sophisticated social relationships.

Inquiry   Process by which a person follows one's curiosity until the mystery is solved or abandoned. According to Lawrence Stenhouse, inquiry can develop into research if it becomes systematic and self-critical and is made public.

In-service   A word descriptive of all those activities and processes that contribute to professional growth and practice. Traditionally, these activities are referred to as *in-service training* as though something was *done to* teachers; more recently it is referred to as *in-service education* or professional development, in which teachers are perceived to be *active agents* in the learning process.

In-service teacher   A term used to denote any teacher actively teaching (as opposed to those retired or preservice—preparing to become a teacher).

Interviews   Discussions with a purpose. Purpose varies from open-ended conversation to highly structured and sequential questions asked of the interviewed person or persons.

I search   A method of inquiry and a type of scholarship created by Ken Macrorie (1980): "Contrary to most school research papers, the I-Search comes out of a student's life and answers a need in it. . . . The paper is alive, not borrowedly inert. . . [The I-Search is unlike traditional research papers where] The expert is up there and they [the students] are down there taking notes" (preface). "A good way to organize an I-Search paper is simply to tell the story of what you did in your search, in the order in which everything happened. . . . 1. What I knew . . . 2. Why I'm writing this paper . . . 3. The Search (story of the hunt). . . . 4. What I learned . . ." (p. 64).

Journal—professional journal   An evolving professional document which serves as a continuing professional dialogue and discussion with oneself (selves) on matters related to one's own practice. It serves as a vehicle for praxis (see subsequent), and for synthesis and analysis of one's work and professional life. It can contain log, diary, and other types of expressive and analytical writing. The author is the sole owner and often chooses to share snippets or sections with others.

Kidwatching   A term coined by reading educator Yetta Goodman in an article by the same name which appeared in the *National Elementary School Principal* in 1978. As an alternative to school testing, Goodman advocated teacher observation, intuition, and knowledge of students as invaluable sources for assessment and evaluation.

Learning communities   Communities by virtue of their aim and ability to learn, together and as individuals, for socially constructive purposes.

Life span development   An approach to studying development from a life-cycle perspective; Erik Erikson's theory of psychosocial development in which he proposes a framework that enables one to contemplate developmental patterns, not only in different periods of life, but also as life continues through time from birth to death. The foundations for each period of development can be seen in the periods preceding it.

Literature circles   An alternative or supplement to basal reading instruction. While basal readers are assembled anthologies, literature circles are a means of implementing a literature-based reading program under a whole language philosophy in which high-quality trade books—picture books, novels, or informational books—become the teacher- and student-selected materials for learning. In student-led heterogeneous groups of three to five readers, students read literature aloud, write journal responses, and hold student-led discussions until the book is completed. Students plan and execute a culminating presentation which they perform or present to their classmates that expresses what the book or story meant to them, without giving away the story essentials (Kasten, 1995). Literature circles are executed in classrooms in a variety of ways that suit the teacher's style and time frame. Sometimes specific roles, such as discussion leader, are assigned to group members. (Daniels, 1994). Literature circles can also be called *book clubs* or other terms invented by students and teachers.

Literature review   Both a process of studying and critically reviewing literature pertinent to one's research topic and area, and the product of such review, usually included in a formal proposal and/or report. More than a listing or presentation literature reviews provide analysis and synthesis of key studies and present these in such a way that the reader learns more about the literature as a whole than about any of its constituent studies and reviews.

Log   Both a verb—to log one's activities or observations—and a noun—a record or a logbook. Activities and observations are often recorded without interpretive text; theoretically, anyone would record the same observations ("the math lesson lasted 45 minutes").

Metaphor   According to the *Merriam-Webster Dictionary* (1974, p. 439), "a figure of speech in which a word denoting one subject is used in place of another to suggest a likeness between them."

Middle school   An organizational structure for the education of early adolescents ages 9 to 15, based on a philosophy of developmentalism, social equity, and academic excellence. Its key organizational features include interdisciplinary teaching, flexible scheduling, block scheduling, teacher as advisor, exploratory and integrated curriculum. It is grounded in the ideas of John Dewey.

Mis-educational learning   John Dewey's term to describe further learning on the topic that is either sidetracked or subverted. An example is that picking apart poems to analyze parts of speech in a poem can extinguish the desire to read poetry.

Modernity   A paradigm and time period when certain beliefs, values, and assumptions are held in common, and these permeate artistic, cultural, social, educational, psychological, economic, and political contexts and practices. It is "based on the premise that the world is objectively knowable, and that knowledge so obtained can be absolutely generalized" (Havel, 1992). Certainty, progress, universality, and regularity are hallmarks of modernity and have shaped many of the rational and assembly-line practices in schools, such as use of time and space and instructional practices or delivery of content *to* students, as receptacles, all needing the same treatment.

Multiply handicapped   Descriptive of a person with more than one physical, mental, or social disability (Harris and Hodges, 1995).

Narrative; narrative writing   "[A]ny form of written or spoken presentation" (Polkinghorne, 1988, p. 13). In this book we refer to *narrative* as the process of narration and its product, the narrative. *Narrative writing* refers to the researcher telling the research story in words and presentation.

Naturalistic research and methods; qualitative research and methods   The terms *naturalistic* and *qualitative* are often used interchangeably and have much in common. Researchers using naturalistic and qualitative methods are not interested in controlling and manipulating the environment, although they are often interested in trying out ideas and observing the results in natural settings. There are few entirely "natural" settings in the sense that there is no intervention into what happens within it, but researchers from this orientation are interested in observing carefully what "is" in as unobtrusive a way as possible. Qualitative research comes from the social sciences and is hypothesis-generating, and the researcher does not presume objectivity. Anthropologists, for example, use qualitative (ethnographic) methods to observe in natural (cultural) settings. Many researchers use quantitative and qualitative methods, referred to as *mixed methods.* For example, biologists go into natural settings and make observations under different environmental conditions, sometimes manipulating the environment to study its effects.

Noneducational learning   John Dewey's term to describe learning that doesn't change anything. For example, cramming for a test and forgetting everything two days later.

Paradigm   A world view or model ascribed to a group of people who hold certain beliefs, knowledge, and understandings in common. It is said that we are moving from a modern paradigm (or era) to a postmodern paradigm (or era). Part of the turmoil in such a process is due to the fact that both paradigms are in existence and conflict; we have a foot in the past and a foot in the future, and today can seem chaotic. Whereas certainty has provided comfort in modern times, today's postmodernists cultivate—and even celebrate—uncertainty.

Philosophy of teaching   According to the *Merriam-Webster Dictionary* (1974, p. 522), a philosophy is "a critical study of fundamental beliefs and the grounds for them." A teaching philosophy may include: beliefs about the purposes of schooling; how children learn; and the roles and responsibilities of teachers, students, and the community. We can use this as a foundation for our thinking about many issues (testing, approaches to discipline, for example) confronting teachers today.

Portfolio   A carefully selected, constructed, and narrated collection of work pertaining to a special topic. It comes from an 18th-century Italian term, porto folio, literally meaning "portare," to carry, and "fogli," leaves or sheets of paper. Current developments in educational portfolios include *teaching portfolios* (pertaining to one's teaching and containing many narrated examples) and *course portfolios* (pertaining to a specific course). A form of scholarship in which one analyzes, synthesizes, and narrates one's work for oneself and to share publically with others. The portfolio can be autobiographical as in the examples cited, biographical, or project-oriented; often used as a form of evaluation.

Portraits: portrayal; portraiture   A *portrait* is a likeness of a person, place, event, or circumstance. *Portrayal* is the way of rendering the likeness. *Portraiture* is now considered to be a "genre of inquiry and representation that seeks to join art and science . . . [it] is a method of qualitative research that blurs the boundaries of aesthetics and empiricism in an effort to capture the complexity, dynamics, and subtlety of human experience" (Lawrence-Lightfoot and Davis, 1997, p. xv).

Postmodernity   In contrast to modernity (see above), a period characterized by difference, particularity, and irregularity. The world is not objectively knowable, nor can one "absolutely generalize" to other situations and people. *Context* matters. Open classrooms based on constructivist principles and flexible and evolving curricula, and some alternative schools are more akin with the postmodern paradigm: Children, adolescents, and adults cannot be *absolutely* characterized as categories of learners, just as individuals within each group cannot be absolutely characterized. Each person is unique and socially constructed. Multiple voices and texts are the "rules" in this anti-rule-oriented paradigm.

Praxis   The critically reflective dialogue that takes place continuously between the professional and her or his practice. In action research this results in new actions and a continuance of the cycle of reflective practice. This process is necessary to continuing the relationship between theoretical understanding and critique of society and its institutions, and the actions necessary to transform individuals and the environments within which they live and grow.

Preservice teacher   A teacher education student who engages in teaching experiences (internships, student teaching, and other teaching experiences) before graduation and employment as a practicing teacher.

Primary data sources   Firsthand sources of information.

Problematize   To explore a topic or phenomenon from a critical stance; to dissect or interrogate in order to uncover underlying causes and or assumptions; to become skeptical of familiar territory. To "question the historical, social, economic, political, and cultural realities that shape our lives" (Leistyna et al., 1996).

Professional development   Anything that contributes to lifelong learning of a teacher, including preservice education, workshops, seminars, professional meetings and conferences, self-initiated and school-sponsored projects and in-service education sessions, professional reading, and graduate study, to name a few! Action research is one of the most potent forms of professional development.

Professional learning   Educational learning (see below) that focuses on the integration of three processes necessary to pedagogical success: human development, curriculum development, and teaching, within a value system of social democracy and environmental advocacy.

Professional routines   The often taken-for-granted practices that structure life in classrooms, such as lesson planning, 40-minute classes, grade-level organization, homework, grouping of students by "ability," standardized testing.

Report formats   Different ways in which to tell one's research story. Action researchers can use or create a growing number of ways to organize and arrange their research stories. These include traditional, scientific, case studies, and newer forms such as evocative forms (see above).

Research   According to Lawrence Stenhouse, "systematic, self-critical, inquiry made public." Research is what scholars *do*. The attitude they take toward research and its conduct is scholarly.

Scholarship   Simply put, professional learning. Scholars are learned and tenaciously inquisitive people. Scholarship is the evolving learning and related knowledge that scholars undertake and "own." It is a curious, skeptical, and inquisitive attitude toward the world and our human places within that world. Research is what scholars *do*. Research is part of scholarship, a way in which scholarship evolves.

Secondary data sources   Sources that are dependent upon something else (primary data sources); sources that build on, quote, and use other people's research.

Story   A narrative, a reporting, a recounting of one's experience or history; a statement or chronicle.

Teacher action research   Action research by a teacher or teachers.

Teacher research   Any kind of research undertaken by a teacher or a group of teachers and others.

Teaching self and **(related self-talk)**   The notion that each of us is not a single, self-contained, monolithic, and congruent "self" who teaches. We are complex beings and have many selves and minds (what Robert Ornstein, 1991, calls "multi-minds" which "wheel-in" on cue) that talk to us and in fact *are* us. We teach with the advice of these "subpersonalities" (Ferrucci, 1982). Self-talk is *listening* to the chorus within and guiding the discussion and outcomes where warranted and possible.

Theory, theorize, theoretical   A *theory* is a systematically organized body of knowledge used to explain a phenomenon; a theory can be *public,* as in Piaget's theory of cognitive development, or *private,* as in our theories of how people learn. Private theories are usually implicit and not articulated consciously, even to ourselves. Scholarship, however, makes it necessary for us to articulate our theories; *praxis* is a method for so doing. To *theorize* is to conjecture, to put forward possible explanations for a phenomenon, and to see if you can gather evidence both pro and con to your conjecture. "If I ask Bridget about her new baby sister, I can probably gauge her feelings on the matter. I think she is upset over the attention she has lost." *Theoretical* refers to a public theory and is used as a basis for conjecturing: "Theoretically, according to Piaget, children cannot learn if they are forced to accommodate more information than they are developmentally able." Often we can test a theory with our own observations.

Vignette   Representation of life on paper or another literary, visual, aural, or composite form that makes apprehension possible; usually brief.

Whole teacher   The person in her or his entirety; social, emotional, physical, motor, and cognitive development and the interaction of these. This is in contrast to singling out cognitive or intellectual growth without reference to how this interacts and is related to other domains.

Writing down, writing up, and writing about   Terms used in this book to call attention to three interrelated processes and functions of writing in action research. *Writing down* refers to developing the art of observation and data collection, capturing rich, detailed information. *Writing up* refers to analyzing and synthesizing the results of our observations and data in writing, to rendering our considered observation in written form (portraits, case studies, research reports). *Writing about* is the process of taking our reports and creating products from these to share, usually moving beyond the report to rendering it in other forms (presentations, articles).

Writer's perspectives   The points of view assumed by the author.

Appendix A

Increasing Social Interaction Between Students with Multiple Handicaps and Their Typical Peers: An Action Research Proposal

Andy Williams

What Is My Research Interest?

I am interested in the interactions between typical middle school students and students with multiple handicaps. My questions are, What are the attitudes of regular education students about students with handicapping conditions? and How can I increase the interactions between typical middle school students and those with multiple handicaps?

Why Am I Interested?

My students in the multiple-handicapped (MH) program are placed in integrated classes for part of their school day. The rationale for this inclusion is for the MH students to gain acceptance from peers and to attain social skills needed to build friendships. I also believe that all students should have access to the rich experiences offered by my middle school. I am not seeing this happen, and I wonder if there are other ways to accomplish these worthwhile goals.

What Do I Already Know? What Do Others Know?

Only limited conversation is occurring inside and outside the inclusion classroom. Occasionally, students pass individuals from my class and say "Hi," but dialogue never grows beyond that point. There was a time when one of the regular education students did not even talk to her own cousin who was integrated into her home economics class. I have observed typical students move from a table where their peers with disabilities were eating lunch. Somehow the relationships that inclusion is supposed to foster are just not happening. The research on peer interactions in special education indicates that the relationships cannot be conjured up at will (Van der Klift and Kunc, 1994). The potential benefits of increased and specialized socialization for students with multiple handicaps are a decrease in their stereotypical behaviors (SoHyun and Odom, 1996) and encouragement of age-appropriate interactions (Janney and Snell, 1996). Typical students believed that they benefited in terms of improved self-concept, increased tolerance, and reduced fear of human difference (Peck, 1990). Some possible solutions found in the research suggested that teacher facilitation increased the interactions between students (Hunt, et al., 1996).

What Do I Expect to Find?

I expect that I will have a few interested typical students in the seventh and eighth grades who might be willing to spend time with their peers with disabilities, but I do not anticipate a long-range commitment from them. It is not unusual for middle school students to lose focus when they are asked to participate in an activity.

What Will I Try Out?

Who?

The participants attend a middle school in a suburban area located near a mid-sized university. The students are mixed culturally and economically due to the influence of the university and its employees and students whose children attend the public schools. Subsidized housing throughout the city affects the social economic status of the group. Approximately 800 students are housed in the sixth, seventh, and eighth grades heterogeneous teams. The 16 students in the two MH classes are diagnosed with Down's syndrome, cerebral palsy, language disorders, vision impairments, and autism. Also involved in this study will be the school principal, regular education teaching staff, and special education staff.

What?

I could formulate a "Buddy Club," and students could come into my classroom to act as tutors in academic classes. Another option is to develop a "Lunchmate" program in which members will be assigned to a student in my class, and they could eat together. The final option is to initiate a "Peer Club" that would resemble an extracurricular club. Students can sign up and participate in organized social events with their partners from the MH classes. The sole purpose of this club is to increase the time these students get for social interactions. I think I will choose the last option because I feel it will bridge the gap between students better. The group will be called the S.T.A.R. (Students and Teachers Advancing Relationships) Club, and interested students can sign up to be paired with peers with special needs. I think the key to success is to have the nonhandicapped students join the project with their own friends. Several existing friends can be paired with a student from the MH program in the hopes that these friends will feel more comfortable together. This peer club may be very time-consuming for me, but will work within the time constraints of the school day. I need to consider students' busy after-school schedules and maximize their availability during class time. Success will be measured through the students' responsiveness to the club, increased positive feelings of regular education students toward their peers with disabilities, commitment to the activities, and the carryover to other school settings.

When? How Often?

The preliminary work to organize this club should be done during the first semester of the year. All the planning and locating of the peers and staff support will take some time in order to succeed. During the second semester, activities will occur for the club members, and they will participate in informational meetings. There should be at least one planned activity per month. Seventh- and eighth-grade students should be recruited for the club because their schedules replicate the schedules of my students more closely.

Where?

The students will fill out forms to state their interest in membership in a club within their classrooms. I plan to have social activities throughout the school building, and students are always welcome in my classroom.

How Will I Document the Process? What Evidence Will I Collect to Show the Consequences of My Actions?

I will keep a journal of my observations of the existing conditions and how those observations change throughout the process of my project. I will recall what I see happening and my feelings along the way. Conversations and information from other professionals will also be noted. A focus group of selected eighth graders can allow me the opportunity to gather data on their feelings about individuals with handicaps. I will also rely upon my 15 years of experience teaching students with special needs. Another data collection method includes reading articles from professional publications that both support and refute peer groups as an effective way to improve interactions. Triangulation of the evidence may occur between the surveys completed by students, my observations noted in my journal, and the student responses during the focus group.

How Will I Verify That My Judgments Are Trustworthy and Credible?

Since I work closely in team-teaching situations with another special education teacher, I know he will offer critique. His perspectives are usually valuable, and he frequently acts as my mentor. The teachers I plan to have in my advisory group also can lend their perspectives and observations. Students who participate in the club will give me feedback about their relationships with the students and their experiences. I shall continually test my emerging hypothesis that this close exposure between the students will branch out to other settings and increase social interactions. Throughout this project, I will need to check for disconfirming data.

How Will I Interpret the Data?

I will interpret the data by looking at my journal, surveys, and focus group comments for categories and patterns. There may be responses that lead to ideas about what makes socialization work for my students. I will categorize the surveys by placing them in piles and highlight emerging categories in different-color markers so I can note patterns. The focus group comments and journal entries should have a distinct marking to show positive and negative impressions of integration. I will write my feelings about my experiences in my journal as I go through the process of developing this club. I will go back and forth between my own thoughts and what I am reading in professional journals. Some individuals feel that friendship clubs cannot foster true relationships. Others have found that a supportive environment in which the teacher acts as a facilitator is best. Under these circumstances, interactions between the students increased.

How Will I Portray What I Have Learned and Make It Public?

I will share my project with my fellow classmates in my action research course. Also, I will show my results to administrators, staff, parents, and students in my school building. My plans also include presenting my project at an upcoming faculty meeting.

How Will These Actions Make Life Better? And What Will I Do Next?

It is my hope that this project changes how my students are included in their school. It would be rewarding to see other middle school students talk to them and greet them by name in the hallways. This project could be a springboard for other activities possibly after school and in the community. I would like to continue the S.T.A.R. Club and potentially pair activities with student council.

Who Will Be My Critical Colleagues?

My special education team partner will be my critical colleague.

What Permissions Do I Need to Gain?

I will secure written permission from the parents of my special education students and from those students who volunteer to be members of S.T.A.R. Club. I will also explain to all these students what my project entails and will gain their verbal permission to use their journals as evidence. I will then have them read over any quotes of theirs that I might use, and I will gain their written permission to use the quotes in my report to my university class.

References

Hunt, P., Allwell, M., & Goetz, L. (1996). Creating socially supportive environments for fully included students who experience multiple disabilities. *Journal of the Association for Persons with Severe Handicaps, 21*(2), 53–71.

Janney, R. E., & Snell, M. E. (1996). How teachers use peer interactions to include students with moderate and severe disabilities in elementary general education classes. *Journal of the Association for Persons with Severe Handicaps, 21*(2), 72–80.

SoHuyn, Lee & Odom, S. L. (1996). The relationships between stereotypic behavior and peer social interaction for children with severe disabilities. *Journal of the Association for Persons with Severe Handicaps, 21*(2), 88–95.

Peck, C. (1990). Some benefits non-handicapped adolescents perceive for themselves from their social relationships with peers who have severe handicaps. *Journal of the Association for Persons with Severe Handicaps, 15*(4), 241–249.

Van der Klift, E. & Kunc, N. (1994). *Creativity and collaborative learning: A practical guide to empowering students and teachers.* Baltimore: Paul Brookes.

Appendix B

Organizing and Visually Displaying Data

We have devoted an entire appendix to organizing and visually displaying data in order to offer possibilities for ways to think about processing data. We will provide examples for both quantitative and qualitative data. In these pages you may find inspiration for your own creative ideas.

Quantitative Data

Quantitative data typically consist of numerical values that are analyzed statistically. Raw data need to be organized and displayed so that they begin to make sense. Organizing quantitative data in lists is a simple way to show what data you have. Figure B.1 shows how student scores on a mathematics test can be arrayed in order from highest score to lowest score. Figure B.2 shows how scores can be organized by range.

FIGURE B.1 *Student percentages on mathematics test*	
Student Name	**Percentage**
Mary	100
Tom	96
Craig	92
Lou	89
Jeff	88
Sam	86
Tabatha	86
Freddie	79
Anne	77
Wil	70

FIGURE B.2	Tally and frequency of scores on mathematics test	
Percentages	Tally	Frequency
90–100	|||	3
80–89	||||	4
70–79	||	3

Displaying numerical values in a graph helps the researcher to see and discuss results. Graphs can be used to compare scores and groups, show trends in data, show relationships between variables, and describe parts of the whole. The following are examples of types of graphic displays that are commonly used by action researchers.

Bar graph.   A *bar graph* compares values across categories. Frequencies are indicated on the vertical axis, while lowest to highest rank-ordered scores are depicted on the horizontal axis. Figure B.3 illustrates the test scores of students on the horizontal axis and frequency of those scores on the vertical axis.

Line graph.   A *line graph* is a line with markers displayed at each data value. It is similar to a bar graph. Figure B.4 illustrates the number of children enrolled in after-school activities in four different grade levels.

FIGURE B.3 *Bar graph showing frequency of test scores*

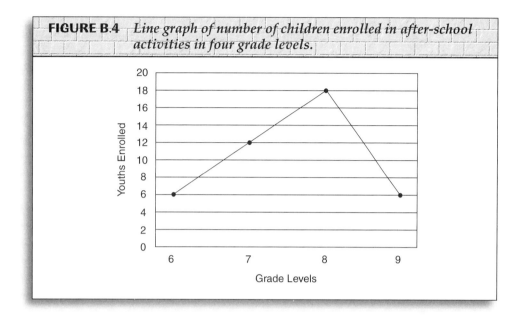

FIGURE B.4 *Line graph of number of children enrolled in after-school activities in four grade levels.*

Scatter plot. A *scatter plot* compares pairs of values and shows the relationship between two variables. The vertical, or *y*, axis indicates performance on one variable. The horizontal, or *x*, axis indicates performance on another variable. Each point is the intersection of two scores for each individual. Figure B.5 shows the relationship of students' scores on an examination and the number of hours they studied. The scatter plot indicates a positive relationship between the variables: students who studied longer had higher test scores.

Pie graph. A *pie graph* displays the contribution of each value to a total and is used to describe the parts of a whole in percent or the equivalent. Figure B.6 shows the percentage of students who favored each of four activities from a consumer science class.

Descriptive Statistics

When we want to summarize data (not generalize from them), we describe the data using the mean, median, mode, range, and standard deviation. Each of these calculations is briefly described.

Mean. The *mean* is the average, and it is computed by summing all scores and dividing by the number of scores.

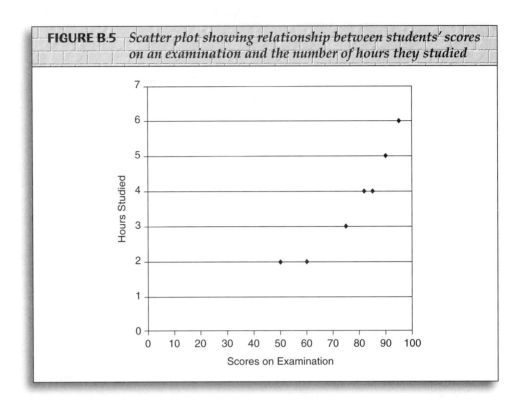

FIGURE B.5 *Scatter plot showing relationship between students' scores on an examination and the number of hours they studied*

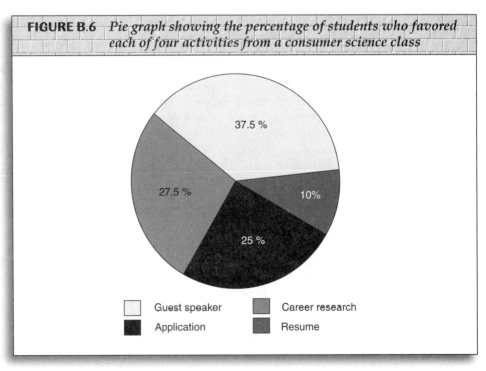

FIGURE B.6 *Pie graph showing the percentage of students who favored each of four activities from a consumer science class*

Median.   The *median* is the midpoint in a series of scores. Fifty percent of the cases lie above the median, and 50 percent lie below the median.

Mode.   The *mode* is the most frequently occurring score.
    Figure B.7 illustrates the computation for the mean, median, and mode for a sample data set.

Range.   The *range* is the span between the lowest score and the highest score. It is useful in summarizing the variability of scores. For example, using the raw data set from Figure B.7, we subtract 2 (the lowest value) from 9 (the highest value) and determine that the range is 7.

Standard deviation.   The *standard deviation* is another measure of variability. It is the difference between a single score in a data set and the mean for the data set.
    All the graphs and summary statistics described here can be easily calculated, displayed, and inserted into the body of your text by using spreadsheets that are included in most computer software packages. Displaying these summary statistics in a table makes it easy to see what is going on. Figure B.8 displays data from Rosie's Democratic Classroom Study in a table that shows the mean responses of students on the Citizenship Survey.

Choosing a Random Sample

When a researcher is studying an entire class, several classes, a team, a grade level, a time period, or multiage grouping, hundreds of pieces of student work may be generated. It is not always necessary to analyze *every* item. By choosing a *random sample* of the data, the researcher can obtain results that are comparable to analyzing the entire data set.
    For example, suppose an action researcher wants to know if portfolios in her science classes are a viable alternative to giving students a final examination. While a rubric keyed to standards, concepts, or competencies can be used to assess student learning, as demonstrated in all the portfolios, it may be impossible to do an in-depth analysis of each. Instead of analyzing *all* of them, a mentor can help you

FIGURE B.7 *Computation of mean, median, and mode for a sample data set*	
Raw data:	2, 4, 4, 6, 6, 6, 8, 8, 9
Mean:	2 + 4 + 4 + 6 + 6 + 6 + 8 + 8 + 9 = 5.9
Median:	2 4 4 6 <u>6</u> 6 8 8 9 = 6
Mode:	2 4 4 <u>6 6 6</u> 8 8 9 = 6

FIGURE B.8 *Citizenship Survey: means for student ratings of importance of characteristics of citizenship*

Characteristic of Citizenship	Number of Students	Mean
Knowledge of current events	17	3.6
Participation in community or school events	17	4.2
Performance of duties	17	5.0
Concern for others	17	5.3
Acceptance of authority	17	4.3
Ability to make wise decisions	17	5.7
Knowledge of government	17	4.0
Patriotism	17	4.2
Moral and ethical behavior	17	6.0

select a representative number from each class or group. But the question then becomes, Which ones to select? A fair way to select them may be *random selection.*

If, for example, you want to select 25 portfolios from the 200 completed in all your five classes, you begin by giving a number to each portfolio. Then you can use a scientific calculator or any number of computer programs to enter the number needed (25) and the set from which to draw (200); and the computer or calculator will print the numbers of the items to select. (If you saved that instruction booklet that came with your calculator, you'll be pleased now!) In the absence of technology, you can use the paper-in-the-hat method (a very technical system). Simply place the numbers of items into a hat, and draw out 25 numbers. No cheating—you can't put back the ones you don't like!

Qualitative Data

Qualitative data consist of the interview notes, descriptive observations written in your journal, and documents and artifacts that have been collected throughout a study. There are fewer restrictions on how these data are displayed and organized for analysis, and we will offer a few ideas to get things started.

Tables with words.   Creating tables with words or concepts instead of numbers can be a useful way to begin analyzing and interpreting data. Figure B.9 presents excerpts from Lauren's journal, which contained her observations and comments from teacher colleagues about the relative benefits of a semitraditional groups (classroom divided in half and students in rows, each half facing the other half) versus cooperative groups (small, heterogeneous groups of students which are flexible depending on the nature of the task) in two sections of Spanish. She separated the data into positive and negative aspects. Lauren, a student teacher, decided that a flexible, heterogeneously mixed grouping of students was the optimal physical classroom arrangement for increasing student speaking in the target language.

Concept mapping.   Concept mapping is useful for showing relationships. In Figure B.10 we include a concept map by Lori, another student teacher, who wanted to understand student views of strategies she used to help them perform better on tests in her honors chemistry class. She also interviewed teachers to find out what they thought of the tests and students' performance on them. In both cases, she quoted what the students and her teachers said.

Lori concluded that students viewed different strategies differently and that she would have to accommodate different needs over the course of the term to ensure each student's success.

Thematic organizer.   After analyzing his data related to when it was most appropriate to use teacher-directed and student-directed teaching, Matt used quotes from students, his mentor, and the professional literature to illustrate two themes that emerged. (See Figure B.11 for an excerpt of his analysis.)

FIGURE B.9 *Comparison of semitraditional and cooperative groups in a foreign language classroom*

	Semitraditional Groups	**Cooperative Groups**
Positive Aspects	More controlled	Positive energy
	Quieter	More student talk
	Better for quizzes	Students take an active role
	Can cover more material	Increased student interaction
	Easy to transition to other activities	Less downtime during oral assessments
	Students are on task	Opportunities for peer teaching
Negative Aspects	More teacher talk	Noise
	Students tune out	Requires more planning
	Boring	Students don't always use target language
	Students can be passive observers	Bad for test taking
	More teacher-centered	Students distracted by others

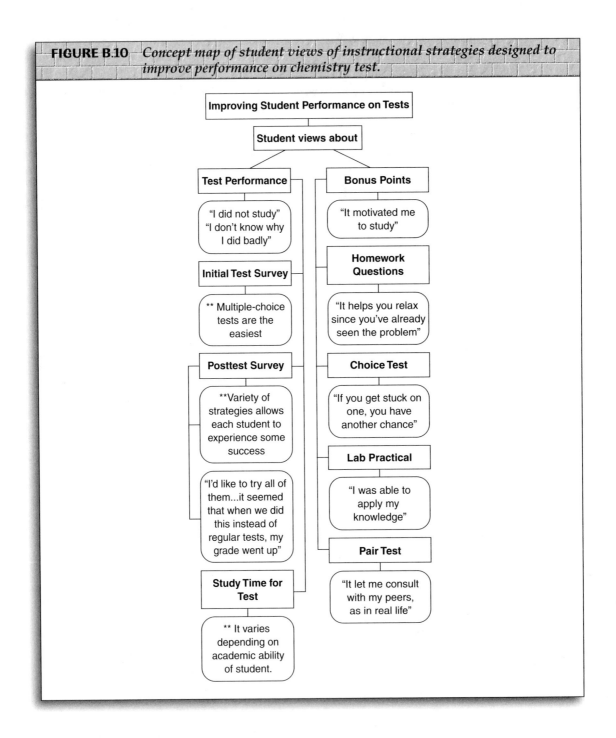

FIGURE B.10 *Concept map of student views of instructional strategies designed to improve performance on chemistry test.*

Improving Student Performance on Tests

Student views about

Test Performance

"I did not study"
"I don't know why
I did badly"

Initial Test Survey

** Multiple-choice
tests are the
easiest

Posttest Survey

**Variety of
strategies allows
each student to
experience some
success

"I'd like to try all of
them...it seemed
that when we did
this instead of
regular tests, my
grade went up"

**Study Time for
Test**

** It varies
depending on
academic ability
of student.

Bonus Points

"It motivated me
to study"

**Homework
Questions**

"It helps you relax
since you've already
seen the problem"

Choice Test

"If you get stuck on
one, you have
another chance"

Lab Practical

"I was able to
apply my
knowledge"

Pair Test

"It let me consult
with my peers,
as in real life"

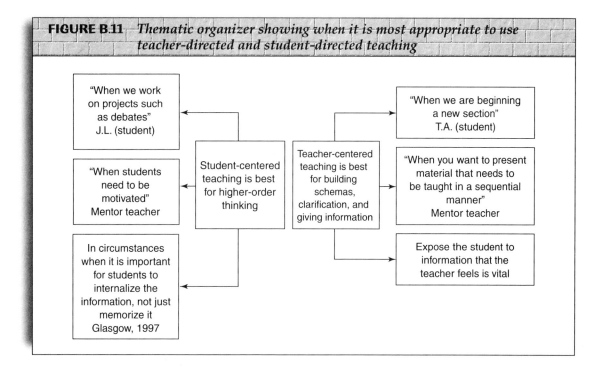

FIGURE B.11 *Thematic organizer showing when it is most appropriate to use teacher-directed and student-directed teaching*

Snake chart. Andrew wanted to show how he went about his action research project and what he learned along the way. He did this by mapping the progress of his study of cooperative learning groups in his social studies classroom from start to finish. (See Figure B.12.)

To summarize the steps she took in her study of helping students to learn the scientific method, Trish created a snake chart that showed the problems she introduced to her science students, what her students learned and did not learn, and what steps she took in her teaching to address the issues that arose. (See Figure B.13.) Both Andrew's and Trish's snake charts were used in presenting their study to other student teachers at the end of the term.

Other ways to organize data and show relationships include classification, cause-effect, and sorting. Several sources may be helpful in visually displaying data: Miles and Huberman (1994), *Qualitative data analysis,* and Hyerle (1996) *Visual tools for constructing knowledge.*

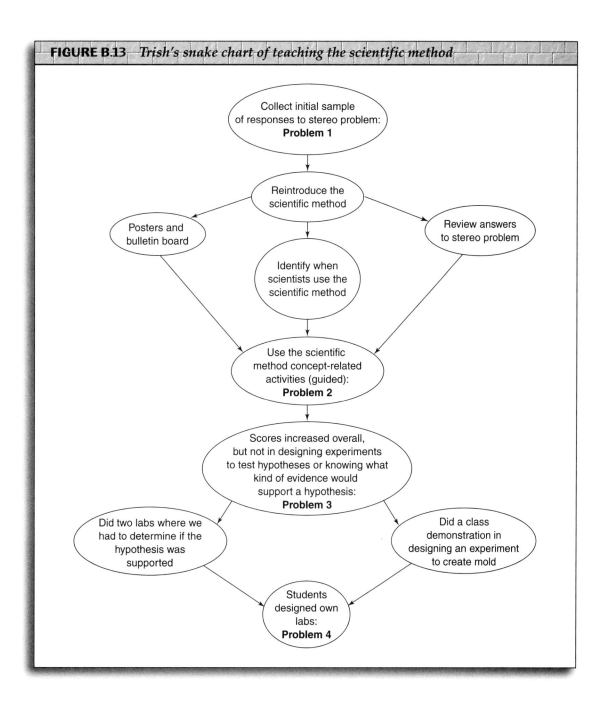

FIGURE B.13 *Trish's snake chart of teaching the scientific method*

311

Appendix C

Analyzing Student Writing and Mathematical Data

Because of the emphasis in education on assessing writing and mathematics, we include specific analytical procedures that may be used to interpret student writing and mathematical understanding. Keep in mind that these are just examples of the ways in which teacher action researchers can approach analyzing student work in these two areas.

Analyzing Student Writing

Written student work may take many forms: responses to an open-ended question, journals, stories, reports, essays, etc. How you analyze student-written artifacts depends upon what your questions are and what you want to find out. You might analyze for spelling development, increased skill in narrative or expository writing, syntactic complexity and maturity, quantity of writing, or use of varied vocabulary. Or you may want to examine student writing for what it reveals about what they are learning in a specific content area, such as social studies. We will make suggestions for each.

Quantity of written work. Keeping in mind that quantity isn't the same as quality, sometimes action researchers are simply curious to see whether students respond to use of a particular teaching strategy by doing more writing. We can find this out by counting words within an entry (such as a journal) or assignment (such as a weekly essay or story). Of course, counting words is not as easy as it sounds. Young students might write as one word what is conventionally several words (e.g., *Onceuponatime*). Some students may break a compound word into two words (e.g., *logger head* for *loggerhead*). As the researcher, you make the decision about how to count such words, keeping in mind that consistency is important.

To help visualize changes over time, teachers might graph the length of written work. Or to compare the length of written work of two classes, a teacher might graph the average length of written work for two classes. This "playing with data" may or may not reveal anything interesting. But it may be worth the effort in terms of insights it provides.

Typically when action researchers graph the length of written work of particular students over several months, they learn that the length varies. Some topics are more interesting to particular students, while others are not. Sometimes on a given day, a student has more to say than at other times (which is true for adults as well). One teacher, in doing this, saw that all students wrote a great deal more on one particular day than other days. When she cross-checked that date with her researcher log, she noticed it was the day *she* began writing while her children were writing. She felt certain the effect was due to her modeling.

Sometimes graphing entries or assignments of a student over time will only appear as an up-and-down pattern on a line or bar graph. However, if the work is segmented by week, by month, by grading period, or by first half or second half of the study, and *then* averages are calculated for each segment, changes may show up that otherwise would not. We call this process of segmenting data *disaggregating* the data. This, too, is what we mean by "playing with data."

Quality of written work.   The criteria for narrative or expository writing are more complex than simply counting words. Narrative writing, for example, is judged by the presence and quality of well-developed characters, plot, and setting. Expository texts are judged on specific features of the genre. For example, journalistic newspaper articles present critical information (who, what, when, where, why) up front, prior to any elaboration. Persuasive writing sequences points of argument, often presenting the most powerful reason at the end. Each type of writing has qualities that merit attention by writers. A review of the literature will often provide rubrics or guidelines that teachers can use. Additionally, because many states and provinces now require mandatory testing of writing, rubrics used to evaluate student writing are widely published.

Once you know what you are looking for in writing, you may want to apply the rubric or other guidelines to all student writing over the period; or you may wish to focus on particular students, such as those who are the least-developed writers, or a combination of more and less proficient writers. Or you may want to randomly select students to represent the larger group.

The development of new or young writers.   Many action researchers follow the development of the writing of young children (ages 5 to 9), some learning a new language, such as Jen. Others are interested in adults coming into literacy for the first time. A review of the literature on the development of writing will provide much description of appropriate expectations for these different kinds of students at different stages in their development. The early stages of young children's writing, for example, have been described by some as *pre-phonetic, phonetic, transitional, invented,* and *conventional.*

Simple forms of analysis may involve keeping track of words the child has conventionalized (by giving an identical spelling test of common words multiple times), by counting the number of words in their connected discourse and then counting those spelled conventionally. This finding can be expressed in a simple percentage by placing the number of words spelled conventionally over the total number, obtaining a percentage of words expressed in conventional spelling. These findings may be graphed for individuals or groups.

The development of more fluent writers. Once writers are more or less fluent in the writing of connected discourse, you may want to know about syntactic complexity by comparing the writing of students in two classes over time, or by comparing classes which have had writing instruction consistently compared to those that have not. One way to examine writing complexity is to look at the scope and breadth of the *vocabulary* being used by the writers. One action researcher tracked all words used by one class of students who wrote frequently and compared them to a class where writing instruction was more limited. By first counting the words in student writing samples (called a token word count) and then counting the different words in the student writing (called a unique word count), action researchers have sometimes noted some interesting patterns. In other words, if a student writes a story in which *the* appears 12 times, *of* appears 3 times, and *friend* appears twice, each of those only counts as one word. Consequently, in a piece of connected discourse that consisted of 50 words, some students might have used only 26 different words by being repetitive, while others might have written with more than 42 different words. The latter shows greater scope in vocabulary and also demonstrates that the writer is willing to take risks to try words that are their first choice as opposed to sticking with words that are easier to spell.

With this type of analysis, it would not be valid to analyze only a single piece of writing from a student as representative of that student's writing. A more logical analysis would be to analyze a range of student writing from an individual or group and compute the average unique word count in a group. By taking the unique count in a group of stories for a class, one might gain some insights about the writers and the curriculum.

A secondary foreign language teacher used an analysis similar to this in a study of French I students who kept dialogue journals. Students wrote freely, without prompts, in their newly developing foreign language. The action researcher responded regularly to the students, writing back, noting incorrect grammar or spelling, and attempting to model conventional grammar and spelling in the responses without ever drawing attention to student errors. The researcher then tracked the journals for *token word counts, unique word counts,* and specific incidents where her modeling influenced the student and resulted in a correction in a subsequent entry. The unique word count became most interesting when words showed up in the count that she had not yet presented in class or had not yet been covered in course materials.

In cases where action researchers have an interest in syntactic complexity, *t-unit analysis,* pioneered by Kellogg Hunt (1965), has been used successfully in many studies. T-unit analysis puts text into an analyzable unit, since sentences are not a helpful unit of measure because they vary too greatly. A t-unit is the main clause and any dependent clauses that go with it. For example, the sentence "I went to the store" is simply a main-clause sentence, and one t-unit. But if the sentence is "I went to the store and then I went to the movies," the sentence contains two main clauses and hence two t-units. But a sentence such as "I went to the store and stopped off on the way home at the dry cleaners" is all one t-unit, but has two clauses.

Writing that has a 1:1 ratio of sentences and t-units is considered undeveloped, choppy writing. Writing that has a somewhat higher ratio of t-units to sentences demonstrates more mature writing. Syntactic complexity has limits, however, and sources such as Hunt should be consulted for this type of analysis. For example, while one can easily say that writing with a series of sentences with 1 or 2 t-units might be considered repetitive and "boring," one cannot assume that writing with five t-units per sentence will win any prizes. In fact, such writing would likely be cumbersome and difficult to read. For the purposes of analyzing student-connected discourse, simply demonstrating that there is complexity and not all one-to-one correspondences is generally sufficient.

First, the researcher counts the number of sentences in a piece of student writing. Next, the researcher counts the number of t-units and then the number of clauses. This analysis should be double-checked by a knowledgeable colleague for agreement. Some unusual sentences will be harder to analyze than others and will need some discussion to come to agreement. Simply calculating the number of clauses and dividing by the number of sentences, and the number of t-units over the number of sentences (simple division), will yield some possibly interesting profiles.

Writing in the content areas.   Many researchers working in music, math, science, social studies, literature, or foreign language have sought evidence in student writing that certain types of learning have taken place. One researcher hoped to see evidence of scientific logic in student learning logs. Another looked for evidence of critical thinking about issues such as prejudice in her social studies classes.

These researchers began their process of analysis by reading and rereading the student work. By identifying the most desirable qualities as well as the least desired ones, rubrics can be created to assess student writing. For example, in a science log, making an observation may be the lowest level of a desired response. Making the observation with added details might be slightly more desirable. Observations with details and evidence of thinking about why might be more desirable still. And the most desired response might include all those features mentioned and the added element of raising questions about "what if" something were done slightly differently.

Using these criteria, we can create a rubric that assigns a point value (say, 1 to 4) to each type of response. As in all analyses of this type, evaluations should be checked by another colleague with similar expertise.

Analyzing Mathematical Data

The *teaching experiment* is a formal research method that can be used by the teacher action researcher. Using initial tasks designed to establish the child's level of understanding, the researcher questions, assesses, reflects, analyzes, and then designs additional tasks to move the child in the direction of more sophisticated thinking. The purpose of this research is to build a model of the mental operations the child employs while constructing meaning for different mathematical content. This model then becomes critical information for teachers in designing lessons in their own constructivist classrooms.

To illustrate this more clearly, let's look at an informal teaching experiment conducted by Judie Mellilo as part of her doctoral dissertation (1999) in mathematics education. Finding the average is typically taught as following the rule. Judie knows that most students develop computational proficiency and never really have an opportunity to extend their thinking beyond the "add them up and divide" procedure. Judie's goal was for her middle school students to develop a more powerful understanding of the arithmetic mean. First, she read research in the area of mathematics education that discussed students' conceptions for the average; what was problematic as they worked with a variety of average-type problems; and what one could expect students to make sense of as they moved away from using the rule and toward applying their understanding of what that rule does to novel problems.

In constructivist research, designing the instructional tasks requires much forethought on the part of the teacher. The task must be structured in such a way that one can assess students' understandings as they move through it. However, the task must be flexible enough to be altered at any moment to accommodate questioning by the teacher, interaction between the students, and whole-group discussion where each child has the responsibility to share and justify her or his thinking.

Judie sequenced the tasks so that the first group of problems acted as her initial assessment. The second group of problems supplied information about how students thought about and were able to discuss the average. The third set of problems moved students away from the use of the rule and toward the decomposition (breaking apart and examining the parts) of the procedure for finding the average. The fourth group of problems provided students with the opportunity to examine and discuss the relationships in the procedure at a more abstract level. The sessions were videotaped, and Judie took notes and collected students' solutions to the problems. Each night, Judie analyzed and reflected on the tapes and the students' written work. Her reflections on what the students were able to understand and do led to new action—new sequencing of problems for the next day, when the process was repeated.

Let's look in on one day of Judie's research. The question she asked of her students was, Can you find five different numbers whose average is 20? Students had to really think about their conception of the average and their understanding of the procedure in order to construct the data set. The following are some of the students' solutions:

MM: [Wrote five 20s on her paper] Take 2 off the first 20, that gives you 18. Give 2 to the next 20, that gives you 22. Now take 3 off this one, 17, and give it [3] to the fourth, making it a 23. Oh, you have a 20 left. We'll take 4 off the 23, make it a 19, and give the 4 to the last 20, making it a 24.

T: So what is your data set?

MM: 18, 22, 17, 19, and 24.

Another two students working together tried guessing five numbers and then used the average procedure to see how close they came to an average of 20. They then made a better guess. Their method was not working, and DM was becoming frustrated. Then suddenly DM had a breakthrough.

DM: Oh! All you have to do is get 100. Once you get 100, you can do it . . . just work backward. 5 times 20 is 100.

T: Can you think of five numbers that add up to 100?

BR: [DM's partner] 50, 25, 5, 10, and 10.

T: Are those the only five numbers that add up to 100?

DM: No, there are lots.

Reflecting on what happened, Judie noted that MM sidestepped the procedure and used mental model-based reasoning to construct the data set. MM saw the average as a leveler, turning everything in the data set into the same number. MM manipulated her mental model of a data set where all the five numbers were the average, 20, to produce the five different numbers.

DM and BR used the procedure but to no avail. Judie noted that they had not abstracted the procedure sufficiently to decompose it into parts and isolate the sum. The breakthrough came after many failed attempts to guess five numbers. Once DM paid attention to the fact that the only way to get an average of 20 when there are 5 numbers is to divide the 5 into 100, because 20 times 5 is 100; DM describes this as working backward. Judie describes it as decomposing the procedure into components, analyzing the components, and reassembling the components to solve nontypical problems such as this. While this type of mathematical research requires thoughtfulness, time, and energy on the part of the action researcher, the results of studies such as this may lead to teaching and learning that are much deeper than traditional "apply the rule" methods.

Appendix D

Creating a Democratic Classroom: An Action Research Study

Rosie Rudesal
May 14, 1997
Research in Secondary Education SEED 62198
Kent State University
Instructor: Dr. Joanne Arhar

It is a contradiction to envision a democratic society when its inheritors, the kids, are forced to live under conditions of unrelieved subordination.

S. Aronowitz and H. Giroux
Education under siege

Free speech is important, not for the words that we like, but rather for the words that we hate.

Senator Bob Kerry
Massachusetts

What Is My Research Interest?

Everywhere people bemoan the state of U.S. society and the destruction of democracy. Pundits argue that civility has declined, aggression has increased, and U.S. citizens grow more cynical of the political process. Fewer and fewer people register to vote; not all those who register actually vote. Fewer and fewer people write letters to the editor, wear campaign buttons, try to convince others about an issue or a candidate, or donate money to a cause. Those who are concerned about these developments say that people are too willing to give up control over the decisions that affect their lives, thereby giving too much power to too few and leaving the citizenry vulnerable to manipulation.

How does this become the problem of the classroom? I believe that rehabilitating democracy requires citizens to challenge the status quo. As William Greider (1991) states in his critique of democracy, this "insurgency" must begin with "ordinary people who find the will to engage themselves with their surrounding reality and to question the conflict between what they are told and what they see and experience" (p. 410). This political will begins in human conversation built upon mutual respect, among people who have learned to question the evidence provided by those in authority and who have learned to listen to the voices that are usually silenced. Such a people can be nurtured in truly democratic classrooms.

Yet, research has shown that social studies classes are those in which democracy is studied but not practiced (Engle & Ochoa, 1988; Radz, 1983). For example, it is essential that citizens know how to verify the truth of what they are being told in order to be socially responsible and to vote intelligently. In class, however, students are concerned primarily with developing the skills necessary to retrieve and remember decontextualized discrete bits of information, rather than constructing their own knowledge in a way that connects their past knowledge with the course content to create new knowledge. They learn how others have made decisions rather than how to use their knowledge to make their own decisions and participate in the implementation of those decisions. Citizens need to balance their rights and interests with their responsibility to others and to society in general, but students are rarely required to examine controversial issues in light of the common good and weigh both the benefits and the dangers of a given policy. Such classrooms are not democratic and cannot create a commitment to democracy that extends beyond lip service.

In the semester before student teaching, my mentor and I noted that the students in civics classes rarely participated in class discussion. Further, a few students tended to dominate discussion, opinions were rarely supported by reference to evidence, and there was little interest in civics as a course of study. Students complained that civics was "boring" and had nothing to do with "real life." I administered a Citizenship Survey to the students in one class in order to discover which characteristics of citizenship they identified as most important. Results from this survey are presented in Table D.1.

Even though the students in this class identified the ability to make wise decisions as the *second* most important characteristic, they identified participation in community or school events, knowledge of government, and knowledge of current events as the three *least* important characteristics, thus demonstrating the lack of connection between knowledge and behavior. Thus my research question became, How can I create a democratic classroom in which students would begin to develop the knowledge, skills, and characteristics necessary for active involved citizens living in a democracy?

What Did I Try Out in Order to Improve My Practice?

Participants and setting.   In this study I chose to focus on three ninth-grade, required, college-preparatory civics classes. Of the 86 students in these classes, the

TABLE D.1 *Citizenship Survey: summary of responses and means for various characteristics of citizenship*

Characteristic of Citizenship	Means n = 17	Least important 1	2	3	4	Most important 5	6	7
		Number of Responses						
Knowledge of current events	3.6	3	2	1	6	2	3	0
Participation in community or school events	4.2	2	1	3	3	3	3	2
Performance of duties	5.0	2	1	1	0	5	3	5
Concern for others	5.3	2	0	0	1	4	6	4
Acceptance of authority	4.3	0	3	1	6	3	2	2
Ability to question ideas	5.0	2	0	0	3	4	4	4
Ability to make wise decisions	5.7	1	0	0	1	4	5	6
Knowledge of government	4.0	1	2	1	10	0	1	0
Patriotism	4.2	3	1	1	1	9	0	2
Moral and ethical behavior	6.0	0	0	2	1	2	2	10

majority were middle- to upper-middle-class and white. In my eighth-period class, two students were of Hispanic ancestry, one was Japanese, and one was Indian. In fourth period, there were 21 females and 8 males; in fifth period there were 14 females and 14 males; in eighth period there were 18 females and 11 males. The study took place during spring term during my student teaching. The school is a large comprehensive high school located in a predominantly white, middle-class suburb between a major university and a mid-sized metropolitan area in northeast Ohio.

The action.   I decided to focus my study on building a classroom community by establishing a collaborative ethos. As one who has long been committed to a more democratic, egalitarian, and just U.S. society, I am also committed to the kind of teaching that develops habits of the heart and mind that make democratic life possible, that asks what it really means to be human, and that finds the answer in listening to each and every voice. In creating a democratic classroom, I wanted to ensure that everyone had the opportunity to participate, that the dignity of individuals was protected by making them feel safe and respected when expressing opinions, that student choice was a primary element of the classroom, that students learned to evaluate carefully the information that we gathered, and that the students and teacher developed a feeling of community within the classroom. I also hoped they would develop empathy for the perspectives of others.

Based on the work of Hutchison (1994), I selected two aspects of collaboration: teacher-student collaboration and student-student collaboration as means of developing a democratic classroom environment. The activities I chose included small cooperative group work; reflection dialogue journals; student choice in assignments, group members, and readings; a classroom compact; a Bill of Rights project; a variety of community-building exercises; and discussions of controversial issues. These activities were also designed to help students construct their own understandings of democratic life.

How Did I Document the Process?

I developed a chart to help me think through my data collection process. I listed the classroom strategies that I planned to use, the data collection methods I could use to document the consequences of my actions, and some ideas about what I would look for when I examined the data (see Figure D.1).

I adapted the Classroom Community Survey developed by Schaps et al. (1996) and had the students complete it at both the beginning and the end of student teaching. I have included it in Figure D.2.

FIGURE D.1 *Data collection plan*

Strategies	Data Collection Methods	What Will I Look For in the Data?
Reflective activities	Student journal written in twice a week and collected weekly	Student ideas about how to create a classroom community and their attitudes about collaborative work
Classroom compact	Student compacts	Evidence of respect for one another; ability to work together and make collaborative decisions
Discussion of controversial issues	Observations recorded in my journal; student journal	Evidence of ability to understand the perspectives of others
Teacher-student collaboration	"Before" and "after" Community Survey	Evidence of student decision making
Student-student collaboration	Community Survey	Evidence of problem solving and respect

Directions:

1. Please do not put your name anywhere on this sheet.

2. Please use marker or pen.

Note: Thank you for taking this survey. It is part of the research project that I am required to do during my student teaching. You will not be graded on this survey. It is designed to let us know how you feel about this particular class right now. Please answer these questions by yourself, as honestly as you can. I appreciate your help.

For this set of questions, use this scale:

1 = disagree a lot, 2 = disagree a little, 3 = don't agree or disagree, 4 = agree a little, 5 = agree a lot

_____ Students in my class are willing to go out of their way to help someone.

_____ My classmates care about my work just as much as their own.

_____ My class is like a family.

_____ The students in my class don't really care about one another.

_____ A lot of students in my class like to put others down.

_____ Students in my class help one another learn.

_____ Students in my class help one another, even if they are not friends.

_____ Students in my class don't get along very well.

_____ Students in my class just look out for themselves.

_____ Students in my class are mean to one another.

_____ When I'm having trouble with my work, at least one classmate will try to help.

_____ Students in my class treat one another with respect.

_____ Students in my class work together to solve problems.

_____ When someone in my class does well, everyone in the class feels good.

_____ The teacher cares about how well we are doing on our work.

_____ The teacher cares about what we think.

Use this scale for the next set of questions: 1 = never, 2 = hardly ever, 3 = sometimes, 4 = often, 5 = always

_____ Students have a say in deciding what goes on.

_____ The teacher lets us do our work our own way.

_____ The teacher is the only one who decides on the class rules.

_____ The teacher lets me choose the kinds of things that I will work on.

_____ The teacher and students together plan what we will do.

_____ Students in my class can get a class rule changed if they think it is unfair.

_____ The teacher asks the students to help decide what the class should do.

_____ Students in my class get to help plan what they will do.

_____ The teacher and the students decide together what the class rules will be.

_____ I get to do things that I want to do.

Adapted from E. Schaps, C. Lewis, and M. Watson, (1996). Building community in school. *Principal, 76* (2), 29–31.

How Did I Verify that My Judgments Are Trustworthy, Credible, and Respectful?

I realized that I would have to verify any judgments I would make to my peers, adviser, and mentor, so I triangulated the data. I used multiple sources of data: (1) interviews of students, (journals, Citizenship Survey, Classroom Community Survey); (2) observations of group work, class projects, etc. recorded in my journal and log; and (3) actual artifacts (classroom compacts, personal-values project; Bill of Rights project) and documents (student journals and other written work). Throughout the study, I also consulted with my mentor, several of my peers and friends, and my university action research supervisor.

How Did I Interpret the Data?

In this section, I will show how I analyzed my data and how I interpreted and verified what I was learning. I will also show the changes that I made in my action during the study in response to what I was learning from my data.

The following items from the Classroom Community Survey were particularly relevant to teacher-student collaboration and student-student collaboration. I numbered them 1 to 5 to make it easy to analyze and calculated the mean scores for each item.

1. Students make decisions about what is going on (teacher-student collaboration).
2. Teacher involves students in decision making (teacher-student collaboration).
3. Students in my class work together on solving problems (student-student collaboration).
4. A lot of students in my class like to put others down (student-student collaboration).
5. Students in my class treat one another with respect (student-student collaboration).

Table D.2 presents the mean scores for each item for each of my three classes in what I call the *before* survey.

TABLE D.2 *Mean scores for selected items on the before classroom community survey*

Class Period	Question 1	Question 2	Question 3	Question 4	Question 5
Fourth	3.2	2.7	3.6	1.9	3.8
Fifth	3.1	2.2	2.9	3.5	2.7
Eighth	3.0	2.5	3.3	3.0	3.0

What I learned by finding the mean scores for each item was that students in my fifth-period class perceived that they had less input into decisions, were less cooperative in group problem solving, and were less respectful of one another than students in my other classes. My own observations recorded in my journal suggested that this was the case.

> Students are laughing when other students debate controversial issues. Students are making comments about clothing, hairstyles, and jewelry, calling students who have different clothing styles the "dirties." I decided to increase the number of reflective activities and discussion that centered on the principles of respect, responsibility, and tolerance.
>
> *Journal, March 15*

With a few weeks left in my student teaching, I decided to administer the same survey again and called it my *after* survey. By comparing the students' mean scores before and after implementation of many of the reflective activities, group activities, and exercises designed to increase collaboration and community, I was able to look again at how my students felt about collaboration. I was particularly interested in fifth period because I had given those students more focused attention after the before survey. Table D.3 compares the means of all three classes on the three items.

While the responses to questions 1, 2, and 3 indicated that students sensed an increase in teacher-student collaboration, responses to questions 4 and 5 indicated that there was an increase in disrespect in all classes, and particularly in fifth period. At this point, I wrote in my journal:

> I wonder if I am cut out for teaching.
>
> *Journal, April 25*

I really thought that I might quit student teaching. I had many discussions with friends, peers, and my university action research adviser who convinced me that I should continue.

In addition to the classroom compact, which I had planned to do next, I added some new activities to address this disrespect, one of which was the Personal-Values Project. So that you can see the changes that I made in my teaching, I have made two flowcharts (see Figures D.3 and D.4). Let me first tell you what happened when I assigned the classroom compact.

TABLE D.3 *A comparison of means on the before and after classroom community survey*

Class Period	Question 1 Before	After	Question 2 Before	After	Question 3 Before	After	Question 4 Before	After	Question 5 Before	After
Fourth	3.2	3.5	2.7	3.7	3.6	4.0	1.9	2.5	3.8	3.5
Fifth	3.1	3.5	2.2	3.1	2.9	3.5	3.5	4.0	2.7	2.1
Eighth	3.0	3.6	2.5	3.5	3.3	3.7	3.0	3.4	3.0	2.7

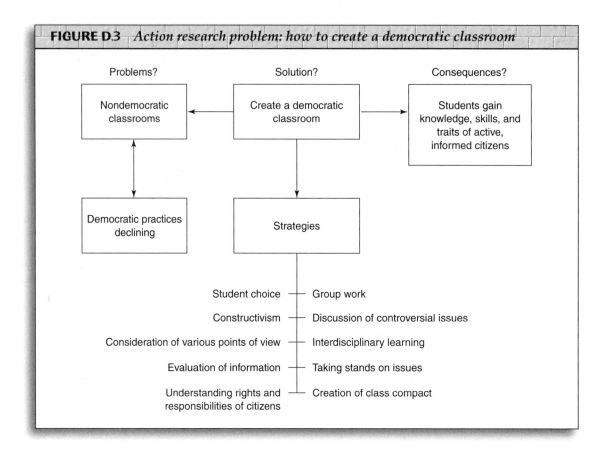

FIGURE D.3 *Action research problem: how to create a democratic classroom*

The classroom compact activity exacerbated an already difficult situation in fifth period. In small groups, students were to develop a classroom compact based on the personal values each had already outlined in her or his journal. Two of the groups (all boys) developed compacts that put down the dirties. I have included one of the boys' compacts to illustrate the situation (see Figure D.5).

I noticed that the other students were visibly upset when this compact was posted. When the boys in these two groups each voted for their own compact (rather than vote as a block for one of theirs), they were out voted by the rest of the class, who chose a compact that reflected a more inclusive and respectful attitude.

The final activity was the Personal-Values Project. Students were to create or select an artistic work which represented a value related to democracy (equality, freedom, etc.) or a value of personal importance. They presented their project to the class. One of the "dirties" acted out a poem by Howard Rollins in which the narrator sees himself in the suffering of another.

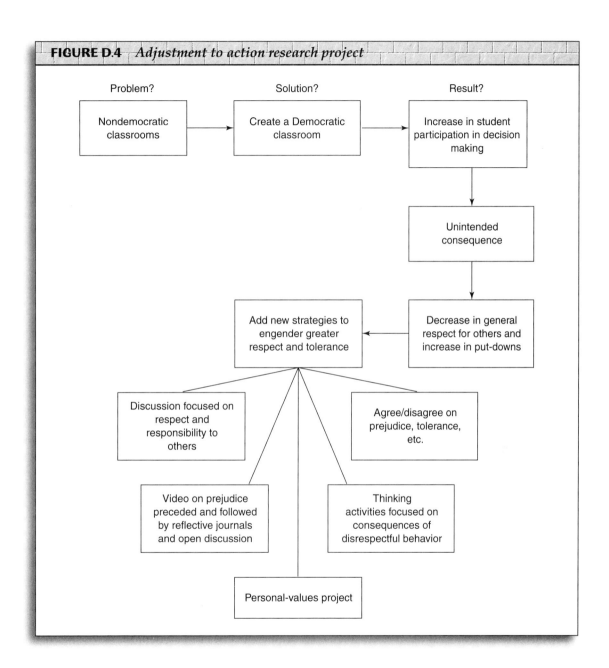

FIGURE D.4 *Adjustment to action research project*

Problem?

Nondemocratic classrooms

Solution?

Create a Democratic classroom

Result?

Increase in student participation in decision making

Unintended consequence

Decrease in general respect for others and increase in put-downs

Add new strategies to engender greater respect and tolerance

Discussion focused on respect and responsibility to others

Agree/disagree on prejudice, tolerance, etc.

Video on prejudice preceded and followed by reflective journals and open discussion

Thinking activities focused on consequences of disrespectful behavior

Personal-values project

FIGURE D.5. *Classroom compact of one group of boys in fifth period*

We the clean people of room 2000 have agreed upon these following rules to make our classroom a better place—

> No DIRTY attire—no jackets, chains, animal collars, ripped and stained clothing.
>
> Students can pick where they want to sit.
>
> No people are allowed to stand outside and look in to see their friends.
>
> Must have a signed note by parent saying that you've washed yourself the night before.

TABLE D.4   *Reflective journal 2: Fifth-period student responses*

What Can We Do in This Class to Create a Sense of Community?	Number of Students Responding
Work together, share work, group work.	11
Help others, take care of those who fall behind.	12
Respect others.	6
Listen to others, make sure everyone has a chance to talk.	4
Other.	1
Total (there are 28 students in class; some students had more than one response)	34

At the end of that day, I recorded in my journal what happened after she read her poem:

> Then she quietly showed them a painting of a girl, all in black, who uses words that describe her good qualities as a shield against the cruel comments of others. There was silence in the classroom when she finished. The entire class erupted in applause. She taught them more in 5 minutes about prejudice than I had all semester.

Rosie's Journal, May 20

I tried to make sense out of what had happened. I reread their journals and carefully analyzed one in which I asked them to write about how *they* would create a sense of community in their classroom. To analyze this particular set of entries, I read over all the students' writings, looked for categories that emerged, and clustered them into what became a pattern of student thinking (see Table D.4).

What I found was that students thought of community as concrete activities such as working together in groups, more so than intangibles such as respect for one another and participation, terms used in the citizenship survey that they rated as least important to citizenship.

I compared what each source of data told me and talked over the evidence that I had accumulated with my mentor, friends, peers, and adviser. I thought back on what I had learned in political science courses about democratic processes and reflected on my own experiences as an activist during the 1960s. I was trying to put all this into a broader context to explain how my good intentions and efforts could have gone so wrong.

What Have I Learned about My Students, My Situation, Myself, and the Action Research Process?

I made the assumption that a democratic classroom would create a caring community. I assumed that if I gave students the opportunity to participate equally, they would treat one another as equals. But what I found was that the more opinionated, more arrogant, louder, and less thoughtful people who never questioned their own judgments were the ones who participated. It happened early in my student teaching, so I had to change my strategies. It was not good enough to just encourage participation. I had to push for respect to save the class because some students were really wounded by the classroom compact and the teasing. I couldn't figure out how to deal with those assertive students and make them want to become part of my classroom. My own experiences in politics and my understanding of the Bill of Rights should have warned me that a democracy that relies too heavily on rights cannot create a safe community.

I also learned something about my own prejudices. When the students responded to my democratic classroom in a way that I had not anticipated, I became angry and depressed. Although I resisted the urge to lash out at them, I blamed them for their feelings; I saw the problem as belonging entirely to the students and not the result of any mistakes that I might have made. I was shocked at the depth of my dislike for certain students. I am going to have to deal with these feelings.

Finally, a close friend with whom I communicated throughout the study helped me to deal with the extreme anxiety that I felt when my actions seemed to ironically turn themselves back on my good intentions. I have always been a type of "savior," wanting to stop the war in Vietnam, wanting to reverse the ills of society in the civil rights movement, and now trying to create a type of classroom that championed the rights of students. To temper my emotional response to what I consider to be injustice so that I can still feel empathy for my students, but not at the expense of my own ability to teach, will be a lifelong struggle.

As for the process of action research, I learned that even though it seemed overwhelming at first, it really kept me focused on my students as well as myself. I could have easily gotten so involved in my own plans and activities, and emotional feelings of inadequacy and anger, that I might have forgotten to remember that these are young people who were perhaps testing me and my ideals. The project forced me to keep a journal, which served as therapy for me and forced me to closely observe what I was seeing in my classroom. Finally, the process heightened my commitment to my ideals. My belief in classroom community is even stronger now than it was before. What I have done is to sharpen those ideals and expand them to include the field of education.

What Will I Do Next and How Will This Make Life Better?

I should have paid more attention to the results of the Citizenship Survey. Had I done so, I might have spent more time at the beginning of the class creating a common ground of the concrete details about what citizenship and a democratic community entailed. For example, I would create a classroom compact earlier on, at the beginning of a class. Then, when students act in disrespectful ways, I could bring them back to the compact and remind them of what agreements they had made.

I will also use some of the methods of documentation that I learned in action research. No matter what my teaching responsibilities might be, from teaching a class to monitoring a study hall, I think that documenting the action and my thoughts and feelings about what is going on will help me to be more responsive to my students and clearer in my thinking.

As far as tempering my savior spirit, I'll keep reminding myself (with a little help from my friends) that I can easily burn out as a teacher if I take everything too seriously. I think that my journal will be my lifelong teaching companion.

References

Aronowitz, S., & Giroux, H. (1985). *Education under siege: The conservative, liberal, and radical debate over schooling.* South Hadley, MA: Bergin & Garvey.

Engle, S. H., & Ochoa, A. S. (1988). *Education for democratic citizenship: Decision making in the social studies.* New York: Teachers College Press.

Greider, W. (1991). *Who will tell the people? The betrayal of American democracy.* New York: Touchstone.

Hutchinson, J. (1994). Creating a classroom community. In J. G. Henderson (Ed.), *Reflective teaching: The study of your constructivist practices* Englewood Cliffs, N.J.: Merrill (pp. 133–145).

Radz, M. A. (1983). Promoting a democratic school climate. In M. A. Hepburn (Ed.), *Democratic education in schools and classrooms.* Washington, DC: National Council for Social Studies. (pp. 67–87).

Schaps, E., Lewis, C., & Watson, M. (1996). Building community in school. *Principal, 76* (2), 29–31.

References

Adelman, C. (1993). Kurt Lewin and the origins of action research. *Educational Action Research, 1* (1), 7–22.

Alvermann, D. E., Young, J. P., Weaver, D. E., Hinchman, K. A., Moore, D. W., Phelps, S. F., Thrash, E. C., & Zalewski, P. (1996). Middle and high school students' perceptions of how they experience text-based discussions: A multicase study. *Reading Research Quarterly, 31*(3), 244–267.

American Psychological Association. (1994). *Publication manual of the American Psychological Association* (4th ed.). Washington, DC: Author.

Anderson, R. H., & Pavan, B. N. (1993). *Nongradedness: Helping it to happen.* Lancaster, PA: Technomic.

Archambault, R. D. (1964). *John Dewey on education.* New York: Modern Library.

Areti, S. (1976). *Creativity: The magic synthesis.* New York: Basic Books.

Aronowitz, S., & Giroux, H. (1985). *Education under siege: The conservative, liberal, and radical debate over schooling.* South Hadley, MA: Bergin & Garvey.

Ashton-Warner, S. (1963). *Teacher.* New York: Simon & Schuster.

Atweh, B., Kemmis, S., & Weeks, P. (Eds.). (1998). *Action research in practice: Partnership for social justice in education.* New York: Routledge.

Ayers, W. (1992). Disturbances from the field: Recovering the voice of the early childhood teacher. In S. A. Kessler and B. B. Swadner, (eds.) *Reconceptualizing early childhood: Beginning the dialogue.* New York: Teachers College Press. 256–266.

Barrell, J. (1995). *Teaching for thoughtfulness: Classroom strategies to enhance intellectual development* (2nd ed.). White Plains, NY: Longman.

Baum, L. Frank (1900). *The wonderful wizard of Oz.* New York: Dover.

Bean, W., & Bouffler, C. (1987). *Spell by writing.* Roselle, New South Wales: Primary English Teaching Association.

Bell, B., Gaventa, J. & Peters, J. (1990). *We make the road by walking: Conversations on education and social change/Myles Horton & Paulo Freire.* Philadelphia: Temple University Press.

Blase, K. (1988). The teachers' political orientation vis-à-vis the principal: The micropolitics of the school. *Politics of education association yearbook.* Washington, DC: Falmer Press.

Bloome, D., & Katz, L. (1997). Literacy as social practice and classroom chronotypes. *Reading and Writing Quarterly: Overcoming Learning Difficulties, 13*(3), 205–226.

Bogdan, R. C., & Biklen, S. K. (1992). *Qualitative research for education: An introduction to theory and methods.* Boston: Allyn & Bacon.

Borich, G. D. (1999). *Observation skills for effective teaching* (3rd ed.). Columbus, OH: Merrill.

Brady, I. (Ed.) (1991). Introduction. *Anthropological Poetics.* Savage MD: Rowman & Littlefield. 3–36.

Brennan, M., & Nofke, S. E. (1997). Uses of data in action research. In T. Carson & D. J. Sumara (Eds.), *Action research as a living practice.* New York: P. Lang.

Brookfield, S. (1984). *Adult learners, adult education, and the community.* New York: Teachers College Press.

Brooks, J. G., & Brooks, M. G. (1993). *The case for constructivist classrooms.* Alexandria, VA: Association for Supervision and Curriculum Development.

Buchanan, E. (1989). *Spelling for whole language classrooms.* Katonah, NY: Richard C. Owen.

Bullough, R. V., & Stokes, D. K. (1994). Analyzing personal teaching metaphors in preservice teacher education as a means for professional development. *American Educational Research Journal, 31*(1), 197–224.

Bullough, R. V., Jr., & Gitlin, A. (1995). *Becoming a student of teaching: Methodologies for exploring self and school context.* New York: Garland.

Canfield, J., & Hansen, M. V. (1993). *Chicken Soup for the Soul.* Deerfield Beach, FL: Health Communications.

Canfield, J., & Hansen, M. V. (1995). *A 2nd helping of chicken soup for the soul.* Deerfield Beach, FL: Health Communications.

Carr, W., & Kemmis, S. (1986). *Becoming critical: Education, knowledge, and action research.* Lewes, Sussex: Falmer Press.

Carson, T. (1990). What kind of knowing is critical action research? *Theory into Practice,* 9 (Summer '90). Columbus, Ohio: Ohio State University. pp. 167–173.

Carson, T. R., & Sumara, D. J. (Eds.). (1997). *Action research as living practice.* New York: P. Lang.

Carspecken, P. F. (1996). *Critical ethnography in educational research: A theoretical and practical guide.* New York: Routledge.

The Chicago manual of style. (1993). Chicago: University of Chicago Press.

Cisneros, S. (1991). *The house on Mango Street.* New York: Vintage.

Clandinin, D. J., & Connelly, F. M. (1998). Personal experience methods. In N. K. Denzin & Y. S. Lincoln (Eds.), *Collecting and interpreting qualitative materials.* Thousand Oaks, CA: Sage.

Coles, R. (1967). *Children of crisis: A study of courage and fear.* Boston: Little, Brown.

Coles, R. (1986). *The political life of children.* Boston: Atlantic Monthly Press.

Coles, R. (1989). *The call of stories.* Boston: Houghton Mifflin.

Coles, R., & Coles, J. H. (1980). *Women of crisis: Lives of struggle and hope.* New York: Delecorte.

Combs, A., & Snygg, D. (1959). *Individual behaviour: A perceptual approach.* New York: Harper & Row.

Connelly, F. M., & Clandinin, D. J. (1988). *Teachers as curriculum planners: Narratives of experience.* New York: Teachers College Press.

Conroy, A. A. (1982). The testing of minority language students. *The Journal of Educational Issues and Language Minority Students, 11,* 175–186.

Creswell, J. W. (1997). *Qualitative inquiry and research design: Choosing among five traditions.* Thousand Oaks, CA: Sage.

Daniels, H. (1994). *Literature circles.* York, ME: Stenhouse.

Delpit, L. (1995). *Other people's children: Cultural conflict in the classroom.* New York: New Press.

Denzin, N. K., & Lincoln, Y. S. (Eds.). (1988). *Collecting and interpreting qualitative materials.* Thousand Oaks, CA: Sage.

Denzin, N. K., & Lincoln, Y. S. (1998). Entering the field of qualitative research. In N. K. Denzin & Y. S. Lincoln (Eds.), *Collecting and interpreting qualitative materials* (pp. 1–34). Thousand Oaks, CA: Sage.

Dewey, J. (1916). *Democracy and Education.* New York: MacMillan.

Dunning, S., Lueders, E., & Smith, H. (1966). *Reflections on a watermelon pickle.* Glenville, IL: Scott Foresman & Co.

Ebbutt, D. (1985). Educational action research: Some general concerns and specific quibbles. In R. Burgess (Ed.), *Issues in educational research.* London: Falmer Press.

Eisner, E. (1994). *Cognition and curriculum reconsidered.* New York: Teachers College Press.

Eisner, E. W. (1985). *The educational imagination: On the design and evaluation of school programs* (2nd ed.). New York: Macmillan.

Eisner, E. W. (1991). *The enlightened eye: Qualitative inquiry and the enhancement of educational practice.* New York: Macmillan.

Elbow, P. (1973). *Writing without teachers.* New York: Oxford University Press.

Elkind, D. (1997). Schooling and family in the postmodern world. In A. Hargreaves (Ed.) *Rethinking educational change with heart and mind: ASCD Year Book.* Alexandria, Va: Association for Supervision and Curriculum Development (27–42).

Elliott, J. (1991). *Action research for educational change.* Milton Keynes, Philadelphia, PA: Open University Press. (50–52)

Emig, J. (1977). Writing as a mode of learning. *College Composition and Communication, 28* (2), 122–128.

Emig, J. (1982). Inquiry paradigms and writing. *College Composition and Communication, 33,* 64–73.

Engle, S. H., & Ochoa, A. S. (1988). *Education for democratic citizenship: Decision making in the social studies.* New York: Teachers College Press.

Ericson, F., & Schultz, J. (1992). Students' experiences of the curriculum. In P. W. Jackson (Ed.), *Handbook of research on curriculum* (pp. 465–185). New York: Macmillan.

Erikson, E. (1950). *Childhood and society.* New York: Norton.

Ferrucci, P. (1982). *What we may be.* New York: Putnam.

Fine, A., & Sandstrom, K. L. (1988). *Knowing children: Participant observation with minors.* Thousand Oaks, CA: Sage.

Flower, L. (1981). Writer-based prose: A cognitive base for problems in writing. In Tate, G. S. & Corbett, E. P. J. (Eds.), *The writing teacher's sourcebook* (pp. 269–293). New York: Oxford University Press.

Flower, L., & Hayes, J. R. (1980). Writing as problem solving. *Visible Language, 14,* 388–399.

Flower, L., & Hayes, J. R. (1981). A cognitive process theory of writing. *College Composition and Communication, 32*(4), 365–387.

Fouts, J. T., & Myers, R. E. (1992). Classroom environments and middle school students' views of science. *Journal of Educational Research, 85*(6), 356–361.

Freire, P. (1970). *Pedagogy of the oppressed* (M. B. Ramos, Trans.). New York: Herder & Herder.

Frost, S. E. (1947). *History of education.* Great Neck, NY: Barron's Educational Series.

Fuller, F. (1969). Concerns of teachers: A developmental characterization. *American Educational Research Journal, 6*(2), 207–226.

Fulwiler, T. (1987). *The journal book.* Portsmouth, NH: Heinemann/Boynton Cook.

Gardner, H. (1993). *Multiple intelligences: The theory in practice.* New York: HarperCollins.

Gardner, J. (1962). *Self-renewal: The individual and the innovative society.* New York: Harper & Row.

Gipps, C., & Murphy, P. (1994). *A fair test? Assessment, achievement, and equity.* Philadelphia: Open University Press.

Giroux, H., & McLaren, P. (1986). Teacher education and the politics of engagement: The case for democratic schooling. *Harvard Educational Review, 56*(3), 213–238.

Goldberg, N. (1990). Wild mind: living the writer's life. New York. Bantam Books.

Goldberg, N. (1986). *Writing down the bones: freeing the writer within.* Boston: Shambhala Press [New York].

Goodlad, J. I. (1984). *A place called school.* New York: McGraw-Hill.

Goodlad, J. I., & Anderson, R. H. (1987). *The nongraded elementary school.* New York: Teachers College Press.

Goodman, Y. M. (1978 & 1991). Kidwatching: An alternative to testing. *National Elementary Principal, 57,* 41–45.

Greider, W. (1991). *Who will tell the people? The betrayal of American democracy.* New York: Touchstone.

Grumet, M. (1990). Retrospective: Autobiography and the analysis of educational experience. *Cambridge Journal of Education, 20*(3), 321–326.

Guba, E. G., & Lincoln, Y. S. (1994). Competing paradigm in qualitative research. In D. K. Denzin & Y. S. Lincoln (Eds.), *Handbook of qualitative research* (pp. 105–117). Thousand Oaks, CA: Sage.

Habermas, J. (1972). *Knowledge and human interests.* Boston: Beacon Press.

Hall, E. T. (1976). *Beyond culture.* New York: Doubleday.

Hargreaves, A., Earl, L., & Ryan, J. (1996). *Schooling for change: Reinventing education for early adolescents.* Washington, DC: Falmer Press.

Harris, T. L., & Hodges, R. E. (Eds.). (1995). *The literacy dictionary.* Newark, DE: International Reading Association.

Havel, V. (1992) The end of the modern era. New York: New York Times, March 1, 1992.

Heath, S. B. (1983). *Ways with words: Language, life, and work in communities and classrooms.* New York: Cambridge University Press.

Henk, W., & Melnick, S. (1995). The reader self-perception scale (RSPS): A new tool for measuring how children feel about themselves as readers. *The Reading Teacher, 48,* 470–482.

Hodder, I. (1998). The interpretation of documents and material culture. In N. K. Denzin & Y. S. Lincoln (Eds.), *Collecting and interpreting qualitative materials* (pp. 110–129). Thousand Oaks, CA: Sage.

Holly, M. L. (1984). *Keeping a personal-professional journal.* Geelong, Victoria, Australia: Deakin University Press.

Holly, M. L. (1989). *Writing to grow: Keeping a personal-professional journal.* Portsmouth, NH: Heinemann.

Hopkins, C., & Antes, J. (1985). *Classroom measurement and evaluation.* Itasca, IL: Peacock.

Hopkins, D. (1994). *A teacher's guide to classroom research* (2nd ed.). Philadelphia: Open University Press.

Horton, M. (1993). *The long haul: An autobiography.* New York: Teachers College Columbia.

Houston, G. (1992). *My great-aunt Arizona.* New York: HarperCollins.

Hubbard, R. S., & Power, B. M. (1993). *The art of classroom inquiry: A handbook for teacher-researchers.* Portsmouth, NH: Heinemann.

Hubbard, R. S., & Power, B. M. (1999). *Living the questions: A guide for teacher researchers.* York, ME: Stenhouse.

Hunt, K. (1965). *Grammatical structures written at three grade levels.* Urbana, IL: National Council of Teachers of English.

Hunt, P., Allwell, M., & Goetz, L. (1996). Creating socially supportive environments for fully included students who experience multiple disabilities. *Journal of the Association for Persons with Severe Handicaps, 21*(2), 53–71.

Hutchinson, J. (1994). Creating a classroom community. In J. G. Henderson (Ed.), *Reflective teaching: The study of your constructivist practices* Englewood Cliffs, N.J.: Merrill (pp. 133–145).

Hyerle, D. (1996). *Visual tools for constructing knowledge.* Alexandria, VA: Association for Supervision and Curriculum Development.

Janney, R. E., & Snell, M. E. (1996). How teachers use peer interactions to include students with moderate and severe disabilities in elementary general education classes. *Journal of the Association for Persons with Severe Handicaps, 21*(2), 72–80.

Kamii, C. (1990). *Achievement testing in the early grades.* Washington, DC: National Association for the Education of Young Children.

Kappa Delta Pi. (1938). *John Dewey: Experience and education.* New York: Collier Books.

Kasten, W. C. (1991). Books beget books. In K. S. Goodman, L. B. Bird, & Y. M. Goodman (Eds.), *The whole language catalog.* Santa Rosa, CA: American School.

Kasten, W. C. (1992). Bridging the horizon: American Indian beliefs and whole language learning. *Anthropology and Education Quarterly, 23*(2), 108–119.

Kasten, W. C. (1995). Literature circles for the teaching of literature based reading. In M. C. Radencich & L. J. McKay (Eds.), *Flexible grouping for literacy in the elementary grades*. Needham Heights, MA: Allyn & Bacon.

Kasten, W. C., & Lolli, E. M. (1998). *Implementing multiage education: A practical guide*. Norwood, MA: Christopher-Gordon.

Kasten, W. C., Lolli, E. M., & VanderWilt, J. (1998). Common roots and threads: Developmentally appropriate practice, whole language, and continuous progress. *Literacy, Teaching, and Learning, 3*(2), 19–40.

Kegan, R. (1982). *The evolving self*. Cambridge, MA: Harvard University Press.

Kemmis, S., & McTaggert, R. (1988). *The action research planner* (3rd ed.). Geelong, Victoria, Australia: Deakin University Press.

Kent State University Human Subject Review Board. *Application to use human subjects in research*. Unpublished document. Kent, OH: Kent State University.

Kotter, J. P. (1996). *Leading change*. Boston: Harvard Business School Press.

Kuhn, T. (1970). *The structure of scientific revolutions*. Chicago: University of Chicago Press.

Lawrence-Lightfoot, S. (1983). *The good high school: Portraits of character and culture*. New York: Basic Books.

Lawrence-Lightfoot, S., & Davis, J. H. (1997). *The art and science of portraiture*. San Francisco: Jossey-Bass.

Leistyna, P., Woodrum, A., & Sherblom, S. A. (1996). *Breaking free: The transformative power of critical pedagogy*. Reprint Series No. 27. Cambridge, MA: Harvard Educational Review.

Lincoln, Y. (1997). What constitutes quality in interpretive research. In C. K. Kinzer, K. A. Hinchman, & D. J. Leu (Eds.), *Inquiries in literacy theory and practice*. Forty-sixth Yearbook of the National Reading Conference. Chicago, IL: National Reading Conference.

Lippitt, R. (1949). *Training in community relations: A research exploration toward new group skills*. New York: Harper.

Lortie, D. C. (1975). *School teacher: A sociological study*. Chicago: University of Chicago Press.

Macrorie, K. (1980). *Telling writing* (3rd ed.). Rochelle Park, NJ: Hayden Book.

Mallon, T. (1984). *A book of one's own: People and their diaries*. New York: Ticknor & Fields.

Maroufi, C. (1989). A study of student attitude toward traditional and generative models of instruction. *Adolescence, 24*(93), 65–72.

Marshall, C., & Rossman, G. B. (1998). *Designing qualitative research* (3rd ed.). Thousand Oaks, CA: Sage.

McCabe, N. (1995). Twelve high school 11th grade students examine their best teachers. *Peabody Journal of Education, 70*(2), 117–126.

McDowell, E. E., & McDowell, C. E. (1986). *A study of high school students' expectations of the teaching style of male, female, English and science instructors*. (ERIC Document Reproduction Service No. ED 278 074).

McKernan, J. (1996). *Curriculum action research: A handbook of methods and resources for the reflective practitioner* (2nd ed.). London: Kogan Page.

McLaren, P. (1992). Collisions with otherness: "Traveling" theory, post-colonial criticism, and the politics of ethnographic practice—the mission of the wounded ethnographer. *The International Journal of Qualitative Studies in Education, 5*(1), 77–92.

McNiff, J. (1993). *Teaching as learning: An action research approach.* New York: Routledge.

McNiff, J., Lomax, P., & Whitehead, J. (1996). *You and your action research project.* London: Routledge.

McTaggart, R. (1991). *Action research: A short modern history.* Geelong, Australia: Deakin University Press.

McTaggart, R. (1997). *Participatory action research: International contexts and consequences.* Albany: State University of New York Press.

Mead, M. (1934). *Mind, self, and society: From the standpoint of a social behaviorist.* Chicago: University of Chicago Press.

Melillo, J. A. (1999). *An analysis of students' transition from arithmetic to algebraic thinking.* Unpublished doctoral dissertation, Kent State University, Kent, OH.

Mezirow, J. (1981). A critical theory of adult learning. *Studies in Adult Education, 32* (1), 3–24.

Miles, M. B., & Huberman, A. M. (1994). *Qualitative data analysis* (2nd ed.). Thousand Oaks, CA: Sage.

Mills, G. (1999). *Action research: A guide for the teacher researcher.* Columbus, OH: Prentice-Hall.

Moffit, J. (1966). To look at any thing. In S. Dunning, E. Lueders, & H. Smith (Eds.), *Reflections on a watermelon pickle* (p. 21). Glenville, IL: Scott, Foresman.

Montagu, A. (1989). *Growing young* (2nd ed.). Granby, MA: Bergin & Garvey.

National Commission on Teaching and America's Future. (1996).*What matters most: Teaching for America's future.* New York: Author.

Oakes, J. (1985). *Keeping track.* New Haven, CT: Yale University Press.

Oakley, A. (1981). Interviewing women: A contradiction in terms. In H. Roberts (Ed.), *Doing feminist research.* London: Routledge & Kegan Paul.

Odell, L. (1980). The process of writing and the process of learning. *College Composition and Communication, 31*(1), 42–50.

Oja, S. (1989). Teachers: Ages and stages of adult development. In M. L. Holly & C. S. McLoughlin (Eds.), *Perspectives on teacher professional development.* London: Falmer Press.

Oliver, M. (1995). *Blue pastures.* New York: Harcourt, Brace.

Palmer P. (1998). *The courage to teach: Exploring the inner landscape of a teacher's life.* San Francisco, CA: Jossey-Bass.

Peck, C. (1990). Some benefits non-handicapped adolescents perceive for themselves from their social relationships with peers who have severe handicaps. *Journal of the Association for Persons with Severe Handicaps, 15*(4), 241–249.

Perl, S. (1979). Creativity and the composing process: Making thoughts visible. *Research in the Teaching of English, 12,* 317–336.

Perl, S. (1980). Understanding composing. *College Composition and Communication, 31*, 363–369.

Perl, S. (1981). Creativity and the composing process: Making thoughts visible. ERIC Document Reproduction Number 202025.

Perrone, V. (1990). How did we get here? In C. Kamii (Ed.), *Achievement testing in the early grades.* Washington, DC: National Association for the Education of Young Children.

Perrone, V. (1991). On standardized testing. *Childhood Education, 67*, 132–142.

Piaget, J. (1926). *The language and thought of the child.* New York: Harcourt, Brace, and World.

Polkinghorne, D. (1988). *Narrative knowing and the human sciences.* New York: State University of New York Press.

Power, B. M. (1996). *Taking note: Improving your observational note taking.* York, ME: Stenhouse.

Radz, M. A. (1983). Promoting a democratic school climate. In M. A. Hepburn (Ed.), *Democratic education in schools and classrooms.* Washington, DC: National Council for Social Studies. (pp. 67–87).

The Random House Dictionary of the English Language (unabridged ed.). (1967). New York: Random House.

Rasinski, T., & Padak, N. (1996). *Holistic reading strategies: Teaching children who find reading difficult.* Englewood Cliffs, NJ: Prentice-Hall.

Richardson, L. (1998). Writing: A mode of inquiry. In N. K. Denzin & Y. S. Lincoln (Eds.), *Collecting and interpreting qualitative materials* (pp. 345–371). Thousand Oaks, CA: Sage.

Roget, P. (1980). *Roget's thesaurus of English words and phrases.* New York: St. Martin's Press.

Rowan, T. E., & Bourne, B. (1994). *Thinking like mathematicians: Putting the K-4 NCTM standards into practice.* Portsmouth, NH: Heinemann.

Russell, T., & Korthagen, F. (Eds.). (1995). *Teachers who teach teachers.* London: Falmer Press.

Schaps, E., Lewis, C., & Watson, M. (1996). Building community in school. *Principal, 76* (2), 29–31.

Schratz, M., & Walker, R. (1995). *Research as social change: New opportunities for qualitative researcher.* New York: Routledge.

Shug, M. C., Todd, R. J., & Beery, R. (1984). Why kids don't like social studies. *Social Education, 48*, 382–387.

Slavin, R. (1988). Synthesis on research on grouping in elementary and secondary schools. *Educational Leadership, 46*(1), 67–77.

Smith, F. (1988). *Joining the literacy club.* Portsmouth, NH: Heinemann.

SoHuyn, Lee & Odom, S. L. (1996). The relationships between stereotypic behavior and peer social interaction for children with severe disabilities. *Journal of the Association for Persons with Severe Handicaps, 21*(2), 88–95.

Spradley, J. P. (1980). *Participant observation.* New York: Holt.

Spradley, J. P. (1979). The ethnographic interview. New York: Holt.

Stake, R. E. (1995). *The art of case study research.* Thousand Oaks, CA: Sage.

Steffe, L. P. (1991). The constructivist teaching experiment: Illustrations and implications. In E. Von Glasersfeld (Ed.), *Radical constructivism in mathematics education.* Dordrecht, Holland: Kluwer Academic Press.

Stenhouse, L. (1975). *An introduction to curriculum research and development.* London: Heinemann.

Strauss, A., & Corbin, J. (1990). *The basics of qualitative research: Grounded theory procedures and techniques.* Newbury Park, CA: Sage.

Stringer, E. (1996). *Action research: A handbook for practitioners.* Thousands Oaks, CA: Sage.

Taylor, K., & Roselli, H. (1993). *Results of student survey: Thomas E. Weightman Middle School—Florida.* Unpublished report.

Taylor, W. (1984). Metaphors of educational discourse. In W. Taylor (Ed.), *Metaphors in education* (pp. 4–20). London: Heinemann.

Tom, A. R. (1997). *Redesigning teacher education.* Albany, NY: State University of New York Press.

Tripp, D. (1990). Socially critical action research. *Theory into Practice, 29*(3), 158–166.

Tripp, D. (1993). *Critical incidents in teaching: Developing professional judgements.* New York/London: Routledge.

Tripp, D. (1996) *The SCOPE Program.* Perth: Western Australia: Murdoch University Center for Curriculum and Professional Development (http://murdock.edu.au/scope/)

Valdes, G., & Figueroa, R. A. (1994). *Bilingualism and testing: A special case of bias.* Norwood, NJ: Ablex.

Van der Klift, E. & Kunc, N. (1994). *Creativity and collaborative learning: A practical guide to empowering students and teachers.* Baltimore: Paul Brookes.

Van Maanen, J. (1988). *Tales of the field: On writing ethnography.* Chicago: University of Chicago Press.

Vygotsky, L. (1962). *Thought and language.* Cambridge, MA: M.I.T Press.

Wasserman, P. (1995). What middle schoolers say about their schoolwork. *Educational Leadership, 53*(1), 41–43.

Weaver, C., Gillmeister-Krause, L., & Vento-Zogby, G. (1996). *Creating support for effective literacy education.* Portsmouth, NH: Heinemann.

Webb, E., Campbell, D., Schwartz, R., & Sechrest, L. (1966). *Unobtrusive measures: Non-reactive research in the social sciences.* Chicago: Rand McNally.

Wheelock, A. (1994). *Alternatives to tracking and ability grouping.* Arlington, VA: American Association of School Administrators.

Whitehead, J. (1993). *The growth of educational knowledge creating your own living educational theories.* Bournemouth, England: Hyde Publications.

Whitehead, J. (1996). Reconceptualizing policy on in-service teacher education. *Teacher education policy: Some issues arising from research practice.* In R. McBride (Ed.), London: Falmer Press.

Wilde, S. (1992). *You kan red this! Spelling and punctuation for whole language classrooms.* Portsmouth, NH: Heinemann.

Wolcott, H. F. (1992). Posturing in qualitative inquiry. In M. D. Le Compte, W. L. Millroy, & J. Preissle (Eds.), *Handbook of qualitative research in education* (pp. 3–52). San Diego, CA: Academic Press.

Wolcott, H. F. (1994). *Transforming qualitative data*. Thousand Oaks, CA: Sage.

Yashima, T. (1955). *Crow boy*. New York: Viking Press.

Zemelman, S., Daniels, H., & Hyde, A. (1998). *Best practice: New standards for teaching and learning in America's schools*. Portsmouth, NH: Heinemann.

Zeni, J. (1998). A guide to ethical issues and action research. *Educational Action Researcher, 6*(1), 9–19.

Zeni, J. (June 21, 1999). Ethics data [e-mail correspondence related to *How to approach ethical issues in teacher research, presentation at the International Conference on Teacher Research*, Magog, Quebec, Canada, April 23, 1999].

Index

About the Authors

Joanne M. Arhar
Kent State University

Joanne M. Arhar started her career as an English teacher at a high school in the Cleveland area. What was most rewarding was working collaboratively with colleagues on interdisciplinary projects. After twelve years, she decided to work as an administrator at both the middle and high school levels, developing curriculum, facilitating the change from a junior high to a middle school concept, and supporting teachers in interdisciplinary teaming. During her doctoral program at the University of Cincinnati, she studied the ways in which teams in both schools and industry developed to create a more supportive and productive working and learning environment. Following graduate school, she taught in the Educational Leadership department at the University of South Florida and later moved to Kent State University where she currently coordinates the Middle Childhood Education program and teaches courses in teaching studies, teacher action research, and middle grades education. Her scholarship continues to revolve around ways in which teachers can provide curricular leadership in an era of standards and accountability.

Mary Louise Holly
Kent State University

Mary Louise Holly is professor in the department of Teaching, Leadership, and Curriculum Studies, and director of Kent State University's Faculty Professional Development Center. Her career began in 1968 as an elementary school art consultant. She became a classroom teacher of young children, and later a professor of curriculum and teaching. Her study of professional development led her as a visiting scholar to two institutions known for action research: the Centre for Applied Research in Education at the University of East Anglia in England, and the School of Education at Deakin University in Australia. Early in her career Mary Lou began documenting and learning from her teaching using artistic and qualitative methods. This introduced her to action research and laid a foundation for later work with adults using life history and biographical methods. Related works include: *Writing to Grow: Keeping a Personal-Professional Journal* (Heinemann, 1989) and *Perspectives on Teacher Professional Development* with Caven McLoughlin (Falmer Press, 1989).

Wendy C. Kasten
Kent State University

Wendy C. Kasten is a professor of Curriculum and Instruction in Literacy at Kent State University, teaching the action research course for the graduate program in reading specialization. At KSU since 1995, Kasten has taught elementary school in Maine, and higher education at the University of South Florida, University of Maine, and at Deakin University in Australia. She earned her PhD degree from the University of Arizona's program in Language and Literacy in 1984, where she was a graduate teaching and research assistant. Kasten is active in the International Reading Association, the National Council of Teachers of English, the National Reading Conference and the Whole Language Umbrella. She is the 1997-2001 President of the Center for the Expansion of Language and Thinking (CELT), an invitation-only collective of literacy educators in multiple countries who share holistic and constructivist views of learning. She is co-author of *The Multi-age Classroom: A Family of Learners* (with B. Clarke, 1993, Richard C. Owen Publishers) and *Implementing Multi-age education: A Practical Guide* (with E. Lolli, 1998, Christopher-Gordon Publishers) and many chapters and articles on literacy topics. Her next book, *A Children's Literature Text* she is writing with Janice V. Kristo will be published by Merrill/Prentice-Hall.